My Life and Rugby

Eddie Jones is the head coach of the England Rugby Union team and led them to the 2019 World Cup final. He took Australia to the 2003 World Cup final as well, and masterminded Japan's famous victory over South Africa in 2015 – one of the biggest upsets in sport. He was also the assistant coach for South Africa when they won the 2007 World Cup.

Donald McRae is an award-winning author of twelve books. He has won the William Hill Sports Book of the Year award twice. He is a three-time Sports Interviewer of the Year winner and has also been Sports Feature Writer of the Year on three occasions, most recently in 2018 and 2019, for his work in the *Guardian*.

EDDIE JONES

WITH DONALD McRAE

My Life and Rugby

THE AUTOBIOGRAPHY

PAN BOOKS

First published 2019 by Macmillan

This paperback edition first published 2020 by Pan Books
an imprint of Pan Macmillan
The Smithson, 6 Briset Street, London EC1M 5NR
Associated companies throughout the world
www.panmacmillan.com

ISBN 978-1-5098-5073-0

Copyright © Eddie Jones/Ensemble Rugby Limited 2019

The right of Eddie Jones to be identified as the
author of this work has been asserted by him in accordance
with the Copyright, Designs and Patents Act 1988.

The picture acknowledgements on page 440 constitute
an extension of this copyright page.

All rights reserved. No part of this publication may be reproduced,
stored in a retrieval system, or transmitted, in any form, or by any means
(electronic, mechanical, photocopying, recording or otherwise)
without the prior written permission of the publisher.

Pan Macmillan does not have any control over, or any responsibility for,
any author or third-party websites referred to in or on this book.

135798642

A CIP catalogue record for this book is available from the British Library.

Typeset in Warnock Pro by Jouve (UK), Milton Keynes
Printed and bound by CPI Group (UK) Ltd, Croydon, CR0 4YY

This book is sold subject to the condition that it shall not, by way of
trade or otherwise, be lent, hired out, or otherwise circulated without
the publisher's prior consent in any form of binding or cover other than
that in which it is published and without a similar condition including
this condition being imposed on the subsequent purchaser.

Visit **www.panmacmillan.com** to read more about all our books
and to buy them. You will also find features, author interviews and
news of any author events, and you can sign up for e-newsletters
so that you're always first to hear about our new releases.

To Hiroko and Chelsea, for your love,
kindness and patience.

And to Mum and Dad, for your bravery,
resilience and love.

CONTENTS

PROLOGUE:
THIS IS WHY WE DO IT

Brighton, England. Saturday, 19 September 2015

This is the hardest time. We are on the team bus driving slowly to the ground. After four years of careful planning and brutal work, I have to let go. I have to trust our preparation and the character of the young men around me. I have cajoled and driven them, encouraged and even changed them. Right now, though, I can do little to control the test of courage they face.

On a beautiful day in Brighton, the sun bounces off the blue sea in a way that happens so rarely in England. It reminds me of the sky above Wedding Cake Island just off Coogee Beach in Sydney. But there is an uneasy backdrop to all this sunshine. Japan are about to play South Africa in our opening game of the 2015 World Cup.

I see John Pryor out of the corner of my eye. John, a fellow Aussie, is our flame-haired strength and conditioning coach, who has worked day and night with me for the last three years. I first worked with John at the Brumbies and then the Wallabies. As soon as I was appointed as Japan's head coach, one of my first calls was to John. I knew that if we were going to make an impact at the World Cup our strategy and tactics required the right physical and mental preparation.

This game against the Springboks has become our obsession. We know that they will try to smash us in the scrum and at the breakdown. We have to match them physically to have any chance today. Our players have to be powerful and hold their body position close to the ground. We plan a high-tempo attacking game, so we cannot drop the ball. Under this immense physical stress, we need remarkable stamina. It is a huge ask.

I look out of the window at the masses of fans in their Springbok and Japan jerseys. We might be stewing in the tense silence, but they're enjoying the friendship of rugby with their fish and chips and beer. I wonder if we have done enough to face down the mighty Springboks.

Japan have only ever won one World Cup game, 24 years ago against Zimbabwe. The Springboks have been world champions twice, in 1995 and 2007. Apart from one draw, Japan have lost every other World Cup match by an average of 35 points, with the most humiliating defeat being in 1995 when they conceded 145 points to the All Blacks. Meanwhile only three teams – New Zealand, Australia and England – have beaten South Africa in the World Cup.

I know all about the strengths of South Africa, having faced them so often when coaching Australia, and during Super Rugby tournaments where I have tried to outwit some of their best players. I was Jake White's assistant coach when the Springboks won the 2007 World Cup in France. Some of the players I became close to during that tournament, including the great Fourie du Preez and Victor Matfield, will play against us today. Du Preez, who was such a revelation for me in club rugby at Suntory, just outside Tokyo, is one of the best players I have ever coached.

Today, returning from a long injury, he will start on the bench. But South Africa have chosen the most experienced starting XV they have ever fielded. Their players have earned 851 caps between them. Even with Pryor's innovative work, stacking on the muscle while retaining our speed and agility, we will be featherweights stepping into the ring against a heavyweight champion.

Our team nickname is the Cherry Blossoms, which I can't stand. Seriously. The Boks must be laughing at the thought of crushing us. They expect, along with the rest of the rugby world, that annihilation is near. Our Brave Blossoms, another little alias that means nothing to me, are supposedly going to be ground into red-and-white petals which are crumpled underfoot.

I know how this feels. I coached the Queensland Reds when we were pumped 92–3 by the Bulls in Pretoria.

In the silence I give Pryor another look. I want to say: 'This is why we do it, mate. This is why we don't put on a suit every morning, pick up a briefcase and catch the same eight o'clock train to a routine office job. This is the feeling you get nowhere else in life. It's this intensity, this fear, this hope, this dread, this thrill, all knotted together in your gut. There is a need for courage in the face of adversity. This is what we do, mate.'

But I don't say a word. I prefer not to talk to anyone on the bus. It's a lonely job and I'm used to its solitary nature. Coaching any international team is difficult. You're supposed to know everything and offer constant belief and hope to a huge number of mostly complex individuals. At the same time, everyone thinks they can do the job better than you. You're never short of someone telling you what you are doing wrong. Most of the time you take it in your stride but sometimes, if you're not strong, it blows you off course. International rugby also lacks the camaraderie of the club game. It's cut-throat – with more distance between you and the players. You are picking men to represent their country, or dropping them, and you need greater detachment. You also know that if they fail, or let you down, you will cop the blame.

When I became Australia's head coach in 2001, two years before we made the World Cup final against England in Sydney, Rod Macqueen, my predecessor, explained the challenges of the job. His final words hit home. 'You're now the loneliest man in Australia,' Rod said with a smile.

He was right. Of course coaching Australia or England is different to being in charge of Japan, where expectations are limited. But, for me, the pressures and demands are the same. I insist on the same commitment, probably even more, with Japan. The inherent disadvantages of working with players who lack the size, skill and experience taken for granted in Australia, or England, need to be overcome. The only way you make progress is through hard work – and more hard work.

Japan are not going to win the World Cup, but I have always believed we can make the quarter-finals. To achieve that sporting miracle we have to beat South Africa. It seemed a pipe dream to everyone else for a few years. But, over the last four months, the team started to believe. Slowly but surely, as we slogged our way through day after gruelling day of training, the players and then the coaches see that it is possible. We can win. We can beat the Boks.

Our plan is simple. If we can keep the score close after an hour, it will unsettle them. Rather than smashing us into oblivion, they will start to have doubts. They will question their tactics and plans. The unthinkable – losing to Japan – will become a possibility. And if that possibility becomes real, you can guarantee that panic won't be too far behind.

We need to play rugby with real pace and intensity, never giving South Africa a breather and making the big men in their pack turn again and again. We will climb into them from all angles and find space which stretches them to breaking point.

Mike Tyson once said that everyone has a plan until they get punched in the face. His own invincible aura was shattered for the first time in Japan. But even Buster Douglas's shocking knockout of Tyson was more believable, in Tokyo in 1990, than the incredible idea Japan might win today. Douglas was a 42–1 underdog against Tyson. A Japan victory over South Africa is 1,000–1.

As we shuffle off the bus and head down into the basement of the Brighton Community Stadium, I keep to myself. The players also prepare for their warm-up in silence. Eventually, they step out into the sparkling sunshine with my assistant coaches. Wisey (Scott Wisemantel) takes the backs and Borthers (Steve Borthwick) works the forwards up into a sweat.

I watch from the sidelines, still saying nothing, feeling helpless 45 minutes before kick-off. It's up to the players now. It always is.

Twenty-four hours ago I had felt they were ready. Then Michael Leitch took the team on his captain's run – a traditional and almost ceremonial workout for the boys on the eve of the game. It was hopeless. The players were edgy and out of sorts. It was so bad I told Leitch, my New Zealand-born but now thoroughly Japanese captain, to end it early.

Watching a warm-up can be misleading. Sometimes your team looks so switched on you feel certain they're going to win. But then the whistle blows, the ball is kicked, one of your players spills it, the other team scores, heads drop, and you're on the way to a defeat before anyone has even settled. On other occasions you look flat in the warm-up and then the game starts, a long pass spins out and one of the boys catches it beautifully and he is away, with the rest of the team hungry to follow.

I remember coaching Australia against New Zealand in the 2003 World Cup semi-final and, just a few months earlier, we had shipped 50 points against them at home. We were hammered by the press and given no chance of challenging the All Blacks at the World Cup. But then, in the semi, we started like a freight train. Stevie Larkham, at number 10, threw every pass perfectly. We had runners steaming onto the ball in wave after wave. For 90 seconds we played almost perfect rugby, which gave the players enormous confidence. You could see the belief surging through them and we went on to win that game pretty easily. But what if one of those early passes had gone astray? What if it had been intercepted and they scored a breakaway try?

This is the beautiful challenge of professional sport. How do you train your players to change, to recover, when things don't go your way? How do you coach a group of athletes to be resilient when the plan goes wrong?

For all its brutality, rugby can be a very delicate game of agonizingly fine margins. A player's confidence can be fleeting and, if it slips once the whistle blows, there is little you can do. After the game starts, your ability to influence the outcome is minimal. We rely on the players to make good decisions, to think on their feet and to adapt, to let mistakes go and get on with the next task. We can relay messages to them but it's infrequent and you need a stoppage in play. All you can really do as a coach in the midst of a game is to be smart in your use of substitutions.

Preparation is everything. If you get it right you improve your chances of success. But, in a team of human beings, nothing is guaranteed.

Thirty minutes before the game begins, I turn to John Pryor and finally say a few words. 'Are three years of work going up in smoke here, mate?'

Gallows humour. He smiles nervously. It's a hideous thought but he knows what I mean. We have worked together so closely for so long. All the obvious parts of the preparation have been pulled apart, examined from every angle, tested, reset and tested again. As we creep towards kick-off the simple and most obvious question remains: 'Will we get the performance we have worked so hard for?'

We could run out and, in the first play, the Bok forwards knock us over. We lose the ball, they hammer some holes in our defence and score a try. It's 7–0 after a minute. They score another. 14–0. Suddenly you're looking down the barrel at 60 points. That might happen. As the minutes start to tick faster, I still believe we have a chance. But the bad angel is now whispering in my ear, telling me to wake up and prepare for the inevitable. My confidence takes a battering similar to the one the Springboks expect to hand out.

I breathe in deeply, calming myself. We have been good for each other, Japan and me. I have helped them improve as a rugby team and they, in turn, have given me new life as a coach. I am 55 years old now and I returned to Japan in 2009, after a bruising five years.

Apart from the high of the 2007 World Cup win with South Africa, it has been a lean time. I was sacked from my dream job as head coach of the Wallabies in 2005 and, on the rebound, made an impulsive decision and took charge of the Reds in Brisbane. After being rejuvenated by the Boks I went through an uneven two years in English club rugby with Saracens. I was starting to build a team I believed would become a powerhouse of European rugby, as they eventually did. But when the ownership changed, so did everything else. A South African consortium walked in and I walked out. It was never going to work.

Then, for the only time in my career, I put my wife, Hiroko, and our daughter, Chelsea, first. They had followed me from one job to another and, with Chelsea at a crucial stage of her education, it felt right to choose stability. I returned to Japan, where my wife and my grandparents were born, to coach Suntory. Chelsea finished her schooling in a settled environment, at an outstanding English-language school in Tokyo – and I got on with life as a club coach in Japan.

Some people thought I was crazy because they considered Japan a backwater of world rugby. But I didn't care. I knew it would be a good move for my family. I could also rediscover the pure pleasure of coaching without being distracted by rugby politics, money, heat from the media or any of the other pressures which always test my passion for the game.

But I would remain an outsider. While I found myself feeling more at peace in Japan than I had done as a coach at Tokai University, as an assistant to the national team and then in my first stint at Suntory 20 years before, I was still an Australian in a foreign land. It's the reality of coaching internationally. Still, by 2011, the desire to coach at the highest level had fizzed back to life and I relished leading Japan.

I challenged the old mentality of Japanese rugby which would be satisfied with defeat as long as the team looked as if it had tried hard. There were moments when I had to rip into the players in public and question their acceptance of being a second-tier rugby nation.

On one infamous occasion, after we lost to the French

Barbarians in 2012, I let them have it. During the media conference after the game, my captain Toshiaki Hirose had smiled and
laughed in answer to a question. I know Japanese people often
laugh when they are extremely anxious, but his response gave
me a chance to ram home the point. My anger was genuine and,
unlike most of my media performances, unscripted. 'It's not
funny,' I snapped. 'It's not funny. They just don't want to win
enough. They don't want to change enough. I'm going to have to
change the players . . .'

When I calmed down, I wondered whether I might have over-
stepped the Japanese cultural mark. But the chairman of the
Japan Rugby Football Union spoke to me afterwards: 'It's about
time someone said that.'

There was a sustained reshaping of Japanese rugby's collective
thinking behind closed doors. It was a fascinating, draining and
inspiring experience. I learnt more about coaching and myself
than I had done in years. Some of this knowledge came from
external sources. Pep Guardiola, when I visited him at Bayern
Munich in 2013, gave me new insights into how to train your
team in intense, concentrated bursts and how to find space on a
field. He told me to be an idea thief. Pep opened my mind and
made me think differently about coaching. But most of the
changes came from within.

There were many difficult days in Japan. I suffered a stroke and
lost my father, the beloved Ted. But I knew I had to keep going.
If Japanese rugby was going to change and we were going to succeed at the World Cup, I had to be resilient and tough. It seemed
fitting that these qualities, which I get from my mum, came to
the fore in Japan. Her grit was forged in the pain of the Second
World War when, after the raids on Pearl Harbor, she and her
family were sent to separate internment camps – despite the fact
that, as a girl in a Japanese family, she had been born and raised
in California. There was no sentimentality in my mother's insistence that I do my best for Japan. She wanted me to do my best
wherever I worked, and she followed me closely, rebuking me if

I was rude or swore or failed to be clean-shaven. It's the same today, even though I am deep into my 50s and she is in her 90s.

Coaching, like life, is cyclical. You will have success and failure. It's the same for a team. They will have strengths and weaknesses. There will be peaks and troughs. You need to build confidence and consistency.

I knew we had practised and prepared far harder than any of my players had done before. I had given my all, as had they, and now we could just wait and see if it would be enough to prevail against the frightening odds stacked in favour of South Africa.

For almost 80 minutes, Japan have been as heroic as they are bold, as quick as they are brave, standing toe-to-toe with the Springboks. The lead shifts from one team to the other and, with less than a minute of regulation time left, South Africa are clinging to a 32–29 lead. They stem one Japanese attack after another. We think we might have scored a match-winning try in the second last minute, only for the Television Match Official to decide that a five-metre scrum should be awarded to Japan.

South Africa send Jannie du Plessis and Tendai 'The Beast' Mtawarira back on to bolster an injured and buckling Springbok scrum. They have 132 Test caps between them but, still, we hammer away at them. With just 13 seconds left, the refreshed Springbok pack reel in the face of relentless Japanese pressure. The scrum collapses. Jérôme Garcès, the French referee who has been excellent throughout, avoiding the usual temptation to favour a tier-one giant over a minnow, has no doubt. Penalty to Japan.

I take a quick slug of water but my eyes remain locked on my captain. Michael Leitch has played magnificently all afternoon. He just needs to point to the posts and a certain penalty will be kicked. A 32–32 draw with South Africa will be a staggering result and count as my proudest achievement in rugby after the 2003 World Cup semi-final victory over the All Blacks. I breathe out in relief. Defeat after such a display would have been cruel.

Leitchy, however, has a different thought in his mind. I can see it and, briefly, it horrifies me. 'Take the three!' I scream. 'Take the three!'

He can't hear me above the bedlam of 30,000 spectators who are roaring as they also realize that Japan are going for the scrum, and the try. My players are searching for victory because a draw would not be enough – not on such a monumental afternoon.

I have been clutching a walkie-talkie all game. It helps me keep in touch with the bench but, most of all, it has been something hard and metallic to grip on to while I deal with the tension. But now, knowing that Leitch has rejected the game-saving penalty, I throw the walkie-talkie down onto the concrete ground in anger. It smashes into a thousand pieces.

I look up and take a deep breath. The mad rage fades and, suddenly, I begin to think clearly again. I feel better as soon as I face the truth.

Leitch has shown real courage. This is more than just the physical courage that my team had summoned all game long, putting their bodies on the line as we rocked the Springboks again and again, driving them back while scoring three tries. Being physically brave in professional rugby is a given for me. This is courage of a different kind. It comes not from me but from deep within Michael Leitch and his players. Risk is attached, because if you fail you will lose the game. Leitch wants the win above all else.

'Good on you, mate,' I say in a silent conversation between my captain and me. 'Go for it.'

In the final minute of a match like no other, with Japan on the brink of history, Michael Leitch shows the courage we all need when it matters most. His decision will reduce grown men to tears and change the course of world rugby, and my own career, yet again. We do not know it now, but the bravery of this choice will be one of the factors behind me leading England into the 2019 World Cup in Japan. Michael Leitch will still be Japan's captain while I will have another crack at this great tournament and maybe, just maybe, reach my third World Cup final with a third different country.

But in this moment, in Brighton, I am thinking only of Japan, and Leitch. The scrum goes down. Two weary packs of men, drenched in sweat, crunch into each other and collapse to the ground. They set it again for a second, and then a third time.

Then, it happens. The ball comes out. Hiwasa and Leitch lead the charge. My Japanese forwards are on a roll and I sense the truth of it all over again.

This is why we do it. This is when we are most alive. This is it. Here we go . . .

1

FREEDOM

On a sunlit Wednesday afternoon in Sydney, early in the winter of 1976, we looked a picture as we ran onto the stone-hard field at Latham Park. We wore our faded blue-and-white hooped Matraville High rugby jerseys and coloured shorts. Most of our boys were in the correct navy-blue shorts, but a few had lost or forgotten their regular kit. They wore replacement white or black shorts which clashed with our motley collection of socks. We looked like a bag of Liquorice Allsorts.

Our small backs were called 'the black line with a red tip', because they consisted of six Indigenous Australian kids and a red-haired winger, Greg Stores, who looked nothing like the three Ella boys playing alongside him. My best friends, the twins Glen and Mark Ella, were six months older than me and they sported big black afros which would have been more funkily suited to The Jackson 5 than an Australian schoolboy rugby team. They were a few weeks away from their 17th birthday, on 5 June, while their straggly haired brother Gary would be 16 that July.

I had turned 16 four months earlier, at the end of January. I stood out, at hooker in our new first XV, because I was small, half-Japanese and talkative. I should have been an outsider at Matraville High because I looked very different. But in 1970s Australia, being good at sport offered a pathway to acceptance. I was pretty good at most sports.

Our school was a mix of Indigenous Australian boys and girls and tough white kids from the working-class suburbs of Chifley and Little Bay, where I lived with my parents and older sisters, Diane and Vicky. The Ellas and our other Indigenous teammates came from La Perouse, where I had first met them at kindergarten. La Perouse was known as Larpa around our neighbourhoods in southeastern Sydney. In the posh suburbs it was called 'the Soweto of Sydney' because it had been used as a dumping ground for Indigenous people since the early 19th century. It was one way of keeping dark-skinned communities away from affluent white Sydney.

Who knew what our opponents, the prestigious St Joseph's College first team, thought when they arrived in a convoy of eight gleaming grey coaches? They came from Hunters Hill, a suburb on the North Shore, 25 kilometres and a world away from Matraville. Our school had opened in 1964, as a way of coping with the overspill of Indigenous kids in and around Larpa and Chifley, while St Joseph's was a Catholic college founded by Marist Brothers in 1881. Joeys, as it is known, is the largest boarding school in Australia and provides the gold standard in schoolboy rugby. In its famous colours of cerise and blue, Joeys has produced more Wallabies than any other school in Australia.

Australian rugby union was a niche sport shaped by the privately educated and moneyed classes. It was only really played in New South Wales and Queensland and, even in these states, it ran a distant fourth behind rugby league, Aussie Rules football and cricket. At Matraville we actually preferred league because we were suckers for the hot skills and raw physicality of the 13-man code. It was just a quirk of fate that Geoff Mould, our first-team coach, had persuaded the headmaster to switch us from a league to a union school.

Joeys were the top team in the elite Greater Public Schools competition. They had been champions 30 times in 50 years. Matraville played mostly against other government schools but, once a year, we could test ourselves against the best in the state and try to win the Waratah Shield – open to all non-GPS high schools in New South Wales.

Mould fancied our chances and so he invited Joeys to play us in a preseason friendly. They swept into Latham Park, which was the training ground used by Randwick, our local first-grade rugby club. We watched their players get off the first bus. They wore immaculate school uniforms and I stared at the expensive grey suitcase one of their players carried. It matched the colour of the bus and it looked as if he was set for a holiday in England rather than playing a game of footy against a team of battlers like us in Coogee. They were also much taller and bigger than us.

'They've got some big cattle,' Glen Ella said as he flipped a ball from one hand to the other. As usual, Glen did not sound worried. We'd had a fair bit of success in previous seasons and were pretty confident that Joeys would never have faced a team like ours before.

Of course, we didn't know that Joeys included a couple of future Wallabies that day. Steve Williams, a hulking lock even at that age, would win 28 caps for Australia while Bruce Malouf, my opposite number at hooker, played a Test against New Zealand in 1982.

When they followed us onto the field in their sparkling kit, we thought they were the smartest team we had ever seen. Their hundreds of supporters lined up in a big tunnel to cheer them on to the field. They had a whole swag of war cries and songs, including 'You'll Never Walk Alone'. Bob Dwyer, my future mentor, sitting among the surprisingly large crowd, thought we were going to get slaughtered.

Bob had been invited to watch Matraville for the first time. Cyril Towers, a former Wallaby who was then 70 years old and acted as our occasional coach alongside Mould, had told Bob he should see the Matraville kids for himself. He promised Bob, who was coaching Randwick and on his way to taking charge of the Wallabies, that he would find it an interesting afternoon.

Bob felt as if he had flicked on a Hollywood movie as the contrast between St Joseph's and Matraville was so vast it looked comical. The privately educated boys exuded health, wealth, strength and an overpowering confidence. They looked like a well-drilled team of all-American jocks who had just stepped out of the gymnasium. Our little Matraville runts with the crazy hairstyles, skinny legs and multicoloured socks either pulled up high, in my case, or rolled around the ankles, looked like we were from the wrong side of the tracks.

Joeys came out fast, like superstars, playing slick and aggressive rugby with a traditional base. They used the familiar deep backline set-up with wide spaces between players, who moved the ball with big swing passes. We came at them from all angles, hitting them hard and low, bringing them down, turning the ball over and then taking the chance to run at them relentlessly. Our backline was ridiculously flat and we ran and passed the ball in dizzying patterns, as if we were playing touch footy on the beach.

The joy and the skill of our team, particularly the Ellas and Lloyd Walker, a silky smooth Indigenous Australian playing at centre, astonished Bob. He could not believe the invention. Even more intriguingly, we had mastered the essential basics, so our passing, catching and kicking were sound and our scrum and lineout operated efficiently. There was a structure and clear alignment to our play which allowed us to run and pass with freedom.

To me it was just another sun-kissed afternoon playing rugby with the Ellas and our mates. We didn't think of the prestige of St Joseph's or the huge advantages they held over us. We just tackled ferociously, won the ball back and zipped it from one set of hands to another as we carved open their defence. Sometimes it would be a jink or a shimmy from Mark Ella which left the Joey boys open-mouthed and on their arses as he ghosted past to set up Glen or Lloyd with a perfectly weighted pass.

We had been playing together for at least eight years. We made the ball our friend as it gave us hours of entertainment, day after day. Rather than practise rugby when we were very young, we just played touch for fun – even if we were using an empty can rather than a ball. We used the same moves we developed on the playground, and gave Joeys a lesson in running and thinking rugby.

The Ellas, and Mark in particular, were extraordinary. Bob Dwyer knew that the brothers would play for Australia. He was right because Mark, Glen and Gary all became Wallabies – as did Lloyd Walker. Matraville played running rugby with the spirit of the Barbarians but, even more tellingly, we emulated the Randwick style. The flat backline was straight out of the Cyril Towers coaching manual; he had first been taught rugby at Randwick Boys High School and later, along with scrum half Wally Meagher at Randwick Rugby Club, he had pioneered strategies of attacking rugby. Now, in his old age, Cyril was passing these same tactics straight on to us at Matraville.

Cyril would walk for 20 minutes every day from his home to our school so that he could share with us his theories which he, in turn, had learnt from the All Blacks before they turned away from the flat backline. He brought coaching sophistication to our sessions because we spent a lot of time learning about the proper alignment of our backline. This even rubbed off on forwards like me. I was taught in those teenage years how to set up your backs and why playing such a bold flat line could open up the field of play in front of you.

The Ellas and Walker would become four of just 14 Indigenous Australian players who have played for the Wallabies so far. Given the impact Indigenous athletes have had in other sports such as rugby league and Australian Rules football, it's an appallingly low number. That statistic proves how rugby union in Australia has failed to capitalize on the ability of an Indigenous community which is represented far more widely in league. My own future was heading towards a lifetime of teaching and coaching inspired by, more than anyone else, Bob Dwyer.

After we hammered Joeys, as the winter sunshine gave way to dappled shadows stretching across Latham Park, we thought nothing more of another game of footy. We just knew we were on the road to somewhere. We loved everything about a journey where even pain was just a short detour back to happiness and our overwhelming sense of freedom.

I was nine years old in the summer of 1969 when my mother, Nell, first showed me how to deal with the bigotry which had blighted her life as a young girl. It was a hot Saturday afternoon and, having finished my homework for the weekend, I was itching to get out and have a bat and a bowl in the park with Mark, Glen and Gary. I was already dreaming of playing cricket for Australia. The idea of a half-Japanese boy one day playing against England in the Ashes felt as natural as it did to any other ordinary Aussie kid.

My father, Ted, loved cricket and he promised to take me to the Sydney Cricket Ground to watch a Test match once he got back from Vietnam. He was a soldier and had been sent to Vietnam as part of the Australian Army contingent which fought in the war. Australia's involvement was deeply unpopular, and split the country, as it entailed conscription. Sixty thousand young Australian men served in Vietnam between 1962 and 1972.

I had no idea how hard and gruesome the war in Vietnam had become. I just wanted Dad to come home and take me to the SCG, the cathedral of cricket in Sydney that wasn't too far from where we lived. That afternoon, as I paced around our modest home in Little Bay, Mum told me we were going to be helped out by a former soldier who was coming over to mow the lawn. The man had been randomly assigned to our family from the local delegation of the Returned Services League to cut the grass and do any other chores my dad normally did.

Mum said that once the man had started to cut the lawn, she would check my homework and, if it was done to her satisfaction, I could head out to the park. My mum set high academic standards for me and my sisters and we accepted them without complaint. She was harder and more driven than my dad, who was a typical knockabout Aussie bloke who loved sport and his family. Mum and Dad had met in Japan and eventually moved back to his home in Tasmania, where my sisters and I were born. Not long after my birth, Dad was posted to the Randwick Barracks in Sydney and we moved to Little Bay.

I respected my mother's firm rule and so I waited patiently for the old soldier to arrive. At last, we heard him push his lawnmower up the drive and then ring the bell.

When Mum opened the door, ready to welcome and thank him, he stared at her in silence. He did not answer her polite greeting or gracious smile. Instead, he looked at her with contempt before he said: 'I'm not mowing *your* bloody lawn.' He grabbed his mower and stormed off.

Mum stayed calm as I stared at her in confusion. I could not understand why the man had been so nasty. She hadn't done anything to him. Mum didn't explain the situation – apart from saying it would be up to us to make sure we kept the grass neat and tidy while Dad was away.

When we were older, Mum told us a few stories. The first one I heard came from the days soon after she and Dad arrived in Australia. Most people in the rural Tasmanian town of Burnie had never seen a Japanese woman before. Whenever she went shopping they assumed she couldn't understand English They followed her and mocked her. Mum didn't utter a word or give any indication that she understood exactly what they had said about her. But once they followed her into a shop, she would shut them up by ordering an item in perfect English with her American accent. When she told us that story it made Mum smile rather than sound angry. She never showed any bitterness.

I only began to understand my mother's past, and all that she and her parents endured, when she gave me and my sisters a copy each of David Guterson's *Snow Falling on Cedars*. It's a beautiful novel about a young Japanese-American man wrongly accused of killing a white fisherman. His trial plays out against the raging anti-Japanese sentiment that coursed through America in the wake of Pearl Harbor and the Second World War.

There is a moving subtext to the plot of whether the protagonist Kabuo Miyamoto will be found guilty of a murder he did not commit. His lawyer, Ishmael Chambers, a former US marine, had fallen in love with Miyamoto's wife, Hatsue, when they were in high school. Chambers wrestles with a new hatred of the Japanese and his love for Hatsue. At the same time the white community bays for the blood of an innocent Japanese man.

When my mother gave me the book I was in my forties and working as a coach in Japan. She did not talk about racism or suffering. Instead, in an understated way, she used the novel to illuminate her own past life. Like many people who had survived the war, she did not like dwelling on it. She preferred to focus on gratitude. I only knew a speck of her history which was littered with prejudice and hurt. But I do know that the forgiveness, love and resolve forged in the internment camps of California is the greatest gift a mother could ever give her son.

After the First World War, life had been tough in Japan. Many families emigrated. They started new lives in Brazil, Peru and, most of all, America. My mother's father joined the new wave of immigrants that arrived in California. He was a hard-working man and, soon after my mother's birth in 1925, in Lodi, 30 kilometres from Sacramento, he began an orange orchard. My grandfather worked hard and, after a few lean years, the orchard thrived. He employed many Japanese immigrants who were thankful for their new lives and determined to be responsible citizens of the United States.

Peace on the orchard, and for my mother's family, was shattered on 7 December 1941, when Pearl Harbor was attacked. On a quiet Sunday morning, 68 people were killed when 350 Japanese planes carpet-bombed the US naval base in Honolulu, Hawaii. President Franklin D. Roosevelt declared war on Japan and Germany the following day.

The consequences for my mother's family in the Sacramento Valley were immediate. Roosevelt issued Executive Order 9066 which led to the forced removal of all people of Japanese ancestry from their homes. This included those who had been born in the US or become naturalized American citizens. Roosevelt said the order was implemented to prevent espionage and, also, to protect people of Japanese descent who were vulnerable to violent reprisals.

Their places of incarceration were known officially as 'Relocation Centers'. Roosevelt was more candid in referring to them as concentration camps. American diplomats avoided the term, but Roosevelt's bluntness mirrored the semantic distortion which meant that the military, who ran the camps, chose not to describe their inmates as Japanese-American citizens. They called them 'non-aliens' – as a sinister way of distinguishing those people born in the US from Japanese immigrants who had yet to acquire citizenship.

My 17-year-old mother, born and raised in California, and my diligent, respectful grandparents had become 'non-aliens'. Among the 117,000 people of Japanese descent who were forced to leave their jobs and homes, they were sent initially to Assembly Centers and then, with random brutality, assigned to camps located thousands of miles away from each other.

White America was overwhelmingly in favour of Roosevelt's order and disdainful of their Japanese citizens. On 20 February 1942, an editorial in the *Atlanta Constitution* declared that, 'The time to stop taking chances with Japanese aliens and Japanese-Americans has come. While Americans have an innate distaste for stringent measures, everyone must realize this is a total war. There is absolutely no sense in this country running even the slightest risk of a major disaster from enemy groups within the nation.'

Eight days later the *Los Angeles Times* was even more venomous. 'As to the considerable number of Japanese, no matter where [they were] born, there is unfortunately no doubt. They are for Japan; they will aid Japan in every way possible by espionage, sabotage and other activity; and they need to be restrained for the safety of California and the United States. Since there is no sure test for loyalty to the United States, all must be restrained. Those truly loyal will understand and make no objection.'

My mother and grandmother were sent to a camp in California, while my grandfather was banished to Arkansas. Living conditions were cramped and dehumanizing.

On 8 December 1942, the *Los Angeles Times* insisted that, 'The Japs in these centers have been afforded the very best of treatment, together with food and living quarters far better than many of them knew before, and a minimum amount of restraint. They have been as well fed as the Army and better housed.'

In April 1943, with racism against the Japanese intensifying as the war escalated, the *LA Times* went further. 'As a race, the Japanese have made for themselves a record for conscienceless treachery unsurpassed in history. Any small theoretical advantages in releasing those under restraint would be enormously outweighed by the risks involved.'

At least my mother and grandmother knew that my grandfather was alive. Even though they didn't see him for four years, they received his censored letters. Words and sentences, even whole paragraphs, were often cut out by army officials who scoured every line for any hint of conspiracy.

After the war ended in 1945, each prisoner was given just $25 as compensation. My mother wanted to return to California, but her father had been embittered by their treatment. He knew life could never go back to normal in the orange orchard. After four torturous years, he left for Japan. As soon as he had settled in his homeland, he sent for his family.

At the age of 21, my mother felt like an outsider in Japan. It didn't help that she looked Japanese and spoke the language. The locals knew she had been born in the USA. The family lived near Hiroshima, which had been devastated by the US atomic bomb on 6 August 1945. The true cost, in terms of death both after the bomb landed and life-shortening illnesses caused by radiation, was calculated decades later. Official studies estimated that over 200,000 people had died as a result of the nuclear attack.

Against such a catastrophic backdrop, it was inevitable that there would be a backlash against anyone who had moved to Japan from America. But my mother said years later that, unless you spent your entire life in Japan, you would always be an outsider. As Japanese society changes in the 21st century, that perception is outdated. But in the late 1940s, when my mother was a young Japanese-American woman, her isolation was obvious no matter how hard she tried to assimilate.

She eventually found work as an interpreter for the British Commonwealth Occupation Forces which controlled Japan after the war. The BCOF headquarters were at Eta Jima, 20 kilometres from Hiroshima, and it was here that she met my dad, Ted. He was a member of the occupation forces. My mum, Nell, was a Westerner, and so she felt at home in Ted's company. They soon fell in love.

In 1947, an Australian soldier, Corporal H. J. Cooke, became the first man to apply for permission to marry a Japanese woman and bring her home to Australia. The application was rejected after Arthur Caldwell, Australia's Minister of Immigration, refused her entry on the basis that, 'while relatives remain of the men who suffered at the hands of the Japanese, it would be the grossest act of public indecency to permit a Japanese of either sex to pollute Australia.'

The following year another Australian soldier, John Henderson, was sent home after he revealed to his officers that, in secret, he had married a Japanese woman. Back in Australia he tried desperately to convince the authorities to relent, but all attempts to bring his wife into the country were blocked. More soldiers came forward and Gordon Parker's pleas for his Japanese wife, Cherry, and their two children to be allowed to join him in Australia were reported sympathetically by the media. In March 1952, with Harold Holt replacing Caldwell as Minister of

Immigration, Japanese women were finally allowed to enter Australia with their husbands.

By 1956, Mr and Mrs Ted and Nell Jones were one of 650 married couples that had left Japan and travelled to Australia. My parents settled in Tasmania and, while they never complained of racism, there was an obvious and widespread bitterness towards Japan after the horrors of the war. Newsreel footage had exposed the terrible torture which Australian prisoners of war had endured in Japanese camps. Hostility towards the Japanese bordered on hatred.

Amid this climate of prejudice, my mother brought up Diane, Vicky and me in a way which spared us her pain. She protected us and, with the help of my dad, raised us with a sense of freedom and happiness. She and my dad made us feel incredibly lucky.

From a young age, I sensed that sport was to be my ticket to inclusion and a way to make my mark. I never felt Japanese because Mum stressed our Australian character but, deep down, I must have known I was different. For starters, apart from my sisters, I didn't look like anyone else I knew.

That difference emerged in subtle ways. It was hard to decide whether our upbringing was shaped by my mother's Japanese heritage or simply a combination of her and my father being very different people. My dad was an uncomplicated Aussie, the best kind of larrikin, who worked hard and enjoyed watching sport and having a couple of beers with his mates on the weekend. Mum was not so laid-back. She was tough on us when we were young, instilling discipline and rigour into our lives. After her upbringing, she was never going to let her children waste their talents. She saw life as a precious gift and insisted that we make the most of it. Australia was a land of opportunity and her children were not going to miss out.

My uncompromising approach to my profession comes from my mother. I never wanted to let her down and I craved her respect and attention. I always did what she asked. I carried those expectations and appetite for hard work into my coaching career many years later. Whether that discipline and attention to detail is inherently Japanese or just in the character of my mother and me is debatable. Mum and Dad handed out praise to me and my sisters in modest amounts. Their generation was very different to parents today who feel compelled to tell their kids how brilliant they are at every opportunity – whether or not it's the truth.

The Japanese influence in our family was obvious. While we never learnt the language, and we were told little about Japan, my mum insisted that my sisters and I should always bring a gift with us when we went to visit our friends. I hated that Japanese ritual because my mates would tease me about the small token of appreciation my mum made me hand over as soon as I arrived. I had to take a present even if I was going over to watch the footy. It was embarrassing.

I was also different to my mates in the sense that my mum ensured I paid proper attention at school. They soon accepted that this was just the way I had been brought up and didn't even rib me about the fact that my mum and sisters all called me Edward – as they still do today.

At first, and in another echo of her Japanese past, my mum was reluctant for me to begin playing cricket or rugby league until I was ten. All my mates, and most Australian boys, started to play sport at the age of five. She eventually relented because I was so persistent. It helped that, on my first day at kindergarten in La Perouse, I sat next to Mark, Glen and Gary Ella. Any anxiety or sadness I had felt at the sight of Mum walking home was replaced by the fun I had with the Ellas.

We would stick together through primary school and all our years at Matraville High. I don't know anyone else who can claim to have grown up alongside three genius rugby players who changed the way the game was played in Australia.

Our part of Sydney in the late 1960s and 1970s was quiet and slow. It had almost a country town feel to it. People were friendly and we always had a good time. I didn't know of any other life, so I never felt like I was missing out.

The Ella boys were just three of 12 children in their family. I don't know how Gordon and May Ella managed it, but they brought up their dozen kids in a small wooden house in La Perouse. There was no inside toilet nor any hot water. When it was bath time they had to heat up an iron tub using boiling water from a relay of kettle runs. My three friends shared one mattress on the floor of their parents' bedroom. It was only a two-bedroomed house, but it rocked with laughter, love and life.

They always turned up to school looking clean and well-dressed and they were polite and well-mannered. They never swore until they were at least 13. The Ellas loved my dad because he had a car and he ferried us from cricket and footy training to matches we played for La Perouse and Matraville. In winter we played rugby league for La Perouse on Saturday mornings and union for Clovelly Eagles on Sundays. I became especially close to Mark and Glen. Their sporting brilliance made them magnetic characters – and they were very witty. Glen was a bit lazy but he exuded charm and warmth. Mark was the greatest rugby player I ever saw, and he was bright too. I did better than them at school – except when it came to maths and our early times-table tests. Mark was the fastest in class and I always wanted to beat him. I never did.

I was so used to hanging out with the Ellas and everyone else I knew from Larpa that I never really noticed skin colour. In the same way I never considered myself to be Japanese, I didn't think of the Ellas as Indigenous Australians. They were just my mates – and outstanding cricketers and rugby league players. I did not have any of their skills, particularly with a rugby ball, but I was tenacious. I was small and light so I needed to work doubly hard to maximize my talents. I also needed to be a smart, determined and purposeful player. Motivation came easily because I was besotted with sport.

I was a better cricketer than footballer then and I captained our team at junior school. By the time we were on our way to Matraville High, and feeling as if I totally fitted in, I'd also developed a pretty sharp tongue. It was my way of getting attention and I loved making people laugh. It was the Australian way. Back then 'putting shit on people', as it was known, was a national pastime. From a young age I was pretty good at it – not that I ever let my mum hear me.

Apart from me, the little Japanese wisecracker, the most exotic kid in our class all through junior and high school was Raymond Bahaja. Raymond's family was of Egyptian descent and he copped some stick because of it. White Australia had long been a crude and tough society. It did not matter that the Indigenous people of Australia had lived in the country for over 65,000 years before the British arrived in 1788. They brought racism with them and, in the 1960s and 1970s, you still needed a thick skin if you were of Indigenous, Arabic, Asian, Black or Polynesian descent.

Of course, Dad kept his word when he returned from Vietnam and, in February 1971, he took me to the SCG to watch the last Test of the Ashes series between Australia and England. It had been a long, tough series, with an unprecedented seven Tests. Australia had to win the final Test to square the series 1–1. It was a baking Sydney summer day and a sense of history hung in the air. This was the first series where the ABC – the Australian Broadcasting Corporation – offered ball-by-ball commentary on the radio. I loved the way the rhythm of the game was captured by the mix of voices, and the roars and applause that echoed from my little radio.

Australia was in a fever. It was bad enough that we were 1–0 down against the Poms, a team which featured Geoff Boycott, John Edrich, Basil D'Oliveira, Ray Illingworth, Alan Knott, Derek Underwood and John Snow. We had been spanked in South Africa the previous summer – losing all four Tests. The South Africans had a great team then, from Barry Richards and Graeme Pollock to Mike Proctor and Peter Pollock, which would soon be lost to cricket because of the sports boycott against apartheid. England were nowhere near as good as the South Africans and yet we were losing the Ashes to them.

The selectors made a bold change before this final Test. Bill Lawry became the first Australian cricket captain to be dropped mid-series. He had played 67 Tests and been a fixture at the top of the order for ten years. His Test average was 47.15, the mark of a very good batsman, and he had not batted particularly badly against England. The Adelaide Test had been rained off without a ball being bowled, but in the five earlier Tests he had hit 324 runs at an average of 40.50. Yet, facing the humiliation of losing the Ashes to an ordinary England side, Lawry had to go.

Even at the age of 11, I understood the brutal realities of international sport. Lawry was far too cautious and conservative. He was not the sort of leader who could inspire Australia to a comeback win. The selectors turned instead to a maverick South Australian – Ian Chappell. In the second innings of the drawn sixth Test, Chappell had hit a thrilling century. That match had also marked the debut of the West Australian, Dennis Lillee, who took five wickets in England's first innings. 'D. K.' would go on to become, at least for me, the greatest fast bowler in history.

On the first morning of the Test I was beside myself with excitement when Dad and I took our seats at the SCG. When Chappell led out Australia for the very first time, having won the toss and elected to bowl, the applause was rapturous. The great saviour had arrived. I could not take my eyes off our new captain. Chappell looked exactly like an Aussie captain should look. He was big, bold and brash – and he had authority as he stood at first slip. Collar up, shirt unbuttoned and chewing gum madly, he was decisive as he set his fields. He was the antithesis of Lawry, who moved slowly and apologetically. It was clear that things were going to be different. He looked the opposite of a bloke who would be tentative in his tactics or happy to accept an honourable draw. Chappell looked every bit the winner we wanted to cheer.

I obviously didn't understand it fully then, but Chappell was changing the culture of his team. It was a task I would take on many times in my coaching career. He didn't care what people thought and he was prepared to rip up convention and do things his own way. Chappell was totally committed to improving Australian cricket and he made everyone want to play for him. Whether they were gifted cricketers, like Lillee or Ian's brother Greg, or more run-of-the-mill blokes, Chappell lifted each one of them. He was hard, driven and uncompromising. He ended some players' careers ruthlessly, but he was full of unshakeable belief. His job was to win cricket matches, and nothing but the highest possible performance was acceptable.

England were bowled out for 186 and that was the start of the transformation under Chappell. He took over a poor Australian side, which had forgotten how to win, and turned them into the best team in the world. It takes time and this was no exception. Despite taking a 78-run lead after the first innings, Australia still struggled. England compiled an impressive 302 in the second innings. Set a target of 223 to win the game and level the series, Australia were bowled out for 160. My new hero only scored six as England won the Ashes 2–0.

It was a salutary lesson for a young boy. In sport, you have to accept the reality of defeat. It hurts but you can always find lessons and hope. Chappell spelt out the main lesson. Australia were not good enough or, most of all, not mentally tough enough. But there was obvious hope. Chappell was precisely the kind of leader we needed to lift the team up by its bootstraps, give it a good old shake, and show us how we could become better. The arrival of Jeff Thomson the following year, to open the bowling in a blistering partnership with Lillee, helped Chappell's team reach the summit of world cricket.

Ian Chappell influenced my thinking about sport and leadership. I have always set out to make my teams tough and uncompromising. I have tried to create tactically smart teams driven by a deep belief in themselves. Chappell and his players were often described as arrogant – which is an accusation levelled many times at my teams. But there is a difference between confidence and arrogance. The confidence of Chappell was rooted in hard work and a positive attitude. To my eye, there was never a skerrick of arrogance in him. It was just a determination to make things work, no matter the situation.

Australia is a big country, with a small population, at the bottom of the world. And for us to become the best in the world it takes toughness, intelligence, competitiveness and creativity. In our own way, a few years later at Matraville High, we did something similar in the context of Australian schoolboy rugby. It was not enough that we had the shimmering virtuosity of the Ella brothers. We had something more.

We were hard and we were smart, and we were always looking for an edge and a way to maximize every ounce of ambition and talent we had in our side. We were the perennial outsiders determined to find the best in ourselves. We were followers of the mighty Ian Chappell, or Chappelli as his legions of fans called him. He really was the Godfather. We were determined to follow him and, as the Matraville Mafiosi, be just as canny and resourceful as Chappelli.

When I remember my life as a schoolboy, my memories are of coming home from La Perouse and Matraville, dumping my bag, and going straight to the park. We would play cricket in the summer and touch footy in the winter. I remember the loamy soil and the underfoot scrub, with the salty tang of fresh sea air and the flame from the Botany petrol plant that would glow as dusk settled over Little Bay.

We would play until it was dark and I'd run home, wash and smarten up for dinner, eat with my family and then do all my schoolwork before bed. Same again the next day – with time on the beach or cricket in the nets or a game of league or union to add variety. It was a simple, sporting life in a working-class area. There were no airs or graces about the people around us. They were just good, honest, hard-working people who also knew how to enjoy themselves.

It sometimes chokes me up now when I think how hard my dad worked to provide for us. He worked very long hours, and he never complained, and he made us feel as if we didn't want for anything. Of course I wanted a new cricket bat or a new pair of footy boots. But we didn't have enough money to get the best bat or the latest pair of boots on offer, so I just used the equipment I already had. Life has changed now but, then, we were totally unmaterialistic. We were happy and free almost all of the time.

2

THE RANDWICK WAY

We played rugby in the shadow of Long Bay jail. From Matraville High you just had to cross Anzac Parade and a patch of scrubland to reach the most notorious high-security prison in Australia. There was a disproportionately high percentage rate of young Indigenous Australians both at our school and in the Long Bay Correctional Centre. And so the bigots and racists, as well as those rugby teams who envied or lost to us, made a cheap jibe. They told us that once we'd finished our schooling, we just needed to make a short walk to start our new lives behind the Long Bay bars. But the Matraville boys had the last laugh, when the Ella brothers, and Lloyd Walker, went on to light up Australian rugby and change it for good.

I remember how the jail seemed to be staring at us when we went out for training. You could just about see the big wall surrounding it in the distance. Being close to the jail, however, was the least of our concerns. We had more problems clearing the rubbish often dumped on the Matraville Oval before we could start practice. It was a shame that they had settled on this location for Long Bay, because the adjoining areas of Malabar and La Perouse had Indigenous settlements stretching back 20,000 years.

Chifley was a real working-class area back then, but these days it's been completely gentrified. Houses that would have been worth $30,000 in the 1970s now cost over $1.5 million. I guess it helps that, located on the southern coast of Sydney's metropolitan area, Chifley boasts stunning sheer sandstone cliffs. They sparkle in the morning sun and offer some of the city's most spectacular sea views. I liked it more back then than I do now, but that's because I loved my childhood and the memories it holds.

I was about to turn 12 when, alongside Glen and Mark, I started at Matraville High in January 1972. We had grown up in a rugby league-dominated area and union was our second winter sport. Rugby was mostly a game for upper-class white boys rather than for Indigenous or mixed-blood kids like us. League was the working man's game and a professional sport. Unlike union, it offered the best young Indigenous athletes a chance to make a dollar from their talents. The Ellas' uncle, Bruce 'Larpa' Stewart, had made a splash in league with South Sydney and Eastern Suburbs in the 1960s. I remembered him mostly as a fantastic goal-kicker who would toe-punt penalties from all over the park.

Glen's favourite sportsman was Arthur Beetson, a legendary Indigenous prop from Queensland who came to the big smoke to play for the Balmain Tigers and then Eastern Suburbs' Roosters. Arthur, or Big Artie as he was known, was a mercurial footballer. He had the body of a front-row forward with the hands of a fly half. He could set off on a bullocking 30-metre run and then make a deft little offload with beautiful timing. I always razz Glen about putting on weight in middle age – saying it must be out of respect for Big Artie. Glen also loved another tough Indigenous prop, John Sattler, captain of the South Sydney Rabbitohs, who is remembered for playing on and winning the 1970 Grand Final with a broken jaw.

We are still mad-keen rugby league fans today. I can't get enough of it. I also think that the fact we played so much league as kids gave us a head start in rugby by developing our core skills of tackling, catching and passing. We were also lucky that, at Matraville, we were exposed to some special teachers. Allan Glenn was our young and charismatic maths teacher who coached us at rugby for three years, from the under-13s to under-15s.

Mr Glenn was schooled in the art of the flat backline and the bold counter-attacking style of rugby which Geoff Mould, our favourite teacher, had learnt from Cyril Towers. Most of all, they just encouraged us to play with freedom. We won most matches by 50 or 60 points. There was no need for any tactical team-talk while we tucked into our oranges at half-time. Looking at the scoreboard Glenn would say: 'Can we double it?' We usually did.

He entered us for the Buchan Shield, which was contested by most of the best under-15 teams in New South Wales – apart from a few like St Joeys. It was the junior version of the premier schoolboy competition, the Waratah Shield, and Glen Ella was convinced we would win it. When our coach pointed out Arthur Buchan, after whom the under-15 shield was named, Glen went up to him. 'Hey Mister,' he said casually to Buchan, a retired referee who looked at him in surprise, 'we're going to win your cup.'

I didn't play in that game but we beat St Ives comfortably in the 1974 final – which was held at the Sydney Cricket Ground. A year later we retained the shield and I was at hooker as we won the final at Coogee Oval. I had grown in confidence. The shy boy who kept his head down had given way to a leader of the pack with a mouth ready for action. I had seen how, when playing cricket, saying a couple of pointed words could unsettle an opposition batsman. As captain of the cricket team it was my job to keep my teammates upbeat and enthused. I found it easy to make them laugh. Usually, I just let slip an in-joke, but occasionally I would take down an opponent in a way that had my teammates roaring.

Rugby soon became more serious. Under Allan Glenn we were unbeaten in our three seasons at junior level. We scored over 1,000 points and conceded less than 50. But as we got older, our opponents were bigger and better, and we started competing against many more private schools. We were lucky that Geoff Mould, or Mouldy as we called him, opened our minds as first-team players. We would sit in a classroom at lunchtime and he would go through some set plays and strategic moves on the blackboard. One of the plays he taught us was called the Baffler and it did totally baffle many opposing backlines.

Mouldy also expanded our education by showing us Five Nations games from the 1970s. He had recorded them at home, as ABC broadcast the matches early on Sunday mornings. Mouldy brought the old Betamax tapes to school so that we could watch the great Welsh team starring Gareth Edwards and Phil Bennett or thrilling French forwards like Jean-Pierre Rives. We would watch Willie John McBride and his gnarled old Irish pack take on the English forwards at Twickenham or Lansdowne Road. The Scots had Ian 'Mighty Mouse' McLauchlan and Gordon Brown. Bill McLaren's unforgettable voice filled the room.

British and Irish rugby was exceptionally strong, as the 1974 Lions had proved on their unbeaten tour of South Africa. But it was also very foreign. The games we saw were often played on the kind of muddy fields we had never seen before. But the passion and intensity of the Five Nations crowds poured out of the screen. The singing, cheering crowds were smiling and the atmosphere was buzzing.

The Welsh loved to run the ball and Edwards, Bennett and J. P. R. Williams had played for the Barbarians against the All Blacks at Twickenham in 1973. We watched the try that Edwards scored – a move started by Phil Bennett near the Barbarians' own line and brilliantly completed at the other end by Edwards after a breathtaking display of skill, agility and speed – over and over again. We reckoned that he would have slotted in perfectly into our style of running rugby at Matraville.

Wales scored another legendary try against Scotland at Murrayfield in 1977. J. P. R. Williams, with his socks around his ankles, scooped up a kick from the great Scottish full back Andy Irvine. Near his own 22, and despite being nailed by Sandy Carmichael, Williams fed the ball to Steve Fenwick who moved it on to Gerald Davies. Stepping a couple of defenders, Davies found

Phil Bennett, who swapped passes with Fenwick and David Burcher before Bennett went over beneath the posts. That brilliant try electrified Matraville High and inspired us to play this style of rugby. At the same time we knew that you needed the ball to be won by your forwards. So we came to love the rigour and the structure of the Five Nations.

The freedom with which all our Matraville teams played was built on a series of non-negotiable factors, like our lines of running and support, our accuracy of passing and catching. We understood that a mastery of the basics led to a mastery of the game. Geoff Mould drilled those essentials into us. He was a highly educated and captivating speaker who loved sport, books, classical music and opera. He had only begun to play rugby late in life, but his instinctive feel for the game was sharpened by the intellectual debates he would have about rugby with the great Cyril Towers. At Matraville he and Towers realized that they were sitting on a goldmine of natural talent; and they liberated us to play with even more flair.

Discipline was key and, as a PE teacher, Mouldy was very strict. I often found myself in trouble when he caught me acting the goat, giving a running commentary as we tossed boots and towels around the gym. He wouldn't stand for it, and gave us two whacks of the cane on each hand. Mouldy was a big man and so it hurt. But he was fair. We respected him and swallowed our medicine.

Even when we were playing softball with the girls in PE, he made sure we paid attention to the catch-and-pass basics. He also honed our natural game by insisting we play a lot of touch. The more we played, the better we performed. He was a very clever coach who taught us so much without our even realizing it.

We won the Waratah Shield in my last two years of school, in 1976 and 1977, and played such an exciting brand of rugby that we became national news. The idea that an underprivileged school, packed with Indigenous kids, could dominate a traditionally elitist sport caught the media's eye and the public imagination. Of course part of our mystique stemmed from the fact that Matraville was found on the reclaimed sandhills and scrubland of southeastern Sydney, in the shadow of Long Bay jail.

When I reflect on those Matraville years now, it seems remarkable that a third of our schoolboy XV went on to feature in international rugby. The Ella trio and Lloyd Walker obviously played for Australia, while Glen and I have coached Test teams for many years.

Modern rugby is almost unrecognizable compared to the game we played in the 1970s, but I have encouraged all my teams to play with the courage and desire of the Ellas. As long as I can see those attributes in my teams, and we win games, I'm happy.

In rugby, as in life, there are always bitter disappointments. Nine of our Matraville team, including me, were picked for two New South Wales selections who played in the annual Australian schoolboys' championships in 1977. NSW and Queensland always had two teams because they were the biggest states. But there was an even more important prize on offer that year. Following the final matches, an Australian schools side would be selected to tour Japan, Holland, the UK and Ireland in 1977–8. Both NSW teams made the final and I was on the winning side with Mark and Glen.

But, as we gathered at the after-match function to hear the squad being read out, my name was missing. I was devastated. I thought I had done enough. I stood there trying to compose myself and not let on that I was crushed. It was just the first serious selection disappointment in my playing career.

Five of our Matraville team – the three Ellas, Darryl Lester and Warwick Melrose – were picked but four of us were left out. Wally Lewis, the future Australian League great, had the good grace to say he had only been picked ahead of Lloyd Walker because Geoff Mould, who was the national schools coach, and the other selectors didn't want the squad to be dominated by Matraville players.

I thought I was good enough to play on that tour, so it burnt to be left out. But in the end, looking back, it was a learning experience. When you endure those tough, bruising moments in life, you never think they're going to help you learn and get better. It's the same when you lose a big game. First the pain, then the experience.

Along with the rest of Australia I followed the tour from a distance. The Australian and British media went into raptures about the brilliance of a schools team they dubbed 'The Invincibles'. Sparked by the Ellas, Australia won all 19 matches on tour. They scored 110 tries and conceded only six. It felt like a turning point in Australian rugby. All of a sudden, our sport was big news, and people were interested in and excited by the game. The flair of the Ellas dominated the headlines and people could not get enough of their 'rags to riches' story – or the genius of their rugby. Up to that point, apart from the occasional team in the 1960s, Australian rugby had been dull and pedestrian.

The Ellas' commitment to rugby union was sealed on that tour. They knew that, while they could make money out of league, rugby union could make them legendary. Their experience with The Invincibles gave them a taste of everything that union could offer. All three boys set their hearts on touring the world with the Wallabies.

After a few months of kicking stones, I resolved to work even harder. For the last two years at Matraville, I had run for three miles every morning at 6 a.m. with our Dalmatian. I intensified my efforts and, besides running, began to lift weights on my own in the evening. I knew that, to play senior rugby at a high level, I needed to become bigger and stronger.

I already had a good understanding of the game, but I studied it even more intently. I loved the fact that rugby was such a technical game you could win in numerous ways. Matraville had given me a good grounding in rugby and the resilience to deal with the knocks and bumps of real life.

I had not become an Invincible, but I was one of only three

kids from Matraville High who qualified for university that year. My mother had drilled it into me that I needed to reach that goal. Disappointing her would have been a bigger failure. More than anything I accomplished on the sporting field, my university entrance made her happy.

I owe every moment of success I've had as a coach to Randwick. At Coogee Oval, a five-minute walk down Dolphin Street to the beach, Randwick Rugby Club provided the foundation to a coaching career that stretches across a quarter of a century. Randwick has supplied four Wallaby coaches over the last 30 years in Bob Dwyer, myself, Ewen McKenzie and Michael Cheika. Bob is my mentor and former Randwick coach, while I played alongside Ewen and Michael.

During my dozen years at Randwick, I learnt everything I know about winning, while having more fun than might be legal, as well as enduring another shattering disappointment which helped shape me as a coach of ambition and ruthless high standards. Randwick was the source of my rugby education and the reason why I have such respect for the game.

But for six months I refused to play for them. On the night we won our second Waratah Shield, in my final year at Matraville in 1977, we were meant to have our party at the Randwick clubhouse. The club cancelled our celebrations at the last minute, which I thought was poor form. Even though my best mates, Glen and Mark, were on their way to Randwick, I thought, 'Bugger it, if they're treating us like this, I'm not playing for them.' My belligerence meter was dialled all the way up to ten.

I began my Bachelor of Education degree, majoring in geography and physical education, at the University of Sydney. I decided to play for the University of New South Wales in the Sydney Rugby Union's second division. It was social rugby; and it was a disaster. I was used to playing with supremely talented and highly motivated sportsmen who were consumed by winning. The university boys just wanted to play a little rugby before getting back to the clubhouse to sing songs, chase girls and drink beers. There's nothing wrong with that, of course, and I have some fond memories of my time there. But, with my ambition to play at the highest level, I was in the wrong place with the wrong attitude. Most of the players didn't bother turning up for training. After six months I got off my high horse and went back to Randwick.

The Ella brothers were already kicking up a storm in Coogee. Ever since he had seen Matraville beat St Joseph's 18 months earlier, Bob Dwyer had been hell-bent on bringing my three friends to Randwick. The twins were 18 and Gary was still only 17 when Bob went to see them and their parents in La Perouse. Apart from persuading them to join Randwick, he was most intent on explaining that they should forget about playing colts (under-20s) rugby. He wanted them to play for Randwick's first team in the new 1978 season. It was a huge leap from schoolboy games to senior first-grade rugby, but Bob made a compelling case.

He is a deep thinker and a very eloquent man. He can charm birds from the trees. But, most of all, Bob exudes clarity and passion in an irresistible combination. Sometimes the most passionate people are muddled, as too much emotion gets in the way. But Bob's insights into the game are generated by the sharpest rugby brain I know. It allows him to talk about complex plays or situations with simplicity and precision. As a coach and a leader this is a critical skill. Whether in sport, business or as the principal of a school, the people you need to direct, motivate and educate have to understand with complete clarity what they are expected to do and how they are meant to behave. There should be no room for doubt or confusion.

Bob was ambitious for himself, for the club and for the boys. So he was compelled to state the obvious. Mark, Glen and Gary were too good to play for the colts. He wanted them to take on the challenge of playing the best.

The brothers were so laid-back that they pointed out that their Matraville mates, apart from me staging my one-man protest against the club, planned on playing for Randwick Colts. They were still boys and their spindly frames looked fragile and breakable when set against the big men of grade rugby, the club competition which is just below state level. They certainly didn't look as if they could withstand the kind of beating they were sure to cop if anyone ever got hold of them. They also knew they would have more fun in the colts.

'But you need to test your ability against the best,' Bob told them, 'and you need to do it now. Not next year.'

Bob was cunning and so he dialled his request back to a suggestion that perhaps they should play grade trials. If they liked it, they would be part of the senior squad and, if the trial left them with any doubts, they could enjoy a season with the colts.

'Fair enough,' Glen said. 'I reckon we'll give it a crack. What do you think, bro?'

Mark, the most gifted of them all, nodded. 'Sounds good.'

All three Ella boys lit up the Randwick trial. Bob said he had never seen anything like it. They found gaps at will. Their running lines, support and linking play meant that no one laid a hand on them. It looked as if they were playing against poor old Joeys again rather than a team of high-quality grade footballers. The Ellas were sold on playing grade rugby.

Despite still being a relatively young coach at 36, Bob knew how important it was to handle the transition of his gifted prodigies to senior rugby with real care. He initially played them in the reserves and then he surprised everyone by picking Gary first. An injury at outside centre opened up a space and Bob didn't hesitate when choosing a 17-year-old for his debut. If you're good enough, you're old enough.

While Mark and Glen had the more outrageous talent, Bob appreciated Gary's subtlety. Outside centre doesn't offer the same scope for flamboyance that Glen could enjoy at full back – nor the multiple touches Mark had at fly half. An outside centre has to think more about the support lines he offers to his inside centre and the space he makes for the wide players on his right.

Gary understood the art of linking play. He moved beautifully and could find a gap himself or create opportunities for his outside men. Like a well-driven Formula One car, he could switch direction with no drop in either velocity or control.

In later years Bob said only two outside centres, Conrad Smith for the All Blacks and Gary Ella at Randwick, could create a try for someone else purely through the accuracy and speed of their realignment. Gary would create gaps by dragging defenders away with his movement and create a hole that another of his teammates would burst through to score. It was instinctive to Gary – but he had also been schooled expertly by Geoff Mould and Cyril Towers.

On his Randwick debut, against our local rivals Eastern Suburbs, Gary set up a try and scored one himself. A week later Mark joined him in the side when Randwick's regular number 10, the Wallaby Ken Wright, played for New South Wales. Mark slotted in so perfectly that the experienced Wright was shifted to inside centre on his return. Glen was called up as a last-minute replacement at full back and he did well in a 36–10 win over Parramatta. But his brothers stole the show by scoring four tries between them, with a hat-trick for Gary.

Building on the interest generated by their performances with The Invincibles, the media went ballistic. Sydney club rugby gained a profile that it had never experienced before. All anyone could talk about was 'Ella! Ella! Ella!' Watching from a distance, I was more excited than they were as the righteousness of my one-man exile had waned. I was desperate to join them. My best mates were having the time of their lives and I was missing all the fun.

The next big challenge for the Ella Brothers was away against the unbeaten Northern Suburbs – who had been the best team in Sydney grade rugby for most of the 1970s. They had giant forwards like the Wallabies Garrick Fay, Reg Smith and Andy Stewart. When Bob announced the team, all three brothers were in the side. Expectations and excitement went through the roof.

The interest was so great that ABC television took the unprecedented step of televising the match live across Australia. The Ellas did not disappoint. Northern Suburbs were drilled 63–0.

The hysteria jumped to another level. Even rugby league coaches were watching and talking feverishly about the mercurial Ella brothers. The main Sydney tabloid, the *Daily Telegraph*, fuelled speculation of a possible switch to the professional code with a headline that screamed: '$100,000 for Ellas!' The boys loved playing league but it was obvious rugby union was the game for them. I knew that – no matter how much money they were offered – they would never leave.

It was pretty funny watching them cope with the adulation. They couldn't work out what all the fuss was about, as they were just playing a game they had loved for the past ten years. The attention never went to their heads.

It was around this time that I decided to end my strike against the club and join Randwick. I had achieved precisely nothing – but, unfortunately, this wouldn't be the last time my railing against perceived unfairness would get me into trouble.

You shouldn't be surprised that Bob made no attempt to talk me into playing grade rugby. I would never make headlines similar to the Ellas as a player, nor would I be picked for the first team as soon as I joined Randwick. I needed a few seasons of colts and lower-grade rugby to prepare me for the big step-up. So at the start of the 1979 season, I played in the colts with my old school pals Lloyd Walker, Warwick Melrose, Darryl Lester and Greg Stores. It was great fun.

I made steady progress and, after two years with the colts, I began playing regular lower-grade senior rugby. In 1982, in my second year of men's rugby, I won the club's 'most improved player'. A year later I was hooker when we won the reserve-grade championship. Jeff Sayle, Randwick's new first-grade coach, encouraged me to aim higher.

Jeff had replaced Bob who, in 1982, had become the Wallabies coach. After coaching Randwick to four wins in five successive grand finals, that first stint as national coach did not work out for Bob. He was in charge of the Wallabies for just two seasons before he was replaced by Alan Jones, from Manly, our bitterest opponents.

It began badly for Bob when, before his debut Test in Brisbane as Australia's coach, he copped a hammering from the press for picking Mark and Glen in place of two Queensland and Wallabies stalwarts in Paul McLean at 10 and Roger Gould at 15. The Queenslanders, and many other Australian rugby fans, called for his head. But Bob wanted Australia to play like Randwick. He was convinced that Australia could become a dominant force in world rugby if they played with the ball in hand and relied on pace, space and guile. Queensland had traditionally dominated Australian selection with a game that depended on kicking for field position and forward power. Bob knew there was a better way.

The Brisbane locals were outraged, and they cheered when Glen dropped a high ball early on in the Test against Scotland. They seemed just as delighted after Mark threw a wayward pass when Glen looked certain to score. The crowd chanted Gould's name throughout as Scotland shocked Australia by winning 12–7. Bob recalled Gould and McLean for the second Test, which Australia won decisively. But this early experience of the white-hot pressure of international rugby had shaken him.

Glen's confidence took a big knock and his international career never recovered from being booed in Brisbane. He won only three more caps. Gary played six times for Australia, while Mark had by far the most successful career. He played 25 Tests, at a time when international matches were less frequent and amateurs balanced rugby commitments with making a living. Mark was a revelation and, after captaining Australia ten times, he masterminded the Wallabies' Grand Slam-winning tour of Britain in 1984. David Campese, another Randwick star, described Mark as the greatest rugby player he ever saw. I thought he retired far too early after that tour. But the game wasn't professional at that time, and Mark needed to build a career outside rugby.

Even after Australia's comprehensive 33–9 victory over Scotland in his second match as national coach, with McLean scoring 21 points, Bob faced controversy. Nine leading players, most of them from Queensland, announced that they were unavailable for the tour of New Zealand. The official line was that they could not take time off work but, privately, they confirmed they were unhappy with the more expansive style of play Bob was trying to impose. Bob could be abrasive and impatient, and steps were taken to oust him at the end of 1983 after he had lost eight of 16 Tests.

Bob was a better coach when he returned to Randwick. And then, from 1988 to 1995, when back with the Wallabies, his genius as a national coach became evident. Australia won the 1991 World Cup, beating England at Twickenham in the final. His record in that second stint as national coach was 39 wins, two draws and 17 defeats.

I was lucky to have played under Bob for four years at Randwick. He transformed my thinking and understanding of the game. The two most influential coaches in my career were Bob Dwyer and Jeff Sayle. They couldn't have been more different, but they taught me so much about coaching. Unlike Bob, who was highly motivated and tactically astute, Jeff just loved the game, loved the laughter and loved the beer. His warm and friendly character gelled his teams together. He was not a great coach, technically or in training, but he cared about his players and showed such pride in the club. I obviously turned to Bob for his wisdom, his strategic insights and his unbreakable hardness and precision, but Jeff showed me the sheer joy of the game. He loved Randwick – so much so that he was the bar manager as well as the head coach for a few years. Jeff was the loveliest man, with an iron constitution.

He had been a decent player, who earned one Test cap against New Zealand in 1967, and he remained a fitness fanatic for years. Jeff was the type of bloke who loved running laps around Coogee Oval while pushing the heavy roller used in the cricket season. At the same time he was a drinker and so, as the years passed, his weight ballooned. In my first year of senior football down the grades, Jeff sometimes played flanker for the third team. I remember him sinking a schooner of sherry in the dressing room before we ran out. He still played a full game.

In 1984, after Bruce Malouf retired as hooker, Jeff promoted me to the first team. I had served my time in a high-quality reserve-grade team and was ready. We had been coached in the reserves by Ian 'Speed' Kennedy. We called him 'Speed' because he had been the slowest forward on the field when he was club captain. He was a policeman and a very good coach who, in 1982, worked us hard. We trained three times a week, rather than twice, and ended up with a great team which produced seven future Wallabies. We finished the season 15 points clear at the top of the table and should have taken the grand final at a canter. But Speed made the mistake of working us far too hard and the team were filthy with him on the day of the grand final. We had lost our spark and were well beaten.

The next season Speed listened to the players a lot more. I often acted as de facto coach as we ran away with the competition and won the reserve grand final in style. By the time I broke into the first team, I was confident. I was playing alongside my best mates, the Ellas, and Jeff Sayle let us run the show. Happy days.

We had a team full of bright blokes and many of them held down pretty big jobs during the day while we trained two evenings a week. Simon Poidevin, our Wallaby flanker, was a stockbroker, while Mark worked for Rothmans, Glen for TNT and Gary for the Department of Aboriginal Affairs in New South Wales. I had a demanding job as a geography and PE teacher. But when it came to training we poured everything into it. We wanted to improve as rugby players and we wanted to win. We were all ruthlessly competitive. Rugby was our passion.

At the same time, we knew how to have fun. Bob Dwyer always liked Randwick's teams to warm up with a 30-minute game of touch football. We had played touch all our lives and we loved it. It often got competitive, but I was the loudest voice and made sure everyone enjoyed themselves before the serious stuff began. I had always loved radio commentary – so during our games of touch, I acted as a commentator and always got the boys laughing.

I gave everyone a nickname. Poidevin was Venus de Milo because he had a great body and no hands. Ewen McKenzie was Link. Despite being an extremely intelligent man, he was a prop forward who looked like a wrestler with the same nickname. Glen chipped in with a quip that Ewen was probably also the evolutionary link between the Neanderthals and man today. It was knockabout stuff because Link was such an analytical thinker. Mark Ella, meanwhile, was God. He was that good.

Everyone called me Beaver. In later years people thought it was because, despite being small, I beavered my way to the bottom of the ruck to get the ball. But my nickname had nothing to do with rugby. I was called Beaver the first time at university when I went waterskiing with my great mate Mick Aldous on the Shoalhaven River on the NSW south coast. On one occasion I came off the skis and, as they turned the boat around to pick me up, they reckoned I was a dead ringer for a beaver. The name just stuck. My oldest and closest friends still call me Beaver.

It was during those games of touch that I honed my skills of straightening people up with a verbal jab. It's common in Australian sport but frowned upon in the UK. British people are more courteous and polite. George Gregan tells an amusing story about Matt Dawson on the 2001 Lions tour. Matt was second choice behind Rob Howley at scrum half, but he finally made it into the Test team. Once the game started George started chipping away at him:

'Dawse, what are you doing here, mate? It's Saturday. You only play on Wednesdays.' (That was when the 'B' team matches were held.) 'You should check the date, mate, because you're a Wednesday player.' It was all good fun and pretty harmless. But then Dawson's dad, whom George knew, asked if he had a problem with Matt. But there was no problem at all. It was just a bit of niggle.

George tells another story which happened after the 2003 Rugby World Cup. George, like me, struggled after we lost to England. He carried the disappointment with him and it was difficult. At Christmas he visited his friend Pat Rafter up on the Sunshine Coast, where he'd been invited to play in the Australia PGA Golf Pro-Am. After his round he was heading to the bar to find Rafter and a few of the other Davis Cup players. The golf pros had gathered. As he approached the bar, they started singing. 'Georgie Gregan lost the Cup, do dah, do dah. Georgie Gregan lost the Cup, oh the do-dah day. Georgie lost the Cup, Georgie lost the Cup, Georgie Gregan lost the Cup oh the do-dah day . . .' And these blokes were his mates. It's a hard school but 99 per cent of the time, when you are 'sledging', it's humorous.

Someone told me the Australian cricket team can't wait to see the latest lyrics of the Barmy Army before they tour so they can rub it into their teammates. Another of my favourite 'sledges' was in a game in 2000 when the Brumbies played the Natal Sharks in Durban. Ollie le Roux, the portly and popular Springbok prop, came charging on to a ball close to our line and dropped it cold. Our number 8, Gordon Falcon, a hard-as-nails Kiwi from Hawkes Bay who didn't often say much, walked over to Ollie and said: 'Hey bro, you wouldn't have dropped it if it was a doughnut.' Both packs of forwards cracked up laughing. In Australian sport everyone does it and, most of the time, it's not with any malice or intent. It's just an accepted way of trying to unsettle your opponent.

David Knox, who also went to Matraville High, was said to be the next best sledger after me. We both learnt our craft as cricketers. Of course I was guilty of misjudging some sledges. No question. But you live and learn. I used to give it out, so I had to learn to take it. Even when they would occasionally go low, I tried to maintain some respect. I remember only one racial slur, playing for New South Wales against Queensland, when their hooker called me a 'Chink' and a 'Chinese bastard'.

'Mate,' I said with a smile, 'you're too stupid to know the difference between the Chinese and the Japanese.'

I usually preferred the more subtle quip or something totally unexpected. Years later, when my career was almost over, I had one last crack playing for Southern Districts. We came up against Randwick whose tight-head prop, Joe Picone, was a good mate of mine. We had played a lot of games together and I knew how good he was in the tight. I thought, 'Shit, Joe's going to give us some in the scrum. I have to distract him.' So, at the first scrum, I kissed him on the cheek. I said: 'Joe, I love you.' He did not know where to look or what to do. He was freaked out the whole game. I said to him later, 'It was just a bit of fun, mate,' and he laughed. He knew I had stitched him up.

Laughter was the soundtrack of my time at Randwick. After games we would end up in the clubhouse and, on winter nights, start a fire in a 44-gallon drum in the car park and sit around it having plenty to drink. We would then go out to the local bars until three or four in the morning. Glen often said he didn't know how we won any matches – but we did pretty well.

Between 1977 and 1992, Randwick reached 16 consecutive grand finals and won 12 of them. Bob Dwyer was the architect of our domination of Sydney club rugby. Over his two spells as head coach, we played in nine grand finals and won six of them.

Bob made me understand that determination and emotional courage had to be at the heart of every endeavour. Any achievement of note would take hard work and application. We had to be prepared to face defeat and come back from it. Mistakes would be made and games would be lost – but as long as we remained brave and determined, we would prevail.

Bob introduced me to the value of sports science in training. His sessions were incredibly well organized and thorough. He was demanding and could be aggressive. He either backed you to the hilt or he burnt you. I was fortunate that Bob liked me. I loved him because he was a great coach. I was not a great player, but he appreciated my efforts and the way I constantly tried to improve. We were also alike in examining the game very deeply.

He could be very hard. I always remember how, after we were beaten by Manly in a first-grade game, Bob tore into us. I probably had about 20 caps for Randwick then and Pat Slyney, our tight-head prop, had played over 200 times for the first team. It was one of those games where they did something a bit different. We didn't react and so Manly beat us. The defeat stung and down at Latham Park, where we trained, Bob growled when he asked why we had not worked out what was happening on the field: 'How in the fuck didn't anybody say anything?'

The players were quiet. Bob pointed at Pat. 'How many Randwick caps have you got, mate?'

'Two hundred,' the prop muttered.

'You've played 200 fucking games for us, Pat, and what did you say in the second half?'

The prop shook his head. 'Nothing.'

Bob nodded in return but, then, he broke down what happened on the field with such clear vision that none of us has ever forgotten that electrifying speech.

I learnt from Bob that it is far better to talk to your players after you've had some distance from the game. Instead of getting caught up in the emotion of the moment, you need to draw breath and step back. Once you have done your analysis you can leave players with a vivid picture in their heads of what they should have done differently. Of course it took me time to understand the value of detachment. As a young coach I sometimes allowed my emotion to get the better of me. I could launch easily into a blistering address. But I soon learnt that, apart from the initial shock of the blast, there is not much point in raving at a team.

These days I always give the players time to work through a defeat, or a bad performance, before I offer my view. The modern player is also much softer and more sensitive than the blokes I played with in the 1980s. Another approach is needed. But Bob Dwyer's clarity, using the simplicity of truth, remains my touchstone. You have to tell it as it is.

In the hardness of my character I also echo Bob. The clichéd view of me in the media is that I'm a tyrant who reduces players to tears or quivering wrecks. Most of those articles rehash the same old stories from my earliest years of coaching and suggest that I am a careless bully or a constant firebrand. Once you get a reputation it's hard to shake, but I've never bothered to try and change these perceptions. It's lazy journalism because all stories need a villain. But I'd rather spend time being productive. I have become more rounded and nuanced in my coaching through experience and maturing as a person and as a teacher. Don't get me wrong. If players or staff deserve a pull-through they will get one. But I'm a bit more diplomatic than I was in my earliest days. I will always remain honest with my players and demand their best effort every single day.

Toughness, candour and straight-talking are the foundation of high performance.

My formative days with Randwick taught me this truth. Away from the hothouse of the training field or a dressing room, Bob is charming and very likeable. He helped me understand that his demands were actually markers of his respect for us. If he expected something of the highest order, then he must have thought we were capable of reaching those high standards. It was a compliment rather than an insult.

Bob never held a grudge. He could tear into you because you had botched something but, once he had said it, and you showed that you heard him, his anger ended. Words that might have sounded accusatory became valuable pointers to change future outcomes. The best coaching, even amid the post-match sound and fury, is forward-looking. If we rake over the errors or mishaps it is not just to rue the agony of defeat. It is more a lesson in how to make our future games better experiences – and, most of all, to help improve the individual and the team.

Straight-talking can be mistaken for aggression. Both Bob and I believe in straightforward language. We don't have time to waste. We're not here to make friends or ingratiate ourselves with anyone. We're here to improve our squads. So we talk straight but, at the same time, we want to listen to alternative views.

At Matraville and Randwick we were continually taught how to play the game and how to respect it. Respect for the game comes from respecting your opponent. Before Matraville High shocked St Joseph's way back in 1976, our coach Geoff Mould said: 'Look, boys, we're a pretty good team. But we're up against other blokes that can play as well.' So while Matraville and Randwick had what might be perceived as arrogance, we were also taught to be respectful and humble. Sometimes that respect and humility doesn't come across publicly with me. But I'm massively respectful of the game, and the people who play and support the game. Rugby has given me a lot and I will always be grateful.

My enduring love of rugby was sealed by the Randwick Way. Bob Dwyer, having been taught by Cyril Towers, said it consisted of four key principles – straight running, short passing, quick ball movement and constant support. These basics were welded onto consistent physicality and commitment, speed of thought, flexibility, and the moral courage to play so close to the opposition defence that, when it clicked, we got the beautifully flat-attack run which the Ellas played so instinctively at Matraville and perfected at Randwick.

Clive Woodward, who played for Manly from 1985 to 1990, wrote about Randwick and what it was like to face the Galloping Greens in his book. His abiding memory made me smile. He said it seemed as if, every minute or two, he had another mass of players in myrtle green jerseys running at him, and he was never sure which of them had the ball.

That echoed a story Bob told about Mike Gibson, the great old

Irish and Lions centre, who asked if he could attend a Wallabies training session. Gibson, who had retired years before, in 1979, turned up in his full kit – which surprised Bob and the Wallabies.

'So you want to take part in the practice?' Bob asked.

'Sure,' Gibson said, as if it was the most natural thing in the world.

'OK,' Bob said. 'You can defend at inside centre.'

'No, no, I want to play in the attack,' Gibson protested, as he had been a sublime playmaker who played 69 times for Ireland and won 12 Lions caps. He was one of those players that the Ellas and I had loved to watch on old Five Nations videos in our Matraville High classroom.

Bob would not budge. 'No, Mike, you can play in attack later. Play in defence at inside centre. I want you to get a feel for what we're doing.'

They practised for 20 minutes and Gibson looked exhausted when they stopped for some water.

'How's it going, Mike?' Bob asked.

Gibson looked up and shook his head. 'I have no idea who I'm supposed to tackle.'

Bob smiled. 'Now why don't you have a go and see how you replicate that in attack.'

Gibson was in his early forties but, still as smart as paint, he picked it up quickly. He absolutely loved it and he was an immediate convert to the Randwick Way.

Professional rugby is now a very pragmatic and structured sport. Teams spend so much time analysing each other on tape, and defences are so organized, that the kind of rugby we played at Randwick seems anachronistic. It would be nostalgia of the worst kind if I were to hark back to Randwick and suggest that my teams should try and play that brand of rugby in the modern Test arena. It just wouldn't work.

But there were times when the Randwick Way helped me as an international coach – especially when I worked with Japan. I took a Randwick mantra that you should always try to pass or run with the ball, rather than kick it. We eventually turned it into a rule. There were occasions when Japan, under my coaching, were forbidden to ever kick the ball. I knew that our smaller, slighter and more nimble players were so much more suited to a running game.

England are different. England are at their best when they stick to their core principles of a forward and set-piece-dominated game, aided by a committed defence and excellent kicking. That's one of the reasons why I love rugby. There are so many different ways to win a game. Having worked with Australia, South Africa, Japan and England, it has been stimulating to utilize the best features of each country. But each time I have relied on the fundamentals passed down to me at Randwick.

Bob likes to say that great leaders produce great leaders. None of us is going to claim greatness for ourselves, but it is striking that three of the seven Wallaby coaches who followed him in the role were coached by Bob Dwyer at Randwick. It is no coincidence.

3

LEARNING FROM HEARTBREAK

C. L. R. James, the great Trinidadian historian, famously wrote: 'What do they know of cricket who only cricket know?' The same truth applies to rugby. A rich experience of the world beyond deepens our understanding of the game we love. So, at the same time I was being educated in the philosophy of rugby at Randwick, I was learning so much about life itself while working as a teacher at the International Grammar School in Sydney. I chose teaching so I could earn a living while playing rugby at a provincial and, hopefully, international level.

Ironically, as a professional coach, I have come to appreciate that my job is actually teaching. If you set aside the media demands, and the logistical challenge of managing an international rugby programme, the similarities are striking. When I get out on the field in my training gear, with a whistle, I'm a teacher.

Life as a student at Sydney University had been an eye-opener. Founded by William Wentworth in 1850, its campus is ranked in the top ten of the world's most beautiful universities. The contrast with Matraville High was stunning. The privilege was coated on the walls of the famous sandstone buildings. There were students from private schools, from state schools, from cities and from the bush, as well as from overseas. But I noticed that the self-reliance and discipline of Matraville wasn't universal. Some of the boys and girls from the private schools struggled to knuckle down. One bloke I knew dropped out and another was there for

seven years and never completed his degree. They did not have
the gift which Matraville had instilled in us – the ability to take
your opportunities.

I found university more a test of application than intelligence.
If you are willing to apply yourself, and you have the basic intelligence you need, you will find a way to the end of your degree.
I also had a good time. It was fun and I made lots of great
new friends from all different walks of life. But it was over in a
flash and I had to find a job as my rugby career continued at
Randwick.

I wanted to work in the eastern suburbs of Sydney so I could
easily get to training after work. I put my name down at all the
government schools in that wide catchment area. But I was told
that, to become a PE teacher at a good school, you could be on
the waiting list for 20 years. No one wanted to leave the good
jobs. I applied to a couple of schools but, while I waited, I worked
as a relief teacher. My career was off to a rocky start.

Then, out of nowhere, I saw an advert for a new school in
Randwick. The International Grammar School had been established by a free-thinking maverick. Reg St Leon was an
educational pioneer who believed that all children should have
the opportunity to learn foreign languages from a young age. His
approach to teaching was unlike the rigid curriculum laid down
by the education authorities. He was intent on helping children
excel academically by encouraging them to learn some of their
subjects in a second language.

Initially, I was drawn to IGS because it was in Randwick. It
was only when I met Reg that I began to think about his vision-
ary approach. During my interview, Reg, a former lecturer at
Sydney University, made it clear that he loved anyone from his
alma mater. He gave me the job.

I've always been drawn towards people with a vision. In 1983,
Reg had approached the New South Wales Department of Education with his ideas for an innovative school. They responded
cautiously. He could proceed with the school but only if he

raised the money himself. Reg announced a public meeting and convinced enough parents to pay a $250 deposit to secure a place for their child at the school.

Reg struck a deal with a group of nuns, the Little Sisters of the Poor, to use their old convent in Randwick as a school. After a year he would purchase the convent and the IGS would be fully established in an ideal location with energetic teachers, an attractive building and spacious grounds. Forty-four children enrolled in the first year and optimism flowed. But the idealism and exhilaration of starting a new venture was soon mugged by financial realities. Reg couldn't afford to buy the convent and, for a while, it looked as if his dream would collapse.

But a desperate search for an alternative site ended successfully with his acquisition of an abandoned Elizabeth Arden cosmetic factory in Surry Hills – which was then a run-down suburb on the southeastern edge of the Sydney Central Business District.

I was 24 when I began teaching at IGS. I was not totally green, as I had done a few years of supply teaching by then. On my first day as a relief teacher I was sent to a primary school in Newtown, which was quite a rough area of Sydney. The kids in my PE class ran wild. My supervisor, an Eastern European man who observed the mayhem, advised me afterwards: 'Next time, tell them that the ball is like their pet. You will control them then.' He was right. It explained a concept in a way that the kids understood. Coaching is the same. When you speak to players it has to be in a language that they understand.

At IGS, I instilled discipline in my teaching. I also got my hands dirty and helped to clear out the disused make-up factory. As we imagined our new future, we turned factory spaces into classrooms and painted them inside and out. Week after week, month by month, it was 16 hours a day of tough work. We were big on ideas and heart but short on cash. The bureaucrats were also on the warpath because, whenever you start something new, you run into opposition. Regretting their earlier permission, they were hell-bent on putting Reg out of business. Citing Reg's unconventional teaching methods, they refused to certify the new school. The move effectively cut off our oxygen because, without certification, we couldn't get federal government funding. It was an act of sheer bastardry.

With the school account sinking deeper in the red, Reg doubted he could keep going. But the parents rallied. Three families accompanied Reg to the bank with the deeds to their own houses to guarantee the loan. It was an incredibly optimistic act of belief and support. Our spirits lifted.

But the bureaucrats weren't finished with us. In early 1986, as the school was thriving with a student population of 350, the NSW Director-General of Education notified the parents of students under 15 that they were liable for prosecution if they allowed their children to attend our classes. Students in Years 10 and 12 would also be ineligible to sit their School Certificate and Higher School Certificate exams. It was a heartless bullying tactic designed to intimidate Reg, his teachers and our community.

Reg fought back and instigated legal action against the state department for a clear restraint of trade. He won the case in the Supreme Court, but the education department appealed immediately. In September, on the first day of a new term, teachers and students were locked out of the school. Reg was carried out of IGS as he refused to leave his principal's chair. Students cheered him and parents honked their car horns in support. There was such a feeling of solidarity as we faced down the authorities.

Reg was exhausted, our coffers were empty, and we owed months of rent to our landlords. More parents stepped in to extend the school loan while Reg made a dramatic decision to step down. His antagonistic feud with the loathsome bureaucrats in the state department was toxic. The school, he reasoned, would be better off with new leadership. Rita Finn [now Morabito], one of my fellow teachers who taught Italian, became the new principal, with me installed as her deputy. It had been an emotional, chaotic, bruising experience.

Rugby still meant so much to me. I wanted to play for Australia. No ifs, no buts, no maybes. Throughout the battle with the education authorities, I worked furiously towards that objective. On my first day in the new job I went in at the usual time. I had prepared nothing for my work as deputy. Within a few days I said to myself: 'This won't work, mate. It's just not good enough. I need to be serious from now on.'

I started going to work early. If I was going to do the job, I wanted to do it well. Rita was the same age as me but she had been on track from day one. We were both only 26 but we were determined and courageous. Rita did not know much about rugby but she reminded me of Bob Dwyer. Her courage and work ethic were astonishing, her organization impeccable. She was crystal-clear in mapping out her objectives and she was prepared to fight for them. From day one of her reign, you sensed that the mighty NSW Department of Education had met their match.

In October 1986, 300 students, parents and teachers marched on Parliament House to protest against the department's tactic of 'waging a carefully orchestrated campaign ... to force IGS into bankruptcy.' Within a week, the NSW education minister Rodney Cavalier certified the school after IGS received hundreds of letters of support, including one from Prime Minister Bob Hawke.

From January 1987, Rita and I worked ridiculously hard, for 12 hours most days, and up to 18 hours when we were really under the pump. Apart from managing the school and turning it into a sustainable operation, we needed to motivate and pay our staff, rebuild our relationship with the Department of Education, liaise closely with the parents, make sure that the bank was happy, write a new curriculum and, most of all, teach the kids who depended so much on us.

At IGS I realized I was resilient and that I had a capacity to work really hard. I learnt how to motivate and manage people – sometimes successfully, sometimes unsuccessfully – and how to multitask and to delegate. I learnt how to plan and put projects together. I learnt about leadership and the unity of a team who shared a belief in the same vision. All these attributes are essential to a successful coaching career and I owe a real debt to Rita and IGS for helping me learn these skills.

When I go to the school now I feel real pride. They have a brilliant campus in the centre of Sydney with around 1,500 students. In March 2019, when Reg St Leon died at the age of 90, it was fitting that obituaries, offering lavish praise for his pioneering work, were published in the Sydney press. Reg, Rita and everyone else at IGS were brave enough to be different. They were strong enough to persevere and reach our objective. It was another valuable lesson that would sustain me throughout my long and tumultuous rugby career.

As much as I loved my work at IGS, rugby was my ambition. I had proved myself at Randwick and I was the first-choice hooker for New South Wales. I didn't talk about it openly but playing for Australia had become an obsession. I felt I was close to making it. I was established in first-grade rugby, winning grand finals and playing alongside some great internationals, week in, week out. I was improving every day.

The biggest obstacle was my size. I was much smaller than every one of my opponents. It forced me to prepare better than everyone else. To eat the right food, lift the weights, put the miles on the clock, study the game, get the right sleep and generally be resourceful, determined and inventive. I did everything in my power to be the best I could possibly be. I'd been proving people wrong since those early days in La Perouse and Matraville. Surely I could do it again.

Bob Dwyer also gave me encouragement and confidence. He pointed out that I was flexible, mobile and strong. I had a mind and a mouth that could get under the skin of those who wanted to bully me. I was also pretty elastic in my movement, and opponents found it hard to pin me down when I wriggled into a ruck and ripped the ball off them. Bob said that, even though I was a hooker, I carried the ball like a flanker. I got through an enormous amount of work in the loose and had a capacity to get close to the ground and twist and turn through tight spaces. I could break past the gain line consistently.

He didn't tell me this at the time, but Bob knew I was going to be a coach. He could spot all the future coaches in his team a mile off. We were the blokes who were the most vocal and the most demanding. And yet we didn't just yell. We spotted the weaknesses in our team and in the opposition. I was clear and confident in barking out orders. I think most hookers have this attitude because we're in the middle of the action. We want to get on top and grind the pack against us down into the dirt. It's a hard and unyielding game upfront and there is no point in shirking the task.

Bob also liked the fact that, away from the mouthy and confrontational stuff, I examined my own game and studied the strengths and weaknesses of my opponents. So while I did not have the physique or the natural talent of so many of my teammates, I was forensic in my analysis and ferocious in my desire to improve.

My biggest test as a hooker awaited. New South Wales against Queensland was always a bitterly contested game. They were unofficial trials for the Test team.

I was first picked for New South Wales in 1987, and one of my early games for the state was against Queensland. I knew I would go head-to-head with Tom Lawton, who won 41 caps for Australia between 1983 and 1989. His grandfather, Tom Lawton Senior, had captained the Wallabies and so, unlike me, he came from a family steeped in the game. But the biggest difference between Tom and me was obvious. He was 5 feet 11 inches tall and weighed 118 kilograms (18½ stone); I was 5 feet 8 and weighed 80 kilograms (12½ stone). I could deal easily with the height difference, but it was daunting going up against a beast of a man who weighed six stone more than me. Lawton was also a serial winner. He had won four club championships with Souths Rugby Club in Brisbane.

On the bus to the game in Brisbane, I went over to Bob and asked if I could have a word.

'Sure,' Bob said.

'How do you think I should handle Tom Lawton?'

'How do you think you should handle Lawton?' Bob said, in his typical way of making the player assess a situation himself.

'I think I should take him very low.'

Bob smiled. 'That would be a very good idea. You don't want to have a stand-up wrestle with Lawton.'

We discussed our plans in much more detail, and I felt ready. I had already worked out my strategy before I approached Bob, but it helped to have him validate my plan. It was another little example of how well Bob coached us. He had encouraged me to analyse the situation calmly, and he was there to boost me and add a few subtle tweaks.

New South Wales beat Queensland that day, and I handled Lawton pretty well. Bob was generous. 'He might be a giant in the Wallaby shirt, but you got the better of him, mate,' he told me after the game.

I felt as if I had taken a massive step forward. Finally, I was going to play for Australia.

Coogee Oval, Sydney. Wednesday, 22 June 1988

On a cold afternoon, with the low winter sun slanting across the field, our little seaside ground was close to bursting. The capacity was 5,000 but there must have been at least 10,000 there to watch Randwick play New Zealand. Every available viewing space was taken, while the roofs and balconies of the close-set apartment blocks were stacked with people determined to watch the game. Others had climbed up trees and walls. Even the fire brigade had arrived. Dozens of firemen stood on top of a fire engine so they could see over the fence. It was an unforgettable atmosphere as the Galloping Greens faced the All Blacks.

This was only their second match on tour and, in the opening game three days before, New Zealand had hammered Western Australia 60–3 in Perth. They had chosen a second string that day but, against Randwick, they selected their Test side – including Buck Shelford, Alan and Gary Whetton, Sean Fitzpatrick, Grant Fox, Joe Stanley, John Kirwan and the rest.

We had some pretty handy players ourselves and, in the first Test on 3 July, Randwick's David Campese, Gary Ella and Simon Poidevin would play for the Wallabies. A young Michael Cheika also played for Randwick that day. It was only his fourth game for the first XV but Cheika showed incredible stamina and toughness at number 8 against the legendary Shelford. Mark and Glen Ella had both retired but they were in the crowd – as was Bob Dwyer.

Bob had met us that morning at the Coogee Beach Lifesaving Club near the ground. He was once again in charge of the Wallabies but he stepped in to give us a little advice as Jeff Sayle, who had replaced him as Randwick coach, was seriously ill in hospital. Jeff had suffered an anaphylactic reaction to an anaesthetic and been close to death. They had even given him the last rites. But Jeff was tough and he was recovering. In his place we were coached by John Quick, another good Randwick man, but it was helpful to have Bob talk to us before the game.

He told us to try and forget that we were playing the All Blacks. Our real opponents were ourselves. We needed to strip away the emotion and play the Randwick Way. Bob reminded us that we knew how to win. We just needed to front up in the set piece and match them as a pack. He looked pointedly at me and Ewen McKenzie. It would not be enough to contain them. We needed to ask questions of them the whole game. If they were good questions it was likely that they would come up with the wrong answers every now and then. When they made mistakes we needed to be clinical. We should have a crack and try to make history.

It was a short and simple speech but it struck a chord. We were ready.

Spiro Zavos, who wrote for the *Sydney Morning Herald*, suggested years later, in 2008, that 'Randwick and the All Blacks
battled out what was, in my opinion, the most memorable game
of rugby ever played in Australia. Anyone who was there will
never forget the intensity of the play, the tribal passion of the
spectators and the thrill of the match . . .'

Zavos described the setting at Coogee Oval and a match that
had a profound impact on him. 'It made a dramatic picture, a bit
reminiscent of those grounds in the valleys of Wales during the
days of the coal mining, when the visiting team quickly realized
that they were playing not only the home team but its supporters
as well . . . Thousands of locals seemed to be pressed within tackling distance of the visitors while maintaining a constant
screaming for blood for the home side . . .

'Randwick charged on to attack from the kick-off towards my
end of the field. I can see it now. There is Sean Fitzpatrick (yet to
become a legendary All Black) taking a long time to throw the
ball into a defensive lineout metres from the All Blacks tryline.
He is plainly nervous. Sitting only metres away from him, I can
see the strain on his face, the slight twitching before the throw is
made.

'Now Randwick are throwing all their famous back plays at the
rattled All Blacks. The noise is overwhelming. David Knox is
master-minding sleight-of-hand backline ploys. David Campese
is popping up everywhere, swerving, side-stepping, goose-
stepping, making no-eyes pop-up passes . . .

'The All Blacks buckle occasionally. But they never break, despite the ferocity and skill of the Randwick onslaught and even
against the immense din made by the Randwick supporters who
can hear the smack of body on body as the tackles are made . . .
Anyone who ever challenges David Campese's courage should
have seen the fearless way he took the impact of the fierce tackles and the ensuing punishment as the All Blacks rucked and
mauled him viciously . . .

'Simon Poidevin for Randwick and Wayne "Buck" Shelford,

the inspirational captain of the All Blacks, were titanic for their sides in the rucks and mauls. An enduring image is of Shelford with his arms around Poidevin's neck almost throttling him in an attempt to get him off the ball . . .'

My memories of the game centre on the battle I had with Fitzy. He was a great player, obviously in another dimension to me, and he and Michael Jones were the first modern forwards who could do everything on the field with real style and punch. But I went toe-to-toe, nose-to-nose, with Fitzpatrick all afternoon. I did well in the set pieces and open play and I matched him in the verbals. Fitzy loved giving it out both physically and verbally. But I gave as good as I got that day. I still remember early on in the game ending up on the wrong side of the All Black ruck and having my back and jersey shredded by the All Black forwards. Fitzy smiled at me as if to say, 'That should quieten you down.'

We took it to them in the first half and they were reeling after we scored the opening try. It was a blind-side attack from one of our rock-solid scrums and Knoxy dived through the gap. Grant Fox was deadly with the boot and at half-time they were 12–9 ahead. It was my fault because late on in the first half we lost a scrum on our line. I missed the strike, Fitzy won it back and they scored. The second half was just as abrasive but the world champions were fitter and a class above us as they ran out 25–9 winners.

A measure of how well we had done was seen after the first Test, when the same All Black team hammered Australia 32–7. They played 13 matches on tour, winning 12 and drawing the second Test, but Buck Shelford said that we gave them their hardest match. New Zealand also vowed that they would never again play a club team on tour. That was a notch on Randwick's belt.

A year later I felt ready for my next clash with the All Blacks – in the Bledisloe Cup at Eden Park in Auckland on 9 August. I was relatively confident that, at the age of 29, I would be called up for my Test debut. The Wallabies had just lost their series against the British and Irish Lions 2–1 on 15 July. Tom Lawton had started all three Tests, as usual, but after the series he announced his retirement from international rugby.

Bob Dwyer, as Wallabies coach, was looking ahead to the 1991 World Cup in England, and his front row needed an injection of fresh blood in the form of combative players. Ewen McKenzie was injured but it was obvious that he would soon make his Wallaby debut. As our former coach at Randwick, and my mentor, it also seemed fitting that Bob would be the man to pick me for the Wallabies.

I knew that I'd had no chance of playing for the Wallabies when Alan Jones had been head coach of Australia between the two Dwyer campaigns. Jones was from Manly and he resented Randwick's influence over Australian rugby. He also disliked me because he had overheard a brutal sledging I gave one of his protégés, the scrum half Brian Smith.

'Eddie Jones, when it suited him, could be the master of filth,' Alan Jones complained later. 'It's something with which I can't and won't identify.'

I thought everything would change now that Lawton had retired and Bob was back in control of the Wallabies. I had been part of the New South Wales side which had easily won that year's interstate series against Queensland. I had also played in five grand finals for Randwick and won three.

The Australian Test selection panel consisted of Bob, John Bain and Bob Templeton. As head coach, Bob had the dominant voice, and it was made clear that the team to travel to New Zealand would be announced on the last Sunday of the month. The selection meeting was held two evenings earlier, on the Friday, and Bob came to find me the following day. He had selected a Randwick hooker to replace Lawton, and make his international debut, and Bob felt it was only right that he should give me the news himself.

He found me sitting alone in the Randwick dressing room

after we had played a club game. 'Mate,' he said, 'I need to have a chat with you.'

He saw the devastation on my face. I just about got the words out: 'My rugby career is finished.'

Bob said later that my face was the saddest he had ever seen and, in that moment, he knew I had already heard the news. Someone at the club told me I had been overlooked and Bob had, instead, chosen Phil Kearns, my young understudy at Randwick. Kearns had just turned 22 the month before and, until recently, he had been Randwick's third team hooker. I didn't know that Bob had persuaded the club to move Kearns up to the reserve team. The former reserve team hooker, who had been friends with Bob, was furious after being dropped for a kid.

I was heartbroken when I heard that my dream of playing Test rugby had been taken by a player few people had ever heard of outside Randwick.

Bob broke the painful silence. 'Mate,' he said again, 'I had to do what I think is right.'

I know how difficult Bob found that conversation. We had been so close, and still are today, and he admired the fact I had made the most of my limited physical resources and unspectacular talent.

My anguish was accentuated by the fact that I knew, deep down, Bob had made the right call. I was not really good enough to play Test rugby. I was also far too small. Kearns was six foot tall and weighed 110 kilograms (17½ stone). So he was four inches taller and 30 kilograms (nearly 5 stone) heavier than me. He was also a bloody good rugby player. Kearns went on to play 67 Tests for Australia and he was part of two World Cup-winning squads in 1991 and 1999. He is one of the best hookers in Australian history. There was no shame losing out to Kearns. But none of that helps in the moment. My lifelong goal, to which I had given everything, was gone. It was over.

Bob had too much respect for me to try and soften the blow. It would have been cruel if he said I needed to just keep working at my game to force my way in ahead of Kearns. We both knew it was hopeless. He could hardly say that I needed to pack on 30 kilograms of muscle to compete with a beast like Kearns.

Kearns made his debut in Auckland two weeks later, playing alongside many of my old friends in Lloyd Walker, Poidevin and Campese. Australia lost 24–12 to New Zealand, but the outcome didn't matter to me. I was just another club player who had done well to get 12 caps for New South Wales. Test rugby belonged to better players than me.

Jeff Sayle, my second favourite coach after Bob, was still in charge of Randwick. Perhaps he did it out of sympathy because, on his return from international duty, Phil Kearns was back in the reserve team at Randwick. The official line from Jeff was that a smaller, more mobile hooker like me suited our running game. I held on to my club place ahead of Phil for the rest of the season, all the way to the grand final which we won by beating East-wood. My fourth championship medal barely raised a smile. I was still crushed and, with hindsight, I am not proud of the way I reacted. I pretty much sulked and went through the motions. I should have shown far more maturity and good grace.

My strop continued into the following season and it was almost a relief midway through the 1990 campaign when Phil replaced me as Randwick's first-choice hooker. I played second-grade rugby the rest of the year and, in a bid to lift my sagging spirits, the club asked me to captain the reserves in 1991. I was also encouraged to get involved in coaching the team.

I felt rejuvenated. Occasionally, when Kearns was called up for international duty, I played for the first team, and even captained them, but I was more fascinated by the challenge of turning the reserves into a better outfit. I took over running the team on and off the field when, midway through the season, we were stutter-ing along in mid-table. 'Speed' Kennedy, who was nominally in charge, said: 'You speak more than me, mate. You might as well coach them.'

I took to coaching easily. After years as a PE teacher I had the basic skills of communication and organization. I changed training and made it much more intense. I had never been able to work out why we didn't train as hard as if we were playing in an actual game. We would focus on silly little aspects that didn't contribute to our preparing for the match, simply because coaches followed tradition. I wanted to make training much more meaningful and impactful. These days, in the professional game, we often put the players under even more physical and mental stress during training. The theory is that the games will be easier then.

We won the competition and my fate was decided. I would become a coach.

The following season, with my role as player-coach of the reserve team made official, I enticed Glen Ella back to Randwick. Glen was working as an assistant to Bob with the Wallabies, but he was happy to come down a couple of evenings a week to help me train the Randwick reserves. Glen was surprised, initially, by my highly organized sessions. Apart from when Bob was in charge, he was used to coaches expecting him to disappear with the backs and run a few moves while the forwards did their thing as a separate entity.

I was much more intent on working closely with Glen. I would discuss the way that the team had played last week and how I wanted us to train to avoid making the same mistakes again. Unlike today, we had no video footage or match statistics to rely on. Everything I did came from memories or notes of what I had seen and my own feel for the game.

Most of the season we were on the cusp of the play-off positions, lying in fourth or fifth place. I wasn't too worried because I knew the season would be judged on whether or not we won the grand final. I was willing to take the odd hit, and defeat, as we built the team and made sure we peaked at the right time. We scraped into the semi-final and won that easily with a smart game plan.

The 1991 reserve grand final, against Western Suburbs, was at Concord Oval. Australia played some Tests there so it was a decent ground and around 10,000 turned up to watch my last game for Randwick. Western Suburbs were favoured to win as they had finished above us in the table.

We prepared well, played intelligent rugby, and I felt good about the game all the way through. It was surprisingly easy how we could control play. They became frustrated and our confidence surged as the players saw the match unfolding pretty much as I had predicted.

We won the game, and the title, and it felt a good way to finish in the myrtle green colours I'd cherished for a dozen years. I had played 210 grade games for Randwick and, at the age of 31, there was no sadness as I trudged off the field for the last time. I knew it was time to move on.

4

THE FIRST STEPS OF COACHING

At my lowest, when absorbing the blow of not being picked for Australia, nothing could console me. I had to work through the pain as if it was a grieving process. It helped that I thrived on the responsibility of being the deputy principal at IGS. It allowed me to forget about rugby for a while, because being a deputy head is a tough task. You're basically running the school for the principal, and so I needed to keep the teachers motivated and in check while forging a relationship with the kids. The parents presented a different challenge, as IGS slotted in between the big private schools and the more routine government schools. We offered an alternative education but the mix was complicated. We covered a wide socio-economic spread from quite poor families to extremely affluent parents. Some parents were pushy and expected us to handle everything.

I did not realize it then, still licking my rugby wounds, but the lessons and skills I picked up at IGS would help enormously in my later career. As a coach you're also dealing with a very mixed bunch of people, and you have to find the right operational mode, one which allows you to move forward as a team while you try and get the most out of each individual.

I taught PE, geography and even maths to the lower-ability classes, where motivation and behaviour were problematic. As they were the opposite of high-achievers, I had to find ways to engage them. I was a pretty effective teacher and I loved it when they became excited about the subject. Their behaviour improved and, with that combination of discipline and enthusiasm, it was inevitable that their grades rose sharply.

My personal life also changed. I'd had a few girlfriends but, between rugby and teaching, there was little time to become too serious about anyone. I guess it was a sign of how consumed I was by rugby that my future wife, Hiroko, and I had been at IGS together for about seven years before I even spoke to her. It was a big school and we rarely crossed paths. I was looking after the high school and she was teaching German and Japanese to the junior students.

The first time I really noticed her, and talked to her, was soon after her father had died in Japan. I met her properly one evening at a school function and, after I had expressed my condolences, we began to talk. Hiroko was fascinating and pretty and I wondered how I had not noticed her for so long. She was good friends with Rita Field, the head, and their friendship continues today. Hiroko had an inquiring mind and a fiercely independent streak which was unusual, then, for a young woman from Japan. She was a qualified German teacher who had studied linguistics at university. Hiroko had completed her Masters and she then worked for a television company just outside Tokyo. She did that for a year, but the hours were ridiculous. Hiroko had had enough and so she quit her job and went backpacking in New Zealand and Australia.

It was then that fate intervened. She found her way to Sydney and, needing to earn some money, applied to IGS. Hiroko loved the school but, as she told me, it had begun to feel like time for a change. We began to go out and it felt just right being with her.

We had not been in a relationship for long when I surprised her with a question. It was not the most romantic proposition but, as casually as I could, I asked Hiroko if she fancied coming to Leicester with me for eight months.

Hiroko had never heard of Leicester before. I had to explain that Leicester was in the heartlands of English rugby.

She looked at me for a while, and then nodded and smiled.

Why not? It would be an adventure and Hiroko was always open to new experiences.

I was thrilled even though, so early in our relationship, neither Hiroko nor I could have guessed that this would be just the first of many rugby adventures we would take together over the decades as a married couple.

Leicester are one of the great clubs in world rugby and, after they had played against Randwick during a preseason tour of Australia in the late 1980s, a bond was forged. The two clubs might have been very different in the style of rugby they played, but Leicester and Randwick were united by their competitiveness. Both clubs were also well run, and so it was natural that we would collaborate.

I was one of the earliest beneficiaries of a player swap. Leicester's Matt Poole, a promising lock who was nine years younger than me, was offered the chance to play a season of first-grade rugby at Randwick while I went in the opposite direction. In Matt's case, it was a significant step in his rugby education. Martin Johnson, for whom Leicester also had high hopes, had become a much better player after his years in New Zealand rugby. I think the Randwick interlude benefited Matt because he and Johnson would go on to lock the Leicester scrum 129 times, which is a club record for a second-row partnership.

My career was at the opposite end of the scale. Randwick offered me the chance to go and play for Leicester in 1991 as a thank-you for my years of service. I had never been out of Australia before and I was keen to immerse myself in a radically different rugby culture.

IGS were also generous in allowing me this sabbatical, but I sweetened the break by agreeing that, while I was in England, I would visit numerous schools. As deputy principal it would enhance my knowledge to see how schools in a different country approached education. I visited most of the big public schools in the East Midlands and I was impressed. They were well set up and there was a consistently high level of education.

I also enjoyed the much more rough-and-ready work I did as an amateur rugby player in Leicester. I helped out Matt Poole's dad, Dave, with his furniture delivery business. A driver and I would go all over the Midlands, and I enjoyed the hard labour and seeing a lot of the English countryside. I remember that, between jobs, we would kick around in the warehouse, having a laugh and drinking lots of tea. Whenever the supervisor walked in, we would jump up and look seriously busy as we moved random pieces of furniture around. We went back to having a laugh once he had disappeared.

I loved the rugby most of all. At Randwick we won all the time. Our mindset was ruthless and our belief unshakeable. I found the same conviction at Leicester. But, rather than playing in the sunshine and sea air alongside Coogee Beach, Leicester rumbled through the cold and the rain on muddied fields. But everyone understood the culture of the club, with a clear focus and strong work ethic, and they had some great players from Dean Richards to the young Johnson. He was pretty quiet then, and there was no sign that he would become one of the great captains of Test rugby and lead England to victory over my Wallabies in the World Cup final ten years from then, but Johnson was already on his way to becoming a seriously good lock forward.

I played three league games for Leicester, and nine reserve matches, and the rugby was interesting. I wore the famous B shirt in Leicester's A-B-C front row. These were still the days when Leicester wore letters rather than numbers on their shirt and I enjoyed packing down alongside two very good props in Graham Rowntree and Darren Garforth.

The conservatism of the game in England was apparent, but it made me appreciate that there was more than one way of playing rugby. During one game I ran to take a quick lineout. One of the forwards growled at me, 'We don't do that at Leicester, mate.'

It was good enough for me to play in a team that had a blend of hardened experience, in the form of Richards and others, and bright young talents like Neil Back, who had just broken into the first team. Tony Russ was the coach, although in those amateur days he was more of a manager, and Leicester echoed Randwick in the way in which the players ensured that high standards were maintained. The experience refreshed me. It would have been much more difficult for me to coach England without that brief taste I had of Welford Road.

Hiroko and I also had a really good time. We saw a lot of England. But our stay was cut short by three months because I took an unexpected call from IGS. Rita Field had already left the school as she wanted to pursue her passion for teaching art. I didn't get on particularly well with the new head. But there had been more changes in my absence, and would I be prepared to step in as acting principal? I was surprised, but flattered, and the lure of a new challenge meant we said goodbye to our life in Leicester after five happy months.

It had been an important time together and, soon after we returned to Sydney, Hiroko and I were married. Our greatest adventures were about to begin.

I decided to have one last season of playing rugby while I settled into my new headmaster's role. It was time for another change so, rather than going back to reserve-grade rugby at Randwick, I joined Southern Districts. They were in the first grade but, compared to Randwick and Leicester, they lacked the competitive edge. Most of their guys were just happy to play and it did not matter too much to them how many games they won or lost. They were lackadaisical because they saw rugby as a mainly social activity. I could socialize and drink with the best of them, but I hated that attitude. Still, I found it quite educational.

The discipline and hardness you take for granted at Randwick and Leicester is not for everyone. Some players are just not willing to put in the kind of effort we did at those two illustrious clubs. I knew I was only going to be there for a season, so it was not down to me to change the culture of the club. We played Randwick twice and, somehow, in the game where I spooked Joe Picone by kissing his cheek and telling him I loved him, we beat them at home. I played all 22 games and I was a busted flush by the end of that 1992 season.

I took a break from rugby and did little in the game throughout 1993. Work at IGS took over. Towards the end of my 18 months in charge, and soon after our daughter Chelsea had been born, Hiroko said I needed to make some changes. I was spending too much time at work. I found a way to increase my efficiency at IGS so I could spend more time with my wife and daughter. It was a valuable lesson that helped me in my later coaching career. You have so much discretionary time as a coach that it's easy to let the job take over your life. I learnt from that experience as a headmaster to use my time well so that my family would not feel neglected.

I made a hell of a lot of mistakes while headmaster, but I learnt that you need a vision – and to implement that vision you have to set standards and continually match them. It was very demanding as the school went from kindergarten to Year 12. I faced problems that stretched from pre-school children to teenagers who were on the cusp of finishing school and heading off to university or work in the real world. I was 32 years old.

After 18 months the school asked me to become their projects director and I set up two new entities. I began an English-language college within the school for foreign students, mainly from Asian countries, and it became a money-spinner. I then set up an international school under the IGS banner in Ho Chi Minh City in Vietnam. I travelled to Vietnam every three months to oversee the school. Most of my problems came from English parents who were working in Vietnam.

Our school was based on Australian lines and some of the snootier parents wanted a system more in tune with English public-school education. I remember one woman would come into each meeting with everything minuted from our previous discussion, and with masses of correspondence covered in coloured Post-it notes. These parents were high achievers, who were paying a lot of money to the school, and so they were challenging. It was bloody hot and humid and I could feel the sweat pouring down my back while I was being harangued. I would look at the overhead fans whirring above us, while I tried to remain patient and diplomatic; it felt like I was in a movie set in southeast Asia.

I had appointed Peter Gibbons, a tough Australian, as the principal. He was a good operator but he could be a bit rough and tumble. I had to find a way to prevent the whole thing from blowing up and reach some kind of consensus instead. It was another great learning experience.

But I knew it was time to get back to rugby.

My nine years at IGS had taught me so much that nothing could faze me when it came to coaching. I applied for the job, which would be unpaid of course, as Randwick's reserve-team coach in 1994. Once I was appointed, I was intent on doing it as professionally as possible.

I had a good team, captained by Paul Cheika, Michael's older brother. James Holbeck, Tim Kelaher and Peter Jorgensen would all play for Australia. With that calibre of player, and me working harder than any other coach in the competition, I was not surprised that we dominated the entire season. We won the grand final at a canter.

Hiroko suggested that it might be a good idea if I could be paid for all the time I gave to Randwick. She had a point, but I had to explain that rugby was still an amateur game. We did not know that the World Cup the following year, in 1995, would be the last tournament before professionalism changed rugby for ever.

Even in the amateur game, opportunities emerged. Tokai University's rugby team flew from Japan to Australia to sample a slice of the Randwick Way. I was asked to take them for three training sessions. I already loved coaching and so I found it easy to make time for the Tokai boys. Apparently they enjoyed my sessions – so much so that, at the end of the Australian season and in the school holidays, in August, they asked me to go over for a month to run a summer camp.

They paid for me, Hiroko and Chelsea to fly to Japan. I loved it even though they were a really weak team. It was very intense and I worked for 28 out of the 31 days I was there, coaching twice a day, up in the mountains in a town called Sugadaira, nearly 200 kilometres from Tokyo. Every high school, university and company team based themselves in Sugadaira in August because there were 130 rugby pitches in the town.

We did nothing but train and play rugby all day, every day. It was heaven for me, even if it was brutally hard and conditions were Spartan. There would only be two meals a day – at ten in the morning and at six at night. We would train in the morning and play matches in the afternoon. It was crazy but it was also the best experience I've had in coaching. At the end of a demanding but exhilarating month I thought: 'I wish I could do this all the time.'

South Africa hosted the 1995 World Cup, which they won by beating a far better team in New Zealand in the final. I had been impressed by the All Blacks throughout that tournament as, beyond the rampaging force of a young Jonah Lomu, they had such smart and skilful players, from Frank Bunce to Zinzan Brooke. Sean Fitzpatrick captained them and they swept into the final where, watched by Nelson Mandela and a fevered home crowd in the bear pit of Ellis Park, they hit a green-and-gold roadblock. The Springboks won 15–12, after extra time, and I admired the way they had been coached so skilfully by Kitch Christie. It was a beautiful reminder that the most talented teams do not always win the biggest games in rugby.

Bob Dwyer, assisted by Glen Ella, had coached Australia, the defending champions. They had lost to South Africa in the open-ing game and had been shocked by England in the quarter-finals.

As the sport turned professional, I was hopeful that I might find a place for myself in this new world. Apart from coaching the Wallabies, there were only three big jobs in Australia – with New South Wales, Queensland and ACT. Glen and I applied for the New South Wales vacancy, as a coaching team, with Super 10 rugby on the horizon. We had no real experience but we got to the final three in the interview process. Chris Hawkins, who was a teacher like me, got the job. Glen and I weren't too disappointed as it had been a long shot.

My life was about to turn upside down anyway. As soon as the call came in from Japan, I was convinced. Tokai University wanted me to return to Japan to become their full-time rugby coach. I said to Hiroko: 'I really want to do this. It just feels right.' She was reluctant at first because the idea of returning to Japan did not appeal. She was settled with me in Sydney and it felt like a backward step to live in Japan again. But, luckily, she loves me and she has always backed me. She suggested we go out for a year and see how we felt then.

It was still a massive risk. I was earning around $80,000 at IGS and I was well established. Working for Tokai would see me take a significant pay cut. But I just wanted to become a professional rugby coach. I went to see Gerry Gleeson, the chairman of IGS, who was a great guy, a six-feet-eight-inch, 18-stone hulk of a man who had previously been a fine Aussie Rules player in Melbourne. We had a good relationship because we respected each other and we both loved sport. I told Gerry about the Japanese offer and that it felt as though I was at a crossroads in my life. If I stayed in education, and wanted to progress further, I needed to get a Master's degree. The alterative was to take a punt and try and become a full-time rugby coach.

Gerry looked at me for a long time and then he said the words I wanted to hear more than any other. 'Mate, I know what you want to do. Go and coach professionally . . .'

We lived in Hadano, 70 kilometres west of Tokyo, and the first six months at Tokai University were probably the toughest of my coaching career. Even though I am part-Japanese, there were cultural and language problems from the outset. There was also a bizarre situation because, while they were paying me to improve their team, they did not want me to do any coaching. At our first training session the manager took me to one side just as I was about to begin work.

'You just watch,' he told me.

I watched the first session, which the captain ran. It was chaotic but I didn't say anything.

On my second day, at the start of training, I said, 'Right, I'll take the session.'

The manager, who was actually a very nice bloke, said: 'No, no. You watch.'

This went on the whole week. On the Friday night I was pretty upset. 'What am I going to do?' I asked Hiroko.

'Resign,' she said.

Hiroko, being Japanese, understood the strictly hierarchical nature of her society. She knew it would never change unless I did something dramatic. And if it didn't work we could go home to Sydney. I knew she was right.

I took my resignation letter into training. The manager was ready to tell me to watch again, but I beat him to it. 'Look,' I said, 'this is my resignation letter.'

He was stunned. 'Why?'

I spelt it out. I had come all the way to Japan to work as their coach. I was not willing to stand by and watch when I should be coaching.

While the training session began with me on the sidelines again, the manager asked if I would wait while he spoke to his superiors. I nodded but shrugged too – as a way of reinforcing the point that I was not in the mood to negotiate.

An hour later he returned with a promise. I could begin coaching the team the very next day.

'Unless I have full control, I'm leaving,' I stressed.

'Yes, Eddie-san,' the manager bowed respectfully. 'Full control.'

They kept their promise and, the next morning, I took charge. There were about 80 kids and their standard of play was hopeless. The positives were minimal, but it was imperative I brought some structure to training. I split them into three groups. I trained the first group from 2 to 4 p.m., the second from 4 to 6 p.m. and the final set from 6 to 8 p.m.

Six hours of straight coaching were physically draining but, as a young coach, it was the best thing I could've done. I was training them on a dirt pitch and by the time I got home at nine I was shattered. It then took me around 30 minutes to wash the dirt and the red dust out of my hair and off my skin. I would have a quick dinner, go to bed and start again the next day.

The mornings were not any easier. I was supposed to be studying Japanese but I found it difficult. I was in a class of 50 and the other 49 students were all Chinese. The Japanese alphabet uses adopted Chinese characters and so they were immediately at home while I was all at sea. Despite having been part of a linguistic school for so long, the sad truth is that I have never had an aptitude for languages.

While I have basic Japanese today, enough to convey instructions to a team, it remains woeful. After all these years my wife forbids me to speak it at home. Our dog in England only understands Japanese and my wife doesn't want me to even speak to him.

In 1996, my Japanese was so atrocious I gave up the classes in Hadano. I concentrated on rugby. The level of play was so low that, early on, I thought: 'What the hell have I got myself into?'

I am often accused now of generating conflict as a way of making an impression on my teams. But I don't seek conflict. Conflict is only useful if it gives you the opportunity to be creative. I learnt that lesson at Tokai. I began to understand that if you wanted to change something there was no point trying to do it at a meeting with the whole group. Players would look at you impassively and nod meekly. But they never acted on your instructions. You needed to get in the faces of small groups and turn them around that way or, even better, target the key guys individually. They would accept it more readily if it was done in private and they did not have to worry about losing face in front of everyone else. My aim became to get the senior players on board. Once I had them believing in my methods, then they would run the team.

I've used the same strategy with every squad I've coached. When I took charge of England I knew that, before I even started to change the mentality of the group, I needed to capture the big characters – Dylan Hartley, Owen Farrell, George Ford, James Haskell and the Vunipola brothers. Once you've got the leaders and the dominant personalities then the rest will follow.

The most obvious change I forced on Tokai was a stipulation that they were not allowed to kick the ball – under any circumstance. I wanted them to run and pass because we had a tiny team. Our biggest prop weighed only 85 kilograms and we played against university teams who had 120-kilogram props. We were getting monstered so we had to move the ball. I tried to instil the Randwick game into them, even though they did not have the skill to replicate that style successfully. But it was better than them playing an orthodox kicking game. I wanted them to play very fast and nimble rugby, attacking with a flat backline, which went against the grain of the methodical style they had been taught. Japanese and English rugby players are not that different – even if the gulf in rugby tradition is vast. In both countries they have been raised on regimented rugby with little room for innovation.

I had to break that down at Tokai and I did it by force. I really pushed the university players hard and insisted they change. I've used a much more subtle approach in England and tried to change the mentality in stages. At Tokai I was draconian – as underlined by my law that they could never kick the ball even if hemmed in close to their own try line. If they failed to listen to me, I would respond ferociously. In England I've learnt to encourage them to discover the right way for themselves.

There was no such subtlety in Japan. I took a dictatorial approach. I knew the players could train hard and absorb punishment. It was part of their cultural make-up. Punishment engenders obedience. It helped me develop the squad but when it comes to leadership you need more than obedience. I faced the same problem with England more than 20 years later. How do you develop leadership? It was testing at Tokai but their previous experience of coaching had been so poor I improved them.

The logistics made it taxing. We only played seven games that season. I needed more time, and many more games, to make the improvements we needed. We came second last in the university first division but, considering our lack of size and my insistence that they run everything, they were a much better team at the end of the year. Our results didn't reflect their improvement, but you could see the pride in their faces. It was gratifying.

It seemed incredible that two boys from Matraville High, Glen Ella and me, would coach Japan in 1996. While I was at Tokai University, Glen drafted me in as the forwards coach of the national team. He was an assistant coach of Japan and responsible for the backs. We worked with Iwao Yamamoto, the head coach who came from Suntory. He loved Australian rugby and wanted Japan to play with a flat backline. Yamamoto was right, but he was not really a great coach and his players lacked the skill and the moral courage to play that style of rugby.

I had watched Japan get smashed 145–17 by New Zealand in the 1995 World Cup. They conceded 21 tries and only started playing a little, and scoring a few points, once the score was humiliating. It was a familiar pattern in Japanese rugby. They only looked like a team once another massive defeat was assured. At 40–0 or 50–0 they got off the floor and played with some gumption. But I always remembered Bob Dwyer saying that it takes no courage to try to win the game when you're beaten. Real courage is to try to win the game when it's on a knife-edge. The Japanese were happy losers. If they tried hard near the end, defeat was acceptable.

After Bob and Glen were fired by Australia, my old friend had taken a circuitous route to Japan. Glen had been coaching Stourbridge, the English club side, when the Japanese Rugby Union contacted him and asked whether he would consider working as a technical coach with the backs. Glen is always up for an interesting challenge and so he said an immediate yes. Soon after his arrival they asked him if he could suggest a forwards coach. Glen laughed and said, 'You've got one of the best coaches I know already in your country.' He was talking about me and so, while coaching Tokai, I worked as a consultant to the national team.

Yamamoto allowed us to do all the coaching. We also picked the team but, the following day, we would discover that someone in the union had changed the selection. We were just young assistant coaches so we had to swallow it.

There were many frustrations. In Japanese rugby, if one team is successful everyone copies them. It's very peculiar. They do the exact same warm-ups as the champions and try to do the same set moves. I was not going to allow that to happen and so, just as I had done with Tokai, I insisted we stopped kicking the ball. They took to the running game but it was difficult to instil the necessary aggression and boldness into their play. I began to understand that the Japanese had been educated to be passive and subservient because, in the past, they had been such an aggressive race. That aggression was obliterated along with so much else by the ending of the Second World War and the atomic bombs which fell on Hiroshima and Nagasaki. It was as if the Japanese had decided that meekness was better than annihilation.

Complexity shrouded that subservience. I could understand rudimentary Japanese but the nuances went over my head. It always felt as if, while talking to the team, other conversations were unfolding. I was told that the Japanese don't like foreigners telling them what to do. I was half-Japanese so I thought I might be accepted – but it was actually harder for me than for Glen.

We had immediate success when we won the Asian championship in 1996. It was the first time that Japan had won the competition without any foreign players. We insisted on picking purely Japanese players and, on this point, the management backed our judgement. We played some beautiful rugby. Glen had the backs purring and we beat Korea who, then, were stronger than Japan. There were some memorable tries and we celebrated properly with the boys after we lifted the title.

The Japanese Union told Glen and me that they wanted to appoint us as head coaches so that we could take the team into the 1999 World Cup in the United Kingdom. We were still young guys and we thought, 'This is bloody exciting!' Three years before the World Cup we could make real progress. But they kept us waiting and then, suddenly, it was announced that they had appointed Seiji Hirao as Japan's new coach. He was a good bloke but our being dumped hit hard. It made me understand that I should never trust rugby administrators.

I also held on to an ambition that, one day, I would return to Japan as their head coach.

5

A NEW WAY WITH THE
BRUMBIES

Japan was isolated from world rugby, and the internet had yet to transform our lives, but I kept in touch with the dramatic changes tearing through the game. Rugby had become professional across both hemispheres and Australia, New Zealand and South Africa were ahead of the northern countries in the format they found for a new competition. Super 10 rugby had been introduced three years before and provinces and states from the three southern hemisphere giants as well as Tonga and Western Samoa played in the inaugural tournament. It was very low key and it needed the injection of a ten-year television deal to transform rugby with the Super 12 in 1996.

Predictably, the island nations of Tonga and Samoa were brushed aside, and all the money poured into the traditional powerhouses. Five New Zealand teams, four from South Africa and three from Australia made up the new tournament. It was obvious the New South Wales Waratahs and Queensland Reds would keep their places, but there been had much speculation over the introduction of a third Australian team.

There was a call to open up the game by starting a team in Melbourne. But Victoria was a state dominated by Australian football – and rugby was always going to be a sideshow in Melbourne. They might have had the money, but they didn't have the passion or the history. So the Australian board decided to back the ACT Brumbies, a new entity in Canberra forged by people from my past.

Canberra is Australia's capital city and the home of the national parliament. Sydney was the first site of Britain's colonization of Australia in 1770 but, by the 1900s, Melbourne was thriving economically. Neither Sydney nor Melbourne would allow each other to become Australia's capital city and they eventually settled on a compromise. Canberra became the capital, despite being initially not much more than a sheep station between the two giant cities.

From the moment it was established, Canberra copped a bad rap. It was the home of politicians and, consequently, the home of everything that was wrong with Australia. It had neither the beauty of Sydney Harbour nor the wealth of Melbourne, and so it was condemned by the wider Australian population as the home of not only lazy politicians but cardigan-wearing public servants. It was a place of intense and widespread ridicule.

But it was also home to some wonderful rugby players. Michael O'Connor played for the famous Canberra Royals. A player of majestic talents, he featured alongside the Ella brothers in The Invincibles and went on to star in both rugby union and league. David Campese was from Queanbeyan, a city just over the border from Canberra that grew out of the European migrant population after the Second World War. So Canberra and ACT (Australian Capital Territory) was a small but proud rugby outpost which sat in the shadows of the established NSW and Queensland unions.

As I followed professionalism in Australia from afar, I had kept in contact with Ewen McKenzie, my fellow front-row forward from Randwick. Ewen had always been the player with whom I'd had the most searching conversations about rugby. We loved analysing the game and gave the lie to the myth that props and hookers were too dumb to ever think beyond their natural tendency to smash into the opposition front row. Ewen was from Melbourne but he was never going to star in Australian Rules football. He was destined, instead, for great things in rugby. He was a rugby intellectual, a deep thinker and an organized man who helped set up a totally new outfit in Canberra as a player and confidant of the coaching and management team.

The Brumbies were coached by Rod Macqueen – a rugby loving businessman from the Northern Beaches of Sydney. His club, Warringah, had started in the Sydney second division but quickly made an impression. Warringah's first president, Bill Simpson, was a devotee of Cyril Towers and the Randwick Way. In homage to Randwick, the Warringah jersey was green and white. So Macqueen was dedicated to the running rugby we loved at the Galloping Greens. Rod made a name for himself as a tough loose forward in the 1970s with similar ball skills to Simon Poidevin.

Randwick and Warringah enjoyed a strong mutual respect. They were clubs full of tradesman, builders and teachers. You always knew that when you headed across the Spit Bridge to play against the Rats (Warringah's nickname came from the famous Australian Second World War unit, the Rats of Tobruk), it was going to be a tough afternoon. Both the Rats and Randwick loathed Manly, Warringah's closest neighbours.

After his playing career, Rod had taken charge of the Rats and coached them to three grand finals without winning a Premiership. He took charge of the New South Wales Waratahs in 1991 and coached them during an unbeaten season in which they played some of the best rugby in the state's history. Their performances had a massive impact on the World Cup-winning team that Bob Dwyer led in 1991.

Rod was also the coach who axed me from the New South Wales squad that toured Argentina that year. But, rather than holding a grudge against Rod, I had been impressed by the way in which he broke the news to me. We didn't know each other then, but he took the time to call before the squad was announced. His reasons for not including me were similar to those which Bob had cited when choosing not to pick me for Australia. I was too small and he had opted for much bigger hookers. I had no complaints.

Five years later, and considering Rod's obvious intelligence, I was not surprised he had become a Super 12 head coach – of the ACT Brumbies.

Macqueen, ever the businessman, arrived in Canberra with a plan to create a new team from scratch by utilizing shrewd recruitment. As luck would have it, Canberra had just hatched a once-in-a-generation group of young players, including George Gregan, Stephen Larkham, Joe Roff, Rod Kafer and Marco Caputo, who all went on to play for the Wallabies. They were Canberra boys and it was a glorious coincidence that a group of supremely gifted, highly intelligent and fiercely competitive young players had come through the ranks together. I was convinced, even then, that they would have a lasting impact on world rugby. At the same time, there were players from Queensland and NSW who, rather than spending time on the bench in their home states, would take the chance with this new Canberra team. Brett Robinson, Troy Coker, Pat Howard and David Giffin from Queensland were joined by Ewen McKenzie, David Knox, Owen Finegan, James Holbeck, Adam Magro and John Langford from NSW.

They took the Super 12 by storm. On notice to perform or risk losing the franchise, the Brumbies faced the famous Transvaal Lions from Johannesburg in their first home game. Louis Luyt, the bombastic South African rugby hard man, had dismissed the Brumbies as unworthy of a place in the competition. He predicted that his team of Springboks would score 100 points in Canberra. But, in front of 8,000 hearty souls, the Brumbies recorded a famous 13–9 victory.

In that first season in 1996 they also beat the Natal Sharks and the Graham Henry-coached, All Black-laden Auckland Blues. The win against the Blues was particularly special as Auckland included Sean Fitzpatrick, Jonah Lomu, Zinzan Brooke and Adrian Cashmore, and they were regarded as, outside the Test arena, the best team in world rugby. The Brumbies caught everybody off guard and finished the season in fifth place, just outside the play-offs.

Ewen was convinced they would be even better the following year and so, over the Christmas break in 1996, I flew to Australia. I wanted to improve as a coach and I wanted a taste of real professional rugby as the Brumbies prepared for a new season. Ewen had cleared it with Rod that I could sit in on their meetings and watch training.

Another good friend was a key member of the Brumbies squad. David Knox had been a teammate of mine for years at Randwick, and he and Ewen were joined by four other players from our old club. These were either blokes who had been sitting on the bench at New South Wales or promising forwards such as Owen Finegan, who had become a Wallaby after that first year at the Brumbies. It was an indication of Ewen's ability to spot a talented player.

Rod understood rugby deeply, but he would never claim to be a highly technical coach. He concentrated on creating an environment that got the absolute best out of everyone involved. Rod was in the mould of John Hart and Nick Mallett, who then led the All Blacks and Springboks. They provided a structure and a culture that allowed their players to express themselves. It was no coincidence that the most successful rugby coaches in the earliest days of professionalism were three very smart managers who were all strong characters.

I was different to Rod as I operate mainly as a hands-on coach who pays close attention to the processes around coaching. But Rod was the right fit for the embryonic Brumbies as he had the vision, entrepreneurial flair and managerial nous to set up Australia's third Super 12 team.

Ewen, who had played under Rod for New South Wales, was the first and the key recruit. He had the respect of every young player in Australia and was a magnet for talent. Ewen also developed the Brumbies in so many other ways. He helped choose their name, designed the shirt, developed the philosophy, and even walked the streets of Sydney and Canberra trying to find sponsors. To this day he still talks proudly of being able to convince his brother-in-law to sponsor the team hats. It was not normal fare for a prop forward.

As the shirt designer, Ewen looked to the All Blacks for inspiration. The black kit of New Zealand always carried an imposing aura, and so Ewen chose the dark blue which dominates the Brumbies shirt around the shoulders and the navy shorts and socks. He was convinced it would make the Brumbies look bigger.

These were simple concepts but, in a still essentially amateur sport, Rod and Ewen were ahead of the pack. They started from a blank sheet of paper and built the Brumbies' processes, style and standards from scratch. In the move to professionalism the Brumbies had a massive advantage over Queensland and New South Wales in not having to deal with the legacy of a hundred years of amateurism.

On my return to Japan I felt a twinge of regret. I had been offered a new job, coaching Suntory, but it felt as if I was paddling into the backwaters of world rugby while Rod Macqueen surfed the booming rollers in a vast and teeming sea of opportunity.

I must have impressed the Brumbies because, four months after I signed my three-year contract with Suntory, I was asked to join them as a development coach. It was a good step back into Australian rugby, but Hiroko was upset I was even considering another move. She pointed out that I had already persuaded her to uproot our lives in Sydney and move to Japan.

We had struggled to adjust but we had made it work. We were now living just outside Tokyo and I was working in Fuchu. Suntory was a giant brewing and distillery company and its owner loved rugby. He wanted me to turn the company team into the dominant force of Japanese rugby. Hiroko reminded me that Suntory had given me a good contract and for us to start all over again in Canberra was too risky. She was right and so I turned down the Brumbies.

Suntory offered a fascinating challenge. My main task was to overtake their fierce rivals Toshiba, who were Japan's equivalent of Leicester. They mauled, kicked and punched their way to multiple championships. They were a defensive, forward-dominated club. Based in Fuchu, 30 kilometres from central Tokyo, Toshiba's players worked for the electronics company. They could be seen around town in work uniforms and on their bikes. They were a working-class club while my players were very different.

Rather than working at the beer factory, my boys were Suntory salesmen. They wore suits and ties and drove around in BMWs. You might think my preferred role would be to coach the working-class club rather than the affluent bunch. But I was on familiar turf as Suntory were the underdogs and we needed to change their attitude that rugby was not important. The president was desperate for us to bring down Toshiba.

For four months I worked our players really hard. They were much better than the students at Tokai – but they were obstinate. I turned up the heat and pushed them through a series of gruelling training sessions. After one particularly tough afternoon a Suntory player came to find me. He was bawling his eyes out. 'Why do we have to train like dogs?' he asked.

'So you can become better rugby players.'

'Why can't we just do things nice and slowly?' he said through the tears.

I sat him down and we had a little discussion. Toshiba were bigger, fitter and stronger and we had to catch and beat them. I had similar chats with many Suntory players and they eventually came around to my thinking. It helped that we improved hugely and made the Japan Cup final. A few myths developed during my various stints in Japan. The stories implied that I was allegedly some sort of devil and the players were so terrified of me they would hide under tables when they heard me coming. It's complete garbage. Whenever I catch up with my former Japanese players today, we get on famously and enjoy the memories of the hard work and successful times. I'm often painted in the rugby media all over the world as some kind of crazed tyrant. I make no apology for getting the most out of my players. It's the only way I know how to be successful. Shortcuts don't work in professional rugby.

As luck would have it, fate intervened. The Wallabies were hammered 61–22 by South Africa in August 1997. It was the end for Greg Smith as Wallaby coach. Rod Macqueen was the obvious candidate to replace him – and his appointment became official that September.

I've since heard that I was one of a final few candidates to become the new head coach of the Brumbies. The ACT board were keen on a local coach while the Brumbies' CEO, Mark Sinderberry, and team manager, Phil Thomson, flew to Christchurch to interview a young coach by the name of Steve Hansen. The World Cup-winning All Black coach was then making a name for himself at the Canterbury Crusaders.

Word started to leak that I was the preferred candidate, but not everyone was convinced. When Rod came to Canberra he brought a few key advisers with him. One of them was David Pembroke – or Pemby as everyone calls him. Pemby was Rod's right-hand man. Ten years earlier he had played in the first team Rod had ever coached at Warringah. Pemby's rugby career ended not long after he visited a close friend in Royal North Shore Hospital who had broken his neck playing for a country team. Seeing the impact of injury, Pemby tossed in his dream of being a Wallaby, reached for his commerce degree and headed off in pursuit of his next adventure. He became a political correspondent for ABC Radio and he was working in the Federal Parliamentary Press Gallery in Canberra when Rod began the Brumbies. Rod, knowing the critical importance of media, marketing and communication, asked Pemby to join the team.

In early September 1997, Pemby got wind of my appointment and headed straight to the coffee shop in Kingston where the players so often met. In the early days of the Brumbies, Queensland coach John Connolly had mocked the Canberra players as the 'Cappuccino Set'.

It was a beautiful spring day and, knowing that the players

would have a real say in the appointment of their next coach, Pemby went to see them even before he approached Sinderberry. McKenzie, Gregan, Larkham, Kafer, Giffin, Roff and the club captain Brett Robinson were having a 'Set' as they jokingly called their catch-ups.

Pemby made a beeline for Ewen. He pulled up a chair and said to the cerebral prop forward: 'Right, so who is it?'

'What's "it"?' Ewen replied wryly.

'Who's our next coach?'

Ewen looked at Pemby and then, knowing how much he could trust the team's adviser, he said: 'Jones.'

'Jones?' Pemby replied in confusion.

'Eddie Jones.'

'Eddie Jones?' Pemby said as he tried to remember where he had heard the name before. 'The bloke you played with at Randwick?'

'That's him,' Ewen said.

'Who does he coach?'

'Suntory.'

'Suntory?' Pemby parroted. 'Suntory, Tokyo?'

He looked at Ewen as if the prop had lost his mind. Was he really suggesting an unknown coach in Tokyo should take over the Brumbies who, under the inspired Macqueen, had just reached the Super 12 final in their second season? The Brumbies were already the best team in Australia. Were the players really going to make such a left-field choice?

'Yeah,' Ewen grunted.

'Are you serious?'

'Yes, Pemby,' Ewen said patiently. 'I'm serious. Eddie Jones is going to be our new coach.'

Ewen explained that I had flown to Canberra a few days earlier. He had pushed hard for my appointment, but it was imperative that the others believed in me as well. Apart from Ewen, I went out for dinner with Robinson, Gregan, Larkham and Kafer at the team's favourite Italian restaurant, La Capanna in Kingston. We talked about rugby easily and passionately. It only needed me to get on with Sinderberry for the decision to be sealed. I immediately liked Sinderberry and he responded well to the players' request that I replace Rod.

I then flew back to Japan to discuss the situation with Suntory. Contracts were being drawn up and, once I had gained clearance from Suntory and we had signed the agreement, Pemby could release the news. Pemby still looked worried as Ewen tried to reassure him.

'Trust me, mate,' he said. 'He's the right bloke.'

Hiroko's backing was critical, and she had agreed to move to Canberra even before I had arrived back in Tokyo. She understood that this was a huge opportunity and so she was willing to start again in Australia with Chelsea and me. The situation was different at Suntory. I had got the club back on track, and the company president was not going to be happy at the prospect of losing me in the first year of my contract. As the owner of a giant company, he was used to getting his own way, so I had to sweeten the blow.

'If you allow me to go for the next three years,' I suggested, 'I'll come back in my holidays and coach Suntory for free.'

I was thrilled when he agreed. I have since returned to Suntory every vacation to coach. I have been a consultant with Suntory since 1998 and I became their head coach for three years from 2009 to 2012. The way in which the president agreed to let me go in 1997 cemented our relationship. I think Suntory were proud that someone from their club had been offered such a prestigious job in world rugby. It explains why the link has lasted all this time and why I spend three months every year in Japan so that I can coach Suntory for the sheer joy of the work.

When news broke of my appointment, the media were as stunned as Pemby. I flew into Canberra via Sydney after travelling overnight from Tokyo. My first commitment was to meet the media at the home of ACT Rugby – in modest offices on the first floor of a building above a topless bar in the semi-industrial suburb of Fyshwick. The surroundings were home to some of the largest blowflies you have ever seen. They bred in the grease trap of the bar's kitchen and buzzed through the office and slammed into windows.

In these unglamorous surroundings, Pemby and Sinders were waiting for me. The media would be with us in an hour, so we needed to prepare. It was clear that this was an important part of my job and, given all the progress made in the previous two seasons, now was not the time to go backwards. Pemby sat me down and ran through some instructions.

'We can't ever be boring,' he said. 'We've got no money so the only way we can get our message out is if we create attention through the media. Make sure you're entertaining. Be clear and precise with your language and whenever possible tell stories. Journos love stories and they love quotes. Put a smile on your face and look happy. Oh, and by the way, have a shave. The unshaven look doesn't work on the telly. You'll look terrible.'

Pemby didn't know me then but, even now, I remain under the iron rule of my mum. She still tells me off if I don't turn out looking as neat as a pin. So I would almost certainly have reached for my razor, but Pemby got his reminder in first. I liked the fact he was so clear from the outset.

I absorbed Pemby's message, read his release and notes carefully, and felt fully prepared for the press conference.

Pemby was pleased I was shaven and looked smart. 'Presentation is everything, mate,' he said.

Once the presser began, I relaxed. People laughed at my jokes and they scribbled away as I spoke about the kind of rugby that I hoped we could play. There were plenty of questions but nothing I couldn't handle. It felt like a bit of fun and I took to it easily.

'How did I go, mate?' I asked Pemby.

'Not bad,' Pemby replied.

I looked at him and nodded. 'I know I can improve. I need you to work with me and show me how I get better at this.'

'With that attitude mate, we'll get along,' he said. 'But it's a big job.'

Pemby and I had a lot in common. His grandparents, aunt, uncle and cousins all lived around the corner from me in Little Bay. I played rep cricket for Randwick with his cousin Marty Gurr, who was a fantastic rugby league player. Pemby and I had both played at the University of New South Wales and matched each other in loathing Manly. We clicked right away and, over dinner, he provided all the background and insights I needed to understand the Brumbies – and why we had to grow our profile not only in Canberra but across Australia and around the world.

I mentioned the tension between the Brumbies and the Sydney media. Pemby laughed. 'Every story needs a pantomime villain, mate, and the Sydney media is ours,' he said. 'They're members of the old guard who see us as upstarts. They don't like the fact we've had success, but none of us really gives a toss. If we keep winning, they have to cover us.'

In the Sydney papers, the Brumbies were regularly described as cast-offs, misfits and rejects.

Pemby explained that Greg Growden of the *Sydney Morning Herald* had started it. 'Growdo wrote it one day and I couldn't believe my luck,' Pemby said with a huge smile. 'It hit the perfect note because it's all tied up with the wider Canberra story – that the rest of the country always bags us. It was the best marketing line we have ever had. It played straight into our "chip on both shoulders" strategy.'

Pemby had also written a wider and more sophisticated plan. It was called 'ACT: Taking on the World.' He gave me a copy and said: 'Sounds better than taking on Australia, doesn't it? By setting up the challenge to be the "best in the world", you push the players to always improve both on and off the field and you give the supporters, the board and sponsors the opportunity to be involved in something really significant.'

Some of the players had laughed when Pemby first outlined his vision – which upgraded Rod Macqueen's aim for the

Brumbies to be the leading provincial team in Australia to an objective that we would become the best provincial team in the world. He explained that the new television deal gave us a massive opportunity to have a global impact.

Today the original Brumby boys still call him 'Global' and tease Pemby about his big-picture thinking. It's all good fun and the boys are grateful. His vision was a powerful driver of ambition, standards and behaviour, and in a few short years we achieved that goal when we became Super Rugby champions – despite being based in a town of only 300,000 people.

That first detailed conversation convinced me Pemby was the sort of bloke I could rely on to tell me the truth and always have my back. Twenty-two years later, we still speak most days, as he ensures I stay on top of my communication. He's a brilliant strategist and helps me shape the right message to the right audience at the right time in order to help my England team succeed.

It's much harder to forge a relationship with the press today because the competition between the various media outlets is so cut-throat that you feel under siege most of the time. Social media has changed everything, and the days when you could have a few beers and a good yarn with reporters have disappeared. The traditional rugby writer now also has so much more to think about with blogs and podcasts, tweets and videos, headline-grabbing stories and internet traffic. Most journalists still want to write decent and even brilliant work, and some outstanding pieces are still produced, but so much of it is mediocre and ill-informed. I also feel that the standard of rugby knowledge amongst the press pack has dipped in recent years.

Back in Canberra, despite overtaking the Reds and the Waratahs, we were still the misfits and outsiders of Australian rugby. I don't think Growden, Peter Jenkins, or any of the other leading Sydney journalists really resented us, but their narrative bound us tightly together. We were misfits to them, but we planned on changing the way that rugby was played around the world. We were the Brumbies – the most sophisticated and accomplished team in the country.

George Gregan epitomized that sophistication and accomplishment. He had a more interesting story than most blond-haired Australian rugby players. George was born in Zambia to a black Zimbabwean mother and a white Australian father – in echoes of my own background. He had grown up in Canberra which, far from being the bland city described by the Melbourne and Sydney media, was actually a melting pot of cultures and nationalities. The clichéd nonsense from the big city media was that dull old Canberra was run by government bureaucrats and full of politicians and roundabouts. Yet, being home to all the foreign embassies, Canberra is a surprisingly cosmopolitan city.

George also had an understated, urbane manner which didn't obscure his ferocious desire to win. He was a great rugby player but, at the same time, the butt of constant ribbing from his teammates. When the game went professional, George shaved his head, started to dress sharply and generally changed his look to match a superstar international player. Joe Roff always teased him when he pointed to George and said: 'See that bloke over there? I used to know him when he was a Kingswood-driving, Afro-haired, purple-suit-wearing physical education student. Look at him now.'

At the Brumbies, no one was allowed to get above their station.

I still knew, after just a few weeks of preseason, that we were in for a testing campaign. The squad was not big enough or hungry enough. Macqueen had made great strides but the set-up was amateurish. With little money to spend and no professional base, we did weight training in a high-school gym with kids running around the hall. It also seemed to me as if the team had peaked, six months earlier, as Super 12 runners-up. Some of the players were too old and they had been clinging on until they were given new contracts.

Rugby, like real life, is not about the surface. The roots, as well as the layers beneath the surface, dictate your chances of success. Macqueen and McKenzie had done an incredible job starting the Brumbies from scratch. The foundations were in place to build long-term success but the middle planks were crumbling. I should have ripped out the ageing guts of the team but I was inexperienced. I had scrambled up five tiers of rugby in one move. So I didn't trust my own instinct and judgement. I decided to wait and see if the players would prove me wrong.

We struggled from the opening day. On 1 March 1998, I took the Brumbies to Sydney to play our biggest rivals, the NSW Waratahs. They had finished fourth from bottom the previous season while the Brumbies ran the Auckland Blues close at the top of the table. We were heavily favoured but ended up being soundly beaten 32–7 on a beautiful sunny afternoon at the Sydney Football Stadium. It was humbling. In hindsight, our preparation had been appalling. The players' mindset was all wrong. They wound themselves up and acted like they were on some sort of revenge mission. I didn't know how to respond. It was a low point.

I worked the players hard on our return and we won our first home game, against the Otago Highlanders, before the Sharks brought us back down again in Canberra the following week. We then beat a very poor Cats team from Johannesburg – but I knew we were up against it with three away games next in South Africa and New Zealand.

We lost 24–7 to Northern Transvaal on a hard pitch in the unforgiving town of Brakpan and then headed for Cape Town. I was plagued by uncertainty – both about my team and my capacity to coach at this level. We faced the Western Stormers at Newlands, one of the great grounds of world rugby. It was a sold-out Friday night game, on 3 April 1998, and the Stormers had very good players like Percy Montgomery, James Small, Breyton Paulse, Chester Williams, Pieter Rossouw, Dick Muir, Bobby Skinstad and Corné Krige. But they were still erratic and I knew we should be able to test them. However, doubt spread through us like cancer.

From the moment the Stormers ran out to the *Men in Black* theme song, a shiver of apprehension rippled through the Brumbies. Forty thousand rabid Cape Town fans kicked up a storm as the black-shirted home team tore into us. It was an embarrassing night as they scored five tries and all we could muster was a lone David Knox penalty. The final scoreline was 34–3 to the Stormers.

Later that night, alone in my hotel room, I sat on the bed and cried. Tears ran down my face as I looked helplessly around that empty room. I remembered some of the words Pemby had said at our first detailed meeting: 'Winning is the first, second, third, fourth and fifth most important thing. If we don't win, the whole enterprise will collapse in on itself.' His words echoed in my head. I rang him but he didn't answer. Exhausted, frustrated and seemingly out of ideas, I thought: 'Shit, what am I going to do? How am I going to turn this around?'

We had lost four out of our first six games and the following day we had to fly to New Zealand. The Crusaders awaited. I knew they were much better than the Stormers and more humiliation loomed. It seemed as if my coaching career at the highest level could be over almost as soon as it had started.

Eventually I splashed water on my face and went for a walk. It was late but it was a beautiful night. I left our hotel in Camps Bay and, in the moonlight, sat on the beach and calmed myself. 'All right,' I thought, 'we're going to change this. We just need to find a way to get out of this mess and then we'll get on with it.'

By the time I got back to my hotel room I was fine again. The next morning no one had any idea that I'd been so distraught. I became firmer and more assertive.

Of course there was still pain. We lost to the Crusaders in Timaru but we played much better rugby during a 38–26 defeat. We were crisper and sharper in attack and scored three tries.

The margins were narrow and while we lost the next three games, two of those defeats, against the Wellington Hurricanes and the Auckland Blues, were each by just three points. The

Blues were an inspiration. They set a benchmark for teamwork, physicality and skill that, if we were going to become the best team in the world, we needed to equal.

As the losses mounted, the locals in Canberra, who had been so welcoming a few short months before, turned on me. We coached from an open box in the Bruce Stadium grandstand and at half-time you had to walk through the crowd to get to the dressing room. People shouted at me.

'Go back to Randwick, Jones. You're hopeless.'

'Seriously Jones, you've got no bloody idea.'

'Bring back Macqueen!'

It was harsh and, while I kept up appearances, the words stung. I knew we would have done better if I had acted more boldly. We eventually finished third from bottom.

The team remained solid but, predictably, the ACT Board started to get nervous. Twelve months before they were in the penthouse, and now I had taken them to the cellar. Sinders started asking questions. Our captain, Brett Robinson, speaking on behalf of the team, was adamant we were heading in the right direction. We just needed more time; the players were 100 per cent behind me. During the season, Pemby, our team manager Phil Thomson and I met each Monday morning at 7 a.m. to go through our weekly plans and to assess our on- and off-field performance. We could see throughout the whole year that things were tracking well. We just weren't getting the wins. There were injuries galore but that's never an excuse. No one cares.

I had made some obvious but difficult changes. One of them was dropping David Knox. We had gone to Matraville High together, played club and rep cricket in the same team and shared so much at Randwick. Knoxy had won the last of his 13 Test caps the previous year and he remained a reliable goal-kicker, whereas Stevie Larkham and Stirling Mortlock were inconsistent. I wanted to build our new and much more structured form of attacking rugby around an axis of Gregan, Larkham and Kafer. Knoxy was one of the most creative players I ever saw but, at three and a half years younger than me, he was 34. He was too old to play at this level and I had to tell him the truth. He was annoyed at the time, but it says much about him that, all these years later, we remain good mates.

Knoxy's contribution to the Brumbies from the first days in 1996 was immense. He's a different sort of character and never quite fitted in at the old-school-tie Waratahs. But on the Brumbies' pirate ship, where opinion, diversity and inclusion were prized, Knoxy found a home. The locals, including the local nightclub owners, loved him. He certainly enjoyed his time in Canberra.

Apart from changing the personnel, I had begun to think of ways we could compensate for the fact we were not as athletic as the Kiwis or as physically strong as the South Africans. We needed to get back to our core strengths of playing smarter rugby. The younger players at the Brumbies were thoroughly engaged in these conversations. Rod Kafer, in fact, became the joint architect with me of how we planned to play the following season.

Wayne Smith, coaching the Crusaders, had already made his own dramatic changes. Until then, Super 12 rugby had often been an unstructured mess where great tries were scored. Smith transformed the dynamics of the game and turned the break-down into a contest. The Crusaders became Super 12 champions that year after bringing a new physicality to rugby. Their innovation spurred us on.

The mood in our team was calm, despite the fact we had won only three out of 11 games. The players trusted me. Trust is not negotiable in any successful team. With this group, the honesty was underpinned by affection. They just knew each other so well. Some of the traditions the team established encouraged the players to be vulnerable. They spoke openly and often emotionally about what the team meant to them. They felt safe with each other. But they weren't scared of conflict. They would argue points of detail but, once the decision was agreed, there was little dissent. It was a true collective. They were deep thinkers, with creative imaginations, and they knew I was curious and searching for on-field innovations wherever I could find them.

I also had not panicked. I could have lost my composure after that brief meltdown in Cape Town, but I was patient as I rebuilt the team. I am not sure now if success would have come any quicker if I had acted brutally. I might have alienated more people than I needed to and we would have finished in mid-table rather than third bottom. The dramatic shifts we planned required time to work.

Towards the end of that first year, as we played some interstate games against Queensland and New South Wales, Kafer and I began to experiment with our new way. Our Wallaby players – Mortlock, Roff, Larkham, Gregan, Finegan and the rest – were given a break between the Tri Nations and the November tour of Europe. Kafer and I were free to try different tactics.

Kafe is the smartest player I've ever coached – at least in his ability to think strategically and laterally. He and I had conversations about the subtle intricacies of rugby which matched anything I shared with Dwyer or McKenzie. We had hit it off straightaway. When I had flown into Canberra to begin the new season, Kafe picked me up at the airport. He was obviously intelligent and so when he confided in me on our drive from the airport, before the 1998 season, that he was thinking of quitting, I spoke strongly: 'Don't be hasty, mate. You'll be making a big mistake if you retire so early.'

He was only 26 but he felt that, having never played for Australia, his international hopes were over. He'd had the desperate disappointment in 1995 of missing out on making his debut for the Wallabies. He'd been selected as an ACT player, which in those days was no mean feat, to play full back in the second Bledisloe Cup in Sydney. In the final training session at North Sydney Oval he broke his ankle in three places. His Wallaby dream went up in smoke. A couple of years later, and despite having played some great rugby outside Knoxy at number 12, Kafe didn't feel he could compete with three outstanding Wallaby centres in Tim Horan, Jason Little and Daniel Herbert. Kafe was a different style of player. He relied on sleight of hand and timing to make an impact. I told him he was definitely good enough to play Test rugby and I saw him as one of my key players.

I was right. Kafe was picked for the Wallabies the following year. He was part of the World Cup-winning squad in 1999 and he ended up playing a dozen Tests for Australia. But, for me, his greatest achievement was the way he helped develop a totally new style of attacking rugby at the Brumbies.

Against New South Wales, in September 1998, we played structured rugby and scored two beautiful tries in the first 20 minutes. It felt incredible. We ended up losing the game heavily, but we didn't care about the scoreboard that afternoon. I can still remember the euphoria as Kafe and I sat in the dressing room and spoke with such belief that we could change the way rugby was played around the world.

At the end of my first season, I convened a session with the team to explore the question of who we were and what we wanted to achieve. While we had the vision to be the best provincial rugby team in the world, and we clearly had a strong culture, we hadn't written it down. So the boys spent a whole day doing team-building exercises and drawing on butcher's paper. Late in the day, they landed on a set of values that matched our name. B was for Betterment, R for respect, U for unity, M for mateship, I for intelligence, E for enjoyment and S for success.

Pemby was ecstatic. In their own words, the players had defined the team ethos. It added further clarity to our identity, another layer to our foundations, and created a new framework for our storytelling.

After a rough start to his Wallaby coaching career at the end of 1997, Rod Macqueen settled into his new role. One of his first tasks was to appoint some hard heads to his national team staff. His strength and conditioning coach was Steve Nance – a grizzled bloke who spoke with raw honesty. Steve had won three Premiership titles in rugby league with the Brisbane Broncos and his work was in demand. I liked him and, even though he was much older than me, we mirrored each other in our pursuit of clarity and excellence through hard work and blunt candour.

Steve knew I was in a tricky spot before the start of my second season with the Brumbies. He respected me and so he pulled me aside to give me some advice. 'Mate,' he said quietly, 'if you don't do well this year, it's probably the end of your career.'

You might think that's unnecessarily harsh, but Steve had been a professional coach far longer than me and understood the reality. It would have been insulting if he had suggested I had another season to fritter away. We both knew if I didn't get the Brumbies back into the top half of the Super 12, the axe was heading my way.

Steve encouraged me to go with my instincts. If I was going to fail, it would be best to stay true to my convictions. I had to take charge of the programme. Our first season had been one where, feeling green at this level, I allowed the Brumbies to drift. The consequences had been dire. I was now in full control and, hearing Steve's stark pragmatism, I felt far more confident in myself and the team.

The next three months of Super 12 brimmed with promise. We had created an exciting new way of playing rugby which would maximize our resources. The old wood was gone and we also had some of the best players in the world in Gregan, Larkham and Roff. My neck was on the block so I was no longer willing to allow the mistakes of the previous year to creep into our new squad. The past had given us a strong foundation, but it was now in my hands to make the new system work. I was convinced we would be successful.

The Brumbies' style became the model for how everyone, at least in the southern hemisphere, tried to play the game. We created a highly structured plan which, in essence, aimed to ensure that our best attackers were running at their worst defenders in the third phase of play. It resembled a game of chess and, when it worked, it was devastating. Defences were nowhere near as sophisticated then as they are now and, ultimately, we were able to beat every team in front of us with something to spare. Physically we were not really a match for much bigger and stronger teams. So we attacked them with our new approach. Eventually, everyone tried to mimic our style, and people all around the world had copies of our playbooks.

Like all innovations it required courage to make it work because, as soon as you try something unorthodox and it doesn't go well initially, you are likely to face enormous criticism. You need to remember that any worthwhile new way of thinking takes time to refine and perfect.

I had always encouraged an attacking style of rugby based around the Randwick philosophy – which is to play as close to the gain line as possible. Randwick were serial winners and so this was not some philosophy devoted to the purity of rugby. It was seriously focused as the best way to ensure we would win game after game. The key was that we believed we could win by unleashing the best in ourselves rather than just by trying to destroy the opposition's attributes. I think there have been two periods in my career when I'd been able to work with our players and coaches to distil the Randwick Way into fluid, attacking rugby which has suited us. We did it with Japan in the 2015 World Cup and, because we had such intelligent and gifted players, we did it best of all with the Brumbies between 1999 and 2001.

In trying to create a pattern where our best attackers target their worst defenders, it's intriguing to reflect on the fact that a system that seemed so revolutionary at the turn of the century now echoes much of rugby today. The leading sides in the game today are very sequenced and their players understand their roles completely and bring a great deal of discipline to fulfilling their set plays. We were quite basic in the way we started our new way.

The genesis of the plan was rooted in rugby league. Kafer and I studied a lot of league games and we developed a system in which, ideally, by the end of the third phase we would have someone like Joe Roff running at their biggest and slowest prop forward with a real chance of carving open the field and going on to score a try.

Sometimes it would take more than the three-phase template and that was fine. The system was not allowed to choke the players. If a gap opened up after the first or second phase, then our guys would break away from the sequence. I was happy to back their judgement if an unstructured opportunity arose. But, for the most part, we stuck to the three-phase mantra. It was incredible how often it worked if the quality of ball was good and the execution of play was spot-on. Today defences are far too organized to be ripped apart but, in those early years, once we had mastered the system, the Brumbies were a step ahead of everyone else.

We were in a tight spot early in the competition. The format was not kind and our first three games were away. Two matches in South Africa, where we had always struggled, followed by a visit to Brisbane to play the Reds. We lost all three matches but each was tight. The Reds only just beat us 19–18. We were fourth bottom, as we had picked up some bonus points, but I was heartened by the fact that, after our third straight loss, only three other teams, out of our 11 rivals, had scored more points than the 56 we had accrued.

We held our nerve and won our next two games at home. Against the Stormers we scored a near-perfect try after we peeled them open in three simple phases. A little criss-cross with one of our runners going to the left, and another to the right, left a gaping space for a third runner to burst through a hole. A week later, we crushed the Bulls 72–9. It was a rainy Saturday, on 27 March 1999, and conditions were atrocious. But we were slick and potent, scoring ten tries. Some of the handling and passing, the line breaks and the interplay between backs and forwards was breathtaking. Even though the rain hammered down, it was as if we lit up Bruce Stadium with sunshine.

We climbed to fifth in the table. Yet consistency requires application and patience and we had to win our last game, away to the Blues in Auckland, to have a chance of making the semi-finals. It was our most memorable performance of the season. We were 16–0 down at half-time but we kept faith in our system and stuck to our three-phase plan. I was immensely proud when we ended up winning 21–16 to move into fourth place.

The Crusaders were fifth; but with a game in hand the following day. We needed them to lose to the Waratahs to ensure our spot in the play-offs. Our mistake had been to leave the fate of our season in the hands of a team as ruthless as the Crusaders. They were the defending champions and I was not surprised when they beat the Waratahs to inch ahead of us in the table. Even as the fourth-ranked team at the end of the regular season, they went on to win the tournament. It could have been us – with a little more composure and conviction.

We also made great strides off the pitch, at both grassroots and corporate level, during that second season. I had a great time. As part of his mad plan to colonize the world with Brumby fans, Pemby knew we needed to start close to home. So whenever time allowed we would stock up his car with second-hand rugby gear, boots and balls, shirts and posters, and head off to the rugby clubs in small towns around the ACT. I would spend the afternoon or early evening training junior or first teams. It didn't matter if it was schoolboy or second-grade rugby. I was just happy to have a whistle in my mouth and watch the boys have a good time. Afterwards, we would get together in their clubhouse or pubs and talk rugby for hours. I always encouraged them to share their views with me and, when the Brumbies had another game coming up, I'd ask them which players they would select. I can't say anyone ever changed my mind, but it was healthy to hear the divergent views from ordinary people who were fans of the Brumbies.

Curiosity is the heart of invention. Whether you are talking to Pep Guardiola, Alex Ferguson or the person sitting next to you on a plane, you can always learn something. If you ask questions and listen with humility, you will learn something. The older you get, the more you realize the less you know, so being genuinely interested in people and their stories is a wonderful way to finding answers and making progress.

On these visits to the bush it was obvious that our style of rugby had won us new followers and it felt as if we were spreading the gospel of attacking rugby one town at a time. To this day, I love coaching at clubs and schools when I get the time. As a national coach of England, my time with the players is limited so I get the chance to run quite a few training sessions at local clubs and schools. I love it. It's just so rewarding to see the joy on the faces of the kids as they play the game we all love. Rugby has given me everything. Doing these sessions is my small way of giving something back.

Ahead of the new season, Mark Sinderberry landed us the sponsorship deal we had needed so badly. Computer Associates, the giant American software company based in New York, were expanding their business to Canberra. They loved our story of rejects becoming world beaters. They loved the exposure they would get with a global television audience. We told them that when on tour in New Zealand, Australia and South Africa, we could do corporate events for them. It all added up to the richest deal in Australian Rugby provincial history: $1.2 million per year for an initial three years.

Finally, our ship had come in and we were able to compete against the juggernauts of the global game. Until then we had been stymied by the fact that the Australian Rugby Union Board did not regard us as deserving of parity with New South Wales and Queensland. The two big states received considerably more funding from the national union as they occupied the traditional heartlands of the Australian game. But, now, we were on our way to becoming giants.

6

LEARNING CURVE

My bond with the squad strengthened week by week, month after month. In an extension of the routine Rod Macqueen had established, my family and I stayed in the same apartment block as most of the players. We met up socially and Hiroko became good friends with George Gregan's wife, Erica, and Rod Kafer's girlfriend, and now wife, Amanda. With many of the other players and their partners, I needed to tread a more careful line. I felt close to them and went out of my way to get to know their families. But I could never forget I needed to make hard decisions every week in terms of training and selection.

I encouraged the players to have a few drinks together fairly regularly, as we were much more relaxed about drinking in those days, but I always made sure I disappeared quietly before they got into the swing. The players laughed about me 'smoke bombing' from social events. They compared me to a magician who disappears in a cloud of smoke in a cartoon. It wasn't far from the truth. I never said goodbye. I just left. I would be up early the next morning and I needed a little distance.

Our closeness was most obvious on Monday evenings during the rugby season. We would meet in one of the player's apartments and talk rugby strategy. In all my years of coaching, only one other group has come close to matching the intellect of the Brumbies' inner circle. The 2007 World Cup-winning Springbok squad, which I helped coach in that tournament, had John Smit, Fourie du Preez and Victor Matfield who were almost as smart as McKenzie, Kafer, Gregan, Larkham and the rest. The Brumbies just about edged it as the most cerebral set of players I've ever coached – but the Boks pushed them close.

The leaders and the best players in the Brumbies were relentless drivers of their own improvement, and of the team. They also had astonishing skills. But, as with any large squad, it was inevitable that others lacked their mental strength and ability. These were the players I worked much harder. I was demanding and my reputation as a hard taskmaster was embedded during this period.

The simpler truth was that I challenged players to fulfil their potential. George Gregan did not need to be challenged because he was already one of the best players in the world and he worked as hard as he could on sharpening his game. But Troy Jaques and Ben Darwin were very different – both to Gregan and to each other. Jaques is one of my favourites and that says a lot when you consider the thousands of rugby players I've coached over the years. But I screamed at Jaques more than any other player.

Jaques was a bruising lock-turned-flanker who couldn't catch a ball. His fingers were almost as big and as useless as bananas. He was a good, tough bloke who was desperate to play professional rugby. He had played club rugby for Easts in Sydney so he understood the kind of game I liked. But Jaques' problem was that, when it came to basic skills like passing and catching a rugby ball, he was well below the standard of our top players. If he was going to stick around, he had to improve.

The way I rode Jaquesy became a standing joke. Twenty years later, former Brumbies still laugh at the memory of the daily shellacking I gave him. They talk about the sound of my voice ricocheting off the tall trees that surrounded our training ground at Griffith Oval in Canberra.

'Jaquesy, fuck me dead, mate. How hard is it? One job, Jaquesy, you've got one job to do. It's not that hard. Seriously, mate. Is that the best you can do? Jaquesy, I'm not sure why you are here, mate.' And on and on and on it went.

Some of my fellow coaches urged me to tone it down. I ignored them. Pemby said you could hear me screaming from the office and wondered if the neighbours would complain. He also suggested that maybe there might be a better way to get the best out of him.

'No,' I would snap. 'Fuck him! He's got to learn.'

The only person who made me pause and change tack was the player himself. After I had ripped him one more time, berating the hapless Jaquesy until the air quivered with the deepest shade of blue, he spoke up. He told me that he didn't like the way I spoke to him or the fact I only called him Jaquesy. 'Call me Troy, and let's talk about it. I'll respond, mate.'

I looked at him for a while and then I patted him on the shoulder. 'OK, mate,' I said.

One of our traditions was that each of the players had to address their teammates and management and speak from the heart about what it meant to them to be part of the Brumbies. There were often tears. Troy, a rough and hulking forward, wrote a beautiful poem about being a rugby player with banana-like fingers who could not even catch the ball. He spoke of his love for the team and their friendship. He even spoke of his gratitude towards me for riding him so hard. When he'd finished there wasn't a dry eye in the house. I loved those moments when players stood in front of their team and opened up. It showed that what we were trying to do was meaningful and people were giving their best effort, every day.

If I was coaching Troy Jaques in 2019 I would treat him differently. The harsh and reprimanding tone I used in 1999 could not be unleashed today. If a modern player received the verbal pasting I dished out to Troy, he would never get up.

That does not mean I wish I could take back the vicious truths and insults I threw at Troy. From being a barely competent rugby player, he turned himself into a Wallaby. Yes, Troy Jaques won two Test caps for Australia in 2000 and, after he played in a Super 12 rugby final for the Brumbies, he enjoyed a fascinating late career in France and signed good contracts with both Brive and Clermont Auvergne. I often cite Troy as an example of a player with limited ability squeezing the very best out of himself. It was the same with players like Jim Williams and Mark Bartholomeusz, who also made the most of their abilities, not only playing key roles in a Super Rugby winning team but being capped by the Wallabies. As a coach, these achievements are the most rewarding.

Ben Darwin also became a Wallaby and, being a much more naturally talented prop forward than Troy was a flanker, he won 28 caps before a serious injury ended his career. In November 2015, just after I had become England's head coach, Ben wrote an article for the *Daily Mail* in London and said: 'Eddie Jones is not my favourite person in the world. Four years as a player being harangued, taunted and dragged kicking and screaming into a professional career means his name does not fill me with an enormous amount of joy. But I would not have played for Australia if it were not for him.'

The first part of that quote has often been used by the media as proof that I'm some sort of monster.

Ben also wrote that, 'Eddie has a history of making life difficult for players and staff. There are still a lot of people in the rugby world where the name Eddie Jones makes them nervous. What seems to scare people the most is not that he screams or yells more than anyone else but that he almost seems to cut straight to your deepest fears that you are not going as well as you could be. He will never allow anyone to coast, not for a second. In training, if any lift, tackle or pass is not up to standard it will be noticed and acted upon.'

Sorry, Ben, but I'm not Santa Claus. That was never my job. I make no apology for not being your friend or making you joyful. As the former Australian Prime Minister Paul Keating used to say about politics: 'If you want a friend, get a dog.' My job is to squeeze every last bit of potential out of the players who want to play for me. I often laugh about Ben's quote because if he had not become a Wallaby, no one would care what he thought.

I could be even harder on my assistant coaches. Tommy Barker had been a decent flanker for Queensland when I was playing for New South Wales, but he was not cut out to be a professional rugby coach. Again, it was the early days of professionalism and we were still in transition. A lot of coaches didn't understand what it meant to be a professional coach. Tommy was a lovely bloke, but he couldn't hack it at the Brumbies. At our weekly management meetings, I'd go around the table and expect everyone in the room to be prepared and able to give a quick summary of priorities, issues and next steps. All pretty simple. But, for some reason, Tommy would always be disorganized and incoherent. He fell apart almost every time. David Giffin would help him get his content together for the lineouts and Pemby used to boost him the night before and try to prepare a decent presentation.

My management meetings were precise and I expected the right amount of detail to be delivered in a short space of time. No matter how much Giff or Pemby had helped Tommy, it was the same old story every time. Tommy would start fumbling and mumbling and I would explode.

We had to let him go. It was a shame because I liked Tommy and I wanted him to succeed. But some people just aren't suited to an environment as harsh as professional sport. It was better for him, and for the Brumbies, that we parted company.

So I didn't always change a player or a fellow coach for the better. My methods did not suit everyone, of course, but they were delivered with the best intentions. I cared about the Brumbies and I wanted to make every single one of us better at our jobs. Most of those I worked with during those three intense and exhilarating years understood that I was consumed by a desire to make us a stronger and tighter team. Did I make mistakes? Of course. You always do, but I learnt and improved and kept trying to be a better coach.

Away from the grind there were still moments which high-lighted why I fell for the game in the first place. They brought the same surge of amazement that I'd felt as a kid. It seemed as if only rugby could do this to me. George Smith offered a prime example.

In the Australian winter of 1999, Ewen McKenzie and I con-tinued to search for fresh talent that would help us win the Super 12 title. We scouted hard and I went up to Sydney every Friday night to watch club games in New South Wales. The desire to find an exciting young player, or a previously ignored journeyman with untapped potential, drove us on.

I even watched schoolboy and colts games. It was at a school-boy game in Sydney that I first saw George Smith. I had been tipped off that he was a real talent but it was hard to decide too much on the basis of schoolboy rugby. I needed to see him play against men.

At the age of 19, in the winter of 1999, Smith made his first-grade debut for Manly. Ewen and I were pretty aggressive and a day after the game we obtained a copy of the video and sat down to watch him. We thought he might be one to keep an eye on in future years.

Ewen and I watched in silence at first. But then, as the play unfolded, I could hardly wait for the next time Smith rampaged into view. Low whistles and loud exclamations fell from us. Smith was still a teenager but he did everything exceptionally well. This would be unusual for a veteran of 29 but, in a kid making his first-grade debut, it was sensational.

Smith was an open-side flanker and our own number 7 and captain, Brett Robinson, had just one more season left in him. Before the game began there had been no idea in our heads that Smith might be a direct replacement for Robinson.

'We've got to sign him,' I said to Ewen after 30 minutes. 'I'm going down to Sydney and I'm not leaving until he signs for the Brumbies.'

Ewen and I met the kid the following week and I had decided

it didn't matter if he was a criminal. Smith was joining the Brumbies. Of course sanity would have prevailed if we had discovered some dark secret to such a shimmering talent. But the opposite was true. George was a good, humble kid. His upbringing had been difficult and he left school in Sydney at the age of 15. His parents took him to Tonga for a while and that settled him down. He had become calmer and clearer. It did not take much talking from me to convince George or his parents that he should join the Brumbies.

I didn't know then that he would go on to play 111 times for Australia, or become the second most capped flanker in the history of rugby, behind Richie McCaw. I had no idea that he would also emerge as one of the kindest and most giving rugby players I've ever known – a great forward, willing to share all he had learnt with anyone who asked him. George Smith could not always explain what he did so well, for he lacked the eloquence off the pitch that he displayed in a very different language on the field. He was also not really a leader nor a dominant character. He was just a genius of a rugby player and, at the end of 1999, as he prepared to move from the warm beaches of Manly to cold old Canberra, I could sense this in the excitement that rippled through me.

George Smith would become the greatest rugby player I have ever coached.

The Brumbies were an edgy team. We were always polite, courteous and professional – until we weren't. We didn't take shit from anyone. It's hard to describe just how much our success irritated the bigger states in Australia and the ARU headquarters. Across South Africa and New Zealand, our rugby was admired and praised. At home, our opponents in the big states manipulated the Sydney and Brisbane media to accuse us of arrogance.

In my mind, we were never arrogant. Arrogance suggests an exaggerated sense of your own importance or ability. Our team leadership would never have allowed it. But we were extremely confident. We played on the edge on and off the field, and lived life to the brim.

In the early days of professionalism, drinking was still a big part of rugby culture and the Brumbies were no different. I didn't see it as a negative. We were just like a successful company that, at the end of a hard week, goes to the bar to let off steam on a Friday evening. Those sessions together were often great unifying gatherings and they did more good than harm. Most nights there were no problems but, occasionally, a few people went awry. It would again be like a business where 80 per cent of your employees leave the bar at a sensible time after having some fun, 15 per cent stay on a little too late and 5 per cent end up drinking for far too long and feel terrible the next morning.

It was on the Sunday night of 19 March 2000, in Cape Town, when the Brumbies briefly went off the rails.

We had begun my third season in charge with the players sharing my conviction that we would become Super 12 champions. It would be an incredible feat for a team that had been in existence for just five years.

Our sequenced play led to accusations that the players were too programmed – which was laughable when we cut loose and scored so many sparkling tries. We had a method that worked, and we had players of such vision and creativity that I never had any fear we would become too rigid. I thought we were the best team in the competition by some distance.

Rugby, however, has a remarkable capacity to cut down any team that gets ahead of itself. We lost our opening match, at home, to the Blues. They were a tough and gnarly team and clung on to win 18–15. It was a reminder that we needed to be totally switched on and ready.

A week later, again at Bruce Stadium in Canberra, we showed our true abilities and slashed the Sharks to pieces. That 51–10 victory set us up perfectly for our brief tour of South Africa. We flew to Cape Town, where we had never won, and where I had been reduced to tears two years earlier. It was a vital game and I felt confident in a way that would have been impossible in 1999. They didn't let me down and, in the end, we were comfortable winners, 29–14. We earned five points that afternoon and denied the Stormers even a single bonus point. The Newlands faithful were muted as they trudged away, knowing that their team had been outplayed.

I had learnt enough by then to know how important it was to savour the sweetest victories. This felt like a landmark moment and I gave the squad permission to have a night out in Cape Town. The way they whooped and hollered, with even a shy kid like George Smith beating his bare chest like a drum, told me it would not be a quiet one. When Smith had arrived in Canberra he brought his 17-year-old girlfriend with him. She was still too young to drink at any of our bonding sessions with the players' families; but George already had a taste for the grog.

That night I enjoyed a meal out and a few glasses of good South African wine with my assistant coaches and Thomo (Phil Thomson), our very efficient and amiable team manager. We went over the game in detail and agreed that we had taken a significant step forward. The Bulls in Pretoria were next, so there was no room for complacency. I went to bed long before midnight.

For most of the team, Sunday was a quiet and relaxing day. The problems happened that night. I was already awake when my hotel phone rang just after 7 a.m. on Monday morning.

Thomo knew I was an early riser and that I would want to hear the news in person. Some of the boys had got into a spot of bother. Could he come up to my room to tell me everything?

I remained calm when Thomo arrived and gave me the players' version of their second big night out. Around one in the morning Rod Kafer, Joe Roff, Owen Finegan, Peter Ryan and Bill Young had got into a taxi. They wanted to pick up some food and then be driven back to the hotel. Instead, they had an altercation with the taxi driver. They claimed that he wanted to overcharge them and, in their drunken state, one of the players pulled his taxi meter loose. Their defence was that the meter was attached to a cigarette lighter and so it had fallen off at the slightest tug. The cab driver had then taken them to Sea Point Police Station to report the incident. They had settled the fare and been released without charge.

It didn't sound too bad to me but Thomo pulled a face. He had first heard the news when a journalist from the *Cape Argus* called his hotel room to ask for an official team reaction. The press were onto the story and so we knew it was likely to start rolling soon – even in those days before social media.

Pemby was back in Canberra as our budget didn't stretch to him travelling every year to South Africa. Thomo briefed him about the news. Over the years Pemby had stood often in front of team meetings and talked about the risk and threat of 'nightmare scenarios'. Players being involved with the police was a definite nightmare scenario. Pemby was calm but he knew that this might be the chance that our critics from interstate and in the media had been waiting for – to straighten out the upstarts from Canberra. We agreed to sit tight and not do anything until we saw which way the story broke.

In the meantime Thomo got word to the entire squad that I wanted to talk to them before breakfast. I was not about to read them the riot act, but I couldn't allow any ill-discipline to blow us off course. A few quiet words would be enough to get across my brief and obvious message that this was the kind of unacceptable incident we should always avoid.

The five players were hungover and contrite but they insisted that they had not acted maliciously. It had just been a bit of fun on a quiet Sunday night.

I raised my right eyebrow at that one – which they always saw as a sign that I was not happy. They were sheepish enough for me to send them out to breakfast. I was ready to put this distraction to one side and, after they had caught up on their sleep, start preparing them for another important game in Pretoria in six days. We had until Thursday in Cape Town to do some serious training.

That plan was soon torn up. All hell broke loose as the South African and the Australian media went to town on the story over the next 48 hours. The *Cape Argus* led the way. They interviewed the taxi driver, Riedewaan Abrahams, who claimed that the players were 'raucously drunk' and 'abusive' and had ripped out his taxi meter and left it on 'a high wall on Beach Road'. He accused them of refusing to pay him and 'maliciously damaging' his cab.

The headline also claimed that 'ACT Brumbies Arrested After Taxi Tussle'.

The Australian press, especially the newspapers in Sydney, were screaming for the five players to be sent home in disgrace. I disagreed. They had let themselves and the team down and behaved immaturely. It was a bad example but I was determined to deal with it internally and fine them for their behaviour. I was definitely not sending anyone home for a minor offence.

The ARU chief executive John O'Neill, under the white heat of media pressure, buckled and announced that we had brought the game into disrepute. We were not close friends and we would clash in the years I was Wallaby coach; but I respected O'Neill. He was a superb businessman and doing a good job in shaking up Australian rugby. Already with an eye on the 2003 World Cup, to be held in Australia, O'Neill was obsessed with the image of rugby union. It didn't help that his hometown newspaper, the rugby-league-dominated Sydney tabloid, the *Daily Telegraph*, presented our players on their front pages like criminals in their Wallaby jerseys. All of a sudden it wasn't a Brumbies' problem, it was a Wallabies' issue, and O'Neill was furious. He diverted the pressure onto the ACT Rugby Union.

I then got the call from my chief executive, Mark Sinderberry. I was close to Mark, who is a very good man, but I was not happy when he said, 'You're going to have to send them home.'

'If they go home,' I said bluntly, 'then so do I. I'll quit.'

I was backing my players to the hilt and I was willing to give up my job, even if the consequences for me and my family would have been catastrophic.

Mark knew I meant it and, to his credit, he immediately switched tack. He backed me in the exact same way I backed my players. We agreed to stand firm against the press and O'Neill.

I then called Pemby. 'How's it looking, mate?' I asked.

'The ARU are pounding Sinders and I also got a call today from O'Neill,' Pemby told me. 'He's filthy. I can see his point that it's damaging but I agree with you, mate. We can't give our blokes up. I'm getting our ducks in a row and trying to drag a statement out of the South African police that will confirm the facts. Once we have that we will start the counter-attack as soon as we can. And when we do, we will go after them with everything we've got.'

The eventual police statement was clear. It said the 'entire incident had been grossly exaggerated. No player was charged and the damage to the meter and car were not serious.'

We had the green light for our offensive. The first target was the *Cape Argus*, the paper that had broken the story and then run a follow-up accusing Thomo of bribing the taxi driver. Our statement, sent to the world's media, accused the *Argus* of having the 'lowest journalistic standards of any newspaper in the English-speaking world.' It went on for days. As far as we were concerned, the statement had exonerated our players and we weren't going to lie down and take it. I shut my mind to the story and got on with the preparation for the upcoming Bulls match that weekend.

Such incidents are a harmful distraction and obviously not to be condoned. But I was determined we would use the furore as a way to instil greater professionalism in the players and to bind the squad more tightly together. We succeeded on both counts. Kafer, Finegan and the other bad boys in the dock were even more diligent in training. They sweated buckets and got all the rubbish out of their systems. The other boys gave them a bit of a ribbing but, most of all, they stood squarely behind their teammates.

We flew up to Pretoria on the Thursday and the drive from the airport to the hotel was a revelation. The local Pretoria newspaper had got in on the act. They had placards hanging on the lampposts: 'Go home Brumby criminals!' It was a circus, and by this time we were starting to see the funny side of it.

More importantly, we saw the quality and maturity of the side when, on Saturday afternoon at the fortress of Loftus Versfeld, we beat the Bulls 28–19.

We flew home to meet the waiting press. But we were ready for them. Pemby was on the phone to us as soon as we landed, and briefed Robbo (my captain Brett Robinson) and I on the plan. We would accept that it did not reflect well on the Brumbies and the game, and the players understood the mistakes they had made. But, beyond that, we would not give an inch.

Pemby had already ripped into the waiting media because they had given little or no coverage of the South African police statement which had cleared our players. It worked a treat. I remember my dad was amongst the large crowd of supporters who were also at the airport. They wanted to welcome us home while my dad, taking a lead from Pemby, was most intent on shouting at the newshounds for giving me such a tough time. He was looking after his boy, who was 40 years old, even then. I calmed Dad down and told him not to worry about the press. It would all blow over.

It was a nice touch that 30 local taxis arranged a guard of honour for us at Canberra Airport. The players were delighted.

That Saturday, we shook off the jet lag and the infamy and thrashed the Cats 64–0. After the game Rassie Erasmus, the respected Cats captain and current Springbok coach, said: 'At one stage I felt like going to Colin Hawke (the referee) to ask him to check whether they actually had only 15 players on the field. It felt like they had 20 because they seemed to be attacking us from everywhere.'

We then beat the Highlanders. After six games, having won five, we were on a roll and top of the table.

We lost only two games all season, winning nine, and finished top of the division, six points clear of the Crusaders.

We played stunning rugby that year. We had the three-phase

sequence trick down to a fine art, and there was a fluidity and courage to our rugby that made me very proud. Perhaps the most satisfying win of all came against the Hurricanes – a team rammed with great All Blacks from Christian Cullen and Jonah Lomu to Tana Umaga and Alama Ieremia. Those players had an enormous athletic and physical advantage, but we stunned them tactically and ran in 47 points. We were flying.

In the semi-final, in Canberra, we romped past the Cats 28–5. The final, against the Crusaders, whom we had beaten 17–12 in Christchurch in front of a sold-out crowd of 36,000 Kiwis on the last Friday night of the regular season, would also be played at Bruce Stadium. The greatest night of my coaching career, until then, awaited.

Bruce Stadium, Canberra, Australia. Saturday, 27 May 2000

As we look at the packed crowd of 26,000, crammed into the arena on a snowy and miserable evening, Rod Kafer reminds me that he had played for ACT against New Zealand in Canberra in 1992. Rod had just turned 21 then and he was thrilled to face the majestic All Blacks. But only 2,500 brave souls watched New Zealand beat ACT 45–13. Eight years later more than ten times that crowd have turned out to support the Brumbies in the Super 12 final. It means that almost 10 per cent of the entire population of Canberra has squeezed into Bruce Stadium.

My eye is dragged back to a noisy corner taken over by the visiting Crusaders contingent. They are covered in plastic capes, in a futile attempt to keep out the sleety rain, but they still wave their red-and-black flags, umbrellas and banners – one of which reads *Float like a Butterfly, Sting Like a Bee, Go Toddy, Go Toddy, Make it Three.*

It's a weak riff on Muhammad Ali but also a cautionary warning that Todd Blackadder's Crusaders are determined to win three Super 12 titles in a row. We might have beaten them two weeks earlier but, coached by Robbie Deans, they will be tough to defeat. However, we will play the same game we have played all season.

Kafe starts at centre, alongside Stirling Mortlock, while Gregan and Larkham are our usual half-back pairing. Joe Roff on the wing and Andrew Walker at full back have scored many tries all season. We have some tough boys among the forwards in Bill Young, Jeremy Paul, Justin Harrison, Brett Robinson and Jim Williams. I've stuck with Robinson at open-side flanker, ahead of George Smith, as he is our captain and this will be his last game before retirement. Robbo deserves the opportunity; he has done a superb job, not only during the season, but in building the team from day one. Smith, even at 19, is already the better player but, in a final, against the Crusaders, I go for experience. Troy Jaques and Ben Darwin are on the bench with Smith.

Despite the freezing cold and the wet ball, we fly at the Crusaders from the opening whistle. We come at them in waves, moving the ball deftly along the backline, and for the first 80 seconds we pin them deep into their territory. But Leon MacDonald, their full back, picks up a loose ball and leads a counter-attack which streams across the length of the pitch and ends up in a Crusaders penalty in front of our posts. Andrew Mehrtens, the All Black number 10 with the deadly boot, is never going to miss: 3–0 to the Crusaders.

We run at them, again and again, sticking to our sequenced play, but the Crusaders are so well drilled they hold us in check. After 20 minutes they are 9–0 ahead, with three Mehrtens penalties highlighting our inconsistency with the boot. Mortlock is a very good player and he will improve as a place-kicker over the years, but this afternoon, amid the swirling snow, he is fallible. He misses four penalties. Mehrtens, meanwhile, slots home his fourth after we are penalized for an infringement in the scrum: 12–0 after 23 minutes.

It is 12–3 at half-time and I encourage the Brumbies. Trust in the process and the scoreboard will take care of itself.

I bring on George Smith seven minutes in the second half. We need some of his magic. His presence immediately lifts the team. A big Smith run leads to an even simpler penalty and, this time,

Mortlock kicks it: 12–6. The stats show that we've had 89 per cent possession in the second half.

The Crusader subs shiver under their blankets as the cold is perishing. But they belong to a bloody good team and their forwards and backs combine and came back hard, forcing us to defend deep in our own half. And then, surprising us with his invention, their number 8, Ron Cribb, bursts through a gap and produces a sublime grubber kick which he runs on to and catches just before crashing over the line. Cribb celebrates by pretending to down a beer before he pours the rest of his imaginary glass over his head. The Crusaders are 17–6 ahead after 52 minutes.

Smith's dreadlocks dance in the cold black air as he cuts back inside, leaving two Crusaders defenders for dead. My wonder kid zips through the gap and scores our first try under the posts. He makes the game look so simple. Mortlock converts the kick and after 64 minutes we narrow the gap to 17–13.

With eight minutes left on the clock, we win another penalty in their 22 and Mortlock is successful again: 17–16. There is a smattering of snow on the touchline but I feel a fire inside. As we attack again, MacDonald is penalized for a high tackle on Larkham by the South African referee André Watson. Penalty to the Brumbies.

It is not an easy kick. Thirty-eight metres out, and midway between the touchline and the centre of the pitch. I take in a deep breath. Mortlock has missed a number of easier penalties and I wonder how I will console him if another drifts past the posts.

We should never doubt him. Mortlock is a study in certainty before striking the ball with such sweet beauty. It sails unerringly between the H.

I clench my fist tightly, give it a little pump and almost jump out of my seat. The Brumbies bench is much less circumspect. My players leap to their feet and punch the air.

Brumbies 19, Crusaders 17. Four minutes left on the clock. Our second-phase possession advantage is 165 to 34. We have already scored 51 tries this year and will keep attacking until the very end.

In our own half we keep playing, driving through one phase after another. After 77 minutes, Patricio Noriega, our tight-head prop from Argentina, is penalized by Watson.

I feel sick to the stomach. Mehrtens rarely misses a kick – and especially not when it matters. He goes through his usual routine, bang in front of the posts and just behind our ten-metre line, and then he steps forward a few paces and swings his right boot. The ball soars high into the black sky, spinning in a seamless arc towards the goal. Even before it sails through the posts I know it is over. My head drops even before the flags are raised. In the Crusaders corner, pandemonium breaks out.

Brumbies 19, Crusaders 20. Less than two minutes on the clock.

Walker kicks off and our pack tear after the ball, hoping for one last twist. The ball spins out to Mehrtens who aims to find touch deep in our half with a raking kick. Roff catches it and sets off on a mazy run. He is brought down on our ten-metre line. Gregan snaffles the ball, slips it to Larkham who finds our talismanic teenager. Smith barrels forward and feeds Kafer who is tackled in Crusaders territory. Gregan begins the next phase. Larkham is given the ball and brought down in a heap.

Penalty to the Brumbies just past our ten-metre line. Walker steps forward and boots it into touch. It is not the kick we want, going out midway in their half rather than deep in their 22. Fifteen seconds are left.

Paul steadies himself and throws towards the back of our lineout. Robinson catches it and gives the ball to Gregan who finds Mortlock running hard into space. He is brought down and the next phase begins. Gregan to Larkham to Kafer who is tackled close to their 22. We go through two more phases and, with a dazzling little reverse pass, Gregan seems to have set Roff on his way. Our best attacker is immediately shut down by the Crusaders' smothering defence. The Gregan–Larkham–Kafer axis slips back into gear. Kafe is in their 22 when he is tackled by two Crusaders.

Scrum to the Brumbies. The clock shows 81 minutes 15 seconds. This is our last chance.

On the monitor I can see that the television cameras are trained on me. My eyes fix on the exhausted forwards. Steam swirls around their heads and bodies as they prepare to go down for one last scrum.

The two packs shudder into each other and crumple to the ground. Watson signals for them to try again. He instructs both front rows to stay on their feet.

Down they go, again. Gregan waits and, when they have engaged and steadied, he feeds the scrum. We win the ball back quickly and Gregan looks up, to his left, and sees Larkham. But Roff is steaming in from the wing and so he is given the ball. Roff is eventually tackled. Gregan is at the breakdown, passing to Larkham who finds Kafer. A defender hits him hard but Kafer manages to turn the ball back to Gregan who returns it to Larkham. Smith is at his side and ready to aim for the line again. But the Crusaders knock him back. Smith gets up, ball still in hand, and runs again. Smith is blocked so Gregan goes again. Larkham has it next and he flips it inside to Roff.

The clock shows 82 minutes 30 seconds. Roff is buried at the bottom of a mass of bodies and cannot release the ball.

Watson reaches for his whistle and gives it a shrill blast. His left hand shoots out in the direction of the Crusaders. Penalty. The defending champions roar in relief while my players sink to their knees. Roff shakes his head as the Brumbies haul themselves up and walk away.

They turn to face the surreal sight of Todd Blackadder, the Crusaders' captain, cradling the ball and preparing to hoof it into touch. But then Blackadder, who is such a sensible and decent man, remembers he is a lock in the very last moments of a Super 12 final. He flicks the ball to his scrum half, Ben Hurst, who has played in place of the injured Justin Marshall. Hurst kicks the ball into touch and the referee's final whistle pierces me.

The Crusaders are a seething black and red party while my players look broken.

I walk out onto the field. As soon as my shoes crunch against the snowy grass I feel the pain burst inside me.

Tears roll down my face. Rod Kafer is the first player to approach me. He is also crying. There is no shame, only the raw and deep hurt that comes after you lose a match that matters so much.

Some lessons can be taught, and some have to be learnt through experiences as bitter as they are tough. I still feel bad about that loss almost 20 years later. There are times when I feel too choked up to talk about it. But I learnt a lesson which will never leave me. We were not good enough that day. The Crusaders were smarter than us.

When they came off the field together, Andrew Mehrtens sought out George Gregan. The All Black and Crusaders number 10 told the Wallabies and Brumbies number 9 that we had been the best team in the competition by a mile. But the Crusaders knew exactly how we were going to play. Steve Hansen, the Crusaders assistant coach, said similar words when he discussed taking over from me at the Brumbies in 2001. Steve, who would choose to coach Wales instead, before moving on to the All Blacks, met with Kafer and some of the other leading Brumbies players. He echoed Mehrtens in stressing that we had been the outstanding team in 2000 but, having beaten the Crusaders two weeks earlier, we fell into the trap of playing in the exact same way. We had been extraordinarily naive in thinking we did not need to adjust our pure approach to the highly structured game we favoured. The Crusaders prepared accordingly. They shackled and suffocated us.

Their hooker Mark Hammett likened the Crusaders strategy to the Maori Wars of the 19th century. 'We ended up taking the same approach to the Brumbies as the Maori did to the Europeans all those years ago. The Maori based all their strategy on defence and used to sneak up on the Europeans and strike whenever they had the opportunity. That's pretty much how we played. We hit them when we could. The rest of the time we defended as resolutely as possible.'

I met with George Gregan two days after the final. We sat down in the usual cafe where the Cappuccino Set gathered and I asked George to take over as Brumbies captain the following season. It was no surprise as Brett Robinson was retiring, and George agreed readily. I moved on to emphasize that we would never make the same mistake again in another final. We had allowed the Crusaders to work out exactly how to nullify our attack and, because we had no alternative plan, we had lost the game.

George and I began to prepare for the 2001 season that very morning. I knew we would be a much better team after suffering such a loss. We would not replicate the experience of a team like the Dutch national side, who played football beautifully in the 1970s and 1980s, but never won the World Cup. We would keep playing beautiful rugby, but we would also be sufficiently pragmatic and adaptable to ensure we won the Super 12 tournament we craved.

It was obvious we needed to develop a kicking game. We brought in Kafer to discuss it and he agreed. He pointed out that George had probably never used a box-kick once in the previous two seasons. So we spent the off season working on box-kicking. We also worked on our place kicking. There had been a misplaced confidence in our thinking that our running game would produce so many tries we didn't need to worry about missed penalties and conversions. Against the best teams we needed to score every point we could. I encouraged Mortlock, Larkham and Walker by putting them on bonuses for successful kicks. They were quick to practise hard and to improve.

We also began to think much more strategically about the games themselves. It was not enough to rely on our sequenced play. We needed a deeper intelligence when we hit a roadblock like the Crusaders defence. In the big matches, against the toughest and best-coached opposition, we had to play differently. And so we began to prepare for the 2001 final in the group games. We went in with a strategy to mimic what we would need to do in the final. We had to play more conservatively and build pressure slowly. Kafer was at the heart of this technique. He had a series of calling strategies that he used at various points in the game. For the first 15 minutes we would play in a certain way and then, after Kafe barked out a call, we would shift the strategy for the next ten minutes. We would use the clock to build pressure and then, when we were ready, we would unleash our most potent attack at certain time slots within the game.

It was considered and detailed. We knew what we were going to do from every position on the field, which is not uncommon today, and from every lineout and scrum. The game was much more set-piece-orientated back then, whereas now it's more fluid. But the same pressure points still apply in the key periods in a match – when fatigue sets in or they make substitutions. We tried to match our game plan to those moments of weakness in the opposition.

If we played the Crusaders again on another wet night, then at least we'd have a kicking game to call on. We would do something apart from attacking in waves, phase after predictable phase. It was also a case of playing within ourselves and keeping something back for the play-off matches. We knew we could win most Super 12 games without drawing on our full repertoire. So while we would not be as dazzling as we had been the year before, our 2001 version of the Brumbies would be a smarter and superior team.

On 23 February 2001, we began the new Super 12 season by facing a repeat of the final. This time we steamrollered the Crusaders 51–16. It got the hurt out of our heads and sent an ominous message to everyone else. Another South African tour was next and the games were hard. We followed our new pragmatic approach in Durban and I was not too worried about losing 17–16 to the Sharks. I had targeted the game against the Cats at Ellis Park as, in a venue where we had never won, it felt important that we should overcome another barrier.

We didn't play great rugby against the Cats, but Joe Roff finally started to find some space. He might have scored a try but the Cats pushed us back. There were just a few minutes left when, with the Cats 17–16 ahead, Kafe called for a running play. George Gregan shouted no. He pointed at Kafe and said, 'Mate, get back in the fucking pocket, kick the field goal, and let's get out of here.' Kafe grinned, said 'Yes, sir!' and went straight back into the pocket.

The scrum held firm, the ball came out nice and clean and George's pass set it up perfectly. Kafe caught the ball, steadied himself and kicked the drop goal. It was an ugly-looking thing, and just crept over, but it won us the game 19–17.

We won eight out of our 11 games in the regular season and finished top of the table ahead of the Sharks, the Cats and the Reds. We had been controlled in an unusual year with no New Zealand side making the play-offs and the Blues and Crusaders ending up second and third bottom. We had played thrilling rugby the previous year, but I preferred that 2001 season. We adhered to the system we had created, and scored 70 per cent of our tries after the third phase, but we were so much more adaptable and mature. Rugby is fascinating because it is never stagnant. The game is always changing, and we were more flexible than any other team that season.

The semi-final was an easy 30–6 victory for us over the Reds; while the Sharks were just as impressive in beating the Cats in Durban. We were in our second successive home final and knew exactly what we needed to do to make amends for the heartbreak of the year before.

Bruce Stadium, Canberra, Australia. Saturday, 26 May 2001

We're one day short of the exact anniversary of our defeat to the Crusaders. But the memory is seared into us and it produces the greatest pre-game dressing-room talk I have ever heard.

The Brumbies' pre-game routine was to gather for our meal, strapping and unit meetings at the Australian Institute of Sport, which is a short walk from Canberra Stadium. Part of the build-up to each game is the jersey presentation. Thomo would hand every jersey to the captain and he would then present it to each player. As each name was called, all hell would break out as the rest of the team and management would hoot, holler, yell nick-names, clap, cheer and celebrate the accomplishment of being given a prized Brumbies jersey. From the first trial match of the season to a final, the same reverence to team selection was shown.

George isn't normally one for words or Churchillian speeches. He prefers action. But tonight he is inspired. He stands in front of the team once everyone has been given their jersey. He starts quietly and slowly, deliberately and carefully explaining what we are going to do. But as he talks he becomes more and more ani-mated. He speaks about our families, the fans, and the journey of the players in the room and those who have come before them. He voices his pride in them and stresses how the job is not yet done. He finishes with a flourish by raising his voice and slam-ming his fist repeatedly into his hand and saying that the mistakes of the previous year will never, ever, happen again. As soon as he says the last rousing word, he picks up his bag and walks out of the door in the direction of the stadium.

The players file out after him. Pemby and I have a tradition of being the last to leave as we walk slowly to the stadium. On this night it is the same as every other game. But in the distance we can see tens of thousands of Brumbies fans streaming into the arena.

We don't speak. And then, halfway there, Pemby breaks the silence with a single question: 'So?'

'We're good,' I reply.

'Why?'

'These blokes are so shit-scared of George, they won't dare lose.'

Only one other captain's speech has come close in all my years of coaching. John Smit found that same captivating power and clarity when he addressed the Springboks in the dressing room before the 2007 World Cup final. They are not easy speeches to make because it's difficult to grab hold of everyone and say words which will resonate so powerfully with such distinct individuals. Smit did it in Paris; and Gregan did it in Canberra.

It is one of those unusual big games where, even before the first whistle, I am convinced of the outcome. This does not happen often because rugby is such a variable and unpredictable sport. But I feel certain now. The Sharks are the fastest-starting team in the competition. They blow teams away in the first 40 or 50 minutes and then ease back. I know that they are nowhere near as fit as us and that we are the best closers in the competition. We are at our strongest in the ten minutes before half-time and in the last half-hour of the game. We call them the championship minutes and so I know we will be at our best just as the Sharks dip. It's important that we let their storm blow out and be close to them at half-time. We will then cruise away from them.

They are a very good team, and feature two of the Springboks with whom I will win the World Cup in Smit and Butch James at fly half. James kicks two penalties and, with Mortlock injured, he is matched by Andrew Walker for the Brumbies. I do not need to say much at half-time, beyond conveying a simple message. At 6–6 we have them exactly where we want. We have completed the precise first-half job. It is now time to go out there and carve them to pieces.

We score three tries, two for Joe Roff and one for David Giffin, while Walker converts them all and kicks three additional penalties. The Sharks are scoreless in the second half and so we win 36–6.

I still treasure the second of Roff's tries. After 54 minutes, with the Brumbies 16–6 ahead, Gregan picks up the ball at the base of the scrum. He passes to Larkham who flips it back inside to Kafer. At the breakdown we smash them back. Gregan finds Giffin who clatters through a gap, bringing down a couple of Sharks with him. Gregan is again ready. It's the third phase and, while he has plenty of runners like Larkham, Kafer and Walker to his left, Gregan goes the other way. He slips a beaut of a pass to Roff who comes flying past him.

'Great ball!' shouts a colour analyst on television before the commentator Gordon Bray screams into the microphone: 'Joe Roff! Nobody in front of him! Joe Cool!'

Roff eats up the 40 yards ahead of him like an express train. He dives over the open try line as Bray yells: 'He's got a double! Oh, it opened up like the Red Sea. They are magic!'

It feels magical when George lifts the Super 12 trophy up into the black sky. Unlike Blackadder the year before, who had looked exhausted, George is exultant as he shakes the trophy to all four corners of the stadium before the team engulfs him.

I watch from a distance, smiling and satisfied, but also aware of a slightly melancholic tug amid the sweetest of victories. Even though I didn't know it then, my time with a team that I love, a team I've helped build and change, is almost over. Rugby will never feel quite the same again for me.

My time with the Brumbies was a sheer joy. I look around the stadium and see the happiness of the fans and the players. We have done something very special for this city and for our supporters in the region, across Australia and around the world. We have played some wonderful rugby and made them proud. And we are now, as Pemby had predicted, 'the leading provincial rugby team in the world.'

7

GREEN AND GOLD

Rod Macqueen had coached the Wallabies to victory in the 1999 World Cup. By 2001 he felt exhausted. He told me that, once the Lions tour of Australia ended that summer, he was taking a long break from rugby. I had been spoken of as Rod's successor for over a year and my credentials were sealed by becoming the first Australian coach to win the Super 12. I had also been asked to coach Australia A against the Lions on Tuesday 19 June 2001.

It was a beautiful warm evening in Gosford, a commuter city just north of Sydney, and the Lions were expected to romp to another decisive victory. They had scored 241 points in their first three games. I had been given just five days to prepare Australia A with Scott Johnson, who is the current director of rugby of the Australian Rugby Union. Scott and I came up with a game plan of playing wide so we could stretch the Lions.

Many of our players weren't good enough to become full internationals but they were committed to doing something special in a game which would be a career highlight for them. They executed our plan almost perfectly. Against a very good Lions team, coached by Graham Henry and led by Lawrence Dallaglio, and featuring Jason Robinson, Mike Catt, Will Greenwood and Austin Healey, we ran them off their feet and hit the lead early. We had been relaxed but concentrated in our preparations and it paid off. Australia A won 28–25 in a milestone match for me.

The quality of our victory was more apparent after the first

1. Very early days with my parents and sisters in Burnie, Tasmania.

2. Living on the mainland at Point Lonsdale with my family (*left*) and
our dog Jimmy (*right*).

3. Dressing up aged five at Point Lonsdale, Victoria.

4. With my old man at Little Bay Beach, circa 1967.

5. The senior cricket team at La Perouse primary school in 1971, where I was captain.

6. The Ella brothers and I played for La Perouse rugby team in the same year. Back then we played league rather than union.

7. The Matraville High rugby team, where my rugby education really began.

8. Getting a bit muddy playing first-grade rugby for Randwick against Gordon in 1985.

9. Toasting victory over Warringah in the 1987 Grand Final.

10. The great Bob Dwyer coaching Randwick in 1988.

11. Here I am sitting in my office during my day job as deputy principal and teacher at the International Grammar School.

12. I tried to duck that punch but he still caught me, as you can see from the photo below with my teammates Ewen McKenzie (*left*) and Mick Murray (*right*).

13. Playing for New South Wales. It was good to get stuck into the Lions on their 1989 tour of Australia. But they won the game 39–19.

14. Over a decade later, in 2001, my Brumbies side should have beaten the Lions. A late mistake cost us the game.

15. Celebrating winning the 2001 Super 12 final with George Gregan, a year after we came so close but failed.

Test on 30 June when, in Brisbane, the Lions won 29–13. They were on a roll and their last game outside of the two remaining Tests would be against the Brumbies. It did not feel much like my Brumbies side as my internationals were with the Wallabies and Rod Kafer was on his way to Leicester in a swap deal with Pat Howard. I could call on just five of the team who had played in the Super 12 final and the Lions were fired up. Four days before the second Test, playing the Brumbies presented a last chance for many of their players to force their way into contention against Australia.

Pat had only returned from Leicester the previous week. He had just played in the Heineken Cup final, which Leicester won by beating Stade Français in Paris. Four of his pack that day – Graham Rowntree, Darren Garforth, Martin Johnson and Neil Back – had played for Leicester when I had turned out briefly for them ten years earlier. Pat had also been one of the founding members of the Brumbies, before he spent three years at Welford Road, and so I was happy to pick him even though he was not familiar with our recent style of play. He was bright and his grandfather was the great Cyril Towers – the pioneer of the Randwick Way and my former coach at Matraville High. Pat had also won 20 caps for Australia then, being a Wallaby centre and fly half just like his granddad, while his dad, Jake Howard, had played seven Tests at prop in the 1970s.

I had asked Jake to say a few words to the Brumby boys earlier in the season, when we played against the Hurricanes. He was a great talker. I've never forgotten the expression Jake used in the midst of that speech: 'Boys, today we've got to be like jackals around the garbage bin.'

In encouraging us to win the breakdown, Jake introduced the phrase 'to jackal'. As far as I am aware, it's the very first time this term had ever been used, and it just stuck. Now familiar in rugby parlance, it became synonymous with flankers scavenging for the ball and winning it at the breakdown. It helped that George Smith, at the Brumbies, became the finest open-side jackal in the game.

We looked set to create another form of history against the Lions as my Brumby reserves played out of their skins. We were 19–3 ahead after an hour and, even though Matt Dawson came on at scrum half and sparked a fightback, we were still leading 28–23 deep into injury time. I felt we were in control when Pat Howard hoisted a high ball with an aimless kick. I was furious as all we needed to do was keep playing through the phases in the Brumby way. But Pat had been steeped in English rugby since 1998, and Leicester thinking had taken over. It gave possession back to the Lions and they came rumbling up the field as they went through one phase after another. I could sense the try was coming but the lack of surprise didn't deaden the hurt when, after nine phases, Austin Healey slipped through a gap and scored. The conversion by Dawson completed our undeserved 30–28 defeat.

The team was gutted, I was gutted and the fans were gutted. We had blown a chance to make history.

My very last game with the Brumbies should have ended in glorious victory over the British and Irish Lions. We had played superbly, only to lose it in a careless moment. I thought Justin Harrison, our lock, was going to murder Pat. He was raging but I calmed him down. It was a good lesson for me as a coach. When a player is under pressure he will revert to habit. Pat did what he had been taught to do for much of the previous three seasons and put boot to ball. We had not had enough time to reacquaint Pat with the Brumbies' strategy.

Defeat stung but my attention had already switched to the Wallabies. I had been invited to help the coaching staff and was up in the box, not far from Rod Macqueen and Glen Ella, his assistant, as Australia fought back to win the last two Tests in Melbourne and Sydney. The Lions had not been helped by Healey's provocative newspaper column in the *Guardian* where he infuriated Graham Henry and called Harrison, who had just broken into the Wallaby team, 'an ape', 'a plod' and 'a plank'. Australia were galvanized and their series victory was the perfect send-off for a shattered Macqueen. Not even the urging of John

O'Neill could persuade him to change his mind about stepping down. The way was clear for me to become Australia's head coach in late July 2001.

I'm not sure how thrilled head office was by the decision, but the sheer weight of my team's performances meant they didn't really have a choice. The Brumbies had delivered time and again and my credentials couldn't be ignored. Through gritted teeth, and with many reservations, they appointed me.

Exactly 12 years had passed since Bob Dwyer decided not to pick me for his Wallabies squad in July 1989. He had made the right decision, of course, and so there was no sense of burning vindication in me when I was finally fitted for my Wallaby blazer. My coaching career was very different to my years as a player. I felt ready to take over the Wallabies despite Macqueen's warning that I would soon feel like the loneliest man in Australia.

My confidence was misplaced. Coaching a national team and a provincial side are very different. I'm not sure anything can prepare you for the top job, as it's a lot more complex and difficult. On taking the role I said: 'There're no more trophies left to win. You go up to the Australian Rugby Union offices and everything that is silver in world rugby is right up there. The aspiration cannot only be to win more trophies. The aspiration must be: "How can we play better?"'

I wanted us to be as ruthless as the Australian cricket team who would 'crush their opponents'.

I had watched the Wallabies closely for two years and I knew that I was inheriting a team that had peaked when winning the World Cup. They were now an old team who had lost some great players and were about to shed some more. John Eales told me that he would retire from Test rugby at the end of the Tri Nations in six weeks. John had been an inspirational captain, and an outstanding player. I was glad to have him lead the team in my first games as Wallaby coach. But I also knew that he was 31 and had just passed the 80-Test mark.

It was a fascinating challenge because, realistically, the team would soon slip into decline. I had been handed a serious task of rebuilding. Macqueen had lost only eight of 43 Tests, drawing one. His winning record stood at 79 per cent, which made him the most successful coach in Australian rugby history. When you become national coach, so much is down to timing. Usually, you're appointed after your predecessor is fired following a poor run of results. This was different. Macqueen had left of his own accord and because, I think, the natural cycle of his World Cup-winning squad was close to its end.

I knew it was going to be very difficult and that we were entering a transitional period which was complicated by the fact that, in just over two years, Australia would host the 2003 World Cup. But I was never going to turn down the chance to coach my country. I had little time to prepare properly, but I reminded myself that it would be very different to coaching a club or regional team. Apart from the intense scrutiny, the burden of expectation and the flood of opinion that trails you every day of the week, as coach of the national team you have less control and less engagement with your players. It's a completely different beast. A national side obviously plays far less than your previous teams. Your day-to-day work changes as you are no longer in regular contact with the players.

This contributed to one of my earliest mistakes as Wallaby coach. I had been extremely close to the Brumbies and I felt that, even though many of them were amongst the best players in Australia, I needed to change the dynamic between us. They had been used to me talking to them openly and freely but now, in charge of the Wallabies, I did not want to look like I was showing any favouritism to my former players. I shut down communication with the Brumbies far too harshly. I should have explained my thinking and the need for change. It was difficult for some of them to fathom; but this was the nature of the job.

I was also without my chief strategist. Pemby had worked with Rod Macqueen and the Wallabies during the 1998 and 1999 seasons, including the World Cup success. He wasn't prepared to make the sacrifice of more time away from his family and so he retired from rugby. When the bloke who has stopped you stepping on landmines every day for the last four years isn't around, the results are often painful. On the upside, I was fortunate that my Brumbies team manager, Phil Thomson, was soon to replace the current Wallaby manager John McKay. Thomo was a superb organizer, a master of logistics and a calming influence. I knew I could rely on him. Glen Ella and Ewen McKenzie were the assistant Wallaby coaches and I felt well supported on the rugby side. But being the new boy on the block, you feel like you can't make too many changes or demand too much.

I chose six of my former Brumby players in my first Test. Andrew Walker, Joe Roff, George Gregan, David Giffin, Owen Finegan and George Smith started for Australia against South Africa in Pretoria on 28 July 2001. Stephen Larkham would have made it seven but he was injured. Ben Darwin, who felt I had been so hard on him at the Brumbies, came on as a substitute.

South Africa were ferocious, as they always seem to be when they play at altitude, and their resolve had been hardened by defeat to New Zealand in Cape Town the previous week. We were 14–0 down at the break but we came back hard in the second half. In a game dominated by penalties, South Africa squeezed home 20–15.

Two weeks later we were in Dunedin, at the House of Pain, as Carisbrook was called, for my first clash against the All Blacks as an international coach. Larkham was available again and we played really well to spring a major surprise. We won 23–15 and became the first team to defeat New Zealand at Carisbrook. Australia had lost all 12 of their previous Tests in Dunedin. It had been a real examination as Jonah Lomu scored a try in the second minute. But we held our nerve and outplayed them. Smith was immense at the breakdown and our pack ensured that Gregan and Larkham had plenty of quick ball, while we consistently managed to slow down New Zealand's delivery.

'Plenty of obituaries have been written the last week but a team like this doesn't suddenly become poor overnight,' I said after the game. 'We scavenged for the ball well and we're pretty happy – both with the performance and the result.'

The following Saturday, in a bruising Test, we drew 14–14 with South Africa. I thought we would win at the death but a 40-metre Larkham drop goal shaved the post. The draw, followed by the All Blacks beating the Springboks, set up a compelling Tri Nations finale.

New Zealand had eight points, Australia seven and South Africa six points. The winner of our battle with the All Blacks would win the competition. On 1 September, 90,978 spectators crammed into Stadium Australia in Sydney as John Eales led the Wallabies in his final game.

It was an epic Test, and a fitting farewell to Eales. We dominated the first half, with Australia leading 19–6 at the break. The All Blacks, typically, came back at us hard. Our prop Rod Moore was sin-binned and two devastating New Zealand tries helped them to a 23–19 lead. We each scored a penalty and there were just a few minutes left as Australia laid siege to the All Black 22. We forced two penalties but, needing a try to win, we rightly kicked for touch. The New Zealand defence was fierce and they kept us out. One last penalty was conceded. Larkham found touch and, from the lineout, we rumbled forward before the ball spun out into the hands of Toutai Kefu. Our big number 8 crashed over close to the posts. Elton Flatley converted the try and we had won 29–26.

Six weeks into my tenure as the Wallabies head coach we had won the 2001 Tri Nations. I was drained but exhilarated. We had defied some mighty odds and prevailed. I walked around that heaving, exultant stadium in my hometown and thought how far I had come from Little Bay and Matraville High. Glen Ella and Ewen McKenzie, my old Randwick teammates and now my assistant coaches, were at my side. Bob Dwyer, having returned from coaching Leicester and Bristol to lead New South Wales, was high up in the stands. Our Randwick mentor looked over us on the field far below. His face creased with a knowing smile. His boys had done it.

Bob Dwyer likes to tell a story about me and my consuming work ethic as Australia's head coach. It bears repeating as it opens a little window on the demands I would make of my coaching staff, even though, during my first two years in the role, I could not have asked for two better assistants than Ewen and Glen. Trouble would only emerge in my last 18 months when I had to find replacements for my old friends.

This story comes from a different period. Three months after we won the Tri Nations, Bob and I were in charge of rival teams. In late November 2001 Australia faced a Barbarians team, coached by Bob, in Cardiff. It marked the end of a long year of rugby and Bob suggested we meet up for a drink during the week. I agreed and Ewen, Glen and I had a few drinks with Bob and Steve Berrick, the Barbarians team manager.

We had an enjoyable yarn and then, after an hour or so, Ewen said. 'I'd better get going. I need to finish writing that report for you, Eddie.'

'Yeah, good, mate,' I replied. 'Slip it under my door when you're done and I'll take a look.'

I was oblivious to Bob's amusement that, even before a fun game against the Barbarians, when everyone else was relaxing, Ewen and I were hard at it.

Bob ordered another round of drinks and we kept yakking away while Ewen was working upstairs.

Glen was the next to say, 'Right boys, time for me to get going.'

'OK, mate,' I replied. 'Don't forget I need your report too.'

'Not tonight,' Glen said.

'Yeah, mate. Tonight.'

'I'm not doing it tonight.'

'Glen, I'm serious. I want it under my door before we go to bed tonight.'

My old friend shook his head. 'I'm not going to tell you again, Ed. I'm not doing it, all right? If you want me to help coach the team against the Baabaas, I'm happy to do it. But if I've got to write a report right now then I won't be coaching them. So don't be waiting up for my report. You won't be getting it, mate. G'night, Bob. G'night, Steve.'

Glen shook hands with the others and walked coolly off while I sat there steaming. Bob enjoyed it immensely. He knew I could be bloody domineering and he felt I sometimes needed people to stand up to me. Only Glen, my best friend for 36 years, since we were five-year-old kids in short pants, could have got away with it.

'It's good, mate,' Bob told me as he suppressed his chuckling. 'You want your coaches to be themselves. You want them to give voice to their feelings and principles. Let it go.'

The Barbarians had some good players and, in the game, Bob had them playing with real snap. They took the lead and held on to it until the second half before, with Gregan captaining a second-string Wallaby team, we reeled them in and won pretty easily in the end.

'That was fun,' Bob said afterwards. 'But I would have still liked to have beaten you bastards.'

Ewen and Glen recall our work together with the Wallabies as being very intense, but they agree that, most of the time, we got on really well and stayed on track. We achieved a lot with a relatively limited squad in the two years and four months that we ran the show. They had a little moan when I expected them to be working at 2 a.m. some mornings in preparation for a 7 a.m. meeting. But those demands were made only in crunch periods and they were almost as driven as me in wanting to get the best out of our players.

My primary fight was with my own union. At first, it had been simple. When I took over I effectively did two jobs. I was national coach and I was also in charge of the high-performance unit for the ARU. I had to cover a lot of ground, but I enjoyed the diversity of both jobs. Trouble only emerged when John O'Neill decided to split the position in two and bring in a specialist high-performance director. I had no qualms about the change because it would free up more time for me to concentrate on the Wallabies. My misgivings centred on the appointment of Brett Robinson as the new head of high performance.

Robbo and I knew each other well. He had been my captain at the Brumbies and we got on well. He's a bright, hard-working bloke who had just returned to Australia from Oxford University where he had studied for a Doctorate of Philosophy in Clinical Orthopaedics. We had worked together on a project called 'Brumbies Europe', where we had packaged Brumbies rugby as 'intellectual property' and sold it successfully to the Scottish Rugby Union. Robbo had also helped scout locations in Spain for our tour and arranged an historic match at Iffley Road between the Wallabies and the Oxford University team. It was one of those great traditional rugby occasions and the last time Australia would play Oxford.

So we were good mates and had been close collaborators over many years. But, in my opinion, he was poorly equipped for the job of high-performance director at the ARU. I'd met so many high-performance directors in Olympic sport, in AFL, in rugby league and in football, and I was sceptical about his experience and credentials. Spending 18 months in a lab in Oxford examining knee operations while captaining an amateur team was hardly the best preparation for developing our approach to high performance.

It was difficult from day one. In my view Robbo was out of his depth, but he had the full support of the CEO John O'Neill. Unfortunately, I couldn't just ignore him because, technically, the Wallabies fell under his remit. Robbo thought he needed to ensure he was doing the right thing by always making me answerable to him. Two short years earlier, he had answered to me. The switch in authority didn't work for me and I don't think it worked for him. I should have been more diplomatic, but I couldn't leave it alone. This was my first job as national coach and I made the mistake of thinking I needed to win every battle. It took up too much time and energy. Ill-feeling emerged between Robbo and me; and O'Neill added to the tension. O'Neill's big criticism of me was that I was immersed in the minutiae rather than taking a big-picture approach. I was also not like Rod Macqueen and you could see that irritated him. It was a challenging time as our planning for the 2003 World Cup was well under way.

Most coach and CEO relationships start well but become strained over time. When results are good, everything seems fine. When results are bad, look out. This was the case with me and O'Neill. I wasn't good at managing up. I was so focused on creating the best possible environment for the players that I failed to control those executive responsibilities. It was a shocking time for all involved and I put my hand up to accept my share of responsibility. Happily, Robbo and I have since squared things away and are now on good terms again. He's currently on the executive of World Rugby and doing great things. He is a good man who has made an important contribution to Australian Rugby on and off the field over many years.

I am much wiser as a national coach now. I know you can't win every battle and you need to pick them wisely. Japan was another great learning experience in terms of concentrating on the battles you can win. I think every coach of Japan before me tried to fix the problems that besiege the game over there. It did not take me long to work out that the only changes I could actually make applied to the Japanese national team. I shut my mind to the wider institutional issues because I was determined not to fall into another war with administrators – as had happened in Sydney.

English rugby offers even more complex political machinations and bitter infighting between the clubs and the union. If I had not learnt some hard lessons while in charge of the Wallabies, I could have become swamped in the mess. But, apart from one obvious example when I became engaged in a spat with the provocative owner of Bath, I have mostly kept a lid on my frustrations with the English game. I cannot sort out the tangled problems that afflict rugby in England and so I've focused on my core task of selecting and coaching the national team. Life has been less stressful than when I was having regular fallouts with Robbo and O'Neill.

With a home World Cup on the horizon, I respected O'Neill and his drive to widen the base of rugby union across Australia, and also to sharpen its profile at a time when league was in trouble with player disputes. He was creative, effective and efficient. He also built a high-performing administrative team inside the ARU headquarters, who were unquestionably loyal to him. He was the boss and he was ruthless. The standing joke was if John was wearing his red pants, look out. It was a sign he was on the warpath. The way he dispatched his Rugby World Cup hosting partners New Zealand – when they got into trouble with the IRB over clean stadiums – tells you everything you need to know about the bloke.

He was hard, ambitious and provocative and deeply unpopular with his own board. They resented his profile and presidential style. He loved the limelight and was close to the media. We also used to joke that the most dangerous position in Australian Rugby was between John O'Neill and a microphone. For him the spotlight couldn't burn brightly enough. In the wake of the Cape Town Five incident, he was suspicious and wary of the Brumbies. He couldn't stand their independent streak. With the Brumbies you don't command respect, you earn it. To the players, he hadn't earned it. After the World Cup success in 1999 he had publicly, if rather stupidly in my opinion, singled out the influence of the Queensland players as a critical factor in the Wallabies' success. The Brumby boys saw O'Neill's comments as being unworthy of the united spirit of a great team and ill-judged from the CEO of the national union.

O'Neill didn't like George Gregan, and it's fair to say George wasn't a big fan of his either. I had appointed George captain after the retirement of John Eales, and O'Neill wasn't happy. George was our best player and a natural leader. He and I share similar traits in terms of our competitiveness, work rate and desire to improve. But he is so much better than me in presenting a charming face to sponsors and the public. George, with his multicultural background, also represented the new Australia as we moved into the 21st century.

The conflict between O'Neill and Gregan deepened as the players became increasingly outspoken. With the World Cup promising a once-in-a-generation financial bonanza for the union, George and his fellow players were determined to hold out for a vastly improved share of the proceeds. I wasn't surprised when the Brumbies players – Gregan, Larkham, Roff and Mortlock – led the Wallabies' dispute. They were intelligent and confident enough to take on the union. They refused to be cowed into giving ground. In a typical Brumby way, they didn't take shit when push came to shove. But with O'Neill having the ear of the rugby media, he went to war.

I always found it amusing that the John O'Neill who was always so ruthless in his dealings with other unions, competitors and World Rugby, became so indignant when he got a taste of his own medicine from the players. John was good at dishing it out – but horrible at taking it.

If you ask me to make a choice between the administrators and players, you can guess with whom I will always side. The administrators decide whether I keep my job, but my loyalty always lies with the players. I've never tried to improve an administrator, while improving players every day is my mission.

I believe the players should receive a significant share of the money that pours into the game. There is big money in rugby because of everything they do on the field. It's not because of work done by administrators or coaches behind the scenes. The players have such short careers, especially now the game has become so brutal, that I support every move to make sure they are paid what they deserve.

Pemby tells a story from his time covering the reunification tour of South Africa in 1992 for the ABC. He was at a fevered Ellis Park when South Africa were readmitted to world rugby after the anti-apartheid sports boycott. Before they played their oldest rivals, the All Blacks, Louis Luyt and the South African Rugby Union defied the ANC and played the apartheid anthem, 'Die Stem'. Pemby then travelled to Port Elizabeth. The Wallabies were on a four-match tour and they played Eastern Province in August 1992.

As he arrived at the game in Port Elizabeth, Pemby ran into his good friend and Wallaby number 8 Tim Gavin and Australia's number 6 Willie Ofahengaue. They were standing at the top of the entrance to the ground waiting for local supporters to arrive. These champions of Australian Rugby were selling second-hand gear from two kitbags. Pemby was embarrassed for the players and offended that they were forced into such humiliation. He rightly felt it was ridiculous that, while tens of millions of dollars were being banked by the unions, these international stars should have to stand like roadside beggars, trying to sell old kit for a little extra cash.

Since 1995, when the game went professional, the players had been battling to get their just rewards. Articulate and educated guys like Gregan were always going to lead the way and I was ready to back them – no matter the fallout with O'Neill and the union. You need to do what is right for your players and deal with the consequences.

O'Neill presumed the head coach would show loyalty first and foremost to the union ahead of the players. During discussions before I took the role, this demarcation had never been agreed or even discussed. If he had bothered to ask, I would have told him the truth. I would be the head coach and not a de facto member of the ARU Board. O'Neill was also extremely close to George's predecessor John Eales, which didn't help. Eales and Gregan have always been good friends but they are very different personalities.

In 2002 I also had to deal with some player dissatisfaction as, backed by O'Neill, we had persuaded Wendell Sailor, the rugby league star, to switch codes. Wendell was a huge star in Australian sport and he had won the 'player of the tournament' at the rugby league World Cup in 2000. He helped the Kangaroos become world champions and he was the top try scorer in the competition. Wendell was loud and brash and, with his gold chains and swaggering style, he could have played American football or been a champion boxer. He had that razzmatazz and I knew he would offer something different to the Wallabies. Wendell always played close to the edge.

At that time of the development of the game in Australia, I was a fan of rugby league players moving to union. I had great success in bringing across Brisbane Broncos forward Peter Ryan and the Kiwi forward Gordon Falcon, who had spent time with the Penrith Panthers, to the Brumbies. They showed the rugby union players how to train hard day in and day out. They set a standard that the union players had to reach.

When you're building a team to win a World Cup, you want a good balance and plenty of consistent players that give you a steady upward curve. But, to become world champions, you need a few X-factor players. These are the mavericks and gifted players who are the most difficult to handle. I've coached a few of them; while they are excitingly creative, their behaviour off the field tends to be more up and down. You can carry only one or two of them. They're insecure and hard to control and you need to give them lots of attention.

Wendell was really powerful, with a massive physique, and we didn't have many big wingers. So I pushed hard for him to be lured across to union. He was a charismatic bloke and, as rugby was on the rise then, O'Neill agreed that he was the kind of signing that could help us take on league. At my instigation the union ended up signing three of the biggest stars in rugby league – Sailor, Mat Rogers and Lote Tuqiri. They were the back three I had in mind for the World Cup; it was an exciting coup which shook up both league and union in Australia.

Yet I had to deal with some resistance from the hardened rugby union guys in the Wallabies. Steve Larkham and Matt Burke were both unhappy that the league boys were being fast-tracked ahead of some promising young union players. They were also probably earning more than some of the established union players, and guys like Burke, Roff, Ben Tune and Chris Latham were under threat of losing their places to the league converts. It's never easy to handle players made to feel vulnerable by the arrival of unexpected rivals but I had to back my judgement. My responsibility was to the team and its success, rather than to any individual player who might have thought it was unfair.

As a close follower of league, I was aware that the 13-man code offered skills and physicality which were superior to union. They are very different games and it takes time for a convert to adapt but, on the whole, our three big league recruits did a decent job. The dissent from the few players who were against the strategy quietened down when they saw that the league boys could make the Wallabies a better squad.

You just need to make a clear decision, back it up, and these prickly little issues usually sort themselves out.

Sailor and Rogers were in my Test squad for the first international of 2002 – against France in Melbourne in late June. Sailor started and Rogers made his debut off the bench while Burke, Larkham and Latham, the three guys who had been directly affected or affronted by the league invasion, scored all our points in a 29–17 victory. We beat the French again the following week and then had a decent Tri Nations, where we won both our home games against the All Blacks and Springboks but lost narrowly in Christchurch and Johannesburg. There were similarly mixed results on the November tour as we beat Argentina and Italy but lost in Dublin and then dropped a 32–31 thriller against England. We outscored England by three tries to two; but

we were becoming acquainted with the deadly boot of Jonny
Wilkinson, whose six penalties and two conversions cost us the
match. It was a theme which, a year later, would haunt us in
the biggest match of my career as Australia coach.

England were the best team in world rugby when they toured
the southern hemisphere in the Australian winter of 2003. Clive
Woodward and I enjoyed sparring with each other before
matches. Along with the rest of the rugby world, I was seriously
impressed by him and his team. He did outstanding work and created a team to win the World Cup. They had size in the forwards
and pace in the backs with plenty of guile from Lawrence Dallaglio in the pack and Will Greenwood at centre. They had a great
try scorer in Jason Robinson and the best goal-kicker in the world
in Jonny Wilkinson – who also brought a ferocious competitiveness to his work, whether he was swinging his boot or making
huge hits as a defender. Woodward was superb in organizing the
team, and the surrounding environment, and he replicated the
strides made by other great managers-cum-coaches in Rod Macqueen and John Hart during professional rugby's infancy.

We played England again in Melbourne on 21 June, a week
after they won a heroic match against New Zealand. Apart from
the fact that they had beaten the All Blacks in successive games
for the first time in history, England's victory in Wellington
seemed all the more remarkable for the resolve of their diminished pack. At a crucial period, with both Neil Back and Dallaglio
in the sin bin, they had just six forwards. Mike Tindall, their
centre, had to play for a while as emergency flanker as they with-
stood relentless pressure from the black shirts. England, led by a
magnificently glowering Martin Johnson, won deservedly 15–13.
All their points were scored by Wilkinson but they had proved
their tenacity and courage.

The following week they were much better than us when winning 25–14. When I look back at that game I am struck by how
settled and dominant England were in a season where they

probably were at their very peak. Four months later England were beginning to creak; but 14 of the players who beat us in Melbourne would start the World Cup final in November 2003. The only change was Matt Dawson starting in place of Kyran Bracken.

I thought, for the first time, 'England really are good enough to win the World Cup.' Until then I had my doubts. They were always difficult to beat at Twickenham, but those games were unbalanced because we were at the end of a taxing season and having to play England in the cold and the wet just as their campaign got into full swing. So even though England had beaten us in November, I didn't see them as the best team in the world. Melbourne changed my mind.

They not only played an efficient driving game but they moved the ball with skill and invention. In Melbourne they drove one kick-off maul for 45 metres. I can still remember it as they drove deep inside our territory with remorseless control. They also scored this beautiful phase try. On top of that they were so physically strong that they monstered us. The scoreboard confirmed they won by 11 points, but the gap was far greater that night. I knew we had an enormous amount to do to catch them.

Unlike England, who had been together with Woodward for six years, and suffered plenty of heartache in the 1999 World Cup and some Six Nations deciders, we were still evolving. Only five of the side I picked in Melbourne would start for us the next time we played England in the World Cup.

England were setting the template for the biggest of all tournaments, but I was more concerned with the immediate challenge of the All Blacks. Under John Mitchell, who would become my forwards coach with England in 2018, New Zealand were playing exhilarating rugby. Carlos Spencer was a magician at number 10, while Tana Umaga and Joe Rokocoko had taken over from Christian Cullen and Jonah Lomu as their talismanic attackers. New Zealand looked like the one team who might be too good for England.

If we were going to reach the World Cup final, almost certainly against England, it was likely we would have to beat New Zealand in the semi-finals. We had to play them twice before then in the Tri Nations, in Sydney and Auckland. It was vital that we could show the Australian public that we were ready to mount a serious World Cup challenge in our own backyard. There would be no better way of doing this than beating the All Blacks at home.

So far, in my brief career as Wallaby head coach, I had faced New Zealand on four occasions. We had won two and lost two. My fifth encounter with the All Blacks felt like an acid test which would reveal so much about where we stood ten weeks before the start of the World Cup.

Amid the embarrassment, humiliation and abuse that you cop when conceding 50 points to the All Blacks, that Test offered so many lessons. Of course we were castigated in the media, shouted at by our own supporters, and wounded by losing 50–21 to New Zealand in front of 82,096 in the Olympic stadium in Sydney on 26 July 2003. It was a terrible outcome but, strangely, I felt encouraged rather than crushed. Clearing through the debris I could see plainly how we would beat the All Blacks when it mattered most – in a World Cup semi-final.

We had conceded seven tries, three of them to Rokocoko, but almost all of them had been scored through counter-attacking. We gave the ball away by kicking poorly and giving them turn-over chances. They had brilliant players but they concentrated on scoring off our return kicks. Their basic strategy was simple. They kicked the ball deep into our half and we'd hoof it back to them. They would then counter-attack with blistering speed. I knew if we refused to kick any return ball our chances of beating them would be higher than ever.

No one commented on this obvious fact. The narrative, instead, veered from the brilliance of the All Blacks to the hopelessness of the Wallabies. I didn't care. I knew what I had seen. It gave me real strength, even though defeat meant we had lost three matches in a row. Between the games against England and New Zealand we had been beaten 26–22 by South Africa. It was not great, obviously, but I knew that our season – and even my permanent reputation as Australia's head coach – would be defined by the World Cup rather than these games. The Tri Nations was an important tournament, but it meant little when set against the quest to become world champions – especially in your home country.

I said nothing about my ambition to win the World Cup because I would have been laughed out of town. The Australian media and sporting public were more concerned that we would be shamed while hosting the tournament. I kept calm and made sure the players shared my conviction. We went over the painful recording of the New Zealand shellacking and I could see how they understood my message. This defeat, I stressed, would be the key factor in determining that we would beat the All Blacks when we next played them in Sydney.

The mood in the team reminded me of the atmosphere around the Brumbies when we had finished third from bottom in my first season. The rest of rugby thought we were useless, and that I had been exposed as a professional coach, but we believed in ourselves. We had known then that if we changed the way we played we would eventually win the Super 12.

I had far less time to seal a similar transformation with the Wallabies, but I had absorbed one of the fundamental lessons of coaching – to always look beneath the surface for the truth. The evidence was compelling. We just needed to apply the lessons to our game.

We snapped our losing streak with a decisive 29–9 victory over the Springboks in Perth the following Saturday. Two weeks later we travelled to Auckland to play New Zealand again in the final Tri Nations match of the season at Eden Park. It was a night where conditions favoured a kicking game, but my new mantra had been drummed into the players. They refused to kick the ball into All Black territory. We controlled the slippery ball, retaining possession on a filthy night, and came close to victory. We lost 21–17 but Steve Larkham almost scored a match-winning try. He pushed the ball up against the padding around the side of the posts and, even though a try would have been awarded today, it was disallowed that night. I was so encouraged because I could see relief in the expressions of the New Zealand players as they trudged off the field. They were Tri Nations champions and they had won all four of their matches but they were there for the taking next time we met.

In the dressing room, the players waited for me to speak. I told them to remember how gutted we all felt in losing. But I urged them to use this feeling to drive us on as we went into World Cup lockdown. We had so much more room for improvement and the same could not be said of New Zealand. I reiterated my certainty that we would beat them when we played again in the semi-finals. The world would be shocked – but we would be unsurprised because we had their number. The pain of a 50-point burial at home and a narrow loss in Eden Park would help seal the sweetest victory of our careers.

George Gregan echoed my words and I could sense the belief in the team as, slowly, they began to unwrap their bandages and peel off their sodden shirts. We absorbed our fresh conviction on that cold night in Auckland.

Alan Jones, the former Manly and Wallaby coach, with whom Bob Dwyer and I had clashed over the years, kept stirring the dissent on his radio programme. Jones is your classic shock-jock. He picks his mark, as he did in future years with former Australian Prime Minister Julia Gillard and New Zealand Prime Minster Jacinda Ardern, dials the outrage and abuse up to 100 and pours on the scorn. Jones, probably with the memory of me giving it to his protégé at Manly Oval all those years ago, unleashed abuse at me day after day.

Closer to the tournament, an email from Jones was circulated in which he said I was 'a dunce, a dope, a fool, a pig and a classic case of a bloke promoted once too often.' But he wasn't alone in his view that I was a dud coach. He had plenty of friends. The media were unanimous that we were hopeless and were going to be an embarrassment during the biggest rugby event ever to be staged in Australia. The newspapers, especially my old friends the Sydney press, maintained the rage. It was comical how wound up they were getting. Happily, it just rolled over me.

Before we went into camp for the World Cup, I took a break in Japan. My relaxation is coaching Suntory for three weeks. I immerse myself in the purity of coaching without any need to front up at a press conference or talk to sponsors or administrators. It's just me, with a ball and a whistle, and a group of young rugby players eager to get better. It's bliss. I've also always been able to think calmly and clearly in Japan.

Suntory were holding a camp in Abashiri on the Japanese island of Hokkaido. Its coastline is the closest that Japan gets to Russia and Abashiri is famous for the blocks of ice that drift around it in the Sea of Okhotsk. I was more interested in the beautiful green fields, which offer the most natural rugby pitches I've ever seen as they are only free from a thick covering of snow for four months every year.

The *Daily Telegraph*, the Sydney tabloid, sent a photographer all the way to Abashiri to track me. I was doing nothing wrong – a rugby coach spending his vacation coaching rugby is hardly outrageous – but their snapper was told to get as many pics of me as he could. I remember spending one whole session staying out of full view of the snapper because I didn't feel as though he had a right to be shooting photographs of me on my holiday. But I was not prepared to play cat and mouse for long, and I asked Suntory to send him on his way. He had got just one proper photograph of me, walking around the rugby field, and it seemed a waste of time for everyone.

Would I have been as hounded if I had chosen to play golf on my vacation? I doubt it, but the fact I was coaching in Japan apparently was news. It was a reminder that, with the World Cup hurtling towards us, we were fair game for endless scrutiny and judgement.

The tournament was being played over 44 days, from 10 October to 22 November 2003, and we were expecting hot and steamy conditions. I decided to take the squad up to Darwin, in the remote Northern Territory, for a heat camp. I had previously taken an Australia A team up there and I thought it was a great spot. I knew the players would be able to relax a little and, as we were about to represent the country, it felt right to prepare deep in the heartland of Australia's first people.

After a few days of heavy and intense sessions in a steamy Darwin, with the temperature at 33°C and an average humidity of 30 per cent, we surprised the team. We flew to Mount Borradaile, in a remote part of northwest Arnhem Land on the edge of Kakadu National Park. Here we were, hundreds of miles from anywhere, on the traditional and sacred lands of Australia's first people. It was the ideal place for the team to connect with each other and their country. On our first day we went out on boats so we could look at the cave paintings and then, that night, Indigenous Australian dancers welcomed us to their country. They danced and painted a few of the boys up as warriors. We then sat around the fire and the conversation unfolded spontaneously.

We began to discuss what the World Cup meant to us. It wasn't planned and, as the players took turns to speak, the team grew tighter. It was another great example to me of how vulnerability drives trust and high performance. It helped that we'd had a few beers to relax before the fireside chats, but the key element was that we had such bright senior guys – Gregan, Larkham, Roff, Giffin, Smith and the rest. They conveyed the significance of the gathering to everyone around them. It's a night none of us will ever forget.

From that special night we took a boomerang, clapping sticks and a painting of a wallaby on ironbark and carried them with us throughout the tournament. In each of our dressing rooms we set them up in pride of place, to remind us not only of the bond we had for each other but for our country and its people.

We did something similar with Japan in 2015 when we went to Kyushu, an island in the southwest. We had a tough training camp, but then we took them to a Shinto shrine on the beach. In the Japanese national anthem, they sing about a boulder as the foundation of the country. This shrine featured the original boulder and we conducted a small ceremony. Even the players who had not been born in Japan were profoundly touched. It was a special night.

Just as we had done in Darwin, when we tapped into the core of Australian culture, we found the essence of Japan in Kyushu.

During my four years in England, while building towards the 2019 World Cup, I tried to discover a similar core, or place, of Englishness. I spoke to so many people to identify a meaningful definition, and spiritual place, of Englishness. It felt strangely elusive.

Sixteen years before, in Darwin, we found the heart of Australia and my World Cup team.

We had been drawn in Pool A alongside Ireland, Argentina, Namibia and Romania. As the host nation we played in the opening match of the tournament, against Argentina in Sydney, and won 24–8. Opening World Cup games are never easy, and I was happy enough with our performance. We then had two gimmes against Romania and Namibia, winning 90–8 and 142–0. I felt a little for the poor Namibians as we ran in 22 tries – and had a lot of fun from the very start at the Adelaide Oval. I had invited Darren Lehmann, the Australian cricketer and future national coach, into the dressing room. Darren was very boisterous and he had the boys rocking with laughter.

We were based at Coffs Harbour up on the north coast of New South Wales, more than 500 kilometres from Sydney, and it was tranquil. We also worked our butts off. I probably demanded even more from Glen Ella and Ewen McKenzie than I did from the players. Glen would groan, 'You bastard', whenever I surprised him at 3.30 a.m. by slipping a piece of paper under his door. He would haul himself out of bed and find a tweaked training programme for the following morning. I also sledged him mercilessly about his weight. He was trying to trim down and sometimes he would give up on the idea of sleep and turn up at the gym at 5.30 a.m. He would find me there, grinning and flicking through the newspapers, as I suggested he get cracking.

The tournament was a smash hit, just as the Sydney Olympics had been three years earlier. John O'Neill and Matt Carroll, the tournament director, deserve enormous credit for the way the event was planned, promoted and presented, with almost every game across Australia sold out. Even in places like Tasmania, where the preferred sport is Australian Rules football, the fans got into the spirit of rugby. We made sure that we made it into the cities at least a few days before games so we could enjoy the atmosphere. The buzz was addictive.

There was a lot of pressure on us and, on 1 November, we had our first real scare. In the final pool match, before a sold-out crowd in Melbourne, we played Ireland to decide which of us would win the group and face a slightly easier quarter-final against Scotland rather than France. It seemed as if most of the crowd had been to the Melbourne races that day, and there was excitement and exuberance before we ran out. The game was watched live on television across Australia and around the world. Only England's pool game against South Africa could match it and it felt like our first big test – even if we were expected to win comfortably.

We were poor and Ireland were by far the better side. With a few minutes left we were clinging on to a 17–16 lead when Ronan O'Gara took aim at the posts with the kind of field goal he slotted consistently throughout his career. This time we got lucky and O'Gara missed.

I reminded everyone that the serious stuff was only just about to begin in the knockout stages, but we were ripped to pieces in the papers and on television. It seemed as if we were, once again, a hopeless joke who had no chance against the All Blacks.

We had to beat Scotland first and, at Suncorp Stadium in Brisbane on 8 November, we won with plenty to spare: 33–16, with tries for Mortlock, Gregan and David Lyons.

England wobbled and struggled to beat Wales, but they earned themselves a semi-final against the mercurial French, who put away the Irish. New Zealand were the most convincing quarter-final winner. They beat South Africa 29–9 to enter our semi-final as the hottest favourites in the competition. We would play them the following Saturday evening in the stadium where they had hammered 50 points against us. We were written off by everyone in world rugby.

The players and I had aimed to peak for this semi-final from our earliest World Cup preparations. I felt relaxed and confident before the biggest game of my coaching career.

8

GLORY AND PAIN

Stadium Australia, Sydney. Saturday, 15 November 2003

Carlos Spencer leads the haka, moving aggressively towards the Wallabies, who stand stock still. George Gregan, personifying icy cool, is at the front as he faces the challenge laid down by the All Blacks. The New Zealanders waggle their tongues, slap their thighs and beat their chests as if consumed by the spirits of ancient Maori warriors. They look straight at the Wallabies, chanting the sacred words of the haka, as the intensity of the occasion grips us. The vast majority of Australians in the crowd of 82,444 respond by roaring 'Waltzing Matilda' in an attempt to drown out the booming haka which is amplified for the benefit of television.

It is magnificent theatre, but I just want the game to start. My certainty feels flimsy now. I am back in that difficult zone every coach experiences just before the opening whistle. All the hard work can go up like a puff of smoke in the sudden heat of battle. A bad mistake can knock your team off kilter in the first minute, scrambling your composure. It is a desperately nervy time.

My strategy is clear. We have worked out where they are better than us – particularly when counter-attacking at great speed and with athletic physicality – and settled on a plan to dilute that disadvantage. It is imperative we impose ourselves on the All Blacks and control possession while putting them under sustained pressure. Possession alone will not win us the game, but I am convinced that if we attack them in cohesive bursts they will crack. We will run at them and play aggressive and fluid rugby. Beyond that basic premise we will make our tackles count and maintain discipline at the breakdown to avoid giving away penalties.

George Smith is also at the heart of my plans as I have given him strict instructions to target Justin Marshall – New Zealand's vastly experienced scrum half. He will do nothing illegal, but George aims to cut off the supply line that makes Marshall such an integral part of the black machine. They are irrepressible if you give the ball away and allow them space to attack. But if we stick to our tactics we will choke their chances and force Carlos Spencer to take risks. He is a brilliant player without any pressure. But we know he is fallible when under the hammer. Spencer always goes for the big play then and he makes mistakes.

I take in a deep breath, as if a lungful of warm early summer air will sustain my hopes. All week I have been planting seeds in the media that I have something up my sleeve. I want the All Blacks to wonder and fret just a little. But I know that one bad decision or error could open us up to a devastating counterattack. My plans could be blown to smithereens.

Spencer kicks off and he sends the ball spiralling high into the night sky as the vast crowd open their throats and seem to bellow as one. Lote Tuqiri gathers it just outside our 22 and, rather than kick, he sets off on a run. One of our three league converts is brought down but, from the ensuing ruck, we filter the ball back cleanly. Elton Flatley, our centre, finds himself at scrum half. He passes quickly to Larkham who finds Gregan, in Flatley's slot at inside centre, Gregan slips it to George Smith who is dragged down. Sticking to our strategy we elect to run again, and a long pass from Larkham hits Mat Rogers at speed. Rogers bursts forward with real impact and it needs three of the black shirts to haul him down.

We retain possession and Gregan sparks the next phase. Tuqiri is tackled but our sense of adventure remains. Gregan sets loose Nathan Sharpe, our big lock, who lowers his scrumcap and charges. He is blocked but he turns the ball back to Gregan for the sixth phase of breathless play. Ben Darwin, my former Brumby at prop, barges forward. Only a big hit from Ali Williams, the New Zealand lock, can knock him down. We recycle the ball and a little reverse pass from Larkham sets Mortlock down a different channel.

The pressure tells. A New Zealand hand wanders into the ruck. Penalty to Australia. Sixty-seven seconds show on the clock and we have already been through eight phases.

'The Aussies are looking razor sharp in these opening exchanges,' the television commentator Gordon Bray confirms on my monitor. I can't hear the commentary, thankfully, but the rest of the watching rugby world can.

From the ensuing lineout Sharp careers forward and then another smart reverse pass from Larkham unleashes David Lyons. The black line holds; but back come Gregan and Larkham, who again switches the line of attack so Mortlock can have another crack from a fresh angle.

New Zealand are resolute and, after two and half minutes of ceaseless attacking rugby, Larkham changes the pattern. His drop goal narrowly misses its target.

I am happy and Larkham has been smart. Three points would have got us on the board but he has also given us a moment to gather breath. The opening has gone like clockwork. I look at the All Blacks and their expressions say, silently, 'Shit, this is not the script we were expecting.'

About 10,000 English supporters, all wearing their team's white shirt, have found tickets to this semi-final and they start singing 'Swing Low Sweet Chariot.' The Aussies and Kiwis drown them out in a cascade of whistles and boos. The players are oblivious to it all. Williams monsters Flatley with a huge hit. Mortlock scoops up the ball but is hauled back for an obstruction. Respite for the All Blacks after they have had to make 28 tackles to keep us out. Spencer finds touch deep in our 22.

Suddenly, it is our turn to feel the pressure as Jerry Collins makes significant ground. The ball zips down the black shirts and Rokocoko hurtles towards the line – only to be taken out by Wendell Sailor with a ferocious hit.

'First points to big Dell,' Bray cries out on the commentary, which I only hear days after the game.

'He's pumped up, big Dell,' his co-commentator, Tim Horan, agrees. 'Most important is that he didn't give Rokocoko any space.'

Our wall defence holds firm from the lineout as McCaw, Collins and Keven Mealamu all have a crack at the try line. The next threat comes from the backs as Doug Howlett arrows into space and releases Mils Muliaina so that he can plunge towards the corner. Tuqiri tackles him just as they cross the line. The All Black full back is convinced he has scored but the referee, Chris White from England, calls for the TMO.

I watch anxiously because we do not deserve to be down after a blistering opening. The replay goes on a loop, as the various angles are considered, and then we are in the clear. Muliaina is adjudged to have knocked on as he dived for the line.

From the next lineout Spencer jinks inside our 22 and spins out a long pass to Leon MacDonald. Out of nowhere, Stirling Mortlock intercepts the pass. He streaks away, a shaven-headed bullet in green and gold, as he crosses our ten-metre line and moves into their half. Rokocoko tries hard and narrows the gap. But by the time Mortlock reaches their 22, it's all over. He dives over the line and under the posts. After ten minutes, we're 7–0 up.

'The Australians are absolutely pumped,' Horan shouts above the bedlam. 'Once [Mortlock] got it they were never going to catch him. It was shut-the-gate stuff.'

Glen Ella is more pumped than anyone. He hollers in my ear: 'Mate, we've got these guys.'

I stare ahead poker-faced and, out of the corner of my mouth, say curtly: 'Shut up, Glen.'

We maintain our strategy and increase our lead to ten points after a Flatley penalty. I feel the All Blacks are buckling as Mac-Donald misses two kickable goals. We crank up the pressure, retain possession and drive through phase after phase. Another easy penalty in front of the posts. Flatley nails it. 13–0 after 34 minutes.

I see on the monitor that the television cameras have panned to me. I keep my expression deadpan as I take a slug of water.

'Just look at Eddie Jones's face,' Horan says. 'He shows so much emotion, doesn't he? It's written all over him like a stone.'

Horan tweaks his metaphor accordingly. 'He's a stone because he knows this game has got so much to go. You can never write the All Blacks off. This is a crucial time. Six minutes out from half-time you cannot allow New Zealand to put points on the board.'

Horan is not wrong. After we snaffle the first New Zealand lineout from the kick-off, Larkham loses possession and the All Blacks are away. Spencer has the ball and, with a shimmy and a dazzling sidestep, he leaves two of our defenders for dead. He cuts deep into our 22 and, instead of going wide to Rokocoko, he slips back inside our drift defence and plays a simple offload to his captain Reuben Thorne, who crashes over.

I want to smash my fist down on the desk in front of me. We know how menacing New Zealand are with turnover ball and yet we've given it to them just before half-time. It's 13–7 at the break and the crowd gives us a standing ovation.

My message in the shed is calm. Retain possession, run through the phases, choke Marshall, turn the screws on Spencer and stick to the strategy. We are on the way to a big win.

Early in the second half, in the 47th minute, Smith clatters Marshall with a legitimate big hit that crunches his ribs. Mortlock gets Marshall again a minute later. I see the scrum half as the All Blacks' spiritual leader and so I am not sorry when he gets up and limps away, gesturing to his bench that his game is over. Smith popped Marshall's rib cartilage with that heavy tackle. Byron

Kelleher comes on and he's a good player – but he's not Marshall. This is a big moment and Marshall looks disconsolate.

Whenever I see Justin now, all these years later, he has a little moan about it. But he smiles too because we got him fairly.

A far more serious injury occurs in the 52nd minute. We're 16–7 ahead but rugby matters little as Ben Darwin is in trouble. I am getting messages in my earpiece which sound worrying. They need to get Ben to hospital. The minutes stretch slowly and the crowd is subdued. Eventually, the medical golf cart appears with the stretcher-bearers.

As sympathetic applause resounds around the arena, and Ben is wheeled away after a ten-minute break, I get my head back into gear. So does the team.

Justin Harrison leaps high to claim the All Black lineout and he gives Gregan clean, quick ball. Gregan finds Larkham gliding through a hole in the New Zealand defence with ghostly elegance. When he is finally brought down, he flips it to Jeremy Paul in support. Our replacement hooker recycles the ball and our backline are away with a spare man on the overlap. New Zealand are desperate. They bring down Mortlock but Aaron Mauger is penalized for handling in the ruck. Penalty to Australia.

Flatley is unerring: 19–7 after 54 minutes.

The All Blacks try to batter their way up the middle for the rest of the second half but we are formidable in defence. We are smart too and refuse to give the ball away lightly. There are no more wasted kicks down New Zealand throats and, denied the chance to run at us on the counter, they grow increasingly frustrated and dispirited. I finally allow myself to enjoy Glen's earlier prediction that we've got them.

At 22–10 we are cruising. We have stuck flawlessly to the strategy and the game runs down with no stress. It's the most comfortable and commanding I have ever seen the Wallabies look against the All Blacks.

'So the Wallabies, massive underdogs in this game,' Gordon Bray tells millions of viewers in the last minute, 'have emphatically answered their critics with a very clinical and professional performance.' When Larkham boots the ball into touch, with 80 minutes on the clock, Bray confirms that, 'The Wallabies are the first team in history to qualify for three rugby World Cup finals . . . New Zealand are shattered. The intensity of the Wallabies was too intimidating. Eddie Jones has been saying all week he had something extra and, my word, did they do it.'

Glen and I embrace, the two Matraville boys who have taken Australia into a home World Cup final. I try to keep my emotions in check. Even after the greatest game of my rugby career, I am thinking ahead to the final.

The media are already rattling down that very track. By the time I face the massed press pack it's striking how much the atmosphere has changed. From earlier in the week, when I was told that I was in charge of a rabble of no-hopers, I am now being exalted and told I stand on the cusp of history. I am fed some arcane stat which says that when Australia first won the World Cup, in 1991, they had struggled to subdue Argentina in the tournament opener and were fortunate to beat Ireland by a single point – just as we have done on both counts in this World Cup. They also raced into a 13–0 first-half lead against New Zealand in the 1991 semi-final – just like us today.

I shrug my shoulders. 'History is for coaches – players live in the present. The lesson of 12 years ago is that things are not always what they seem. We were smart in our preparations for the All Blacks, but you never know how things are going to turn out on the field. England will offer us a sterner examination in the set pieces and the game will be more of a grind, but they have brilliant individuals like Jason Robinson who can quickly turn a match, as he did against Wales, and I think the final will be decided by a moment or two of sublime skill.'

I am asked how I dealt with the deluge of criticism after our poor performances against New Zealand in July and against Ireland in the World Cup. 'Criticism is only an opinion and I really mean it when I say it does not bother me. When things go bad, it is right that I should cop it. When they go well, as they did against New Zealand, the players should receive the credit.'

I look up and grin. 'OK, boys. See you before the final.'

I head through the throng, thinking of John Mitchell, who is next in line for a media grilling. We all know he will never coach the All Blacks again. The hurt runs far too deep in New Zealand to allow a reprieve for a very good coach. Another long period of national grief has already begun. The All Blacks have not won the World Cup since the inaugural tournament in 1987 and, today, at the final whistle, George Gregan let the emotion pour out of him.

'Four more years, boys,' he shouted at the All Blacks. 'Four more years . . .'

You can say George was being cruel; but sport is a cruel business. I understood. George had been hurt badly, just as I had been, when we shipped 50 points back in July. We had suffered often against New Zealand teams – as in the 2000 Super 12 final when the Crusaders beat us by a point. We needed to savour this victory.

I go in search of my dad, the great Ted, the man who taught me so much, and worked so hard with my mother to raise me and my sisters to be such lucky and happy Australians. Dad always stays in the shadows after my big wins. I remember him coming into the dressing room only once – after a first-grade game for Randwick when I got poked in the eye. He wanted to check on his boy then.

Now, I want to check on my dad. I want to find him and share these moments, after a momentous match in which I got everything right. It takes a while but, finally, I see him.

'Dad,' I call out. My father turns and smiles. He stretches out his hand. I can see how Dad feels about me in his crinkly eyes. I can feel his pride and happiness.

'Good work, mate,' he says simply. And then, with a little smile, he confirms another truth as he thinks of his son coaching Australia in a World Cup final. 'Big game next week . . .'

*

Rugby is a beautiful game but it can have brutal consequences. That night the elation ebbed with news from the doctors treating Ben Darwin. Emergency surgery was considered as scans revealed a prolapsed disc in Ben's neck was touching the top of his spinal cord. The full extent of the damage had yet to be established, but there was a danger that Ben could become a quadriplegic.

We had just begun to piece together the chilling story from earlier in the evening. In the 48th minute, John Mitchell had replaced his tight-head prop, Dave Hewett, with Kees Meeuws, a real scrummaging machine. Meeuws was fired up to do some damage – but not this kind of damage. Four minutes later the scrum had wheeled and collapsed. As they hit the ground, Ben screamed: 'Neck! Neck!' Meeuws, to his immense credit, stopped pushing. In removing that pressure, he saved Ben from likely paralysis.

The doctors were still worried as, while lying in a crumpled heap on the field, Ben lost all feeling in his arms and legs. This explained why the paramedics took so long to get him into the correct position before lifting him onto the stretcher. He had since felt pins and needles in his hands and feet, which was good news, but the proximity of the prolapsed disc to the spinal cord was unsettling. More scans were undertaken.

Life is precarious and it can change in an instant. Even the hardened neck of a Test prop forward is not meant to withstand such pressure. If Ben had broken his neck, the glory of winning a World Cup semi-final would have been meaningless.

All my battles with Ben at the Brumbies, when I had to bully and cajole him to find the necessary toughness, were forgotten. He had just turned 27, and the immature boy I had first coached in Canberra had long since grown up. In the World Cup semi-final he had been in the midst of his 28th Test. Ben was tough, fast, aggressive and, at 118 kilograms, strong too. He had it all but, suddenly, the challenge was to ensure he might be able to walk again and lead a normal life.

There was great relief in the second set of scans. The threat of paralysis retreated and, with careful treatment, the prognosis was excellent. Ben would never play rugby again but, in time, he would make a full recovery. The rest of his life stretched out before him.

Later that week I asked Ben to consider handing out the team jerseys before the final. I was not sure if it would feel right for him, but I was pleased when he said it would be an honour. It felt important to maintain his link with the team as the countdown to the final intensified.

Away from this sobering business of real life, the Australian press had got stuck into England. It was the usual rabble-rousing stuff. The back page of the *Australian* printed a photograph of Jonny Wilkinson lining up a kick at goal with a banner headline: 'Is That All You've Got?' The *Herald Sun* had a long piece called 'Why We Hate England'. The Sydney *Daily Telegraph* called England 'Grumpy Old Men', while their columnist, Mike Gibson, took aim with some outdated clichés: 'So, England play boring rugby? You're kidding. What else is new? The Pope is a Catholic? Hitler was a bad guy? Kylie has a cute rear end? It's only halfway through the week but, already, I've had it up to here with rugby fans complaining that England are boring.

'News Flash. England have always been boring. England sporting teams have turned boring into a fine art. In a country that produces bores like we produce blue heelers, England's sporting super-bore was Geoff Boycott. When Boycott took to the crease, cricket fans used to designate a member of the crowd to wake them when he finally got out . . . and you thought they were planning to play entertaining rugby? Hey, we're talking about a nation where the most popular actor is that tedious twit, Hugh Grant. We're talking about a nation whose idea of excitement is to join a queue.'

Clive Woodward said he had been kept awake by Australian fans chanting, 'Boring, boring, boring . . .' He then joked: 'It wasn't from my wife in bed. It was from the street.'

The *Sydney Morning Herald* asked Martin Johnson if 'England are killing rugby?' while there were photographs of a notice posted on Manly beach which targeted Woodward's players: 'Warning: Boring Rugby Teams Train Here.'

Woodward and I had been jabbing away cheerfully at each other for two years. When we faced England for the first time with me as head coach in November 2001, Woodward had just selected Henry Paul, a New Zealander who had recently switched codes from rugby league.

'Our guys have to earn a Wallaby jumper,' I said. 'England obviously have a different selection policy.'

Woodward was a smart operator and he responded with a sneaky little jab of his own. 'Does Eddie have the balls to pick Mat Rogers and Wendell Sailor?'

Rogers and Sailor were Aussies to the core, but they had just left rugby league. I was not about to ask them to play their first game of senior rugby union in a Twickenham Test. From then on we bumped up against each with regular amusement. There was also an edge – which was to be expected when we were both striving to become world champions.

When England played Australia at Twickenham in 2001, Woodward used his press conference to wheel out videotapes of our alleged cheating. 'Australia used the old Eddie Jones trick of having decoy runners in front of the ball carrier,' he griped.

When the English reporters found me, I said: 'I'm glad Clive is so in tune with the laws. Have you seen what England are doing in the lineout?' We spent the next ten minutes talking about English infringements and I notched it up as a small victory when the reports the following morning were more about my lineout observations than Woodward's talk of decoy runners.

A few months later, when I was asked if I'd had a chance to meet the match referee Paul Honiss, I smiled. 'No. Apparently he's still looking at Clive's videos.'

England were a bloody good side and so I did what I could to try and get under their skin. I knew Clive bridled at England being called defensive and conservative. 'England do not have to be boring,' I insisted. 'They choose to be.'

Woodward sniped back after they beat us midway through 2003. 'Eddie obviously spends more time planning his press conferences than his training sessions. Everything seems to have changed in Australia since I lived here. I thought you Aussies were all about winning, and not about marks out of ten for performance. Eddie has been trying to wind us up all week about what an old, tired, slow and boring team we are. Well, that's all bullshit. I wanted the roof shut so the game could be played in perfect conditions for a great running game. Eddie wanted it open to introduce the uncertainty of weather conditions – and you call us boring?'

I could be just as sarcastic. 'They're probably the best side in the world, mate,' I said in a mocking tone. 'They know how to do everything.'

There was plenty of talk from the English press that Woodward would be honoured with a knighthood if they won the World Cup. 'Is that so, mate?' I said. 'Will I have to call him Sir Clive from now on?'

At my last press conference before the final, I laid down a challenge to England and their aspiring knight. 'Our natural game is to attack,' I said of the Wallabies. 'We'll keep our side of the bargain – I promise you that. If you can get England and the referee to do the same, we should have a great spectacle. It could be the world's greatest game of rugby.'

We gathered together early in the afternoon on the day of the final. There was applause and a few choked-back tears when Ben Darwin walked slowly into the team room. Ben wore a neck brace and he moved stiffly and painfully. But the fact he was walking made his entrance uplifting. There was a poignant moment when Al Baxter, winning only his second cap, was called up to receive his jersey. As Ben shook the hand of his replacement it must have hit him again that his career had ended with shuddering sadness.

I was impressed by Ben. He spoke about some of the sights he had witnessed in the hospital spinal unit. He had seen young men who would never walk again and it made him feel lucky he had been discharged from hospital. Ben said he had been fortunate enough to play in a World Cup semi-final. The boys now had the chance to play in the final. Ben urged them to enjoy the occasion and feel lucky to be so fit and healthy.

George Gregan, his Brumbies teammate and Wallaby captain, stood up to answer. There was so much emotion that George couldn't get his words out for a while. George is strong, though, and unafraid to show his feelings. He talked through the tears and told Ben how much he meant to the team. He also conveyed how much it meant to all of us to have made the final. We had been written off all year but, against the All Blacks, we had shown our true selves. George asked us to fulfil Ben's wish that we enjoy the occasion – while winning the World Cup.

Stadium Australia, Sydney. Saturday, 22 November 2003
There is even more emotion four hours later when 44 rugby players link arms as the anthems are played. 'God Save the Queen' for the 22 Englishmen and 'Advance Australia Fair' for the Wallabies. A cold drizzle has swirled around Sydney all day but it feels fiery inside the arena.

My primary concern is whether we can get up again for a massive challenge. It's easy to say you should peak in a World Cup final – but, after an outstanding performance, the next game is always tricky. You need to get the right balance of driving your squad in the week but not pushing them too much. We prepared well but it's hard to know whether we're right on the edge of where we need to be to beat a team as good as England.

We have a different strategy. England are a much more rugged, disciplined and better team than New Zealand – but they're also older and slower. I want us to move the ball more, and play wider than we had done against the All Blacks. It's important we display the same courage to attack but we do not need quite the same possession-dominated game. I encourage the boys to mix it up and stretch England. We also suspect Wilkinson is carrying an injury. His right shoulder is crook and we'll target the number 10 channel and play right through him. At the same time we need to move their forwards around and avoid as much set-piece play as possible.

From the very first minute we have the bravery and zip we need. We are almost as sharp as we had been in the opening minutes against New Zealand. Larkham looks full of invention and daring and England are pinned back.

Receiving the ball from a rock-solid scrum, Gregan passes to Larkham. Rather than sticking to the same pattern, Larkham hoists a towering kick towards the corner flag. This is the kind of kick I had forbidden him to use against the incredibly athletic All Blacks. But now I am happy. As the ball hangs in the air I see Lote Tuqiri racing down the wing. He and Jason Robinson leap for it but there's only going to be one winner. Tuqiri plucks it out of the air and plunges over the line: 5–0 after six minutes.

It settles down into a tough, gritty and often scrappy game. This is not pretty rugby. England are not a pretty team. They're full of gnarled old warriors like Johnson, Dallaglio, Back and Hill. Wilkinson is already immense. He might have a dodgy shoulder but, boy, he is producing big hits, as if he is made out of concrete rather than flesh and bone. His boot is, as usual, flawless. After 15 minutes, and two Jonny penalties, they are a point ahead. They blow a chance to score a try when Ben Kay spills a simple pass a few metres from the line; but another penalty makes it 9–5.

England keep coming and, two minutes before the break, Dallaglio bursts through a pocket of space. Wilkinson takes the pass and immediately switches it outside. Robinson hits the line with blistering timing. Sailor doesn't have a hope of catching him. Robinson scores in the corner. His face is contorted with passion. He looks like a very angry volleyball player as he uses a spare hand to smack the ball in the air, making it 14–5 at half-time.

I tell the boys to keep chipping away. The scoreboard will take care of itself.

Test rugby is so hard to win when you are playing away because history proves the home team always gets a little subconscious help from the referee. There is a huge English presence in the stadium, and 'Swing Low Sweet Chariot' rolls down from the soaring stands, but it's still a home game for us. There is much more gold than white, wherever you look, and André Watson, the South African ref in charge of his second successive World Cup final, makes some calls that help us. We keep England scoreless in the second half and Elton Flatley kicks three penalties – the last, under colossal pressure, with less than a minute left on the clock. It's a simple kick, on their 22-metre line, but it takes heart to make it.

It's 14–14. Extra time.

Everyone is shattered. They've given everything they've got and have to dredge something more from deep within themselves for another 20 minutes. I tell them to feel proud of coming back. I urge them to go big one last time. England are out on their feet. We can win it.

I am more precise with Matt Giteau when he comes on to replace Larkham briefly. Larkham has taken a blow to the head and Gits has a huge responsibility. Having just turned 21, he is very young. My head is clear and my instructions are on the button. Gits does well and then Larkham returns to the fray.

England have been the better team but, somehow, we're still there at the death. Glen Ella and I have spent the whole of extra time on the sidelines as coaches are allowed to be pitchside after the regular game is over. We're having fun, even if it feels like torture at the time. Occasionally I sneak a look over at my oldest mate. This is Glen, an Indigenous Australian kid from La Perouse, my best mate, with whom I have coached Randwick, Southern Districts, Japan and now Australia. We're in extra time of the World Cup final. We've played imaginary World Cup finals in extra time as kids on the beach or the park. Now, we're doing it for real.

Glen looks back. He sees old Beaver, his mate who drives him mad with his 2 a.m. work demands, and the tiny Japanese kid who went with him to kindergarten and primary school before we had such fun at Matraville High. These are only fleeting thoughts because the match is so consuming. We are so close, yet still so bloody far.

Play grinds on and we make a break down the right. It might be on. Glen and I jump up together but Lote is bundled into touch. We groan and sigh together. As we go to sit down again on the fold-up seats, we have our World Cup comedy moment. Glen forgets to push down his seat and we both fall to the ground. We sit there laughing in the middle of an excruciatingly tense final.

Wilkinson kicks a testing penalty in the first half of extra time, but we keep exerting pressure. England make a mistake deep in the second half. Flatley has another relatively simple chance but the consequences of missing are severe. He holds his nerve: 17–17.

There is a minute left but, as soon as Rogers misses a long, raking touch, we're in trouble. Lewis Moody is on as a substitute for England and he has the energy to make significant ground before the ball goes out. Moody wins the lineout as England drive forward again. Larkham is screaming orders, knowing that Wilkinson is being set up for the field goal. But Dawson foxes us. He darts ahead, instead of making the pass, and gains a precious 15 metres before he is scragged.

We see Jonny drop back further into space. He wants the field goal. He wants to win the World Cup with one last swing of his boot. Wilkinson has missed a couple of attempts but this one is made for him. His weary pack remain patient deep in our 22. They retain the ball.

Dawson is still at the bottom of the ruck. Neil Back steps in at scrum half and wisely goes for the simple offload to his captain. Like a rumbling old tanker ending its final voyage, Johnson makes one last charge. He is brought down. Dawson is up. He has the ball.

George Smith, Larkham and our boys have no hope of closing

down Jonny. I want to shut my eyes but I have to keep watching and hoping that, somehow, he will miss. I have clocked that the field goal will be attempted with his weaker right foot. I clench my fists into little balls.

Wilkinson has been hunched over, hands on his knees, as if gathering himself for this moment. He straightens up and takes another step back. He is positioned perfectly, 25 metres out and just to the left of the posts. Dawson spreads his arms towards the referee as if to warn him that the Wallabies need to stay onside. We have a gold line of defenders waiting to hurtle towards Wilkinson in the hope they can close him down. We're all waiting for the long pass.

Here it comes. Wilkinson catches it and steadies himself. He looks up and then down before – in a moment he has practised thousands of times in his fanatical training routines – he drops the ball onto his right foot. As soon as it leaves his boot and climbs into a black sky illuminated by the glaring floodlights, I know he has caught it right. The ball loops and spirals towards the posts.

A third of the stadium bellows with ecstasy, while two-thirds let out a muffled moan of despair. I am silent as the ball dissects the H.

Fuck. We've lost the World Cup final in the very last minute of extra time.

Woodward and the English bench go crazy. Glen and I are glazed as we sit on our fold-up chairs.

Our boys pile into them desperately from the kick-off. These are the very last moments. England control the ball while Dawson waves his arms like a demented air-traffic controller.

Mike Catt is ready, and when he receives the final pass, he hoofs it out into touch. His arms are raised in celebration even before Watson reaches for his whistle.

The final blast is shrill and piercing. Amid the bedlam, England run around and jump into each other's arms.

I get up and reach for Glen's hand. I pull my old mate up and we turn to meet our bereft boys and to congratulate England.

This is the worst way to lose a World Cup final, but still I feel proud. England have been the best side in the world for 18 months, while we have been derided and mocked. But we've slugged it out for 100 minutes and pushed them to the brink. England are the best team in the world – by 30 seconds.

Back in the dressing room, surrounded by broken and beaten men, I remind them to feel proud of their gigantic effort. No one is really listening. I circle the room, trying to find the right words to console and praise my players, one by one, as if I might, somehow, soften the pain.

9

ROCK BOTTOM

I was dazed by the match and the result – but immensely proud of the players. It had been a performance of the highest order. But, as is my way, I was already moving on. At the media conference following the final, I thought it was the ideal time to start talking about the future. After all, we had a tournament to win and only four years to prepare.

'I'd say 70–80 per cent of our squad will be strongly in contention for the next World Cup, so there are some real positives for the future,' I said. I also wanted George Gregan to stick around as captain but only 'if he has the enthusiasm to keep improving as a player.'

On the Monday night after the final, we were invited to The Lodge, the prime minister's house. We had drinks with John Howard and his wife and, afterwards, when it was just me and the players sitting around late at night, some of the boys opened up. They said it had been one of the best experiences of their lives but they still felt sad. I understood those tangled emotions because they matched mine. We'd had a great tournament and, for a team that hadn't been expected to do well, we had surpassed expectations and captured the imagination of the Australian public.

Within days of the loss, I got the feeling that John O'Neill wanted to sack me. He never said anything to me directly, but you get the vibe, don't you, when things aren't quite right? For whatever reason, John and I never discussed the matter directly.

But, just as I was beginning to worry, the karma bus ran straight over the top of him. With the tom-tom drums beating louder that the ARU board were going to punt him, O'Neill got in first and decided to 'move on' and end his contract a year early. Lovely words about mutual decisions were sprinkled liberally over a media release. To me it looked like the hatchet men on the ARU Board from NSW and Queensland had finally had enough of him.

The struggle to come to grips with losing a World Cup final took me two years. It ate at me. On the surface I was fine and already planning for the next World Cup but, deep down, I was hurting.

I would not change many things about my life but, if I could, this would be one. I should have resigned after the final. I should have walked away on a relative high and taken a break from the game. It was a mistake to continue but, in retrospect, I understand how much I was struggling. I wanted to atone for that heartbreaking loss by winning the next tournament. This happens when you come close and fall just short. You carry the burden of defeat with you for the next few years. It might be buried deep inside you, but it twists your thinking.

There are lessons to be taken from other World Cup coaches. Apart from Steve Hansen, it seems as if anyone who has won a World Cup has not gone on to coach again with any great success. Rod Macqueen did exceptional work when Australia became world champions but, two years later, he stepped away from the game for a long time. His return with the Rebels in Melbourne did not go well. Clive Woodward led the Lions on a disastrous tour of New Zealand, in 2005, and never coached again. Jake White won the World Cup with South Africa in 2007 but his subsequent career has not been a roaring success. Graham Henry masterminded the All Blacks belated victory in 2011. Since then he has helped Argentina as an assistant coach and has worked as a consultant. It's very difficult to sustain the intensity of World Cup success.

Coaching the losing finalists occupies more complex terrain. But, at the very least, the sapping experience should have persuaded me to step back and replenish myself away from the game for a year. I chose the opposite path. I went at the job even harder than before. We did well in the 2004 Tri Nations – which turned out to be the tightest in the history of the competition. All three teams won their home games but were beaten away. Having defeated the Springboks and All Blacks in Perth and Sydney, we travelled to Durban for the tournament decider.

We were 7–3 ahead at half-time, and we scored three tries to the Boks' two, but we lost 23–19 to Jake White's team. South Africa were champions, on 11 points, while we were second on 10. The All Blacks, still mourning the World Cup, only scored one bonus point to finish third – with eight points.

Another narrow loss and runners-up position added to my frustration. I knew that I had to rebuild the team. We had done a temporary job as we had helped some of the players involved in the 1999 World Cup triumph make it to 2003. But 2007 would be beyond many of them. It remained difficult. If you were to get rid of them, you'd get criticized. If you allowed them to stay on, you might be left with players past their best. I also struggled because there wasn't much young talent coming through. As an international coach, you're a prisoner of the talent that's emerging or failing to come through quickly enough.

Woodward resigned less than ten months after winning the World Cup, and England were rocky under his former assistant coach Andy Robinson. We beat them at Twickenham that year and also defeated Scotland twice – while losing in Paris.

I changed the way we played and trained – and focused on getting Australia ready for the 2007 World Cup. I knew there would be pain while we waited for new players to establish themselves. New Zealand were also suffering, even though, usually, they are the only country that can produce a winning team year after year because the whole nation is willing on the All Blacks. All their resources are poured into the objective of improving the national team. That priority has now been copied by most tier-one nations – with England being the exception.

I was hell-bent on putting together a team that could win the World Cup. We had many injuries in 2005 as we intensified training. I think we were the first team in the world to use GPS devices and we began pushing them harder in practice than in matches. They were under far greater physical and mental stress in training. This technique is used by many international teams now, but the Wallabies were the first to be shocked by it. The new strategy cost us some big players in key games but I was willing to take the hit to have them ready for 2007.

We would move the ball far more than previously. Studying how France played, I tweaked our backline so we had a formation which resembled a 1-5-1 which, at that stage, hadn't been played before. Physically, we couldn't compete with the bigger sides, so I wanted more fluidity.

Using this new system we scored a record number of points while winning our first four games of 2005. We racked up 210 points against Samoa, Italy, France and South Africa. But the mood behind the scenes was tense. Trouble broke out, which was caused partly by my selecting the wrong staff, and partly by my losing perspective as the demands and frustrations of the job led me down a rabbit hole of relentless work.

I was increasingly frustrated with my new assistant coaches. Roger Gould and Andrew Blades were pushed by the union and had come in for Ewen McKenzie and Glen Ella. Ewen had taken over as head coach of the Waratahs while Glen was enjoying a well-deserved break. I had approved their replacements, but that turned out to be a mistake. Roger had never coached at any level and Andrew had only done a little work. They are good blokes, but they just weren't equipped to coach an international team. As a way of trying to overcome their shortcomings, I drove them hard and they battled to cope.

In recent years they have both been very public in their sustained personal criticism of my efforts without ever once reflecting on their own contributions. Enough said.

The team were also about to implode. Our first defeat came at Ellis Park, the spiritual home of South African rugby. We were under the pump even before the game. The bus that took us to the stadium arrived suspiciously late. And when it did, this huge Afrikaans guy in a Springbok jersey walked up to the front of the bus and gave it the world's hardest Liverpool kiss. He split his head wide open and blood poured from the wound. Only in South Africa. Instead of arriving 80 minutes before the game, our police escort got us to Ellis Park with just 40 minutes to kick-off.

After a quick warm-up, we tried to get back to the dressing-room – but Nelson Mandela's golf cart blocked our path. We were about to play South Africa in the Mandela Cup and they had parked the great man in our way. We couldn't just ask Nelson Mandela to get out of our road. So we waited. Finally they moved Mandela on and we rushed madly to get ready for kick-off. I realize now that I didn't do enough as a coach to prepare the team for that kind of situation. Ellis Park is such a tough ground anyway and we were 23–8 down at half-time. We did well to come back – but still lost 33–20.

A few days later I sent Matt Henjak back to Sydney. He was our reserve half back and he and Lote Tuqiri had an altercation. They were in a nightclub in Cape Town with Wendall Sailor and Matt Dunning when Henjak and Tuqiri started arguing. They were all drinking and Henjak admitted he had thrown the contents of his drink. I was not happy. A few of them were skating on thin ice; but Henjak was a serial offender.

Five years earlier, when some of the Brumbies had got boisterous in a taxi on a raucous night out in Cape Town, I had made a point of refusing to send them home. It had been a minor incident, as even the local police had confirmed, and – crucially – a first offence for all of them. The word 'serial' told us everything we needed to know about Henjak's record. I fined the others but had no compunction in sending Henjak home.

At least Henjak was contrite on his arrival in Sydney. He told the waiting pressman that, 'I've acted inappropriately as a Wallaby. I'm going to cop that on the chin and try to get back in the side as quickly as I can.'

Taxigate had helped bind the Brumbies closer together, but this incident knocked us off track and we lost 22–16 in Pretoria that Saturday.

A dismal run of seven straight Test defeats had begun. We ended up losing three times on the spin to South Africa, twice to New Zealand, and then away to France and England. It was disastrous as the media tore into us. You've got all these great ex-players, or great former coaches, who suddenly become media experts. I've done a few gigs as a pundit and it is such easy work. You can be the smartest bloke on earth because you're always dealing in retrospect and you can change your opinion from week to week. And they all try to 'outrage' each other by searching for sharper and steeper insults and slurs. It's part of the territory, and if it grows the attention and support for the game, well, that's good. But you sometimes wonder about people's motivations. I do my best to ignore it.

If there is something I need to pay attention to, Pemby will generally be in touch pretty smartly. The older I've got, the more I've tried to distance myself from the chatter. You hear about it because your mates tell you that you're taking a kicking, or your mum asks you what's going on. But if someone sends me a link containing punditry about me or my teams, I don't even open it. I hit delete. Whenever you're trying to do work of ambition and commitment, you can't worry about the guys who don't support you. I take the same attitude if someone sends me a link which is effusive about my work. I won't open it because it's invariably wrong.

At the start of my coaching career I went to see an excellent rugby league coach, Brian Smith, who was in charge of the

Parramatta Eels. Brian gave me some advice I've never forgotten: 'Just remember, whenever they say you're good, you're never that good. When they say you're bad, you're never that bad.' I've thought of those simple, but wise, words many times during my career. When England lost six games on the bounce in 2018, and the media was screaming, after lauding me as the second coming at Twickenham 18 months earlier, I recalled Brian's words. I knew that, then, we were 3 per cent from being a great team and 3 per cent from being an average team. The margins are that small.

The situation, however, was dire with Australia in 2005. It came from the top down. Gary Flowers had replaced John O'Neill as the CEO of the ARU. I didn't have a great relationship with O'Neill, but I thought he was outstanding in his job. He had a vision of turning rugby union from being a rather boutique, elitist sport into competing with league, Aussie Rules and cricket for mainstream attention across Australia. We made some magnificent inroads and pushed rugby to the forefront in 2003.

The man who replaced O'Neill didn't have a matching vision or flair. Gary was a lovely bloke, with good intentions, but in my opinion he was seriously out of his depth. There is a vast difference between being the chief executive of a law firm and the chief executive of a national union. The scrutiny of professional sport is searing. You have so many people whispering in your ear and screaming at you in the media. You need to be selective in terms of who you take counsel from. As each day passed, he become more ineffective. Even though he didn't deserve it, the jackals of the press, fed by a few cowards in the shadows who had an axe to grind with Australian Rugby, started to devour him one mistake at a time. It was painful to watch.

I was more concerned with the team. We were hit hard by multiple injuries that year. Elton Flatley was forced to retire after suffering blurred vision, and Steve Larkham, Stirling Mortlock, Dan Vickerman and David Lyons missed huge chunks of the season. I pressed on with the new style I was determined to have ready for the 2007 World Cup. We could have played safe and stuck to the old ways but, two years from rugby's defining tournament, it was time to innovate.

We did not have the tight forwards to take on the best Test packs and so the aim was to spread play across the full width of the pitch with our number 10 roving and linking with the back-row forwards. The first receiver, generally the 10 or 12, would take charge of three or four phases which would allow our attackers to position themselves so that we could switch from left to right depending on the play in front of us. We wanted to play a looser style of passing rugby rather than the direct, more structured game we had developed with the Brumbies and then Australia. The fallacy was that this curbed George Gregan at scrum half; but I actually encouraged his running options.

Rugby was in the midst of slowing down. It would reach ludicrous proportions in 2007 when we regularly had games of over 100 kicks. This didn't help because, with the breakdown being so tough, George was not getting the quick ball he loved. He struggled to adapt to the new system. My strategy was correct, for the time, but to make it work we needed a world-class team. Losing Larkham hindered us and I made a mistake in sticking to my guns. In the November 2005 internationals I should have been more pragmatic.

George and I had a brief argument because he went against team orders when we lost to France in Marseille. He was unhappy that I had criticized him openly to the media after the game. He felt, rightly, that we should have kept it within the team. But we played poorly and were under a lot of pressure. Teams revert to old habits when they're feeling the squeeze, and I felt the senior players should have shown more leadership. I was under pressure myself and I made the error of talking so bluntly in public. It was not really a big deal between George and me. We cleared it up quickly and our mutual respect for each other was undented.

The following week, at Twickenham, we got destroyed upfront. I had two woefully inexperienced tight-head props in my squad.

Al Baxter, who had replaced Ben Darwin in the World Cup final, had still only played a handful of games in Super Rugby. At that stage of his career he wasn't a Test prop. We worked hard with him all week but Al just wasn't ready. He got pulverized in the scrum by Andrew Sheridan and we lost 26–16.

We snapped the seven-match losing streak by winning in Dublin, but the criticism was unrelenting when we travelled to Cardiff for our final game of the year. Alan Jones, the former Wallaby coach with whom we'd had such run-ins when he coached Manly against Randwick, kept up his deliberately controversial talk-show drivel.

'The Wallabies have problems,' Jones said, 'but they are not player problems. They are coaching problems. Sometimes, what Eddie Jones says borders on the indecipherable. God only knows how the players work out what he means. Sometimes it's better not to be coached than to be badly coached. Australian rugby is full of talented players but our talent is being betrayed. The real tragedy is that Eddie Jones, the unsuccessful coach, permeates right through Australian rugby. What on earth does this man do for the money he is paid?'

I was too busy to get caught up in a spat with my namesake. But, in an indication of how I was not thinking entirely coolly, I responded to criticism of our scrum at the Twickenham press conference by pointing out that the board had refused to give me the money we needed to run a scrummaging camp for our props. My temper had got the better of me and Pemby, whom the ARU had employed six months earlier to bridge the gap between me and them, ticked me off.

'You shouldn't have said that, Beaver,' he told me. 'You don't publicly criticize the board. Ever. Once you're home, you need to apologize and set things straight.'

'Really?'

'Yeah, mate, really,' Pemby said dryly, before reminding me that, once again, my appalling political judgement had got me into trouble and might cost me dearly. I had little goodwill to call upon.

I had planned to head to South Africa after the tour to scope facilities for next season, but Pemby was having none of it.

'Mate, you're coming home,' he said. 'I've got a bad feeling about this. We need you home and ready to explain how we are going to get out of the hole we're in.'

I accepted his advice and thought I had better make sure we beat Wales. Flowers was in Cardiff and the messages he gave to the media alternated between a vote of confidence and hinting that the die was already cast. An interview he gave to Peter Jenkins certainly suggested I was gone. There was nothing I could do but prepare the team as well as I could. We led 14–6 deep into the game but our scrum imploded again. A penalty try was awarded against us after we had collapsed once too often. Wales won 24–22 and celebrated their first defeat of Australia in 18 years.

We had lost seven out of our last eight Tests and I flew home to Sydney under a dark cloud.

I often reflect on that time and think about how different people and players reacted. I put my hand up for my contribution to our lack of success. But it surprised me how quickly it turned toxic. Players with agendas started to leak to the press, board members were no longer wearing their gold scarves in the team hotel and the administrators were thinking about their future. It was not Australia's finest hour.

Gary Flowers was later quoted as saying that 'I had lost the dressing room', which is a trite cliché uttered by administrators and journalists who have never been in professional sport. Teams just don't act that way. In rugby you generally have 15 people who are happy. They have been picked to play. Then you have eight who are not as happy as the chosen 15, but happier than the balance of the squad who are in the changing room in their suits. As you would hope and expect, they are unhappy because they are not playing.

These are complicated ecosystems, and if you are looking for people who want to have a whinge they are easy to find. It's just simplistic nonsense that I had 'lost the dressing room'. Clearly there was more than the usual amount of unhappiness because of our losing streak. That's to be expected. Our Australian squad was not great then, but the best teams stick together and fight through it. The challenge is to reflect honestly on your weaknesses and get on with solving the problems – which is exactly what I planned to do.

On Thursday, 1 December 2005, five days after our defeat in Cardiff, Pemby and I had prepared hard for my end-of-season presentation to the board where I was going to have the opportunity to update them on my plans. But I took a call from Gary Flowers early that morning asking if he could see me first in his office. Pemby was about to fly from Canberra to Sydney for another business commitment. We agreed that Flowers was probably going to talk about my presentation and go over the rules of engagement.

Our plan was in place. I would apologize to the board and address the various issues the Wallabies needed to overcome. I would also take full responsibility for the poor run of results but stress my belief that we were making the right strategic plans for the 2007 World Cup.

Everything changed as soon as I walked into Flowers's office. I respected the fact that he didn't waste any time. He was sympathetic but direct. They were terminating my contract.

I heard him out and didn't argue. I was not about to beg for another chance and so we shook hands. It was very civilized. But it happened so fast I was in shock.

The first person I called was Pemby. He was still in the air and his phone switched to voicemail. 'Mate,' I said, 'don't worry about the plan. He's just sacked me.'

Pemby called me as soon as he landed. 'Mate,' he said, 'what happened?'

'I walked in there and he told me I was done.'

'Who's your lawyer?'

The only lawyer I knew was the solicitor who had helped Hiroko and me buy our home.

'Listen, Beaver,' Pemby said patiently, 'that's not the kind of guy you need right now. We need an employment lawyer who can make sure you get the right kind of settlement.'

The money mattered far less to me than the fact I had just lost my position as Australia's head coach. I told Pemby I'd leave it to him.

Pemby called a friend who was CEO of one of the biggest ASX-listed companies. Pemby explained the situation and then asked, 'Who is the most ruthless lawyer you know?' He was given the mobile phone number of Rupert Murdoch's lawyer. When Pemby called him, it went to voicemail. Time was of the essence, so he changed tack.

This time he tried a school friend who was a partner in the Sydney office of Baker McKenzie, the big global law firm. Pemby's mate confirmed he had people in his office who could deal with the ARU. Pemby drove me over to meet them. I was shattered so I just nodded along to everything they suggested. They got onto the ARU and the deal was sorted over the next six hours.

The next morning was announcement day and Pemby was all over Flowers and his executive team. We needed to set ground rules of what would and wouldn't be said by both sides. The ARU official media release had to meet with our approval. The ARU agreed. Pemby and the ARU then spent the morning thrashing out the details. They haggled over words acceptable to both parties. It took a few hours before we reached a compromise. None of this mattered much to me but I knew it was important to get it right.

A media conference was called for two o'clock that afternoon. Pemby prepped me so that I could handle it with as much dignity and grace as I could muster – even though I was reeling. Flowers was up first and Pemby went into the presser to make sure the ARU didn't trash me.

'All good, mate,' he said ten minutes later. 'They kept their side of the bargain. Your turn now.'

Pemby had reminded me that, in 1997, I had been coaching rugby in Japan. In the ensuing eight years I had won the Super 12 and the Tri Nations and lost the final of the World Cup in extra time. My win percentage against the All Blacks was 45 per cent – which was better than any other coach in Wallaby history. In total, the Wallabies had won 33, lost 23 and drawn one game under me. So I could hold my head high. The last year had been a failure but at least I had been working on a long-term strategy. I had taken a risk and lost. But I had given everything to the Wallabies – maybe too much so, because I was burnt out.

I handled the press conference well. I was generous to the ARU and the media. I got them laughing again and spoke without anger or bitterness. There were handshakes all round and even a little applause. At the same time, there was the whirr of camera shutters and flashes. Every snapper wanted to get one last shot of me leaving for the last time as Wallaby coach.

Pemby gave my arm a squeeze and said, 'Good job, mate. Let's go.'

The lift doors opened and we stepped inside. It was just the two of us as the doors closed again with a soft swish.

We had just started to descend when the first tears fell. I couldn't stop them. I cried in the lift.

'Mate,' Pemby said quietly. He did not know what else to say.

I shook my head as the tears kept rolling down my face. My mouth was crumpled into a little ball which I eventually managed to open. I wanted to tell Pemby how I felt.

Finally, just before we reached the ground floor, I got the words out: 'I *will* coach at this level again.'

'I know you will,' Pemby said.

Pemby understood. My dream job had been taken away from me. He knew it would take me a long time to recover.

We reached my car. I was in control again. 'Where are you staying tonight, Pemby?' I asked.

'At my mum's. But I'll get a cab there.'

'No,' I said. 'I'm happy to drive you.'

We made the drive through the lower North Shore of Sydney, mostly in silence, but there were no more tears. When I pulled into his parents' driveway, Pemby's mum came out.

'Hello, Eddie,' she said in surprise. 'How are you?'

I don't think she had any idea what had just happened. 'I'm well, Mrs Pembroke,' I replied. 'How about you?'

We exchanged a few more pleasantries before Pemby ushered his mum away. 'We'll talk tomorrow, mate,' he promised.

I climbed back into the car. I felt relieved I was driving home to Hiroko and Chelsea. A weight had been lifted off me. The previous evening, when I'd arrived home and told her I had been sacked, Hiroko had been great. 'So, where are we going next?' she asked.

Hiroko was serious. She was not fazed for a moment and she showed me she was ready to get right back on the rollercoaster and go wherever rugby took me.

As I wound down the window on that summer evening, I had time to think a little more. I didn't mind that Pemby had seen me crying in the lift. He knew how much rugby meant to me. What mattered more were the words I had said in my deepest sadness: 'I *will* coach at this level again.'

Those words echoed in my head as I pressed my foot down a little harder on the accelerator. I wanted to get home and start again.

Bankrolled by the millions – and the rugby-fuelled passion – of their chairman and owner Nigel Wray, Saracens had become one of the most intriguing stories in English rugby. They had been a very minor club that had moved from one small ground to another for decades. But the arrival of Wray coincided with the advent of professionalism. Wray enticed a stunning trio of international players to join the club in 1996. Philippe Sella, Michael Lynagh and Francois Pienaar, who had led South Africa to the

World Cup the previous year and shared such a rapport with Nelson Mandela, transformed the club.

A decade later, early in 2006, Saracens were fourth from bottom of the Premiership and desperate to avoid relegation. Their idea of having joint head coaches in Steve Diamond and Mike Ford had not worked. The two men did not get on and a change had to be made. Diamond left the club and Ford took over – and Mark Sinderberry, their chief executive who had been in the same role with me at the Brumbies, convinced the board that I should act as a consultant from February until the end of the season.

I had already made what would turn out to be the worst decision of my rugby career when I impulsively accepted an offer from the Queensland Reds. It was 100 per cent my own fault. I didn't talk to anyone, I just said yes. I agreed, verbally, to join them in the middle of 2006 on a three-year contract. This would give me six months to prepare for the start of the expanded Super 14 season in 2007. A short stay in England would clear my head of the Wallaby fallout and set me up for my return to Super Rugby.

A day after my arrival in England I was with Mark when I took a call from Greg Growden, one of the Sydney rugby writers who had given me a tough time over the last year.

'How can you speak to him?' Mark asked.

'Mate,' I said, 'he's just doing his job.'

It was a sign that I had begun to piece myself back together. I also remember walking into the Saracens dressing room that first day, in March 2006, and feeling comfortable straightaway. I told the players that, while I would only be with them a short time, I would give everything I had to ensure we pulled away from the relegation zone. They responded well and our first game was on the Friday night of 10 March – away to Sale who were the league leaders and on their way to becoming that season's Premiership winners. Saracens showed a lot of grit and we won 15–9 on a cold and rainy night up in the north. It was our first win in nine games.

I was just coaching again. Freed from media, sponsorship or administrative commitments, both the club and I thrived in our six weeks together. Saracens were very good in agreeing to my one stipulation – that I should be director of rugby for that crucial period. It meant every rugby decision had to go through me. This decision brought clarity to what had been a confused situation. Leicester were still the powerhouse of Premiership rugby and had a strong contingent of English players. I could see Saracens needed to follow them by tweaking their model and relying less on foreign players in future seasons. But then, in the mire of a relegation battle, I had to clean up the mess.

Kyran Bracken was the scrum half and outside him, at 10, was Glen Jackson. Bracken wanted to play English rugby; Jacko wanted to play New Zealand rugby. Neither of them would bend so I found a way to make it work. I sat them down and said, 'Kyran, you look after what's in front of you. Jacko, you look after what's behind you. If you both do that, we'll be all right.'

It was basic stuff but it worked. We also had some good overseas players in the side. Cobus Visagie was our tight-head prop and Taine Randell was at number 8. Both were good men. Thomas Castaignède was an intelligent man but, boy, he could be difficult. He had lost a lot of pace and he struggled at full back. We were up against Leicester, who were in the top four, and challenging for the title. I said, 'Thomas, this week you're going to play on the wing.'

His lip dropped and he asked: 'Why?'

Castaignède was upset and so we had a discussion. I explained that this would allow him to have a roaming role to do whatever he wanted. I knew this would suit him, but he gave a very Gallic shrug. The rest of the week he was pretty shitty but then, on the evening of the game, he walked into the dressing room with a big smile on his face.

'Tonight, Eddie,' Castaignède said, 'I am Joe Roff.'

I laughed and Castaignède went out and played brilliantly. He was a revelation.

Having had such a good time, winning four out of our six games and just missing qualification for the Heineken Cup, I thought, 'I could do a good job here.'

Nigel Wray thought the same. He flew out to Portugal to meet me at a late-season camp on the Algarve and he got straight to the point. He had a substantial four-year contract to offer me.

I turned him down with regret, telling him I had agreed my deal with the Reds.

'Have you signed their contract?' Nigel asked.

'No. But I gave them my word.'

This might sound noble, but I can't brag about it. I had already started working with the Stormers in Cape Town in 2015 when England came calling. It made me feel very uncomfortable, but I took the big job that seemed right for me. So I am not always as virtuous as I was in honouring my commitment to the Reds.

It was time to fly back to Australia – and complete the biggest mistake of my career.

A former national coach should never accept a lower-ranking job in his own country. Once you have coached your nation in Test rugby, it's a mistake to return to work with a regional or club side. It simply doesn't feel right. This truth was made even more obvious by the problems I discovered at the Queensland Reds.

A new Australian team had been introduced into Super 14 rugby in 2006 with the emergence of the Western Force in Perth. Twelve players from the Reds, including their captain Nathan Sharpe, were shifted to Perth as the ARU bolstered the new franchise. It didn't help either the Reds or the Force. The new team finished bottom of the table and the Reds were just two places above them.

Before I went to England to work with Saracens, I met the Reds CEO and he promised me a $500,000 player budget to boost the squad. By the time I returned, he and the chairman, as well as the high-performance manager, had all been sacked. The new management team told me we had no money and I had to make do with what I had.

We had some promising young players, but the mature heart of the team had been transplanted to Perth. I would have thought about the troubled situation at the Reds much more clearly if I had not been so rattled by my experience with the Wallabies. I had jumped at the first offer which came my way and I soon had cause to regret it.

There was little I could do but try to prepare the Reds during preseason. I took them to Japan for training and some warm-up games and, for a while, it looked as if I might be able to do something with them. We had young future Wallabies in the squad like James Horwill and Stephen Moore, who would both eventually captain Australia, and I tried hard to convince the union to help me by bringing in some league converts. They agreed on our signing Clinton Schifcofske, who I had watched playing rugby league for the Canberra Raiders for years. If they had backed the recruitment of two more league players, the season would have changed markedly. I also needed a second row forward and I had the perfect player lined up. But the Reds and the union vetoed the signing of Luke O'Donnell.

So I made a bold decision to bring in two kids from high school, Will Genia and Quade Cooper, to play Super 14 rugby. They were both 18 and, while Cooper's talent was obvious, no one had ever noticed Genia. He was a dumpy little Papua New Guinean half back, who played in the third string of the academy. Soon after I arrived, I had watched an academy session and seen Genia. His passing was razor sharp and I was astonished by his raw talent. I spoke to the academy coach who dismissed him: 'The kid's lazy and fat.'

'Yeah,' I said, 'but look at his potential.'

I had to jump though all sorts of hoops to obtain clearance for Genia to move up to Super Rugby, but he excited me in a way that no other young player had done since I first laid eyes on George Smith. From the start, as soon as he was in my Super 14 squad, Genia changed. He got the bit between his teeth and worked like a dog. The weight fell off him and, after training, or even on our free days, he would grab a bag of balls and go out and kick by himself. He was a committed, dedicated, great little half back who went on to play over 100 Tests for Australia. Cooper won 70 Test caps for the Wallabies.

So out of the carnage of that season I had unearthed some diamonds.

Four years after that, in 2011, Ewen McKenzie would coach the Reds to a Super Rugby title. I always remember a text I received that night from the Reds kit-man: 'Mate, no one will know this all started with you.' It was very kind of him to say so, but the future championship-winning potential of the Reds did not really help us much in 2007.

At least we started well. In early February we won our opening game against the Hurricanes. We then lost narrowly to the Blues before travelling to Canberra to play the Brumbies – still being driven by Gregan and Larkham. Despite having such a young and limited side, we shut them down completely. It was 3–0 to us at half-time, and we were pumping them in the scrum. But then, in my opinion, the referee changed the way he controlled the scrums. We were penalized in the first three scrums after half-time. It allowed them back into the game and the Brumbies won 6–3. Afterwards, I sprayed the referee. I was furious. I was sure he had been got at in the break because we weren't supposed to win that game. This happens in rugby. Referees are only human and they buckle when put under pressure by the bigger teams. A quiet word and interpretations change.

We won only one more game that season – losing nine in total. I remember we played the Highlanders at Dunedin. Murray Mexted, the old All Black number 8, said, 'Shit mate, you've got a high-school side today.'

I could have done a better job nurturing such young players. I coached badly that season. I was too aggressive and pushed them too hard because I wanted to win there and then. I didn't want to wait. Cooper became a brilliant player, but he was a complex boy. It was a difficult year for him because, as a young kid, he was targeted. The Chiefs went really hard at him because he had been born and raised in Waikato until he was 15. He struggled that day and lost his rag. So it was a long, hard season which ended in catastrophe.

Our final game of the Super 14 season was in Pretoria. The Bulls aimed to finish top of the table while we were already condemned to last place. They were a great side and would go on to become Super 14 champions that season. Later that year, players like Bryan Habana, Fourie du Preez, Bakkies Botha and Victor Matfield would help win the World Cup for South Africa.

We took the lead with an early penalty. The Bulls then went on the rampage. Everything went for them. Nothing went for us. We threw the dice and went out there to play extravagantly. I thought it was the only way we would get something from the game. I wasn't interested in aiming for a narrow loss. I wanted us to have a real go and throw the ball around in the hope we could score a few tries. They tore us apart.

The Bulls scored 13 tries and the final score was 92–3.

I had suffered a worse defeat. At Tokai University we were once beaten 110–0. We then lost 75–0 in the very next game.

But that was Japanese university rugby. This was 12 years on in Super Rugby.

It was a painful day in Pretoria. We had been belted at the end of a miserable season. I knew I was out of luck and out of another job. It felt like I had hit rock bottom.

10

THE SHAPING OF
SOUTH AFRICA

Four months and nine days later, on 14 September 2007, at half-time at the Stade de France in Paris, I stood close to the heart of South Africa's dressing room. I looked around at these incredible players, including numerous members of the Bulls team which had decimated my callow Reds on 10 May. I had never been involved with a leading side that had been as dominant as the Springboks were against England, the defending world champions, in the opening 40 minutes. England were extremely poor but South Africa steamrollered them in our second Pool A game of the World Cup. We were 20–0 ahead at the break.

I had learnt to say 'we' because, after eight weeks with the squad as South Africa's technical director and effective number two to Jake White, I felt an integral part of the Springbok set-up. It was an unbelievable turnaround, from the disaster of Pretoria to the masterclass of Paris, and proof that the life of an international rugby coach is anything but predictable. I was engrossed in the game and fascinated by the player-led discussion in our dressing room.

No one seemed to care that we were 20 points clear – the gulf between the teams was so wide it felt as if we could end up winning 100–0 if we wanted. Instead, the leading players made a startling tactical choice. They were happy to cede possession for much of the second half so that the Boks could practise their defence.

This wasn't arrogance but simply the decision of an intelligent team focused on their aim of going deep into the tournament. It also aligned with the South African mindset which relishes the physicality and brutal hits of rugby.

I didn't object to their plan because my role was not to dictate strategy; it was to offer alternative ideas to make them less formulaic. My other responsibility was to support Jake. I would try to ease the pressure on him by offering tactical advice and another voice for the players while also helping him deal with the media.

The Springboks were much brighter than the clichéd stereotype of the South African rugby player. They were the opposite of the unimaginative hulks who clobbered anyone who got in their way but could be outsmarted by more thoughtful teams. I learnt that Jake, John Smit, Fourie du Preez, Victor Matfield, Schalk Burger, Bryan Habana, Jean de Villiers and the rest had an insatiable curiosity about world rugby. The way in which they grilled me about the attacking style we had developed at the Brumbies was a clear sign of their open attitude and enquiring minds.

There were no Thomas Castaignède-style imitations of Joe Roff amongst the Springboks in Paris in the second half. They played within themselves and followed their half-time decision to allow England more of the ball. Their tackling was clinical and ferocious and England didn't score a single point. South Africa won 36–0.

It was a terrible humiliation for English rugby and early evidence that South Africa were among the clear favourites to win the 2007 World Cup. I was pretty sure we would go all the way to the final where I expected we would face the All Blacks. I was less interested in the sideshow that suggested if we had success it would be some sort of personal redemption for me after the 2003 World Cup final. I couldn't care less. Jake and the players had given me the massive privilege of being a part of their team. It was an honour for which I will always be grateful. All I could think of was how best I could add value to help the team continue to improve.

I had spent the last nine years scheming how to beat South African rugby teams. It was fascinating to now sit in the belly of the beast. Of course I had had many clashes with the Boks which had veered between the ugly and the comic. In August 2003, after my Wallabies had beaten South Africa by 20 points in Brisbane, I was furious. I called the Springboks 'a disgrace to international rugby' after my players accused them of biting, spitting and gouging. There was enough proof for Bakkies Botha, the great lock, to be banned for eight weeks after a disciplinary panel found him guilty of 'deliberately attacking the face' of our hooker Brendan Cannon. Robbie Kempson was suspended for four weeks for hitting our number 8 Toutai Kefu with a high tackle. I did not hold back. 'It's a deliberate tactic from the Springboks and it puts a slur on the game. We're absolutely filthy about what they did. We need to expose them. They really need to have a good look at themselves, because that sort of rubbish should not go on.'

My anger was intensified by the fact that Kefu was taken off on a stretcher with his neck in a brace. He spent the night in hospital, suffering from spinal concussion. My players were just as outspoken. 'It is frightening when someone is gouging your eyes,' Cannon said. George Gregan told reporters that, 'They don't have a real positive attitude. They play the player and you have the leader of their team spitting at blokes. Look at the Tri Nations the last couple of years. Any time there has been an incident there has been one common denominator: them.'

Corné Krige admitted he had spat out a mouthful of blood, some of which landed accidentally on our flanker Phil Waugh. He said he had apologized immediately. We were not impressed and I stressed that there was no place for spitting, biting and gouging in rugby. Krige warned that he would consider taking legal action and that, 'If any of the Australian players can look me in the eye and say I spat on them [deliberately] I would like to speak to them. It was an accident.' He then said he was glad to be playing next in New Zéaland – 'a rugby country' which understood the game's physicality.

More usually, my ire towards the Boks was laced with humour. Before the 2005 Mandela Cup at Ellis Park, when it seemed as if South Africa did everything they could to delay our arrival at the ground, I had reached for *The Simpsons'* cast of characters to take a shot at Jake White. I compared the Springbok coach to Sideshow Bob. Apart from being Bart Simpson's arch-enemy, Sideshow Bob is a self-proclaimed genius and reactionary.

It was just a bit of fun after Jake had been shooting his mouth off all week – claiming that the Wallabies 'don't particularly like scrumming, they don't particularly like mauling, so they have adapted their game according to their strength.' I laughed it off by saying that, 'I predicted at the start of the week that Jake would want to take attention off his team. I said he would do enough talking for both of us and he's turned into Sideshow Bob.'

The reality was that Jake and I had been good mates for more than seven years. I had first met him when he was part of a South African delegation, led by the then Springbok coach Harry Viljoen, who flew to Canberra in late 2000. They wanted to study the Brumbies' new three-phase form of attack. Since Rod Macqueen had first invited me into his team way back in 1996, I have always been open to other coaches visiting my training camps. I don't give away all my secrets, but I think it's in the spirit of rugby to share ideas.

Jake and I stayed in touch and met as often as our schedules allowed. In November 2004, when the Boks and the Wallabies toured the UK, we swapped notes and helped each before we played England and South Africa faced Scotland. The previous week we had beaten the Scots and the Boks had lost to England. It was a really productive meeting and we both won the following Saturday.

I also got a chance to see, first hand, the immense pressure Jake was under as Springbok coach. A few months before, in

August 2004, the president of the South African Rugby Union had refused to ratify the selection of Jake's team to play the All Blacks in Johannesburg because there was only one black player, Breyton Paulse, in the starting XV. Jake was forced to replace his scrum half, Fourie du Preez, whom I have always regarded as South Africa's best player. Bolla Conradie was a decent number 9 but he was not in the same postcode as Du Preez. Jake still had to accept the quota system.

After apartheid, I understood the need for transformation. But as a coach, knowing you are judged on wins and losses, I felt for Jake and the players. Coaching South Africa is clearly the most difficult job in world rugby – closely followed by New Zealand and England.

In New Zealand, the expectation is off the charts. The national mood swings with the performance of the All Blacks. For me, it is the world's greatest rugby nation. I know they always get stuck into me and I always get stuck into them, but beneath the banter is a deep and mutual respect for the game and its values. New Zealand is the spiritual home of rugby. Currently, they are facing many challenges. They have begun to lose lots of players in their prime as huge offers roll in from France, Japan, England and Ireland. They will cope but it is increasingly difficult for them. The question of what the All Blacks jersey is worth will come into sharper consideration as the Euros, pounds and yen pile up.

The challenge and complexity of coaching England is different. Unlike New Zealand, rugby is not the national sport, but it is a growing and important game. The structure doesn't help and pits club against country. A cultural reticence also inhibits the rise of natural leaders in English rugby. When players move from club to national team, the links are hard to break. In Australia, it was easy. In England, it has been one of my most difficult tasks. If I have improved the transition from club to Test rugby, it would be a satisfying part of any legacy I leave. England should always be among the top teams in the world and the current group of players and administrators are committed to making that happen.

But South Africa presents an incredibly tough situation. While the country's rugby followers expect to win most matches, with an intensity that boils around 90 per cent, the head coach is probably only allowed to operate at 50 per cent of his capacity. The politics of post-apartheid South Africa shadow the game and the Springbok team at every turn. But it's inspiring to see the benefits of the development programmes, where black and 'coloured' (mixed-race) players emerged in the build-up to the 2019 Rugby World Cup. They have asserted themselves and demanded selection on the basis of their performances. South Africa is the sleeping giant of world rugby and could grow into an ever-greater superpower if they maintain their development programmes.

Back in 2006, Jake's problems continued as Springbok head coach when he narrowly survived a vote of no confidence from the board. That year South Africa lost four out of six games in the Tri Nations – including a hammering at Suncorp Stadium where I would coach the Reds.

I remember having coffee with Jake in Brisbane in the week of the game and he asked for some insights. 'Mate,' I said, 'there're always plenty of points on this pitch. It's a really fast ground. Get your defence ready.' Perhaps Jake didn't quite believe me because the Boks got slaughtered 49–0. I think that memory stuck with him and he learnt from it. Afterwards, he showed greater trust in my judgement.

In the 2007 Tri Nations, South Africa lost three out of four games and were well beaten, 33–6, by New Zealand. The All Blacks were once again the runaway favourites for the World Cup, despite not having won it for 20 years. The Springboks were dismissed by the rest of world rugby and able to prepare for the tournament without any attention. I think that's a great position to be in before any World Cup – written off and without undue pressure.

In late July, soon after the Tri Nations, I had been in Japan on one of my coaching holidays at Suntory. My next job in rugby was meant to be as general manager and coaching adviser at Saracens. Mark Sinderberry and Nigel Wray had not been put off by my experience with the Reds and they had enticed me back to England to start working with Sarries from August 2007.

I had been ready to stay on at the Reds for another year because the team were in a mess, which was largely my fault, and I liked the chairman. I was prepared to go through another hard season to help build the new foundations that the Reds needed. But the chairman and I went out for a very nice breakfast and he said, 'Might be best if you go, mate.' I smiled: 'Good idea.' So we finished breakfast and I was relieved to move on.

Fired by the Wallabies and politely asked to move on by the Reds, I now had a fresh start in England to energize me. My previous stint at Sarries had been a success and I was looking forward to facing the obvious demands of Premiership rugby.

Then, out of nowhere, Jake White called. I was just off the training pitch at Suntory when he surprised me: 'Would you like to bring the family over for safari?'

I knew Hiroko and Chelsea would love to spend a few days in a South African game reserve. So I accepted his generous offer and agreed we would stop off on our way to London to join Saracens.

We met up in Durban and, after a few days away, Jake asked if I would take a couple of sessions with the Boks. 'Really?' I asked. 'I'd love to, mate.' The idea of running around on a field with the Springbok players had me feeling like a kid on Christmas Eve.

At the first session I watched them go through some shadow plays and I could tell they were pleased with how they were looking. I was relatively impressed with some aspects, but there were many areas of their play which could be improved.

We gathered in a circle afterwards and John Smit, as captain, addressed his boys. He was complimentary and then he looked over at me. 'What do you think, Eddie? How was that?'

'It wasn't bad, mate, but if I were giving you a score out of ten, I'd say it was about a four.'

John looked at me. He was checking to see if I was joking. 'A four?'

'Yeah, mate. There's a fair bit to work on.'

It was true. They deserved little more than a four because of the talent that was on the field. They had so much more in them. I've never been one to pull my punches and I didn't really care if they were offended. John had asked me my opinion and I had given it to him.

I went through some set moves and showed the Boks how I would do things differently. We did more of the same at the next session and they must have liked it because Jake made me an intriguing offer. Would I consider staying on with the Boks until the end of the World Cup as their technical adviser?

As the words came out of his mouth, I tried to stop myself from giving Jake a hug. A technical adviser to this group of players on the eve of a World Cup? Seriously?

It's hard to describe just how excited I was by the offer. Here was Jake offering me the chance to be involved in a team that clearly had the potential to go all the way. I had done none of the heavy lifting of the previous years and now, with the tournament in touching distance, I was invited along for the ride.

Of course I loved the idea and said I would just need to square things with Saracens. Sinderberry and Wray were supportive and agreed to release me for Springbok World Cup duty even before I had begun working at the club. Hiroko also agreed to fly to London ahead of me – as Chelsea's new school year would begin in September. Flexible and accommodating as always, my wife and daughter set off for England while I moved into camp with the Boks.

Inevitably, there was flak from South Africa and Australia. Some ardent Springbok fans didn't embrace the idea of an Aussie, especially one they had never liked, infiltrating their set-up. Some of my old sparring partners in Australia had a pop at me. John O'Neill, no doubt attracted by the opportunity to speak into another microphone, described my appointment as 'a clinical and rather sad reflection of where the game may have ended up', while also rubbishing my ability. 'The combination of Jake White and Eddie Jones is an interesting one. Sideshow Bob and the Beaver. I don't think it should alarm the Wallabies in any way. It might help them.'

I didn't respond to O'Neill's remark because, like most people in rugby, I sensed the looming train wreck of the Wallabies' 2007 World Cup campaign. After I was sacked, John 'Knuckles' Connolly was finally rewarded with the role of Wallaby head coach. Connolly, a successful coach for the Queensland Reds, had first missed out on the top job after the 1995 World Cup. He should have been appointed on merit, but he fell victim to the political rivalry between NSW and Queensland. NSW won that battle and their candidate, Greg Smith, was preferred. Connolly never recovered from the disappointment and spent much of the next decade sniping from the shadows at Greg Smith, Rod Macqueen, myself and the Wallabies. Gary Flowers, O'Neill's predecessor, understood the history, but he still made the appointment. Letting a mongoose loose in an enclosed space is dangerous and, deep down, once he was back in the job, I thought that O'Neill might have known it. As for his crack at me and Jake, revenge is a dish best served cold. I looked forward to giving him a decent-sized plate.

Less than a year later, O'Neill appointed Robbie Deans, a New Zealander, as the Wallabies' first foreign coach – and Deans let slip to a reporter that O'Neill had tried to recruit him for the role even when I was still Australia's head coach.

Once my role with the Springboks had been agreed, I couldn't wait to get started. I was surprised to find the team so well versed in the rugby I had developed with the Brumbies and Wallabies. It was fascinating to hear John Smit reveal that the structure of the Bok attack was built on our Brumby template. After training and over shared meals and a few beers, they quizzed me about the rugby that had been born and built in Canberra. In my experience, only the Brumbies could match these Boks when it came to an intellectual curiosity about the game. I already knew that Victor Matfield, Fourie, John and the leading Boks were great players. I discovered that they were great men as well.

At one of our first meetings Victor came up to me and said, 'We want to play much closer to the gain line. Do you remember that five-man lineout you had with the Brumbies? Where you had the winger at the front of the lineout? I think that would suit us.'

We spoke frankly and I added another element to the Boks – particularly in terms of their backline play. I had been fortunate to coach Gregan and Larkham for so long and Fourie and Butch James, as the Springboks half backs, were like sponges when I spoke to them about playing flat, counter-attacking rugby.

It enabled them to create an attacking game that suited their strengths. Their game was based on savage defence. Their attacking plays tended to be pieced together from other teams. They were on the right track but we could help them become gain-line focused. We needed Fourie and Butch to have a clearer vision of playing flat against the line.

The second fly half in the squad was André Pretorius. He was a talented but flighty player. To win the tournament we needed a solid guy playing like a modern-day Henry Honiball. In my opinion, Butch was that man. In consultation with Jake, we tinkered with the alignment of the backs as the Boks tended to play very deep. We got them playing flatter behind that big pack. It was simple stuff and the Boks took to it with conviction.

Jake and I just clicked. We had a mutual obsession with rugby. We also liked each other's company and loved working hard on improving a squad of players. I think I helped Jake in two obvious ways. As an outsider, coming into such an established set-up, I could see the big picture much more clearly. Jake had coached guys like John and Fourie from under-19 national level and, while they appeared close, there were tensions and disagreements. For the players, my arrival meant they had a new sounding board. They spoke to me in a way that they could not have done with Jake. I was much more relaxed than Jake, or how I would have been if I had been their head coach, and so we had a terrific relationship. There was not a single player I did not get on with in the Springbok squad. I was not responsible for selection and so they could just be themselves with me and ask for advice in a totally open way.

I also tried to ease the media pressure and expectations on Jake. It helped that I had been all the way to the World Cup final four years earlier and I could pass on some of the lessons I had learnt about preparation and tension. When my Springbok experience ended, I vowed that if I was ever to start again as a head coach in the Test arena, I would always have an independent guy, a right-hand man, who is not directly involved in the coaching. International head coaches need advisers they can trust.

With England I turn to Neil Craig, a former Australian Rules footballer and coach. He doesn't have the technical knowledge that I could share with the Boks, but he is my trusted right-hand man who offers a fresh pair of eyes. My work with the Boks helped me learn how to support a national team.

I liked Jake's coaching staff. It was a strong unit with a good blend of characters. Jake's an English schoolmaster, while Gert Smal is a very serious Afrikaner who is brilliant on detail. Allister Coetzee would briefly become the Boks' head coach in 2016. He is a reserved bloke, from South Africa's 'coloured' (mixed-race) community, and he has some good insights and a gentle sense of humour. Derrick Coetzee, their strength and conditioning coach, is a very bright guy who is full of laughter. He is an earthy Afrikaner from Bloemfontein with about four degrees to his name. They all welcomed me and allowed me to make a contribution.

It turned out to be one of the great experiences of my life because it was the first time I'd been involved in the coaching of an elite team from another rugby culture. You could not compare my work with Tokai University, Suntory and that fleeting stint with Japan in 1996 to working with the Boks in 2007. It was enlightening and, on my return to Japan and with England, I relied on some of the fundamental lessons learnt from my time with South Africa. It made me accept that there are certain characteristics unique to every rugby-playing country. The Springboks are intuitively conservative and defence minded. If you study the history of games between South Africa and New Zealand you know that every time the Springboks get under the pump they go back to their old style of 'Let's put the ball up in the air . . . let's run hard at them . . . let's smash these *okes* [which I learnt is Afrikaans for blokes].' But Jake and I could discuss with them that the important stuff is what happens after you revert to an old habit.

Jake was very smart and we shared a view that everything boiled down to the World Cup. He was willing to take a few hits along the way to peak in the biggest tournament of them all. I admired that courage because even when he was getting heat during the Tri Nations, he only chose his best team once. They won that game but he held them back for the World Cup.

As a consequence, he became unbelievably nervous as we approached the tournament. John Smit and I saw it as our role to ensure his contributions to the team were positive.

I began to understand how much Jake was struggling during our opening match at Parc des Princes in Paris on 9 September 2007. John admitted later that the players also felt suddenly anxious as they lined up against Samoa. They were taken aback by the size of the Samoans – they had some absolute monsters in their pack.

For the first 20 minutes the Samoans beasted us around the park. They were 7–0 up and it was such a physical contest that we looked to be wilting.

'What the hell is going on here?' Jake muttered.

'Relax, Jake,' I said. 'The storm will blow over. They're big guys and they can't play at this intensity much longer. We just need to keep our composure.'

We were fortunate that John, who is such an exceptional captain, told his bewildered players the exact same thing down on the pitch.

The storm passed and we ran out easy winners. We scored eight tries, four of them by Bryan Habana, and the final score was 59–7.

With Jake seeking my input, my World Cup experience helped manage the pace of the team through the tournament, especially during the pool games. After Samoa, we drilled England before we eased back and beat Tonga, a little too narrowly, 30–25, before putting 64 points on a weak USA team.

It was interesting because it was probably the most defensive tournament of all the World Cups we've had. Not a lot of rugby was played. It was dominated by slow play, committed defences and the boot. Since 2003, New Zealand had been, by far, the best team. They looked miles ahead of everyone. Australia were looking reasonably sharp on the surface, but I knew the players and I knew the signs. The scrum and forward play that had let us down in 2005 hadn't been fixed. I knew they would offer a limited challenge. The Springboks weren't in consideration – until the Boks' first 40 minutes against England. That made everyone take serious note.

The tournament also opened up beautifully for South Africa. After France, the hosts, had been shocked by Argentina in the opening match of the World Cup, our route was clear. You could not have had a better run-in to a World Cup final. The only problem was that I was not happy.

On Saturday 29 September we were in Marseille, preparing to play the USA in our final pool game just down the road in Montpellier. We were staying in one of those old-style hotels, where the rooms are connected like flats, and you could hear the noise of all the televisions blaring out. Everyone was watching Wales v Fiji in the final Pool B game. The winner would qualify as group runners-up and play South Africa in the quarter-finals. We assumed it would be Wales.

I had done all my analysis work on Wales and so I was fuming just as the Boks were cheering wildly when Fiji shocked us all by winning 38–34 with a try in the third last minute.

I obviously redid my video analysis but, nevertheless, in the quarter-finals, South Africa nearly lost to Fiji. It was a strange match because after 56 minutes we had scored three tries and led 20–6. Fiji were also down to 14 men as Seru Rabeni had been sent to the sin bin. Complacency took hold and, within three minutes, the electric Fijians had scored two converted tries. Suddenly the score was locked at 20–20 after 59 minutes. We were in serious danger of losing.

It was a beautiful sunny day and the predominantly French crowd were totally into the game and supporting Fiji. The momentum had swung horribly in just a few minutes. Every pass the Fijians threw stuck, and they were playing with sudden belief. The Boks looked as if they could go down in a World Cup shock.

It took a masterclass of leadership to steady a sinking ship. John gathered the team around him and spoke with brilliant clarity. 'Right boys. This is pretty simple. We need to play everything in their half from now on and we maul everything.'

That sounds so simplistic, but it was an inspired intervention from John. He helped the reeling Boks get back onto familiar territory where our pack would take charge. As long as Fiji were starved of possession by the rumbling South African forwards, there would be an easy winner. John was right and we strangled the game. Juan Smith and Butch James scored late tries while Percy Montgomery added a penalty and two conversions. South Africa won 37–20 but the score masked the truth that, but for John's calming influence, we could have blown it.

The semi-final was less nervy. I knew we just needed to target Agustín Pichot, Argentina's talismanic scrum half, who led their kicking game. If we could smother Pichot, the Pumas lacked an alternative strategy. We did exactly that and won 37–13.

South Africa were into their second World Cup final. This would also be my second final in a row.

A player revolt against their coach Brian Ashton had forced changes in the England team, and they shocked everyone by beating Australia in the quarter-finals in Marseille. England smashed the Wallabies at the scrums and breakdown. They won 12–10, with Jonny Wilkinson, having been injured for most of the previous four years, kicking all four penalties.

There was an even greater shock later that night in Cardiff, as the French continued to haunt the All Blacks in the World Cup. Having beaten them in 1999 at Twickenham, they came from behind again to stun New Zealand 20–18.

England, back in familiar territory, played the semi-final in Paris and just squeaked past the hosts. At 9–8 down with five minutes on the clock, Wilkinson came to their rescue with a late penalty and then a drop goal to seal a 14–9 victory and another World Cup final.

As Jake White's number two, my primary task in the week of the final was to reassure the Springbok coach and his team. Some of the leading players have since spoken about their doubts around Jake in that last week. It's a really tough position and Jake's nerves were exacerbated by the fact that England had come back from the dead.

Logically, the way in which we had crushed England just five weeks and a day earlier should have built our confidence. But even hardened and experienced rugby men get nervous when the stakes are so high. Were England ready to complete the most surprising World Cup comeback of all? They had certainly become much more organized and compact, and played to their core strengths of forward power and Wilkinson's boot. But I knew the Boks were better than them on all fronts. We were well structured, highly efficient, and Montgomery's place-kicking had proved even more accurate than Wilkinson's. Habana and Du Preez also brought a spark to our backline which England lacked, as Jason Robinson was on his last legs in his final match as a rugby player.

From where I stood, at his side, I thought Jake stepped up to the plate and coached really well in that final week. His nerves were natural, but he overcame them when it mattered, out on the training field and in the key team meetings. He selected well, thought clearly and did his job. Jake and the players clashed over minor matters because they were all tense. But that's why I had been brought in – to give technical insights, but also to act as a buffer and to smooth away any last-minute doubts.

It was still an eye-opener for the Boks when the entire squad was compelled to be at the main media conference. There were at least 300 journalists and 150 cameras and the boys suddenly knew that this was no ordinary week. The players were fine but Jake started seeing potential speed bumps at every new corner. Even a minor distraction, like a player's wife arriving at the hotel, became an issue for Jake. I had to quietly remind him that the players were fine and our role was to focus on winning the World Cup.

He's a very good coach, with strong insights into the game, but the players sometimes turned to me as the game came close. I was able to help them by being much more chilled out and approachable. I also could go over the game plan in calm detail. The Boks felt reassured. They felt ready.

The World Cup final on 20 October 2007 was an even less attractive game than the taut and tense battle from four years before. A couple of tries were scored in 2003, but South Africa and England fought out a try-less grind on a chilly autumn evening in Paris. To the neutral, the rugby probably seemed cold and clinical, shaped by pragmatism from both sides, but Jake and I liked the way the match unfolded. We were a step ahead, and in control, while Matfield and Botha were majestic in the lineouts. It felt to me as if we didn't need to do too much to win the game. England had to find a spark to knock us off kilter and I doubted they had it. We just needed to play tough, conservative rugby and hold them in the scrum. They could have gained an advantage in the set piece, but we maintained parity. Montgomery was also deadly with the boot and he kicked all three penalties to take us into the break with a 9–3 cushion.

England thought they had made a sensational breakthrough early in the second half. Mathew Tait cut through our previously impregnable defence with a slashing run which seemed to set up Mark Cueto for a try as the winger plunged towards the corner. But Danie Rossouw produced the tackle of the tournament. It was outstanding defence from our number 8, and all the more impressive when you remember that a man who weighs 120 kilograms is not meant to move so fast. Rossouw tackled Cueto just as he dived for the line. England's players and supporters were convinced he had scored; the South Africans were sure Rossouw had forced him into touch.

It was touch-and-go and it took the video referee, Stuart Dickinson, a couple of minutes to replay the footage over and over again. Eventually, he ruled that Cueto had put a fraction of a foot into touch. The try was disallowed, but England had the small consolation of a penalty for an infringement earlier in the move. Wilkinson kicked it. Rather than leading 10–9, England trailed 9–6.

If Rossouw had not made that tackle and England had scored a try then perhaps the game would have changed. South Africa might have buckled. But I still think the Springboks would have found a way to win.

Three more penalties were kicked and, crucially, two of them were for South Africa. After an hour the Boks were ahead 15–9 and we shut England down. The score did not change for the rest of the game because we played smart, percentage rugby. It was not a game to live long in the memory of the casual fan. But I admired the way the Boks had played so intelligently and efficiently. And I was thrilled for the men to whom I had become so close in such a short time. They were world champions.

Fourie du Preez has gone on to record to say that South Africa would not have won the World Cup without me. That's very generous of him, but I believe that the Boks would have still become world champions. I saw my contribution as being similar to a guy who comes in after a new house has been built and he takes care of the small defects in a very solid structure – sorting out a minor issue here or there and adding a coat of paint.

The 2007 World Cup, in coaching terms, belongs to Jake White. He spent three hard years, in the toughest job in world rugby, building a team from players he had nurtured since junior level. He came through so many challenges to reach the very summit of the game. I hope I made his job easier in the 13 weeks I was there – but the brevity of my stay is a reminder not to overplay my impact.

I was touched, however, by the solidarity the squad showed towards me. At the World Cup final dinner they refused to wear their Springboks blazers because, as a non-South African, I had not been given one by the union. They removed their treasured green-and-gold jackets. It was a powerful gesture of gratitude from the new world champions.

Bryan Habana was also incredibly kind to me. About a month later, once I had settled into my new job at Saracens, a huge package arrived. I could not work out what it might be and so, with some amusement, I opened the parcel. It did not take long to see Bryan's generosity. He had framed his World Cup blazer, and surrounded it with photographs of us all together, as a big thank-you for the small part I had played in South Africa's success.

As part of the official coaching team I had been awarded a World Cup-winner's medal after the game. It certainly made me feel like I belonged to the victorious squad and it wiped away some of the pain from 2003. The memories matter more than the medal – which I've left behind in Cape Town. The pictures I carry around in my head of those 13 weeks with such an impressive group of men will always be more vivid than a shiny gold medal.

South Africa gave me three months of respite in a testing five years. For the rest of that time, I struggled to find any joy in my work. From December 2003 to the week before Christmas in

2008, it was a grind. That's appalling when you consider how much I love coaching. My last two years with the Wallabies had been grim. A six-week interlude as a consultant at Saracens had been my only buffer between being fired by Australia and then plunging into the mistake of coaching the Reds. The fun and harmony I experienced with the Springboks was then sucked dry by the next 14 months of grinding away on my return to Saracens. I hated my second spell in English club rugby.

I had arrived in England full of hope and even excitement in November 2007. Rejuvenated by the World Cup, I was set to resume my great English adventure with Saracens, a club with a leadership and playing group I admired. I had high hopes, even though I would be the general manager and do little of the day-to-day coaching. In my previous short stint at the club I had come away feeling optimistic about Saracens and the state of English rugby. On my departure I had argued strongly to Mark Sinderberry and Nigel Wray that Alan Gaffney, an old mate of mine from Randwick, was the right man to be head coach.

On my return, Alan was still head coach and I concentrated on managerial issues as well as finding new players. Stepping back into Premiership rugby, I was stunned by the shockingly low standards. The game had gone backwards in England. During my first stint at Sarries I didn't think the standards were too flash; but it had become much worse. There are some outstanding clubs in England now, Saracens being the best of them, but they had a long way to go a dozen years ago.

Even today, when I watch so much English club rugby, I often wonder: 'Is it ever going to change?' Whether it's cultural, the length of the season, the weather, the different competitions or the number of games, the widespread lack of imagination and skill is an anchor that the competition seems unable to lift. Friends often ask me if I get disheartened when I am watching such stodgy games week after week. I always say, honestly, that I don't. It's not my job to change English club rugby and, after all these years, it's clear that this is the kind of game the clubs and their supporters like. I let them get with on it. But, when working as a general manager at Saracens, and not even coaching, the Premiership slog took the joy out of the game.

Of course, there are many very special people in English club rugby, and that first year had some highlights. Sarries did not do well on the field, finishing eighth out of 12 teams. But behind the scenes we began to lay the foundations for a subsequent revolution at the club.

When I had been at Saracens previously, I had seen that they were a team without leadership. They lacked a talisman on the pitch. So one of my first tasks was to find a player who could change and galvanize the club by the example he set. All my research pointed in the direction of Steve Borthwick at Bath. The lock forward and new England captain was soon to be out of contract and so I went to see him in Bath. He had been at the Rec for ten years and all my reports suggested that, apart from being very intelligent, he was loyal and dedicated. His character was said to be exemplary.

When I sat down with Steve it was clear that everything I had heard was true. He was also more thorough and organized than any rugby player I had ever met. Steve made it clear that, at the age of 27, he wanted to improve. His next move would be his last as a player and so he wanted to ensure he got everything right. He arrived at the meeting with a large notepad, filled with detailed questions. Before I could even begin to sell the idea of Saracens to him, he quizzed me hard.

'Aren't I supposed to be the one doing the interview here?' I said wryly.

In truth, I loved the fact that he was so searching in his questions. He also exuded an integrity and diligence, which explains why, in subsequent years, I appointed Steve as my number two and forwards coach with both Japan and England. It also became plain to me that he was the exact player I needed to begin changing the culture of the club. My time at Saracens was soon over but Steve spent six outstanding years at the club from 2008 to 2014.

The difference between Saracens in 2008 and 2019 is vast. Many people have contributed hugely to their transformation and their current position as the powerhouse of European rugby. But no one did more than Steve to change the approach of the players and ensure that they took responsibility for the direction and ethos of Saracens.

There were other deeply impressive men at Saracens. Andy Farrell had just arrived at the club when I did my first consultancy stint. He had gravitas and, in 2008, I saw more of the qualities that had made him one of the greatest rugby league players of all time. Andy is well organized, a leader and an astute thinker. While his career at Saracens was badly affected by injury, I encouraged him to do some coaching as he recovered. He is steeped in rugby league and he was then adjusting to a new code – but it was obvious that he would have a significant impact in union. So I have been unsurprised by his subsequent success and the fact that, from 2020, he will be Ireland's head coach.

Owen Farrell, Andy's son, and England captain from 2018, also stood out. I was Saracens' new head coach, having swapped roles with Riff (Alan Gaffney) at the start of a new season. Owen made his debut in a cup game against Llanelli having just turned 17. From day one, he was class. Apart from his talent, and despite being a teenager, he already had a big voice and a real presence on the field. Owen was not afraid of barking out instructions to men who were ten or more years older than him. He and his dad were proud of their home town of Wigan in the north of England, and of their heritage in the working-class game of rugby league. They were different to many of the other players, who'd enjoyed the privileges of the English private school system. There remains much to do to grow and promote the game in the north. Mark Wilson is the latest world-class player to come out of the north and he really had to work hard to be noticed.

Owen came from a very promising academy group at Saracens, which included George Kruis, Jamie George, Jackson Wray and Will Fraser. All of them went on to make an impact in the first team and, in the case of George and Jamie, play for England. So there was plenty to celebrate at Saracens and I was just getting into the swing of the second season when life changed.

Mark Sinderberry, the chief executive, called to ask if he could drop by my office. He walked in with this other bloke I had never seen in my life. His name was Edward Griffiths. He had been part of South Africa's management team when the Springboks won the 1995 World Cup. Mark got down to business quickly. They'd had a board meeting the previous night and he would be moving on. Mark didn't look very happy, but he gestured to Griffiths and said, 'This is the new CEO.'

The more I got to know Griffiths, the more he reminded me of John O'Neill. They're both brilliant operators but not the sort of people with whom I have a natural affinity. The first words Griffiths said to me were very peculiar: 'If you don't want me to be the CEO, I won't be the CEO.' He knew I was in no position to make that decision and that he had been appointed by the new Saracens board, as the club had just been taken over by a South African consortium. I shrugged and waited for him to continue – which he did at great length. Griffiths was one of those blokes who says, over and over again, that they're not going to interfere with the rugby side of the club while soon proving that this is exactly what they plan on doing.

While I tried to keep an open mind, I was determined that, after my experience at the Wallabies, I would never work again for a CEO I didn't trust. By Christmas it was clear that the leadership of Edward Griffiths was not for me and I made my decision to leave at the end of the season. But I didn't last. I thought the way the new regime treated the players was appalling. Once Griffiths had his feet under the desk, he arranged a series of individual meetings with squad members on a Monday afternoon to let 20 players know whether or not they were being kept on or sacked. From my perspective it was bad because I was meant to be preparing them for a game that Saturday.

I saw good men looking desolate after their contracts had been terminated. Chris Jack, the former All Black lock, Glen Jackson, another New Zealander and the club's leading points scorer, and Census Johnston, the Samoan prop, were among the 15 players who were culled.

Mosese Rauluni, the Fijian half back, was another of those about to be axed. His close friend Kameli Ratuvou, the wing who was also from Fiji, was on the list the club wanted to keep. But Kameli said, 'I'm not staying unless Mosese stays.' So Mosese got called back in and his contract was reactivated. The players and I retreated to the pub. We were all upset. It was then that I decided to leave immediately. I told Saracens I wanted out in February 2009.

Hiroko and I had already decided we would go back to Japan. As luck would have it, Suntory were having problems of their own. They sent over a small delegation to meet me and asked if I would return to take over. Professionally it was a big step back, but personally it was the right move. We had jumped around so much as a family and we needed some stability. It was fine for me to do various jobs in different countries, but it was hard on the people I loved most. Chelsea was 14 and she had three years left of senior school. She had gone to a good school in England, which she loved, but we needed to give her a settled period. It was vital for her and for us as a family to be in one place for the next three years. We knew there was also an excellent American international school that Chelsea could attend in Japan. We needed to look after her rather than think about my career.

I had changed as a father. In the past I had made some poor decisions. I wanted Chelsea to be tough like me and I was far too hard on her. Whenever she was upset, I would just tell her to shrug it off and move on. It took me a while to understand that she was not the same as me and that I needed to soften my approach. I remember that, when I was with the Reds, we went up to the Gold Coast. We were playing tennis on a hot day and, aged about 12, she was struggling. I urged her to keep going. I said,

'C'mon, Chels, let's play another set.' She got a bit upset but we kept playing and she ended up getting heatstroke. I was mortified. She was still only a girl and it was wrong to be so hard on her. I think that softening actually benefited my coaching because I was much more sensitive to younger players after that incident.

Just before I left Saracens, and not wanting there to be any ill will, I sat down with Dominic Silvester, who owned a 10 per cent stake in the club. He was a lovely bloke and we got on well. 'You know, Eddie,' he said, 'this is not a great decision for your career. Japan is a backwater of world rugby.'

'Yeah,' I said, 'but I need to do this for my family. It's about time I put them first.'

11

THE MAKING OF JAPAN

After so many poor decisions, frustrations and disappointments, I simply wanted to enjoy coaching again. I loved Suntory; and I still do. The company and club will always be a part of my life and I am grateful for their support. But I also had another plan. I wanted to coach Japan. I had watched them closely and seen how they had repeatedly tried, and failed, to play rugby like New Zealand. I knew they would be successful if they played the game in a distinctively Japanese way. They needed to back themselves and trust their own character. Suntory would be the perfect place for me to begin the experiment – as they had similar problems to Japan. They had a small pack and were not great athletes. They needed to find a new way to be effective because they had not won a trophy for nine years.

I made some simple changes to the culture of the club. Many of the players were lazy and felt an entitlement to play for Suntory – a prestigious company in Japan. Yet the more successful teams were linked to factory-based companies. Their players had the same hard-working approach. In contrast, some of our boys were arrogant and complacent.

I set a new vision for the club. We would become the most aggressive attacking team in Japan and we would not kick the ball. We lost the first three games in preseason, playing 12 versus 12 on a full-size field to make it harder for the boys. Slowly, our fitness and toughness improved.

Our B team played a match on a Wednesday, and they were

under instructions to follow this new style of rugby. We were behind at half-time but I told them to stick at it. In the second half it suddenly clicked and we won by 50 points. It felt like a turning point for the club. In the next game the first team won by 70 points and, from then on, we started to fly.

We improved the spirit of the club. The previous coach had not been a drinker and the players had given up socializing. I insisted that, after every game, we all went to a bar in Tokyo and had a drink together for an hour. This had always been part of the Suntory culture in previous years and I was keen to revive the camaraderie that is so important in successful rugby teams. It worked because we had some great characters at Suntory – including George Gregan, who was in his second year at the club.

I had paved the way for George to join Suntory. At first he had been shocked when I had called him to suggest that he finish his career in Japan, even though I was still based at Saracens. But George loved his time in Japan and he was, yet again, a great asset to me. We turned the club around very quickly. After we were hammered 30–0 in preseason to Toshiba, our old rivals and a dominant force in Japanese rugby, we did not lose to them again in my years at Suntory.

It was a really happy time for me and the club. I didn't mind that I was out of first-class rugby. I even got used to rugby's low profile in Japan. Almost all our supporters were Suntory employees. It reminded me of the distinction I often made when considering football and rugby. I had always been struck by the feeling that football fans love their team while rugby fans love the game. In Japan it was the opposite. The fans loved their company team but they didn't have an affinity for the game.

Suntory moved up a couple of levels when we signed George Smith and Fourie du Preez. George was at Toulon when I went out to meet him with our Japanese head of rugby. I don't think he was too impressed because George had taken the opportunity to enjoy an off season and was not in peak condition. We met after a game and the sweat poured off him. I managed to convince my

Japanese boss that, beneath the layers of poor conditioning, we had a champion rugby player who could be an inspiration once he was back in shape. My boss looked sceptical but trusted my judgement.

George was easy to persuade. He wasn't enjoying France and he was looking for a fresh start. It helped that George Gregan had been at Suntory. George Smith is fiercely loyal and respectful. I remember being in the Brumbies' changing room after we won the 2001 final. As a mark of respect to Brett Robinson, the team's first captain who had retired after the devastating loss to the Crusaders the year before, the players pooled the money to fly him back from Oxford so he could attend the game. In the shed, with all the yelling and cheering and crying going on, George Smith took off his prized number 7 jersey, walked quietly over to Robbo and handed it to him saying, 'Here, have this. It's yours. You deserve it.'

There was also the time at the Stade de France in 2000 – after his debut against France when he stunned the rugby world with a 'man-of-the-match' performance. After the game, the media were clamouring to speak to him. One of the Australian journalists, Peter Jenkins, was among those keen to talk to him. When George asked his name and he said 'Peter Jenkins', our magnificent flanker turned his back and walked off. George knew that Jenkins had led the media's unjustified and savage assault on the Brumbies' reputation and those of the Cape Town Five. Jenkins had also relentlessly criticized his captain, George Gregan. George Smith wasn't having a bar of Jenkins. That says everything you need to know about George Smith and his commitment to his teammates.

George played brilliantly for Suntory. He started working at 100 per cent and he was great with the players. You would never think that George is one of the greatest flankers in history. He is humble, down to earth, and ready to stay late after training to work with individual players. George is also a bit of a drinker and so our post-game time in the Tokyo bar suited him.

In our first season we lost the league final to Panasonic, coached by Robbie Deans, but won Japanese rugby's equivalent of the FA Cup. Once Fourie joined us, we won the double. Fourie had heard that George Gregan was leaving and called to ask if he could join the club. It was a bold move by Fourie. At 29 years of age he was the best scrum half in the world. Fourie remained as driven as ever. He wanted to keep playing for South Africa but felt he and his family needed to have a complete break. He was a genuine superstar on the streets of Pretoria so the more anonymous life in Tokyo appealed.

Once we had our running game sorted, we needed to develop a kicking game. Fourie was a canny box-kicker and I knew he would add a new dimension to our rugby. With Fourie and George Smith in the team, it was like having two coaches on the field.

Fourie is a more serious character than George and he had never lived outside of Pretoria. But he embraced life in Japan. Our families lived in the same apartment block, right in the centre of Tokyo, and so we became close. Fourie learnt Japanese, and he and I went out for lunch every other week so we could talk rugby.

Danie Rossouw, who had also played for the Bulls and the 2007 World Cup-winning Springboks, joined us at Suntory. His time in Japan was less successful because he's a big unit and the game didn't suit him. But Danie's a good guy and he tried really hard.

Fourie and George Smith drove the team and, rather than just being a very good outfit, we developed into an almost unbeatable force. I had learnt from my Japanese assistant coaches, and from spending time in the country, that our real strength lay in the local players. If the Japanese boys felt that they were being dominated by foreigners, it would not work. It might seem fine on the surface but, deep down, they would not put in the same effort.

We were captained by Takemoto Juntaro, a small Japanese bloke, who was our number 8. Despite being only five foot eight, Takemoto was a very good player who trained hard, set a good example for the boys, led them well and provided the essential link between our star foreign internationals and the Japanese core. George Gregan and Fourie were always clever enough to rely on Takemoto. Rather than barking out orders, they allowed Takemoto to share their thoughts with the squad. It helped maintain the very Japanese identity of the club which was critical to our success. We were powered by foreigners – in the form of me, Gregan, Smith and Du Preez – but Takemoto made sure Suntory always felt very Japanese.

I took that same approach when coaching Japan. I had to make sure that the Japanese players felt as if they owned the team. The foreign boys had to earn the right to play for Japan – and to understand the importance of that Japanese essence. I learnt a lot about Japanese sport, and culture, from reading Robert Whiting's classic book *You've Gotta Have Wa*. It's an American writer's take on Japanese baseball in the 1980s. The book flows with so many sharp insights into the sport in Japan, often seen through the eyes of the American imports he follows, and key differences emerge between the contrasting cultures. Unlike the Americans, who prize individuality, the Japanese revere the team, and the concept of '*wa*', meaning 'group harmony'. Whiting quotes the Japanese saying: 'The nail that sticks out gets hammered down.' In other words, no individual can ever stand above the team.

Wa is about sacrifice and hard work as well as team unity and collective harmony. These ideals align with the ethos of rugby. So I could never understand why the Japanese weren't good at rugby. Rugby is not about superstars. It has always been a team game for all shapes and sizes who work together as a seamless unit.

Yet Japan is complex. My Japanese was never more than functional, so I developed other skills. I became much better at reading people because, generally, you are dealing with players who do not show emotion and feel unable to speak to you freely. I became quite skilled in reading the meaning of the unsaid and then, with the help of Takemoto and other Japanese leaders in the team, getting to the heart of a situation with specific players.

We played some beautiful rugby and won the league by beating Panasonic in the final. Under Deans they played Crusaders-style rugby, but we were too fast and aggressive. That victory gave me great pleasure and I sent a video to Bob Dwyer back in Australia.

Bob spoke effusively about our speed of movement and quick passing and complimented the alignment of our play. We had the flat backline that Cyril Towers and Bob had drummed into us at Matraville High and Randwick. He spoke about how our rugby at Suntory had blossomed – and made a typical Bob joke about Japan being a good place to blossom. Bob believed I had become too structured at the Brumbies and he loved this reversion to the Randwick Way. I felt it just proved I could coach differently in divergent cultures and with players of varying abilities. Our Brumbies style was perfect for the Super 12 at the start of a new century while this fast and fluid rugby was perfect for Suntory – and Japan.

In 2012, after almost three happy years with Suntory, I was asked to become Japan's national coach. I had regained all my confidence and enthusiasm – which had been dented by those frustrating years at the Wallabies, the Reds and Saracens – and felt ready to do something dramatic during the three years before the World Cup.

Japan also offered an invaluable opportunity to consider all that my parents, and especially my mother, had endured in the past. I was coaching Suntory when my mum gave me and my sisters David Guterson's *Snow Falling on Cedars* – that beautiful but often very sad book about the racism that Japanese-American people suffered in the wake of the Second World War.

I knew the basic story of how my mum, as a girl, had been sent to an internment camp with her own mother in California, while her father had been sent to Arkansas. As Chelsea was 16 when I read Guterson's novel, it meant she was only a year younger than my mum had been when she'd been separated from her dad. I imagined how impossibly hard I would find it if I could not see Chelsea for four years.

I could understand why my grandfather had moved the whole family back to Japan after the war. He had been scarred by his experiences in the United States. In the humid and miserable swamplands of Arkansas, my grandfather and his fellow prisoners had been made to drain the swamps while dealing with the embedded racism of America's southern states. The Jim Crow racial laws, which discriminated harshly against black people, spilled over into anti-Japanese sentiment.

In 1943, the Arkansas state legislature passed the Alien Land Act 'to prohibit any Japanese, citizen or alien, from purchasing or owning land in Arkansas.' That prejudice was seen also in handmade signs hanging from porches: *JAPS KEEP MOVING: This Is A White Man's Neighborhood*, and *JAPS KEEP OUT: You Are Not Wanted*.

The last Japanese internment camp was closed in March 1946, after an earlier Supreme Court ruling in the case of Endo v The United States. Mitsuye Endo, the daughter of Japanese immigrants from Sacramento, just like my mother, refused the government offer to free her. Filing a writ of habeas corpus, and using her own circumstances to test the legality of the US government's incarceration of Japanese-Americans, Endo's lawyers proved she was a practising Christian who had been born in California and had never been to Japan. She spoke only English and her brother served in the US Army.

In an emphatic ruling, the Supreme Court declared that the War Relocation Authority 'has no authority to subject citizens who are concededly loyal to its leave procedure.' The judicial statement was made a day after Franklin D. Roosevelt declared the camps would close – giving the president a chance to make his announcement first.

Of course the pain did not end there. My mother's family

returned to Japan and, because she sounded like an American, one form of prejudice replaced another.

My mother, by then, was in love with my dad, an Australian soldier in Japan. I learnt that the US government was conciliatory towards their men; and the War Brides Act of 1945 meant that around 35,000 young Japanese women entered the US with their new husbands. No such concessions were made in Australia. It took years before Australian soldiers could return home with their Japanese wives.

The wartime generation were stoic, regarding it as self-indulgent and pointless to rehash the pain of war. But my respect for my parents intensified once I was living permanently in Japan. I had time to reflect on all they had done to give my sisters and me such fortunate lives.

Mum and Dad came over twice to see me, Hiroko and Chelsea while I was at Suntory. It was the first time either of them had been back to Japan since leaving in the 1950s. My mother still had a family house in Hiroshima, but the connection with Japan had lessened as she had only a few relatives and friends left in the country. I remember Mum and Dad trying to find the house where they had lived together in Tokyo as a young married couple. It is now one of the most affluent areas of the city and they could not locate it; Tokyo had changed so much in 60 years. That was a bit of a disappointment, but you could tell how happy they were to be walking around the city again. Even though they made little fuss about it, I was proud to have become the national coach of both Australia and, now, Japan, my mother's homeland.

Coaching the Japanese rugby union team presented the most fascinating challenge of my career. They called themselves 'The Brave Blossoms'. To me that absurd nickname said: 'You go out there, boys, and try your best. As long as you do that, and score a few points at the end of the game, everyone will be happy.' I was never going to accept that mentality.

I was more interested in the business of technology and the fact that the Japanese had long been great inventors. Yet in rugby we were shameless copiers. I wanted to change that. We needed to develop a new way for the Japanese national team and we created the template with Suntory. Japan had small players, so we had to play quick and aggressive rugby. We needed to be super-fit and our set piece had to be incredibly smart.

A week after I took over, in May 2012, Japan's under-20s played Wales's under-20s. They lost 119–7. I gathered all the development coaches together the following day. I said: 'We're a country of 120 million. Wales are a country of three million. How can a vast country get beaten so horribly by a tiny country? I want you to come back with the reasons.' I split them up into groups and they returned with three points.

1. We're not big enough.
2. We don't train hard enough.
3. We've got a farmer's mentality.

I obviously understood the first two, but I didn't have a clue about the third point. It was explained that, before the Second World War, 75 per cent of Japanese people grew rice for a living. They lived in rural villages where a dominant boss drove them hard as they had a quota of rice to grow. Anyone who rebelled or upset the production line would be kicked off the farm or out of the village and left to fend for themselves. So everyone toed the line and did what they were told. My development coaches told me that Japanese people, even in a society transformed by technology, had not shaken their farmer's mentality. They lived to please their boss and showed little to no instinct for leadership.

I didn't buy it. The Japanese had demonstrated extraordinary leadership in transforming their economy into a powerhouse in the wake of the devastation of two atomic bombs. So we needed to find and develop the essence of this leadership in our own squad. Clearly we also needed to train much harder to get fitter and stronger and to improve our rugby skills.

My backup staff consisted of just two Australians – Scott Wisemantel and John Pryor. I looked after the scrum, the line-out, general attack and general defence. Wisey focused on the backs' lines of attack. JP looked after our strength and conditioning. It was a complex task for John because if you run harder and longer you strip away muscle. But we needed to put on muscle – especially among our forwards. John is brilliant and he studied hard. He used a lot of strength-and-conditioning ideas pioneered by Frans Bosch, a Dutch biomechanist, who talks about differential systems which help the body organize itself so muscle mass can be added at the same time that endurance and explosive fitness are intensified.

The hardest task was to break the farmer's mentality. Time and again we created opportunities for the players to lead. Once the referee's whistle blew, they couldn't rely on me, Wisey and JP. They had to find leaders amongst themselves. So I put them in unusual situations.

We would set up secret cameras in a room, call a meeting and not turn up. From a distance we would watch how they reacted. In another little trick we would tell them to wait at a certain spot so that they could be picked up by the team bus. I would make sure that the team bus never left the garage. It was interesting to watch them milling around, not knowing what to do. Eventually one or two of the more resourceful guys took charge. They showed the leadership we needed.

I started to spread my plans for the team through these emerging leaders. Just as at Suntory, the Japanese players had to own the plans. The goal was to lift Japan into the top ten of world rugby. At the time, Japan was ranked 16th. Rugby tradition said that the Six Nations and the Tri Nations occupy nine of those places. Argentina were far stronger than Italy and so the top ten seemed locked down – even before you considered the credentials of more rugby-orientated island nations like Fiji,

Samoa and Tonga. But I believed that Japan could crack the leading ten nations and oust Italy and reach the quarter-finals of the 2015 World Cup.

My predecessor as Japan coach, New Zealand's John Kirwan, favoured foreign players in his selections. He included plenty of New Zealand- and Pacific Island-born players. I headed in the opposite direction. I wanted a Japanese-driven team, and the only foreigner I would consider initially was Michael Leitch – who spoke better Japanese than some of the local boys in the squad. Michael was a Kiwi but he had lived in Japan since he was 15. I liked him and sensed he would become a dominant leader. But he had been assimilated so completely that he was too Japanese for my liking. He was too passive when I really needed him to show the bark and bite of a Kiwi mongrel.

We had easy victories in a poor Asian Five Nations Cup in April and May 2012. Kazakhstan, the United Arab Emirates, Korea and Hong Kong were dispatched as we scored 312 points, conceding just 36, in those four games. Narrow losses to Fiji, Tonga and Samoa in the Pacific Nations Cup gave us a better indication of our progress. Our transition to a Japanese style was in its earliest days and the change was slow. I stuck with a pure Japanese team to make sure everyone understood I was serious. At the same time, I knew that eventually we would need the bulk and experience of a few select foreign players. I wanted the Japanese to see that we required a blend which would be led by the local players.

But I had not been expecting a disaster when we played the French Barbarians straight after the Pacific tournament. We had arranged to play two matches against the visitors. The first was on Wednesday, 20 June 2012 in Tokyo. We had lost 16–14 to Samoa just three days earlier and so I changed the team. A local website, meanwhile, suggested that, 'Rumour had it that the Barbarians, who arrived on Saturday, had mapped every bar in Roppongi and would tire in the second half.'

Before the break we were abysmal. We allowed a decent

French team to look like world-beaters as they blasted huge holes in our defence and scored their first try after just two minutes. My players looked as though they were waving them through. We looked weak and gutless and lucky to be just 32–7 down at the break. After I gave them a severe pull-through at half-time, Japan showed more spirit and, as predicted, the Barbarians eased off.

A match report summed up the problems with our mindset. 'In the end, Japan won the second half and ended up losing honourably 21–40. Let's see if the Cherry Boys can bounce back for the return leg on Sunday and give the French a proper fight. It would help, of course, if the audience would cheer their boys on with more than polite tennis applause.'

I was sick of the lack of fight, the politeness and the complacency. It dishonoured Japan. We would only fire up once the game was well and truly lost. It was ridiculous. I had tried the softly, softly approach and it wasn't working. I was now furious and, at the subsequent press conference, I lost my rag.

'It was a really poor performance by us,' I said. 'We showed no fight. Basically, in the first half, the French Barbarians did what they wanted. We were completely outplayed in the set piece and I was really disappointed with the players' attitudes. We'll have a real rethink on selection and the players showed that they probably don't want to play for Japan. We have young guys who should've been out there smashing their players, so I yelled at them at half-time. They just don't want to win enough. They don't want to change enough. So I'm going to have to change the players . . . I want to apologize for the performance. I take full responsibility. But I guarantee I'm going to change things.'

My captain, Toshiaki Hirose, let slip a nervous laugh. I liked and respected Hirose, and we still meet up for a coffee whenever I am back in Japan, but that set me off. It also gave me the chance to make a calculated point. I decided to crank up the stakes in an icy attack on the complacency of Japanese rugby.

'It's not funny,' I said before, after a loaded pause, repeating myself. 'It's not funny. That's the problem with Japanese rugby. They're not serious about winning. If we want to win we've got to go out and physically smash people. Some players are never going to play for Japan again – unless they change, unless they grow up. What are we going to do with Japanese rugby? Do you want to carry on like this, or do you want to go down the path of choosing a side half-full of New Zealanders?

'The players need to grow up, take responsibility. It's got to start happening quickly. We've only got three years till the World Cup. But we have no sense right now of what winning means. We've got to get a group of players quickly who do know.'

My expression turned stonier. 'I made a mistake. I tried to pick the best young players in Japan. I tried to develop them. Do you want me to resign now? I'm happy to take full responsibility for the defeat and the performance. It's my fault. It's my bad coaching. I will put six New Zealanders in there to win the game. Do you want me to do that?'

In the cloistered world of Japanese rugby, my words exploded like an earthquake. Everyone knew I was serious. There was fear but, far more importantly, there was clarity. Any future player for Japan needed to show commitment and courage, dedication and determination, from the very first to the very last minute. These were the non-negotiable basics of playing for Japan.

Four days later, in the return match against a much stronger French Barbarians, we lost more heavily, 51–18. The Barbarians were determined to send off their retiring hooker, William Servat, who had played 44 times for France, and former Test prop Lionel Faure, in style. They took an early lead but we were brave and fierce. Early in the second half, we trailed 17–11, but the class of the French took over. I didn't care about the score. I cared about the improved performance.

'Look,' I said, 'sometimes you get beaten by a better team. Most of the points they scored came from our turnovers. But the great thing is that we played against a superior team and actually got ourselves in a position to win the game. Unfortunately, we made some mistakes. But I'm really proud of the boys today. They competed as hard as they could. The score shows the reality of where we're at. We know clearly where we have to improve.'

I knew we had an opportunity to do something courageous, different and inventive. I just needed the right blend of players and management. I wanted to make sure that, amid the hard words, I could give them enough sunshine and water to grow. The skill of coaching is to create an environment that inspires players to reach for their best each and every day and to strive to continue to improve.

In November 2012, I took them to Europe. We beat Romania in Bucharest to record our first ever win on European soil. And then, the following week, we beat Georgia in Tbilisi. They were a good, tough side and it was a massive moment for us. They tore us apart at the start but we just hung in there and kept playing fast, aggressive rugby. I was thrilled when we scored a try from deep in our 22 in the second half. We then did something similar to win the game 25–22. I was so proud, and the boys were even prouder.

We ended my first year in charge of Japan by playing the French Barbarians for a third time. We met them in Le Havre, a week after Georgia, and we were even better. We were behind 26–20 at the break but we had pushed them hard. In the second half we again gave everything we had to the game. They won easily in the end but the transformation in our attitude from five months before was staggering.

The players returned home but I continued my European tour. From Le Havre I travelled to Paris. I was on the hunt for a new scrummaging coach and felt the answer for this Japanese team would be in France. I've always admired the way the French scrum. They are technically sound, physically strong and nice and aggressive. I met three potential recruits. The last was Marc Dal Maso, the former hooker who played 33 Tests for France. Marc was 45 when we met in December 2012 and his passion and knowledge of scrummaging was obvious.

Even if I could barely understand much of what he said, I could see the joy in his eyes. He tried to calm down and reached into his pocket to bring out a piece of paper. I noticed how badly his hands shook as he struggled with the paper. I wondered if he'd had a nervous breakdown. But as soon as he began to read his ideas out loud, from the notes he had scribbled, I was seriously impressed. Marc's attention to detail was outstanding. English might have been his second language, but French scrummaging was his first.

I offered him the job on the spot and he agreed just as quickly. It was only much later that he revealed to me he had Parkinson's disease. I told him not to worry because he had proved his worth. I warmed even more to Marc as he had a darkly comic way of referring to his Parkinson's.

'My new fiancée,' he calls it. 'She is not pretty, but she has helped me . . . I was lucky to meet her. Without this disease, I wouldn't have achieved what I have . . . She has taught me to take on every opportunity in life. She will be with me until the end – so I don't worry about the future. Why would I? We're all degenerating. Everyone is getting older, balder, slower. Maybe I've aged a little quicker but that's what happens when your fiancée breaks your balls every day.'

I admired Marc's attitude and loved his sheer craziness about scrummaging. We soon learnt that any place, any time, was good for Marc and a scrummaging clinic. I lost count of the number of hotel corridors where I would find him overseeing a full-tilt scrum between our props and hookers, with the poor old locks looking bemused at having been dragged into these impromptu sessions. He would also lie in the tunnel beneath the front rows to assess their binding technique or stand on top of our scrum and jump up and down, roaring like a mad artist.

Our scrum improved markedly. Marc was emphatic that, rather than being a disadvantage, the smaller Japanese frame helped produce far more supple scrummagers. He insisted that, when the scrum went down, the Japanese have the best body position in world rugby because they are much more flexible. It helped compensate for our lack of power compared to the French, the English, the Argentinian and the South African scrumming machines.

Marc gelled with Steve Borthwick, who transformed our line-out. My old Saracens captain kept popping back and forth between Hertfordshire and Tokyo, even though he was still playing. Steve was outstanding in finding new ways for our forwards to overcome their lack of height against some of the giant lineout men of world rugby. When he retired in 2014, I moved quickly to appoint him as Japan's full-time forwards coach. Apart from his precision and dedication, Steve bonded with all the forwards. They revered him. He also put me to shame because, even though I had lived in Japan far longer than him, he soon spoke the language more fluently than I ever would.

So much of our thinking was geared to the collective and, in Japanese terminology, we soon had our own form of *wa*. The team grew tighter and tighter. But I also took time to look after the more individualistic player – those 'nails' that usually get hammered down in Japanese sport. I wanted them to be part of our *wa*, but I didn't want to lose their maverick qualities.

Akihito Yamada was a really gifted wing. I would have backed him to sidestep his opposite number in a phone box. I always said he had ninja foot movement because, despite being so much bigger than most Japanese backs, he was fast and nimble. Before I even moved back to Japan, I had mentored him. I would see him whenever I went over to Suntory to do some holiday coaching. But he was a wild kid. Yamada had coloured hair and wore different coloured boots. At 23 he drove a Mercedes-Benz because he was a superstar. While he was at Keio University, which is one of the most prestigious in Japan, I organized for him to spend some time at the Waratahs Academy in Sydney because he was that good.

But Yamada lost his way. Honda, who were a poor team, signed him for a fortune (US $300,000), but his rugby faltered. He then moved to Panasonic, who were a good team. It was assumed that when I became national coach he would be one of my first picks. But his attitude was poor so I left him out. It was my way of giving the stuck-up nail a bit of a tap with the hammer. I brought him in soon after, but he didn't perform so I dropped him. He was in and out of the team because I was waiting for the message to sink in.

I knew he understood when I took a call from him. He put in an urgent request for me to have coffee with him. I met him in a cafe and when he walked in I nearly fell off my chair. He had a military haircut and I thought, 'Boy, we've got a change coming here.' We started to talk. Yamada began to cry and, between the tears, he told me how he wanted to play for Japan. He was now willing to put in the work. I told Yamada we would start with a clean slate. I picked him for the next squad and, while he was diligent and concentrated, I was delighted he had not lost his individuality.

Yamada would repay us in spades and at the 2015 World Cup, against Samoa, he scored an incredible try. He was up against Alesana Tuilagi and it looked as if he had no space. But, using his old phone-box sidestep, he left Tuilagi for dead and scored one of the tries of the tournament. Those players are so important, in any team, and I will always look for a way to include them. At international level you need players with this X-factor.

I also rediscovered some lost talent for Japan. Ayumu Goromaru, an excellent full back, had been left on the scrapheap after John Kirwan didn't pick him for the 2011 World Cup. The two men had clashed. Kirwan favoured a foreign-influenced Japanese squad and Goromaru, who is extremely patriotic, resented all these English speakers taking over his national team. I knew he was a bloody good rugby player, and a decent goal-kicker, and so I wanted him back in the fold. But, in the beginning, he was cold and distant. You could tell that he saw me as yet another foreign coach – and he hated foreigners. He sat in the back of team meetings and never said a word. He was a sullen presence.

I persevered and got the more amenable Japanese players to

talk to him on a one-to-one basis. They conveyed the sincerity of our mission. I wanted a predominantly Japanese team to play a distinctively Japanese brand of rugby. Slowly, he bought into this vision, and he was soon sitting in the front row at team meetings and asking excellent questions. The change was striking.

Less than two and a half years later, Ayumu Goromaru was named in the 2015 Rugby World Cup's team of the tournament.

I had also discovered the soul of my team. Michael Leitch, my new captain, was a leader every bit as inspirational as George Gregan or John Smit. When he was just 15 he had been invited to study in Sapporo on the northern island of Hokkaido on a student exchange programme. Michael, who is of mixed New Zealand and Fijian heritage, left Christchurch to live with a Japanese family. Rugby helped him find his way in Japan and, apart from the odd spell back in New Zealand, he spent much of the next 15 years in his adopted country. He was an excellent flanker, who played Super Rugby for the Chiefs. But his leadership qualities set him apart. Michael understood that I needed him to be more assertive. As he did, he became the perfect link between the team and me and we started moving in a new and exciting direction.

I began working the players harder than ever. The regime was necessarily brutal. If we were to achieve our goal of playing in a quarter-final at the Rugby World Cup, we had a lot of work to do.

Some days we got up at 4.15 a.m. The players would have a protein shake at 4.30 to ensure they didn't lose weight on these intense days. They would walk to training, warm up, and then drills would begin at 5 a.m. We would train for an hour then have breakfast. They would rest and sleep before more training. Lunch would follow, with more rest before the next session. After dinner there would be time for some weights before winding down, then the players would head for bed after a long day.

As coaches we still had a couple of hours' work to do before sleeping. In those two hours we would look at training videos, plan meetings, discuss progress and drills for the next day. The coaches were terrific in their commitment and enthusiasm.

During a high-altitude camp, we would train five times a day for two weeks before easing off. The players might have moaned privately about the workload but, feeling their new strength and fitness, they felt proud and more confident. Our hard work transferred to our improved performances.

In June 2013 we played Wales in back-to-back Tests in Osaka and Tokyo. We played brilliant rugby in the first game and had them on the ropes. We were 11–6 up at the break and were in control for much of the second half. Wales were missing some of their best players, who were on the Lions tour of Australia, but they were still a decent team. Against us, Wales were reeling and unable to find a way back. And then our little winger, Kenki Fukuoka, made a mistake.

Kenki is tiny but I reckon he's the quickest wing in world rugby. He's also a very bright guy. He was a medical student when I first saw him, and was playing for his university. They were a very weak team and I could see that Kenki didn't know much about rugby. He was incredibly raw – but he had pace and power. I had picked him for the first time when Japan had played the Philippines two months earlier. I wanted to give him the gentlest of starts. He came off the bench and, in a hopeless mismatch, scored two tries in a 121–0 demolition. Wales was a huge step up for him. We were cruising when he made a bad error on the kick return. They scored their only try of the game and got a lucky win, 22–18.

I was furious that we'd let the opportunity slip but this time kept it to myself. Unlike against the French Barbarians, when we had been embarrassing, I was happy with the way we had played. We just didn't close it out and gave away the decisive try through a simple mistake. I didn't sleep that night. Instead I sat up thinking of how to stop the errors. We were improving; but not fast enough. The clock was ticking.

We were in a hotel in Osaka and due to get on a bus to the

train station the next morning. The second Test against Wales would be in Tokyo the following Saturday.

As soon as we gathered in the hotel reception area, I put up a white board and said: 'Right boys. We should have won yesterday – but that's gone now. Before we get on the bus, we're going to walk through how we're going to beat them next week.'

The key message was that we were going to play relentlessly attacking and aggressive rugby. We would go at them in waves with intensity and purpose. We would maintain our concentration and not give them a moment to recover. I laid out the tactical plans and I could see that the ordinary Japanese people milling around the lobby were thinking: 'These blokes are mad. What are they doing?'

My intentions were clear. I wanted to get the idea in my players' heads that we were ready to beat Wales. Even before we stepped onto the bullet train back to Tokyo, I needed them to believe it.

On 15 June 2013, Japan beat Wales 23–8. I kept Kenki Fukuoka in the team and he did well. We scored two tries and Ayumu Goromaru kicked 13 points. 'I'm very proud of the team,' I said at the press conference. 'We've created history by becoming the first Japan team to beat a top ten country in world rugby. We understand Wales are without their best players, but we played a very good game of Test match rugby and this is another step forward for us. It was all about the players' attitude to keep fighting, to keep getting back on their feet and making tackles and line-breaks. It's a great result for us.'

We were five days short of a year since we had capitulated against the French Barbarians. The change in the team had been profound and I had high hopes for our next Test – against the mighty All Blacks in Tokyo that November. It felt as if we were on the road to somewhere special.

12

LIFE-CHANGING MOMENTS

Life knocks you down just when you think you have cracked it again. On Tuesday, 15 October 2013, I was feeling weary after flying back from South Africa. I had been in Durban, persuading a young full back in the Sharks academy to commit his rugby future to Japan. He was of mixed Japanese and South African heritage; and, as always, I was on the hunt for promising young players. From Tokyo I would head to our training camp to begin preparations for the biggest challenge in world rugby – our game against the All Blacks.

In Tokyo, I felt queasy during lunch with members of our management team. I blamed the jet lag. I got through the lunch and closed my eyes while we made the three-hour drive to the training camp. I tried to sleep but I couldn't. A dull headache throbbed. When we finally got out of the car there was a tightness down my left leg. I had run a lot in Durban and my left hamstring felt tender. Again, I thought it was nothing unusual, just stiffness after a long drive.

As we walked around the camp, my movement was less controlled. 'Shit,' I thought, 'what's going on here? This feels strange.' But I didn't say anything and concentrated on trying to move normally. I thought it would pass.

Once in my room, I sat on the bed and looked out at the ocean. Dark, ominous clouds were rolling in from far out to sea. I tried to lift my left hand. It was then that I knew something was wrong. I willed it to move. I managed to lift it, but my arm was now ridiculously heavy. I got up, found my phone and rang Hiroko.

I was relieved to hear her voice but I also felt anxious as I told her what had happened. She spoke clearly and told me to lie down. I ended the call when she said she would phone the team manager. Lying on the bed, my head and the left side of my body were numb. There wasn't any pain, just a creeping heaviness.

When the manager arrived, I started to feel a little better. He said we should get the next flight back to Tokyo as a typhoon was on its way and we didn't want to be stranded so far from home. He asked me if he should call a doctor, but I said I would rest.

I slept and felt calm when I woke up. Within a few hours we were at the airport, ready for the short flight. On the plane I still had a pounding headache and my left arm wasn't working properly. I closed my eyes and the flight passed peacefully. But as soon as I tried to stand up, I knew I was in real trouble.

The entire left side of my body was frozen. I struggled to get down the stairs of the plane, leaning heavily to my right. My left arm and leg just dangled. At the bottom of the stairs I was asked to see if I could touch my nose with my left hand. No chance. I knew then that I was having a stroke. It was like a computer system slowly closing down. Bit by bit, another part of me was retiring from use.

They moved quickly and, within minutes, I was in the back of an ambulance. I was dimly aware of the siren screaming as we raced to hospital.

They sedated me and I slept for most of the next three days.

When I was finally fully conscious, I managed to have a conversation with Hiroko, who had been feeling sick with worry. The doctor arrived at my bedside and explained what had happened to me. He then suggested I should stay in the hospital to recover.

'But doc,' I said, 'I can't stay here for long.'

'You must stay in hospital,' the doctor said again.

Instinctively, I reacted to what I thought was terrible news. Trying to lift myself up I said, 'I've got to get ready for the game, mate. We're playing the All Blacks.'

The doctor shook his head gravely. 'No, Eddie-san,' he said softly, 'you won't be coaching in this game. You must rest.'

They kept me in intensive care for another five days as my speech was slightly slurred and my left arm was still paralysed. My blood pressure was also high. I lay there and wondered how long it would take to start coaching again. There was never any thought in my traumatized head that my career might be in jeopardy. But I hated the feeling of lying there helplessly. I also wondered about what part of my lifestyle and my work habits might have contributed to the stroke. How much of this was down to me? Could I have avoided it?

I still knew I would make a full recovery. I was taking Japan to the World Cup. No ifs, no buts, no maybes.

It was easier when they moved me from intensive care to a normal ward so I could begin my rehab. 'This isn't great,' I said silently to myself, 'but I'll beat it. And I'll beat it fast.'

Rehab began but, in my opinion, it was too slow. I thought the physios were being too soft on me and that I could always be doing more. They warned me to take it nice and slowly. I would nod and agree with them, but once they were gone, I'd continue my rehab at night. Finally, after plenty of nagging, they allowed me to take a short walk with a stick around the ward at eight o'clock each night. I did lap after lap of the circular top floor of the hospital. After ten nights I began sit-ups and push-ups. The nurses would shout at me in Japanese to slow down and not go so fast. I would smile and say 'Yes, yes,' and then go back to what I was doing.

I was clearly making progress and was well enough to go home – but they suggested I spend another two weeks in hospital to complete the rehab programme. As much as I wanted to be home with Hiroko and Chelsea, my priority was my recovery. I took the advice to stay in hospital and work on my rehab. It was a wise decision. By the time I was discharged, I had made huge progress. I was a long way from being fully recovered, but the paralysis had eased and the reboot of my system was well under way. The frightening experience was suddenly nowhere near as daunting and I felt as though I was starting to put it behind me.

Someone described recovering from a stroke as being similar to walking into a library and finding all the books have fallen from the shelves. The job then is to put the books back in the right order. You have to relearn simple movements and actions.

It was challenging. The stroke had messed with my brain and the simple task of listening and talking to people was difficult and irritating. My limited movement was another source of frustration. Slowly but surely I started to improve; but it took me almost six months to recover fully.

I held my first coaching session again in April 2014. It was a start. I was lucky that John Pryor had put me on a specialist training programme to beat the last numbing consequences of the stroke. I lifted weights and I ran. I got fit and strong again and a dark time turned into a good period. I became much healthier. I ate even better than before and I cut back on drinking. I now only have the occasional glass of red wine.

People always ask if the stroke changed me. And it did. When you are sitting in a quiet room recovering from an event like that, all kinds of thoughts whirl through your head. I think I became less intense and learnt to relax more. I'm sure the England players will find that amusing but it did give me pause for thought. But, most of all, it supercharged my love of family, friends, rugby and coaching. I was grateful to be working again – and fortunate to be in a job that gives me such pleasure and satisfaction.

I also started to go to a church near our home. I had never been a practising Christian, but I found peace in church. It was not some dramatic conversion – but, rather, a place where I could reflect and give thanks for my returning health, my family and my work. I began to strongly believe that there is a purpose for all of us in our lives.

My purpose is coaching rugby. I'm not much good at anything else. I don't have a long list of interesting hobbies or a bucket list of crazy adventures to complete. I just like living a simple life and coaching rugby. It's hard to explain the joy I get out of it. I resolved to make the most of my talent and, instead of getting weighed down by frustration or worry, simply give it a real hot go. I did not become any more, or less, dedicated and hard-working. But I became clearer in my thinking.

In Tokyo, the church was a ten-minute walk from my home. I went there every Sunday and it was a lovely coincidence that the pastor was a South African. He was a big Afrikaans guy who loved rugby. I think he was pretty pleased that I turned up. I'd always sneak in late and sneak out early. But I went, yes, religiously, every week.

I haven't really found the right place since then. Whenever I'm in a new town now, and I see a church, I'll step inside. It's very low-key but I've retained that gratitude and faith. It's simply a belief in something higher and greater than all of us. The clarity of thought that I had during my illness has since served me well. I know what I want to do and how I want to do it. And I also know that none of us can afford to waste a single second. Life is precious.

A few months earlier, following ongoing reflection about my strengths and weaknesses as a coach, I'd taken steps to ease my intensity. I had invited Kaori Araki into the inner sanctum of our team. It was a radical step as Kaori is a female sports psychologist. Japanese rugby is very conservative and parochial and devoid of femininity. In truth, I was less interested in Kaori's gender than the fact that she seemed to be such a bright and incisive psychologist. I was intent on using all available techniques to know my players better and to help them become more decisive in their thinking.

Kaori did some fine work with the team but perhaps her most penetrating comment was directed towards me.

'Eddie-san,' she said respectfully but firmly, 'you are too grumpy.'

I gave her a suitably grumpy look in return, then asked her to explain.

'You walk around with a scowl on your face most of the time,' she said. 'You look very intense and bad-tempered. Often the team don't understand why you are in such a bad mood. Even when they please you, you are still in a bad mood. It would help everyone if you lightened up.'

I protested that I was rarely in a bad mood but, when pressed, I admitted that I worried a lot about all the work we needed to do to get the squad ready for the World Cup. I am not, in ordinary life, a worrier. But the relentless nature of international sport occupies your mind. As head coach it is extremely difficult to escape the demands and stresses of the job.

'You must try,' Kaori said. 'It will help you and it will help the players.'

Of course she was right, and so, even before the stroke, I made a conscious decision to try and lighten my expression and the surrounding atmosphere. I also made attempts to include the odd rest day for both the players and the staff as we continued the remorseless work we needed to do in 2015. Our plan was clear and we were monitoring our progress. I knew exactly where we were and exactly where we needed to be. It was a huge gap. But with Kaori's new information, I resolved to smile more and make the programme more interesting.

I enjoyed studying martial arts in my spare time and, in 2014, I asked Tsuyoshi Kohsaka, a former UFC fighter, to come into camp so that he could teach the players how to stay low in contact. The boys loved it because Tsuyoshi offered something different while preparing them for the battle I had begun to discuss – against South Africa in our opening World Cup match.

Slowly and carefully I began to plant the seeds of how we would beat the Springboks. In my new and less frenetic way, I opened up conversations to explore the players' views. In June and July 2014, we held a training camp which coincided with the football World Cup in Brazil. It was fantastic. We watched games between training and, while Japan had finished bottom of their group, the pulse and excitement of the tournament became a great way for us to understand what was ahead of us at our own World Cup in another 14 months.

Costa Rica were the surprise team in Brazil. They were low down the world rankings and most experts predicted they would finish bottom of a group containing Italy, England and Uruguay. In the end they finished top and Italy and England were sent home in shame. They beat Greece in the last 16 and only just missed out on the semi-finals – losing on penalties in the quarters to the Netherlands.

I used Costa Rica as an example. We, too, were expected to do little of note in the World Cup. But I told the players we could shock the world. We were not good enough to win the World Cup but we could be the team of the tournament. To do this we needed to reach the quarter-finals. Our first two games were the hardest of all – against South Africa, the two-time world champions, and then Scotland just three days later. Rather than targeting Scotland and playing a second-string team against the Boks, as some people had suggested, I said we would carve our way to the quarter-finals by beating South Africa in the tournament opener.

No one believed me at first, not even Steve Borthwick and my fellow coaches. But, without them knowing, I had already launched Operation Beat the Boks.

In the European winter of 2014, after another November tour in which we lost to Scotland but easily beat Russia and Spain, I went to Munich to meet one of the great coaches of world sport.

Pep Guardiola turned out to be the biggest influence on me during my time with Japan. Pep had just taken a year's break from football, having left Barcelona after he won so much with a brilliant team in which Lionel Messi, Andrés Iniesta and Xavi proved that comparatively small men could become the greatest footballers in the world. I was fascinated by tiki-taka, that Barça style of football characterized by short passing, deft movement and controlled possession of the ball until the opposition defence are opened up and helpless. I wanted to talk to him about these attributes, because Japan had to find a way to beat bigger teams. We were so much smaller and the only way we could win was by moving the ball quickly into space.

Pep was incredibly generous and gave me a lot of time. He also allowed me to watch his training sessions with Bayern Munich. It was intriguing because he was coaching some of the best players in the world, and talking to them in various languages, while working with striking intensity. After a routine warm-up he split them into three groups and had them working on concepts of space with relentless focus. One particular session only lasted for 30 minutes but, as they came off for a break, the players were mentally and physically drained. Despite the freezing temperatures, sweat ran down their gaunt faces. Pep's razor-sharp instruction and expectation pushed the players to their limits. But with purpose, intensity and clarity, they had achieved more in half an hour than most teams would in a traditional two-hour training stint.

I had also started to structure our training in short concentrated bursts. But, rather than feeling proud that Pep and I had the same views, I squirmed at how amateurish my sessions seemed when compared to Guardiola's sophisticated and intricate coaching patterns. I liked the way he could move from coaching the team, talking to everyone in ways that opened their minds, to individualistic moments when he would take a player to one side and show him exactly what he meant. He sometimes even used his hands to move a player physically so there could be no misunderstanding about what they needed to do. It was impassioned and it was inspirational.

At the end of a long day, which finished at 7 p.m., Pep gave me two hours in his office. He talked about space, movement, passing, training and winning. I left Munich feeling almost dazed. It was exhilarating to watch, listen to and speak with one of the masters of our profession but, at the same time, it was embarrassing to know how far ahead of me he was. Prior to visiting Bayern Munich, I thought I knew something about professional coaching.

Sitting on the plane back to Tokyo, I realized how much I had to learn. It's a great lesson in business as well as sport. If you think you're going OK, you're probably not. Stay humble and curious and use every minute of every day to improve your attitude, your skills and your contribution. It's the only way to stay relevant and have a constant impact.

These rare encounters with great coaches in different sports are invaluable and, in later years, I gained a lot by talking to men as distinct as Sir Alex Ferguson, Louis van Gaal and Ric Charlesworth. I explored new training ideas, such as tactical periodization. I went to Qatar to meet Alberto Mendez-Villanueva, who explained that the concept was created years ago by Vitor Frade at the University of Porto.

Tactical periodization is a system of training that focuses logically on certain moments in play; the resulting levels of improved fitness and skill levels will transfer directly to a game. Tactical thinking drives your training; it is shaped by four key areas – defensive organization, offensive organization, the transition from defence to attack and the transition from attack to defence. Every aspect of training targets ways to sharpen the physicality and mentality that your team will need on match day.

Rugby and real life collided again for me in May 2015. We were about to play Korea in the third and last game of the Asian Cup in the Japanese city of Fukuoka. We had won our first two games in the tournament and were building towards the more important Pacific Nations Cup and then separate tours of Uruguay and Georgia to get us ready for the World Cup. I knew that the crucial preparation would be done in our training camp – but the games were important because we were already playing the style of rugby with which I knew we could beat South Africa.

Five days before the Korea game, my sister Diane called from Sydney. Dad had just a few days left.

The news hit me hard. When I had last been home to visit Mum and Dad, I could see he had reached that stage where he'd just had enough. All the life had drained out of him and he was waiting to slip away. But you can't make such choices in life, or death, and so he lingered in a deeply shadowed world.

Dad was 96 when I took the call. It felt almost merciful to know that the end was near.

I was torn between the desire to see Dad one last time or to return home for the funeral and stay on longer with my mum, Diane and Vicky. In the end I decided to be at the game against Korea on Saturday 9 May and fly home straight afterwards.

On 6 May 2015, Dad died, less than 24 hours after I took the call. I would have made it back in time to see him, but nothing would have changed. I could not have saved him and I would just have seen a ghostly image of my father on his death bed.

Three days later it did not matter that we had beaten Korea. I just wanted to get home.

On the long flight back to Sydney, I thought of everything my dad had done for me, and for us as a family. I could see him clearly again – the good, decent, hard-working and selfless man who was gone for ever. I choked up, as I still often do now when people ask me about my father.

I think of that old Harry Chapin song about a father and his son. In the first part of the song the father is too busy working hard to give the time he should to his boy. And then, as he ages and retires, and has ample time, his son has become a man with his own commitments and constraints. It echoes life and our interaction with our parents and then with our children.

If I had the chance again, I think I would have flown home to see him one last time. I am not entirely sure. All I really know is that I wish I had done more for him in the last years of his life. The consuming nature of my work means that so many sacrifices are made at the expense of my family.

My mother, meanwhile, battles on remarkably. In 2019, four years after my dad died, she turned 94. She still watches out for me and, thankfully, she still keeps me in check.

On my own, I think often of those days and realize all over again that family matters more than anything. And, yes, there are times like now when, as I try to talk about my dad, my eyes fill with tears. They are tears of gratitude, of love, and loss too.

I knew the players had bought in totally to our World Cup plans when, rather than saying they were going to training, they echoed my rallying call. 'We're going to Beat the Boks,' they said as they trotted off to another session. Training was actually called 'Beat the Boks'. Steve Borthwick took it even further. I could hear him urging the players on by saying we had already beaten the Boks four times. They looked puzzled and then he reminded them that we had played the exact style of rugby we needed to defeat South Africa while dispatching Hong Kong, Korea, Canada and Uruguay. When we played Georgia in our final warm-up game before the World Cup, we would run out against them as if they really were the Boks. We would stick to the Beat the Boks game plan we had honed to perfection. Of course, none of these teams were in the league of the Boks, but that didn't matter. It was more important, at this stage, that we drilled such belief into the players.

The game plan was simple. We would play the same fast, aggressive rugby we had worked on the past three years. It was vital that we maintained the speed of the ball and kept it in play, staying away from set pieces and striving to keep the score as close as possible so that doubts could begin to fester in Springbok heads. We would take them low and tackle in numbers – with our physical bravery matched by an emotional courage that we would play flat and attacking rugby. We would play to win rather than to limit the damage.

The closer we got to the World Cup, the more we analysed the Springboks as individuals. Each of our players knew their opposite numbers inside out. It became easier to imagine an his-toric victory if they stepped away from gazing in awe at the collective mystique of the Boks and looked closely instead at players who were, just like them, fallible human beings.

I really did believe that we had a serious chance of winning – but we needed South Africa to have an off-day and we needed to be better than we had ever been before. If they turned up at their best then they would beat us. It was as simple as that. But, in the opening game of the World Cup, we could catch them cold.

They had so many advantages over us – in terms of size, strength, power and experience. But I was so familiar with the Boks – I knew they wanted to play the game as if they were a heavyweight boxer. They wanted to play relatively slowly and pound us into submission. They wanted to use the power of their set piece, and the sheer bulk of their forwards, to physically domi-nate us. We could not allow that to happen. Once we came close to matching them physically, we could crack them mentally.

When we had possession, it was vital we moved the ball quickly so that they would also have to move fast. How many times could we make them move against their will? How many times could we make them have to get off the ground? We needed to play the game lower and quicker. And even when they did hit us, as they surely would, we could never allow them to trap us. They wanted to hunt us down but we had to keep them on the run.

Our Beat the Boks camp began in July 2015 and, for 12 weeks, I worked them harder than ever before. At Miyazaki, on the island of Kyushu in the far south of Japan, the players went through a punishing schedule. It was not merciless training because, with John Pryor's help, we were pretty scientific in the way we stag-gered the levels of intensity. The players had also grown used to the kind of sustained and ferocious commitment I demanded. They were hardened. But this regime was rigorous both mentally and physically. We did not flog them for the sake of flogging them. The sessions were as sharp as they were brutal. I think it was more gruelling for the players because we pushed them emotionally to the brink. They could handle the one-off sessions without undue difficulty – but it became harder for them when there were five sessions in a day and we trained for the first five weeks without a day off.

Every hour of every day was mapped out. They were stretched and engaged constantly, whether working on basic handling or scrummaging skills, wrestling and boxing, cycling or problem-solving exercises. It was fascinating to be at the heart of it, to watch them suffer and yet, at the same time, grow in strength and resolve. The Japanese players, even more than the foreign imports, took to the regime with messianic zeal. They radiated commitment and conviction. The 'Beat the Boks' call echoed around Miyazaki with a haunting power.

Our final game before we played South Africa was against Georgia at Gloucester on 5 September 2015 – exactly two weeks before the Boks. Georgia came at us like beasts. Their formidable pack just wanted to crush us. It was the perfect preparation. In previous years we had lost many close games to them because they had bullied us. This time we turned over their scrum and scored a try in the last minute. Japan won a bruising contest 13–10. Once again, we told the boys that they had beaten the Boks.

The mood in the camp was eerily calm the closer we came to a match that had consumed us for a year. I only felt the first twitch of uncertainty on the Friday afternoon before the game. Michael Leitch took them out for his largely ceremonial captain's run and all the players looked terribly edgy. I told Michael to call it off before we did any damage.

There was nothing left to say. I just had to trust in the work we had done, and in the character of the young men with whom I had shared so much.

On the Saturday morning, on a beautiful day in Brighton, Michael and I went down to a cafe on the gleaming beachfront. We had a coffee and all the unease was gone. Michael did not say a lot but I sensed the certainty within him – a clear conviction that we would play boldly and courageously.

Leitchy was ready. Japan were ready.

I felt moved by the transformation he and all the players had undergone over the last three years. Suddenly, it all felt worth it.

I looked at Leitchy and said: 'Listen, mate, we've got nothing to lose. If you think we should have a go, have a real go.'

My captain looked up and nodded intently. 'Yes,' he said quietly. 'I will.'

Brighton Community Stadium, Brighton, England. Saturday, 19 September 2015

This is the hardest time. The minutes drag during the long coach journey to the ground and, at the stadium, I feel the uncertainty wash through me like a muddy river.

History is stacked against us. Japan have only ever won one World Cup game in their entire history, and beating Zimbabwe 24 years before will not help us today. Our average loss in the tournament is by 48 points. I know none of this matters now – unless we suddenly crumble beneath the weight of this woeful legacy or the shuddering force of the Springbok assault.

There is little I can do but trust in the players and in our preparation.

In the dressing room the last few words are said. Leitchy is terrific, taking the lead. The players are calm but, as importantly, they are intense. They look ready.

There is a steeliness in Leitch's gaze as, after giving me a nod, he says, quietly, 'Let's go . . .'

The players head down the tunnel. I watch them leave, one by one. I then follow them along that echoing and gloomy corridor.

They walk purposefully, rather than run, into the glaring sunshine. I like the way they look in their pristine red-and-white hooped shirts and white shorts and socks.

The Springboks wear tracksuit bottoms even though it is a scorching afternoon. But their familiar green-and-gold shirts are short sleeved. They look ready to start bashing us.

We know that they want to smash us. They want to pulverize us with heavy hits. So I have tweaked the game plan. We are still intent on dictating the pace of play, but I tell the boys not to be afraid if the Boks have early ball. South Africa is a defence-minded rugby country. They are at their happiest when putting in crushing tackles and knocking their opponents back. Let them come at us because their game is built on defence not attack. They won't be comfortable with too much ball and they will be less comfortable when we chop them down.

But, most of the time, Japan need to use the ball quickly and move the heavy Boks across the field, back and forth, up and down.

Jérôme Garcès blows his whistle and the roar from a sold-out crowd of 30,666 settles my nerves. At last I can lose myself in the game.

From the kick-off we look fiery and composed. The first real test comes when Zane Kirchner, the Boks' full back, picks up Ayumu Goromaru's raking kick and sets off on a run. He unleashes Bryan Habana and my old Bok friend flies down the wing. This is exactly the sort of movement their supporters had paid to see. But we know what's coming. We chop down Habana and then Male Sa'u, our outside centre, sparks a counter-attack from the breakdown. Moving through the phases, quickly and aggressively, we gain 35 metres. The Boks can see we are not going to wilt at the outset.

After six minutes, and sustained Japanese pressure, Goromaru nails a penalty: 3–0, Japan.

Joel Stransky, the former Springbok number 10 whose drop goal had won the World Cup for South Africa 20 years earlier, is the co-commentator as the cameras lock onto me. I stare ahead, not wanting to show any emotion, and it helps that the commentary can't be heard by me. 'You've got to love the contrast,' Stransky says to the rest of the watching rugby world. 'South Africa – big, strong and powerful, playing the one-off running game, trying to almost bully Japan into submission. This man, Eddie Jones, has his team playing fast and furiously with pick-and-goes, moving it quickly and dictating the speed of the game.'

After 17 minutes, with the Boks rumbling though the gears, we are pinned close to our try line. Victor Matfield soars majestically at the lineout and wins clean ball. The green-and-gold pack drive a wedge around him and the ball is funnelled back to Francois Louw, the Boks' canny blind-side flanker. Ahead of him, Tendai 'The Beast' Mtawarira, Schalk Burger, Bismarck du Plessis and Ruan Pienaar drive towards the line. Louw, like a jackal, scavenges low behind them, the ball cradled in his huge hands. Masataka Mikami and Hiroshi Yamashita, on early as a sub, are helpless against the sheer size of the five Boks. Our other defenders scramble back too late. The Boks crash over, with Louw clearly grounding the ball.

We are 7–3 down after 18 minutes. I look at our captain and Leitchy is just as I want him – talking calmly and looking more determined than ever.

Eleven minutes later, Leitch transforms the game. It starts with a rolling ten-man Japanese maul that oozes resolve and menace. The South Africans are driven back and we keep going. The ball is somewhere deep inside my red-and-white mauling machine and the Springboks are trying grimly to stop our momentum.

I control the urge to jump up in sheer admiration as my pack bullies the Boks. We're getting closer and closer and then, suddenly, Leitch peels away from the cover of the maul and dives for the line. His left hand stretches out and the ball is over the whitewash. Try.

I leap from my seat and raise my right hand. This feels so good.

It takes a while for the bedlam to die down and then Goromaru kicks the conversion. It's 10–7 to Japan after 31 minutes.

The Boks are into it now. They know they have to respond and, from the restart, they hit back hard. They produce their own rolling maul and, within a minute, Du Plessis is over for their second forward-dominated try.

This is a key period with seven minutes left until the break. South Africa come close to another try but our defence is magnificent. We keep them out: 12–10 to the Springboks at half-time.

At the break I'm happy, really happy. The boys are sweating heavily but they don't seem to be breathing too hard or looking anxious. Everything is going according to plan. If we can keep the score this close for another 20 minutes, the Boks will be under real pressure.

'This is Eddie Jones at his best,' Francois Pienaar says at the break, praising our high-tempo game. For me, it's more important that this is Japan at our best. We have been outstanding for 40 minutes.

Two minutes into the second half, a Goromaru penalty restores our lead. It doesn't last long. Pienaar feeds Lood de Jager, the Boks' powerful second-rower, just outside our 22. The lock finds an unexpected hole in front of him and, showing startling pace for such a big man, he scorches over the line, just to the right of the posts.

'He's a giraffe,' Gordon Bray the commentator yelps before, as the tall Afrikaner rises to his full height again, he tempers his image. 'A human one.'

De Jager is mobbed by his teammates and he smiles in delight. I can see how relieved the Boks are to be in front again. Pat Lambie kicks the conversion: 19–13 to South Africa.

After 51 minutes, and another successful Goromaru penalty cutting the deficit to three, we drive deep into Bok territory. Burger is penalized. Penalty to Japan. Fumiaki Tanaka, our little scrum half, looks for the tap and go but Leitch calms everyone down. He points to the sticks.

Goromaru is in the mood; it's 19–19 after 53 minutes. Television footage cuts to Japanese fans. A middle-aged man looks as if he is about to cry in happy disbelief. 'Delirious!' Bray shouts.

We are past the sacred hour mark, our first aim, and still on target after Lambie and Goromaru swap penalties: 22–22.

The Boks dig deep now, trying to kill us off. Fourie du Preez, recovering from injury, is on in place of Pienaar. He feeds another substitute, Adriaan Strauss, and the beefy blond hooker barrels into space and then over the line. 'Well, we had the giraffe,' Bray suggests. 'Now we have the rhinoceros.'

Handré Pollard, on as a replacement number 10, converts, and the pressure eases for the Boks as they savour a 29–22 lead. They win another two penalties and both times they kick for touch. Another try would finish us off. But we hold on and force them back.

Then, with some sublime and exhilarating play, we turn the match inside out. Attacking fast with the exact flat backline we need, Harumichi Tatekawa, our inside centre, delays his little peach of a pass until just before he is smashed by Pollard. Kosei Ono, our number 10, is away and then, with a lovely sleight of hand, he switches play with a reverse pass which dazzles the Springboks and finds Kotaro Matsushima. The quicksilver left wing arrows diagonally towards the right corner flag and releases it to Goromaru who is absolutely flying. He has Akihito Yamada on the overlap but Goromaru does not need him. The try line is open and he dives across it as if plunging into clear water.

Brighton rocks in disbelief and the boys embrace Goromaru. I am up on my feet. This is not good for my heart.

Goromaru steadies himself – and the galloping inside my chest – and lands the conversion. Seventy minutes on the clock. South Africa 29, Japan 29.

Whatever happens from now on, I know that we have already produced the most extraordinary game of the World Cup.

Pollard gives the Boks the lead again with a 73rd-minute penalty to make it 32–29 to South Africa.

We are not done yet. We are on the attack. We are coming at them in the red-and-white waves we had planned.

Seventy-eight minutes 55 seconds on the clock. We have a lineout just five metres from the green-and-gold line. As Matfield organizes the Boks, drawing on his vast experience and expertise as the world's premier lock, I reach for my last throw of the dice. I bring off Yamada, who has had a good game, and send on Karne Hesketh, my New Zealand-born replacement wing.

Michael Broadhurst, another Kiwi, leaps high and takes the ball cleanly. The maul is on and all the forwards and even some of our backs pile in. We roll and drive for the line.

Ten Japanese men crash over and on top of a green-and-gold pile of defenders. A couple of boys shoot up their arms to claim the try. No one knows for sure and Fourie du Preez walks away as if he might persuade Jérôme Garcès to be equally resolute in refusing the appeals for a try.

Garcès retreats and then uses his hands to draw a square in the air. He needs to go upstairs for the Television Match Official to take a look. We can hear Garcès's voice on the monitor. He says he did not see the ball being grounded but could the TMO check on the screen.

'Where's Clark Kent when you need him – with X-ray vision,' Bray quips as angle after angle fails to reveal a clear sight of the ball.

'He's underground there somewhere, trying to see,' Stransky says.

'There's nothing clear at all,' the TMO eventually tells Garcès. 'It's going to be a scrum five – red ball.'

Heyneke Meyer, the Springbok coach, speaks urgently into his mouthpiece. Jannie du Plessis and Tendai Mtawarira, the Beast, are called back into action. They had been substituted but they return to bolster the front row of an injured Springbok scrum. They have 132 Tests' worth of know-how between them. Meyer has called in the heavy artillery but my pack don't even notice. They are in a huddle, talking intently.

I am on my feet, churning with emotion. Hope mingles with pride, as I will my boys on for one last giant effort. 'Eddie Jones,' Bray says, 'on the verge of this colossal upset . . . if it comes off.'

Atsushi Hiwasa, our replacement scrum half, feeds the scrum. 'Thirteen seconds to go,' Bray cries.

We hook the ball back just as the referee's left arm shoots out.

Penalty to Japan, but he waits to see if there is an advantage. The scrum wheels and he whistles.

We've got the draw, as long as Goromaru can hold his nerve.

I look up and pause. I can see Leitch consulting with Garcès, asking him how much time we have left.

This is sensible. But kicking the goal is even more sensible.

Bray asks Stransky what he would do – secure the draw or go for the win. 'I don't know,' Stransky admits. 'But, famously, Dr Danie Craven once said a draw is like kissing your sister.'

I would happily kiss both my sisters on the cheek to celebrate the most famous draw in World Cup history. But Leitchy, tugging at his cauliflowered ear and thinking hard, has a different idea.

I shake my head at him. He can't see me. 'Take the three!' I shout. 'Take the three!' Of course he can't hear me.

The crowd has gone into meltdown, fuelled by ecstasy and hysteria, as they also understand that Japan are going for the scrum, and the try.

I hurl my walkie-talkie onto the ground in fury. It hits the concrete and breaks into shattered fragments.

I soon compose myself because I know Leitch has shown real bravery, and belief. He is not up for kissing his sister. He's going for the full-on smacker of an historic victory. He is prepared to risk defeat to get the win.

He has remembered our chat over coffee this morning. He is ready to trust his instinct.

This is leadership. Leitch had once been quiet and subservient. But now he is leading his team towards a courageous and potentially match-winning act.

'Good on you, mate,' I think. 'Go for it.'

Matfield claps his hands. He is not applauding his opposite number as captain. It is his way of urging the Boks to make one last effort to keep out Japan.

'This would be the upset of all upsets,' Stransky says.

'Of all time,' Bray confirms.

'In the history of sport,' Stransky concludes.

The scrum goes down. Two packs of men, soaked in sweat and reeking of desperation, smash into each other again.

Hiwasa puts the ball in and he zips around to the back of the scrum, Du Preez shadowing his every step. Amanaki Mafi, our substitute number 8, has the ball at his feet as the scrum wheels again.

Garcès orders them to set the scrum again. Leitch and Matfield both have a word with him, checking the ruling, knowing that the next scrum will surely be the last of the match. We're a minute into injury time.

Down they go, again. 'Crouch,' Garcès shouts. The two packs crouch and wait.

'Bind,' Garcès instructs. Both front rows dig their heads in beneath opposing shoulders.

'Set!' The packs engage and immediately, under immense pressure, the scrum collapses.

Garcès whistles and, patiently, he put the tips of his fingers together to indicate that they should try again.

Leitch comes round to talk to his front row, telling them to retain their composure.

The camera cuts away to the crumpled face of a Japanese fan weeping openly with anxiety and, as Stransky says, 'a huge element of joy.'

I know how this feels. There is nothing I can do but wait, and hope.

'A glorious performance by the Japanese team,' Bray says. 'This is rugby at the very summit.'

They set it again for a third time, and I can hear the bellow of both packs as the scrum locks.

Then, it happens. The ball comes out of the mess of a wheeling scrum. Hiwasa has it with his captain, the imperious Leitch, on his shoulder.

We are on a roll and I sense the truth of it all over again.

This is why we do it. This is when we are most alive. This is it.

Hiwasa darts forward and then offloads the ball to a charging

Leitch. Du Preez, my old friend, blocks his path. Leitch is dragged down. Hiwasa is waiting. His captain lays back the ball and Hiwasa funnels it into the arms of Broadhurst. The lock is tackled by two big Bok defenders.

We go through two more phases and South Africa keep us out. Hiwasa changes tack and switches play to the right. His backline is primed and ready. He passes to Shinya Makabe, who is tackled. The ball comes back and Hiwasa plays a clever little reverse pass to Leitch.

He drives for the line and it needs the blond rhinoceros, Strauss, to bring him down.

Hiwasa goes again. He moves it down the line to Tatekawa, who misses two backs with a long pass that hits Mafi running at speed.

'Here we go,' Bray screams into his microphone as Sa'u and Hesketh run hard on the overlap.

Mafi throws a spiralling ball to Hesketh who takes it without breaking stride, Sa'u, the outside centre between them, points helpfully towards the try line.

Hesketh does not need any help. He has eyes only for the corner and the gleaming white try line.

I jump as Hesketh dives. '*History!*' Bray screams as Hesketh scores the winning try.

I am lost in a boiling sea of men hugging and crying. I am smiling and high-fiving rather than crying. We have done it. Thanks to the courage of Leitch, and the bold imagination, resilience and audacity of the players, we have won the game at the death.

'Japan have been immense this afternoon,' Stransky enthuses as replays of the try spool across the monitor again and again. 'They were courageous in not kicking the goal. They went for the try. Mafi showed good strength and timed the pass to perfection. In at the corner went Hesketh to seal the game for Japan. One of the most famous victories in the history of sport – not just in the game of rugby union. And victory it will be for the Cherry Blossoms.'

It does not matter that Goromaru misses the conversion. The final whistle blows.

South Africa 32, Japan 34.

'Our eyes have seen the glory,' Bray shouts out to millions of disbelieving viewers around the world as I congratulate my beaming, exultant staff. Our lives have changed in the space of a beautiful, crazy, sun-filled afternoon.

'It's a rugby miracle,' Bray hollers again. 'Eddie Jones is the president of Japan.'

13

THE NEXT ADVENTURE AND A GRAND SLAM

I don't do regret. Any time spent thinking about what could or should have happened is indulgent. The past is gone and there is nothing you can do to change it. But I still reflect on things I might have done differently – as on the Sunday afternoon of 11 October 2015. I was so drained I could not find the words I wanted to say to my players in the dressing room at Gloucester. Japan's World Cup campaign had just ended and I was cooked.

It was a mistake. The players deserved to be shown how much I appreciated their efforts and how much they'd done for their country. It would have been the right way to bring down the curtain on an incredible tournament. They had thrilled tens of millions of sports fans all over the world with their triumph over South Africa and changed rugby in Japan for ever. I've since thanked almost all the players on an individual basis, but it was a lost opportunity to praise them as a squad while the heat of battle could still be felt.

Just four days after beating South Africa, we had faced Scotland. I barely had time to enjoy the euphoria after we'd shocked the Boks. Thirty minutes after the game I was focused on all we needed to do to beat Scotland. If we could sustain our momentum, and defeat another tier-one nation, our quarter-final place would have been virtually assured as group winners.

It was another mighty challenge – and even harder to achieve because we had such little time to recover and prepare. Scotland's first World Cup game was against us and any danger of complacency had evaporated after they saw our performance against South Africa. They were primed and ready.

We played brilliantly in the first half and were ahead 7–6 after Amanaki Mafi scored a try which Ayumu Goromaru converted. At the break the score was 12–7 to Scotland but it was too much for the boys in the second half. Their heroics against South Africa just 96 hours earlier caught up with them and we ran out of juice. Scotland scored five tries and won 45–10.

There were ten days off before our next match, in contrast to the tight turnaround for Scotland. We took advantage of it and beat Samoa comfortably, 26–5.

Our impact on Japanese rugby was obvious. Thirty million Japanese viewers, a quarter of the country's population, watched our game against Scotland. The sport had gone mainstream and so it was important that we finished the job with another win – but the USA were desperate to get their first victory in our last match.

I could see the energy levels of the players were dropping. My response was to push them harder. We could no longer make the quarter-finals but we had to keep building our reputation. The players responded. It was just as well because the Americans were tough and physical and it required another big effort to win 28–18. We had matched both South Africa and Scotland in winning three out of our four pool games – but they qualified for the knockout stages having scored more bonus points.

We flew back into Tokyo to a heroes' welcome of thousands of cheering fans. It was in stark contrast to the fewer than a hundred people who had seen us off at the airport six weeks earlier. The players' performances had stirred national pride and come to represent all that is good and great in Japanese society. Our players had demonstrated the virtues of the Samurai code of loyalty, courage, compassion and honour, and the Japanese people were rightly proud of them. It was a special moment and a reminder of the power of sport to unite and inspire people.

Whenever I return to Japan now, I am struck by the latest statistics detailing the number of kids playing rugby. The increase, since Japan beat South Africa in 2015, is between 150 and 200 per cent.

I had thought I would remain in charge of Japan until the end of 2019. I had even signed a new four-year contract extension early in 2015. But a month before the World Cup I realized I couldn't stay on. I worried that my coaching would stagnate and I knew that Japan would benefit from a different coach with fresh ideas. I also carried the painful memory of the mistake I made with the Wallabies when I should have moved on after the 2003 World Cup. Furthermore, a new chairman and chief executive of the Japanese union were appointed and I felt no connection with them. They were happy to let me out of my contract. I was grateful, because I had fallen for a new challenge which had captured my imagination.

I was going to become the head coach of the Stormers, in Cape Town. I couldn't remember too many occasions when I had been more excited by such an opportunity. Maybe the Brumbies edged it – but I was now much more experienced and clearer in knowing how to build a high-performing team.

I have always wanted to coach in South Africa. The attraction is strong because, for me, the two greatest rugby nations in the world are New Zealand and South Africa. As an Australian I'm never going to be given the opportunity to coach the All Blacks, and so the chance to take over the Stormers, in a city as beautiful as Cape Town, was unmissable. There is so much raw talent in South Africa, especially in the Cape. My experience with the Springboks in 2007 had also given me confidence that I could get the best out of South African players.

I was convinced that the Stormers could become Super Rugby champions. I liked their players and I had already forged a positive relationship with my new support staff. After one meeting with the squad, and one upbeat training session, I was even more convinced I'd made the best possible choice in swapping Tokyo for Cape Town.

Jake White was even more excited than me. He called me with the news that England were looking for a new head coach after the departure of Stuart Lancaster. We all knew that Stuart was a very talented coach, but it seemed to me that England's failure to get out of the group stages, at a World Cup held in their own country, meant that it was impossible for Stuart to continue.

Jake had always wanted to be England head coach. He told me he had applied, while I confirmed I had no intention of putting myself forward. I was committed to the Stormers. Jake and I share an agent, Craig Livingstone in Johannesburg, and it sounded like the wheels were turning. Jake had an interview for the job on the Friday. 'That's great, mate,' I said, and wished him good luck. I didn't think any more of it.

Then, out of the blue, Craig called me on the Thursday. He said Ian Ritchie, the chief executive of the RFU, had asked if I might meet him in Cape Town on Saturday. We agreed that I would be crazy not to hear what he had to say – especially as Ritchie had initiated the contact and seemed very keen to talk to me.

'OK, mate,' I said to Craig. 'There's no harm in chatting to him. Go ahead and set it up.'

I took another call from Jake on Friday night. I got the feeling that his interview had not gone so well because he spoke mostly about the possibility of our doing the job together. After we had worked so successfully as a team in 2007, we had spoken occasionally about doing the same again one day in the future. I was open to it, as I knew England was one of the most taxing jobs in world rugby. I told Jake I'd definitely mention it to Ritchie when we met.

Craig, who brokered the deal with the Stormers, had placed a clause in my contract saying that I could terminate the agreement in the event of a job offer from a tier-one country. But I still felt a twinge of guilt when I got up on Saturday morning to meet Ritchie. I was very happy in Cape Town; but the possibility of being offered the England job was both intriguing and compelling. Even the thought of coaching England gave me butterflies.

Ian and I met at a fancy hotel on the waterfront. Craig had arranged everything and the room had a beautiful view of Table Mountain. It gave me the perfect response when, after we said hello, shook hands and made some small talk, Ian asked if I was interested in coaching England. 'Well, mate,' I said with a little smile, 'who wants to swap Cape Town for London?'

Ian laughed and joked about the impossible task of competing with the Cape sunshine and the majesty of Table Mountain. I liked him and I was soon seriously impressed. He was better prepared than any chief executive I had ever met; he had clearly done his homework and spoken to people who knew me in all my previous jobs. He had been very discreet and professional.

I explained that Jake had been in touch and raised the option of our doing the job as a team. But Ian wasn't interested. He was polite in that very English way but clear that he thought it would be too complicated and messy. He was convinced that England needed one man with one vision. That man would be 100 per cent accountable to Ian, as the CEO, for the performance of the team. He also made it clear that he thought I was that person.

We talked about the job and English rugby, about the World Cup failure, and his vision for the future. As the minutes ticked past, I became more and more excited by the prospect of working with Ian and the RFU to build the best team in the world. I made no attempt to play hardball or disguise my interest in the job. As far back as 2003, and before the World Cup final between my Wallaby team and Clive Woodward's England, I had been interested in the position. Earlier in that tournament, on a quiet evening, Glen Ella and I had enjoyed a good yarn. He asked me which other country I would like to coach one day and my response had been instant: England. They had vast resources and a huge pool of players; and yet England had never fulfilled their potential. Of course they ended up winning the World Cup a few weeks later, but England had since slipped back into inconsistency and even mediocrity – particularly during the 2011 tournament.

England had played some decent rugby under Lancaster from 2012 to 2015. They had excellent players, but in my opinion the team lacked leadership and a differentiated style. I knew I could help England be more consistent. I reassured Ian that my experience with Saracens had given me insight into the unique challenges of English rugby. My focus would be on improving England's best players, and creating a winning team.

Ian politely raised my 'management style'. He had heard of my abrasive and demanding reputation. He wanted to know if I had mellowed over the years.

'Yes,' I said honestly, 'especially since the stroke.' I discussed the impact of my illness and, more importantly, how I maintained friendships with the majority of my former players. A few still popped up in the media to talk about the way I might have shouted at them years ago – but even they tended to say that they had become better players in the process. I stressed to Ian that rugby had changed hugely in the past 20 years, and that it was no longer possible to speak to players in the way we had done in the early days of professionalism.

As the conversation drew to a close, it was obvious that things had gone well. We shook hands and, three days after we met, on the Monday, a deal was in place for me to become England's head coach until 2019.

When he heard the news, Jake was upset. He didn't say it directly to me, but I was sure he felt I hadn't supported him or the idea of doing the job together strongly enough. But Ian had stressed that the RFU were never going to appoint a two-man coaching team. Ian said later that he had flown to Cape Town with the express intention of appointing me. My conscience was clear. I knew Jake was seriously disappointed, but I'd earned the offer to coach England through my own performance over many years. I certainly wasn't going to turn down the opportunity of a lifetime because it might hurt Jake's feelings.

I was more concerned about breaking the news to the Stormers. I felt terrible that, after just two weeks, I was asking to be released. The irony was that the Stormers had been a dream job – until I fell into an even better and far bigger dream. The management and my fellow coaches at the Stormers were disappointed but understanding. They recognized the huge opportunity I had been offered and they made the hard task of saying goodbye so much easier.

It had been a whirlwind. On Thursday evening I had been setting up my office and new life in Cape Town. By the following Monday night I was on a plane and heading to London as coach of the biggest team in the world.

It's hard to describe how excited I was. During the 2015 World Cup, England, Australia and Wales were in the same pool, so Steve Borthwick, Leigh Jones – our Welsh defence coach – and I watched the games closely. I thought England looked confused in the way they played the game. Their fitness was also way below par. As I sat on the plane to London, I got straight to work. The first task was to identify a style of play that suited England.

I knew the 'tactical periodization' model (where you decide a game style and tailor your training to support it), which had worked so well for Japan, would also suit England. Our style would have to be built on the foundations of English rugby, which include a strong set piece and aggressive defence. The last piece of the puzzle would be how we attacked.

I didn't have a lot of time to be successful. It's a cut-throat job and if we didn't start winning quickly, it was unlikely I would make it to 2019.

I looked dishevelled when I arrived at Heathrow on 19 November 2015. I'd left in such a hurry that the only clothes I had were a T-shirt, shorts and scruffy shoes, which got me into trouble with my mother. The British media were on hand to greet me and

Mum was not happy when she saw photographs in the Australian newspapers. She reminded me once again of the importance of looking smart and wearing proper shoes. Mum was right. I was ill-prepared and hadn't given my presentation enough thought. It was careless and an early reminder to me of the scrutiny I would be under in this new job.

My chaotic look was matched by the rearranged plans on arrival. After being picked up at the airport, we were supposed to head for Pennyhill Park, the hotel that England use as their training base in Surrey. But the press had already arrived and were waiting for me outside Pennyhill – so I was whisked away to a little hotel in Windsor, not far from where Ian lived. I spent the night there and had a meeting the following day with Ian and Rob Andrew, who was director of rugby at the RFU. They showed me around the RFU offices in Twickenham. It was an eye-opener to see their massive offices with over 600 staff. It was a thrilling day and, in my time with England, the RFU have been great employers. There has always been a genuine desire to improve and grow the game.

The media conference announcing my appointment was on 20 November. This time I was ready. I wore a dark pin-striped suit and a red tie in a nod to England, and shoes with a military-grade shine. I had to make a good impression. The powerful and influential British media would play a big role in my success or failure, so I was friendly and optimistic. Being England's first foreign coach, being Australian and being Eddie Jones, meant I would get no free passes. They would pounce at the first sign of hesitation or weakness. In describing my relationship with the media, I've often used the metaphor of a Western gunslinger who walks into a bar full of locals. They look you up and down, very slowly, and at the first sign of trouble they kick the tables over and blast you with their six-shooters. That's life with the British media.

The mix of highly paid and opinionated former England internationals and the supporting cast of hyper-competitive journalists from the newspapers, radio, television and online media means you have to be very careful about what you say and do. Every word counts as they compete to see who can be the most outraged. When I visited Sir Alex Ferguson in Manchester, after our loss to Scotland in 2018, his first and best piece of advice was, 'If you still read the papers, stop. It will drive you mad.'

With the media room at Twickenham full to bursting, I said, 'It's quite clear from talking to Ian that the desire is to build a winning team that has Twickenham buzzing. We have to systematically make sure that, over the next four years, we bring through young players to play in the next World Cup.'

I acknowledged Stuart Lancaster because, apart from making the players more grounded and hard-working, he had uncovered a wealth of talent which would be the foundation of my 2019 squad. I also stressed, as Ian had asked, the need to develop coaches. 'One of our goals is to have assistant coaches who by 2019 are ready to take over. I'm sure we can do that. There are good coaches in England.'

It went smoothly, as the failure to get out of the pool stages of a home World Cup had been a chastening experience for those involved in the sport in England. While it was clear that many people didn't like the idea of getting in a foreign coach, I felt I was going to get a fair go. But we would have to win matches and I would always need to be on my guard.

I was keen to get cracking, but I could not begin work quite yet. My start was delayed by work-permit issues and the fact I had already committed to giving a World Rugby workshop to ten tier-two rugby countries in Los Angeles in late November. Bill Beaumont, who was then the RFU's chairman, joked that he was not aware England had slipped down as far as tier-two level. But he and Ian appreciated that my appearance at the workshop was a way of me giving something back to the game while sharing Japan's success with other developing rugby nations. It was also a demonstration of the RFU's genuine commitment to expand the global game.

My visa had still not been cleared once I finished my work in LA. So I flew back to Tokyo to see Hiroko and make final arrangements for her to join me in London in early January. She had not even had a chance to see Cape Town but, as always, she was ready for our next adventure. It was another example of her great contribution to my life and work.

I officially started work as England head coach on 1 December 2015. My first task was to speak to the key Test players. I then wanted to visit the directors of rugby at the Premiership clubs and to watch as many games as possible. I would soon discover that most of them were happy to work with me to find and develop the best talent. I was also keen to immerse myself in English culture to better understand the national character. As with Japan four years before, we had to instil the unique essence of the English character into our game style.

On my first Saturday afternoon on the job, I left my Twickenham hotel room and made the short journey across the road to the Stoop on a freezing cold day. Harlequins were at home to London Irish and their team included current England players in Mike Brown, Danny Care, Joe Marler and Chris Robshaw. James Horwill, who had won 61 caps for the Wallabies after being a young player for me during that disastrous season with the Queensland Reds, was in their side at lock.

It was a poor match, with Harlequins thumping Irish 38–7. Conditions were atrocious and London Irish were weak. But the home crowd of almost 15,000 seemed to enjoy themselves, and Care and Robshaw were among the more impressive performers. I had arranged to meet Robshaw for a coffee that evening. It felt right he should be the first England player I spoke to on a one-to-one basis. He was England's skipper and, despite leading them during their disappointing World Cup, he had captained his country more times than anyone else apart from Will Carling. Even Martin Johnson had not captained England as often as Chris Robshaw.

I respected Chris – even though remarks I had made about him might have suggested otherwise. After England lost to Australia, and crashed out of the World Cup, I told the *Daily Mail* that, 'David Pocock [Australia's number 7] is an out-and-out fetcher. There is no one in the world better than him over the ball. Stuart Lancaster doesn't have that sort of fetcher. To me, Robshaw is an outstanding club player, but at international level he just doesn't have that point of difference. He carries OK, he tackles OK, but he's not outstandingly good in any area. I think that's his limiting factor. He's a good workmanlike player, but he does not have the specialist skills and the instinct of an open side like Pocock.'

I still think that's a reasonable assessment in the context of Robshaw's professional capability as a number 7. But the British media saw my comments as signalling the end of his Test career and another example of big-mouth Eddie Jones rubbishing a good bloke. The truth was more nuanced. I had an open mind about Chris's future with England as a player. It was important for me to get to know him. In my view, he was a number 6 and he had proved it that afternoon with a performance which was at a higher level than most English club players.

Chris clearly carried an unusually heavy burden after England's failure. I admired his stoicism. He is a quality bloke. I told him that, as a player, we would start with a clean slate. As long as he was playing at 6, I would be interested in him. He just needed to get his head down and play well for Quins. If that happened, he would have a good chance of making the squad. I didn't discuss my thoughts on the captaincy with him and, instead, made it clear that my priority for him was to play well.

Chris was sincere, down-to-earth and passionate about England. He listened to what I had to say and I got the feeling that he was motivated to become the best blind-side flanker in England.

Privately, I had already decided England needed a new captain to change the mood around the squad. Chris was diligent and hard-working, but we needed a more forceful personality. England, to me, have always been at their best with a powerful leader. Winston Churchill, Mike Brearley and Martin Johnson are three very different men who spring to mind when I think of leaders in this country. All the great English teams seem to have had special and often larger-than-life captains. Some countries, some people, need strong leadership. I felt England did, especially in the wake of 2015.

I went to watch Northampton next and I had barely settled into my seat in the stand when a woman came over. She was a Northampton fan and, bold as brass, said: 'You've got to pick Dylan Hartley as England captain. Whenever he captains Saints, our team changes for the better.'

Despite Dylan's disciplinary record, I was interested. He was clearly a leader of men. My first experience of him as a player had not been a positive one. When I coached Saracens he was a young hooker for Northampton with a bad attitude. I thought he was a nasty bastard. But there was something about him. I was looking for someone with a hard edge, and he had that in spades. I wanted and needed someone with real experience to captain England.

Dylan had a decent game that night and I invited him for breakfast at Pennyhill Park the following week. I had moved into the hotel while I waited for Hiroko to join me. I liked the hotel but had to put up with walking to breakfast each morning along a corridor that celebrated the success of the 2003 World Cup-winning team. It was a constant reminder of one of my most painful defeats. But I was happy to know that those photographs might serve as motivation for the players ahead of Japan 2019.

I waited for Dylan in the restaurant and, a few minutes before we were due to meet, a chubby little bloke walked in. He was bookish and wore glasses. He walked straight towards me and, looking more like a fourth-year philosophy student than a rugby player, Dylan Hartley offered his hand. I was taken aback but his firm handshake made me smile. He looked nothing like the ogre depicted by the media.

I was intrigued. Dylan was calm and intelligent and spoke well about himself and where he thought he and England needed to improve. Talking a good game is one thing, but I'm always looking for other insights into a player's character. Dylan was considered, engaging and sincere. Our conversation was interrupted by a call I had to take. As I moved away from the table, I noticed that Dylan went out of his way to talk to one of the ladies who worked in the restaurant. Doris had been at Pennyhill for years. I was struck by how engaged Dylan had been while chatting amiably to an elderly hotel worker. I liked that about him.

Later, after Dylan left, Doris came over for a chat. Like many of the hotel workers at Pennyhill, she knew I was always up for a chat. Doris loved Dylan. She said Dylan was one of the players who always said hello and spoke to the staff. Beyond the fact that he was obviously a decent human being, I was interested in his ability to engage positively with different people. It was clear he would be able to bring the players together.

The world has changed so much, with young people spending so much time on social media, that connecting authentically in person while bringing a group together is a dying art. Dylan was a street-smart rugby player with an old-fashioned approach. He spoke well about his background in New Zealand and his transition to England. He also fronted up and admitted his mistakes. I liked his honesty. As someone who has made more than his fair share of mistakes, I admire people who don't make excuses and can explain the lessons they have learnt.

It was hard to reconcile the bloke sitting across from me at breakfast with a player who carried one of the game's worst disciplinary records. It didn't fit. He was a fine communicator and had, I knew, the intelligence and guile to interact well with the referee. In rugby there are contests over the ball all the time and the referee is constantly making judgements. The captain's ability to have a good relationship with the ref, even to subtly influence him, is an important part of Test rugby.

Dylan also matched the kind of rugby I thought England should play in our first year. He was not a great athlete – but a tough competitor who understood the psychology of rugby. He brought an edge which England lacked. I wanted a hard-nosed team, with a strong set piece and a good defence that could squeeze an opposition to death. We needed to win games to build confidence. The 2015 team had lacked self-belief and confidence. Dylan looked to have both these qualities. The more I thought about it, the more convinced I became that he was the perfect candidate to help me change the team's mindset.

It was a straightforward choice as Owen Farrell did not feature in my thinking as captain at that stage. I had known him at Saracens as a teenager and watched plenty of games when he had been outstanding for England. He would certainly be one of my key players and he was maturing as a leader. But he was still young.

Having settled on my captain, it was time to finalize the coaching staff. I had given Andy Farrell his first experience of coaching while at Saracens in 2008. After his inspirational rugby league career, he had made his union debut for England, but his time in the new code was dogged by persistent injury. Andy was too strong to mope about his bad luck, and he responded well to my suggestion that, while going through rehab, he should do some coaching for Saracens. His sharp insights and organizational skills were obvious, and he went on to become England's defence coach from 2011 to 2015.

I would have liked to keep Andy on because he's a very good man and a very good coach. But the situation was complicated because he was Owen's father and so I decided that he had to go. Two and a half years later, with Owen having come into his own and captained England on our tour of South Africa in 2018, and with Andy being a key contributor to Ireland's Grand Slam-winning coaching team, I approached Andy. My defence coach

Paul Gustard had decided to step down from England and take over at Harlequins and I was keen for Andy to rejoin the set up.

He was seriously interested, and I think we would have got the deal over the line, but Andy knew he would replace Joe Schmidt as head coach after the 2019 World Cup. He was keen on that challenge and so, understandably, chose to remain with Ireland. Whenever we see each other now, Andy and I get on well. His past disappointment at losing his job is no longer an issue.

Once I had spoken to Andy in December 2015, I made the same decision in regard to Graham Rowntree and Mike Catt. They had both achieved a lot in the game. Catt won a World Cup winners' medal in 2003 and Rowntree, after earning 54 England caps, had already been a forwards coach for the Lions on their successful tour of Australia in 2013. But it was time for a clean break. I wanted my own coaching team, and so I broke the bad news to Catt and Rowntree.

A head coach wants his assistants to provide a balanced back room. There needs to be diversity, so I always look for personalities who are different to me and can add something new. My first choice was nailed on. Steve Borthwick had been exceptional with Japan and I admired and trusted him. He'd accepted the head coach's job at Bristol but, as soon as I arrived at Twickenham, I wanted Steve at my side. Steve felt the same about joining England, but we still had a very difficult task extracting him from his contract. Bristol were in the Championship, the second tier of English club rugby, and Steve had joined them straight after the World Cup. By mid-December, having accepted my offer, he told Bristol of the changed situation.

They were not happy and issued a strongly worded statement: 'Steve Borthwick has today indicated to the club that he wishes to join the RFU coaching team. Bristol Rugby want to make it clear that we have not agreed that Steve Borthwick can leave our employment. Steve Borthwick is subject to a recently signed long-term contract. Bristol Rugby did not give the RFU permission to speak with Steve Borthwick. Bristol Rugby will take all reasonable actions necessary to protect the club's position.'

The next four days were tense. I knew the RFU would have to compensate Bristol, but I was also sure that we would prevail. The ensuing rancour demonstrated the divide in England between club and country. Bristol's owner Steve Lansdown claimed the RFU were 'totally unprofessional' in their approach and accused them of trying to 'ride roughshod over everybody. I cannot believe the governing body acts in such a way.'

This situation would never happen in Ireland, Scotland, New Zealand, Australia or South Africa, where the success of the national team is everyone's priority. I know the ownership structure and cultures are different in England – but in those countries the national interest comes first. That's not the case in England.

In the end, an agreement was reached. Ian Ritchie did his best to smooth over the situation: 'We very much appreciate that our approach for Steve has come at a challenging time for Bristol, and in such circumstances I thank them for reaching this agreement.'

We took a lot of flak, and the battle lines between club and country had been drawn again. We were also accused of trying to poach Alex King from Northampton, but I'd decided to look after England's attack while I wanted Gustard as my defence coach. I knew Gussie from my time at Saracens and always enjoyed his approach. Perhaps the most famous example of Gussie's personal style was when he brought two wolves into training at Saracens. It was his way of making the point that he wanted the players to 'hunt like a pack of wolves'. But Gussie was also a serious coach who worked extremely hard. Fortunately, my old club were much more amenable than Bristol when we approached them.

Gussie's personality profile is almost the exact opposite of Steve's. He is an extrovert, whereas Steve is much more reserved. Steve is thorough and analytical while Gussie enjoys developing the social side of the group. They had spent years together at Saracens and I knew they would complement each other.

It was generous of Stuart Lancaster to meet me within three weeks of my taking his job. He was approachable, friendly, and shared all the information he'd gathered over four years. I was impressed by his humility, diligence and professionalism. Having been fired from the Wallabies job some years earlier, I felt real empathy for him. I knew he was hurting. But there he was – right up until the end – giving his very best effort to English rugby in the most difficult of personal circumstances. Four years on, I'm sure he will still feel a certain disappointment at the way his time as England coach ended. Stuart had done fine work with England and they had carried high hopes into the World Cup – only for two matches against Wales and Australia to slip away. It should always be remembered that Stuart was the coach who identified and gave the first opportunities to many of the players who are in the 2019 World Cup squad.

Stuart's classy behaviour was not matched by the press. Ian Ritchie asked me to attend a function where many of the leading rugby writers would be invited. It would be a chance to get to know the journalists in a relaxed atmosphere over a few drinks. I was assured the event was governed by 'Chatham House rules' (a convention whereby all parties agree to leave the details of any conversation in the room). But knowing that many journalists struggle to keep new information a secret, I thought I would let it slip that I had decided Dylan would be the new captain. I wanted to see if the journalists could be trusted to keep a secret. One of them asked me if Robshaw would retain the captaincy.

'No, mate,' I said. 'I'm going with Hartley.'

Sure enough, one of the journalists just couldn't help himself and rang Dylan to ask him how he felt about taking on the captaincy. I hadn't as yet told Dylan that he'd got the job. It was a clear early sign that I needed to be careful with the media. I didn't make a fuss about it and I also didn't care that there was a mixed reaction to Dylan's appointment. I knew I had chosen the right bloke to captain England for the next few years.

By early January, with the Six Nations starting in a few weeks, there was still a heap to do. But it was exciting. The early stages of putting a project together are always the most enjoyable. We were racing to get things done. But, as with many jobs, you never seem to have enough time in coaching.

My first training session with England was a surprise. I was seriously taken aback when I saw that, after just 20 minutes, many of the players were blowing. They were not used to the pace and intensity of our drills and, physically, they looked in poor condition compared to my Japanese players. I had not been expecting such a low standard of fitness. They were conditioned to play slow, stop-start rugby, and you're never going to win consistently at the highest level playing that way. But we were working with good players – and players of this standard catch up fast when they are in a proper training programme. Within six months they were dramatically fitter.

Their skills levels were pretty good, but English players rarely show great movement. They play a controlled game which stifles movement and they lack the spontaneity or zip of the New Zealanders or Australians. During my four years in England, I've never once seen kids play touch footy in the park. I see plenty of boys kicking a ball, because football is king, but I've yet to see English kids flipping a rugby ball around for the sheer pleasure of passing and running with it. When I visit the club academies and schools, they all push a very structured game – which means the average English rugby player is not a natural mover. But they've got the potential to improve very quickly.

I was more concerned with the mentality and the lack of leadership in the squad. It was obvious that, because of the intense media scrutiny, many players didn't show the same freedom and energy with England that they produced for their clubs. They worried about making mistakes. So, instead of wanting the ball, they tended to hang back. They reminded me of a certain kind of fielder in cricket. Once you drop a catch, the good player wants the ball to come his way again as soon as possible. The less gifted and more tentative player thinks: 'Please, don't hit it my way again.' Some of the England players reminded me of those fielders. They lacked confidence and were afraid of getting completely involved.

I needed to change their mindset before we did much else. The easiest way to do this was to increase their fitness and prepare them to play rugby in a very simple, robust England style. It's always important to have clarity – in terms of your preparation and philosophy. The quicker these ground rules are established, the quicker the players grow in confidence. We set up a simple framework and I encouraged the players to drive it to a large extent and to make decisions for themselves. Once they start taking charge, they really begin to grow and the team becomes more cohesive.

It took a while because the culture of modern sport does not produce enough dynamic and assertive leaders. Everything is so organized that players don't have to show initiative. This impacts on leadership. The two are entwined because to show leadership you need initiative. You have to be prepared to do things to create movement and progress. If you show initiative then people will follow you. But the problem is that players are becoming robotic. They are followers rather than leaders, because they get told what to do all the time. They're told what time they need to arrive and what they need to wear. There is no need for them to worry about their kit or their food because that will be provided for them. They're told what to think and what to say. The contemporary argument is that you are taking away all distractions and allowing them to concentrate on the game. But you're actually robbing them of the opportunity to grow as people. They follow blindly even if they are being led badly.

In 2018 a few players in the Australian cricket team decided to use sandpaper to tamper with the ball. Australia had been the most hard-nosed, self-driven team in world cricket, but they ended up in a mess. I couldn't believe that no one in that team had been brave enough to stand up to a couple of guys who wanted to do something against the spirit of the game. But it wasn't really their fault because they had not been properly prepared to be courageous.

As a coach you've got to create an environment where it is acceptable to fail occasionally. You need to give the players opportunities to make decisions, and to lead, and not to fear the consequences. When you've got control of a national team for a short period of time it can be difficult to influence behaviour. But I was determined to change the culture of comfort, shake them up and find some leadership amongst the players.

I injected some chaos into the usual routine. The players would be told to turn up at an important meeting starting at 8 a.m. the next morning; meanwhile I had made sure that we had set up hidden video cameras in the training centre. My fellow coaches and I would be in a different part of the hotel monitoring their behaviour when they turned up and began milling around. After 15 minutes of waiting aimlessly, it began to dawn on them that we were not joining them. It was fascinating to watch how, after the initial confusion, a couple of players stood up and led the way.

Dylan and Owen set about making sure that the players turned that time into a productive meeting. It replicated the technique we had used with my Japanese players. I used it a few times with England. One time they gathered in a room which was empty but for a white board on which a couple of points had been written down. We watched which players fed off those pointers and led the squad in a different direction.

It would be the same if they had ended up on a deserted island. They'd sit around and wonder what to do and then, eventually, a few people would step forward and decide how best to cope with the situation. We were trying to replicate that dynamic. We needed to see who wanted to lead.

Every team in elite sport has to deal with failure, and they need leaders to find a way out of chaos and confusion. And when the team moves into a great position, and the wins are rolling, complacency is your next threat. So it's important you have leaders who can identify these transitional periods and deal with them quickly. It's how you build success.

I also tried to get inside the heads of individual players to find out what made them tick – and to encourage them to think for themselves. During our training camps I held a series of one-to-one sessions as I wanted to shake them up or bolster their fragile confidence. I approached each player differently.

Scrum half is a key position and the two standout players in England were Ben Youngs and Danny Care. I liked Care. He was a chirpy Northerner who could make things happen. But Ben Youngs was the better player and the more likely World Cup number 9 in 2019. I thought he should be our first-choice scrum half, but he'd had a poor tournament in 2015. He was not in the best physical condition and that reflected his distracted mental state. I decided to have some fun with him. He walked in the room and, even before he could say anything, I threw a big bag of sweets onto the table.

'I heard you like these, mate,' I said with a little smile.

Ben didn't look too pleased and he was not quite sure how to respond. I helped him out. 'You've got a choice here,' I said. 'You either keep enjoying these or you start paying proper attention to being a Test match rugby player.'

The message was absorbed very fast and, since then, Ben has been good. He has done the hard yards and, even when I picked Care ahead of him, he kept the same attitude and work ethic. He was soon established as my first pick at scrum half.

Luke Cowan-Dickie was our third-choice hooker, behind Hartley and Jamie George. You couldn't miss him. Luke had one of the worst mullets I've ever seen on a rugby player. He was a good working-class bloke from Truro in Cornwall and he played for Exeter. I'd heard Luke was a bit of a drinker. So when he walked in, I put a crate of beers on the table. He made me laugh because, after we'd had our chat, he walked off with the beers.

I learnt that Luke is an obsessive guy. He goes at everything 100 per cent, so when he does drink he really lets rip. More importantly, Luke soon found a way to control himself, and he cut out the drinking because he understood the opportunity in front of him.

One of the many fascinating challenges of coaching is the diversity of characters in your squad. George Ford is a born footballer, a hugely resourceful player with immense talent. I remember first seeing him play when he was a 17-year-old kid for Leicester. I was in Japan, coaching Suntory, when I saw him on television. It was typical of me to relax by watching rugby from another country. My eyes opened wide as soon as I saw George playing. He had an incredible feel for the game and I thought, 'Boy, this kid can play. He's going to be the real thing.'

George was Mike Ford's son. Mike had been at Saracens before I took over as their director of rugby on a short-term basis in 2006. Like his close mate, Owen Farrell, George had moved with his family from the north of England when his dad switched codes from league to union. Owen and George spent their teenage years in Harpenden, a genteel town in the Home Counties. Apparently George often did Owen's French homework so that they could get out and play rugby. It was a story which matched my own past.

Owen was a much more physical player and, in the way he barked out orders and carried an abrasive edge, he almost had the mentality of a gnarled forward. They gave me plenty of options. My hunch was that Owen would eventually become my chosen fly half, but George is such a good player that I was equally comfortable with him at 10 – and Owen at 12.

I also knew we needed fighters and Mike Brown was a born fighter. He was a great competitor and probably the best defensive full back in the world. The closer we came to the World Cup, the more we needed an expansive number 15 with speed and skill to burn. It was always going to be hard for Browny to match Elliot Daly and Anthony Watson but, in 2016, he was just the kind of player I needed.

The media were hammering me to pick Alex Goode at full

back. He's a very good player. No question; and for his club Saracens I would agree that he has been a great player. But I needed
something different. The distinction between club rugby and
Test rugby is pace. You need absolute gas at the top level, and
Goode didn't have it. Brown had much more of it and a feisty
attitude to match.

I was worried that the English boys might have been a bit
reserved for my liking, but James Haskell made enough noise for
the whole squad. I initially suspected that Haskell was quite an
insecure character who tried to hide his vulnerabilities by
making a racket and kidding around. Every team needs a joker
and Hask did it for us. He wanted to be loved and we embraced
him. He had also been around the block and, after failing to fulfil
some extravagant early claims about his talent, he had learnt a
lot by playing rugby in New Zealand and Japan before returning
to England. Haskell was playing well for Wasps. I thought he
could provide a short-term solution, given the shortage of open-
side flankers in England. I envisaged a situation where, in the
absence of a natural fetcher in 2016, I could play Robshaw at 6
and Hask at 7. They brought a commanding and powerful presence to our back-row play, with Billy Vunipola giving us some
magic at the back of the scrum.

It did not take me long to work out that the Vunipola brothers
were going to be instrumental to our long-term success. Billy
was a star – a player blessed with an incredible skill set. He had
strength, speed, power and skill. Off the field he was very different to his older brother, Mako, our loose-head prop. Billy was
rebellious and funny. He was a very jovial character who would
turn up to training with the kind of attitude that says, 'Everything is amazing!' Mako's only a couple of years older but he
seems to belong to a different generation. He was almost like a
father figure to Billy. He is very calm and controlled and a cohesive presence at Saracens and England.

After working with him for four years I rate Mako as one of
the most complete props I've ever seen – all he is missing is a

turn of speed. He and Billy are two of the best players I've ever coached. The obvious perception was that Billy would become my key player, certainly among the forwards, but I soon learnt that Mako was just as important. In terms of the team it seemed to me as if Farrell, Brown, Haskell and Billy would give me the fire I needed while Mako would provide the calming influence to make sure everything flowed.

Maro Itoje, who played for Saracens, alongside the Vunipolas, Farrell, George Kruis and Jamie George, was another player I paid close attention to in our earliest sessions. He was still only 20 when Lancaster picked his World Cup squad. Itoje just missed selection. In early 2016 he was being hyped as the best prospect in world rugby – which seemed a stretch to me. I knew that in England, where the media are in an eternal competition to outdo each other with facile predictions about who is the biggest, greatest and fastest, players get hyped as 'world class' way too soon.

Itoje was intriguing. When I first saw him play, I wasn't convinced that he was that good. But when he came into camp, that assessment changed pretty quickly. He was a great athlete – big, strong, reasonably powerful and with, most importantly, a desperation to win.

It was obvious that he would become a Test player of the highest class, and that his athleticism would add a new dimension to a typical English pack, but he needed to be brought along slowly. His striking physical presence had made him a darling of the media and he was having his tyres pumped up almost every day. In their eyes, he could do no wrong. But it was clear to me that, at times, he was struggling to manage his pin-up-boy status. He needed to mature and, over the years, I've really enjoyed watching him grow and learn how to be coached.

I remember Pep Guardiola once told me the best players face their most difficult challenge when joining the national team. They are surrounded by much better players than at their clubs and they realize that there are areas of their game they need to improve. It takes courage for the gifted player to change. Itoje was excellent in this regard. He impressed me the most in terms of his courage to change and to understand that he needed to add more to his game.

Now, four years on, if he stays fit, he will establish himself as a dominant figure in world rugby. Unlike in 2016, he is a now a very good attacking player. When he first came into the squad, he was more a destructive force. Today, having become more construct-ive, he has a better balance to his game. I've learnt that Itoje wants to be more than a good player. He wants to be the best.

I'm often asked if I rode him hard in those early camps, but in fact I adopted the opposite approach because that's what I thought would work for him. At first, when we spoke, his eyes never connected with mine because he wasn't really hearing the message. In the past, I might have interpreted that as a sign of in-difference and become angry. But, in Maro's case, I understood that he needed to learn how to be coached. I would often encour-age Maro, but he didn't give me much feedback. I soon realized that – before he could respond to me – he needed to find himself first.

I use the analogy of the young horse that wants to run fast. Sometimes you've got to pull them in and sometimes you've just got to let them go and let them organize themselves. Maro was one player we needed to let go. We allowed him to develop and we waited for the time when we could control him more effectively. He's now developing as a leader and becoming influ-ential. It's happened quite naturally.

In early 2016 I approached my first tournament, and opening games as England coach, with gathering confidence. After my initial surprise at the players' lack of fitness and confidence, I was now satisfied by their growing assertiveness. They were less worried about making mistakes and more determined to have a go. It was gratifying; and it filled me with real hope as we set out on our first challenge together, the Six Nations, the most historic tournament in world rugby.

There was a real urgency in camp: 2015 had hit hard and these boys were going to do something about it.

I'd been so busy focusing on the players and the programme that I hadn't really taken the time to think too much about what was about to take place. I remember one morning early at the gym when it hit me. I was about to coach England in the Six Nations. I felt a real sense of pride, accomplishment, honour and humility. Here I was, a half-Japanese, half-Australian bloke from Little Bay in Sydney, about to coach the biggest team in the world in the most famous tournament in rugby. It was one of those moments where you just think: 'How did that happen?'

While the standard of play can be variable, especially in the depths of a European winter, the Six Nations is, without question, rugby's greatest annual tournament. In my experience, nothing comes even remotely close to it. As we approached the opening match, you couldn't help but get drawn in. I was surprised by the wall-to-wall coverage in the build-up. Apart from all the newspaper supplements and radio podcasts, I kept seeing Dylan Hartley's face whenever we turned on the television. Glossy commercials reminded the public that the Six Nations was on its way.

I was soon struck by the toughness of every match. This is particularly true if you're coaching England. For every other team, playing England is like their final. You cannot be off your game in the slightest because they will catch you out – and if they beat England they've had a good tournament.

We had a difficult opening game and had to travel to Murrayfield to face Scotland on the Saturday evening of 6 February 2016. You could not miss the intensity of the rivalry. But I am not sure the players understood why there was always such animosity towards them in Edinburgh. As an Australian – fan and coach – who had always wanted to beat England, the reasons were obvious.

I found similarities between England and Japan. Both countries were colonial powers that had built their empires ruthlessly. Their reputations suffered. As a consequence, both England and Japan have become quite passive. Their aggression remains buried until they are really put under the pump. It's always there but, as a coach, you have to dig deeper to extract the aggression you need in a combative game. I knew that the Scots would come flying at us with hostility and intent. Their mission was to settle age-old scores.

All I cared about was getting the win. It was desperately important that we ground out a victory to bolster the boys' fragile confidence. I got us organized and set us up to play a very English brand of rugby. I chose an experienced team and went for Brown at full back and Ford and Care at half back. Farrell was in at 12, Hartley was hooker and captain and Robshaw, Haskell and Billy Vunipola were my rumbling back row. I decided to save Itoje's debut for an easier occasion and sent the whizz-kid back to Saracens to play a game of club rugby.

Vern Cotter, Scotland's venerable Kiwi coach, didn't like me saying that the home team were the favourites. I knew we were better than the Scots but, in a media game, it's far better to paint yourselves as underdogs. I could also point to the fact that England were ranked a lowly eighth in the world.

It was a real arm-wrestle in horrible conditions. But I was pleased with England's attitude. I already knew that they were good players, but they showed me real grit that day. Hartley set the tone and the team responded to his lead. Robshaw, meanwhile, was outstanding. He worked really hard and never took a backward step. We won 15–9 and my sweetest memory is of a brilliant piece of skill from Mako Vunipola. I think he is the only prop in the world who could have played such a beautifully deft inside pass to Farrell, which checked the Scottish defence long enough to create room on the outside. Jack Nowell finished the move by diving over in the corner – but the try belonged to Mako's soft hands.

We moved on to Rome and we weren't great. The players were

too comfortable for my liking. But Italy is always a difficult game. If you beat them by a big score then everyone says. 'What do you expect?' But if the score is much closer everybody says you're terrible. You can never win with the English media. A lot of them, particularly the more experienced ones, are miserable when we win and miserable when we lose.

England won easily enough, 40–9, and the headlines focused on the fact that Itoje came off the bench to win his first Test cap. I immediately doused the plaudits. 'Maro's like a Vauxhall Viva now. We want to turn him into a BMW. He's got a lot of work to do but he's got potential.'

Itoje showed his youth by admitting that he had to turn to Google to discover what a Vauxhall Viva looked like.

After two wins on the road, the media were already banging the Grand Slam drum for England. I had to adjust to the fevered attention. In the previous six years in Japan I had worked in blissful isolation. The Japanese media had no impact on me. But here it was the complete opposite. Media is a significant part of the job and the demands are unrelenting. Of course I had the experience of big media demands at World Cups, but this was at another level. There is no other job like it in world rugby. The sheer scale and demands are vast. I was out of practice, which led to me making a bad mistake in the build-up to the Irish game.

I wanted to divert attention from my players and so I went after the Irish. I pointed out that, under Joe Schmidt, they kicked away between 60 and 70 per cent of their possession. I was stirring them up deliberately. I said that I'd be taking my boys to watch Stoke City so we could get used to the ball being hoofed high in the air. It was knockabout stuff but, with the game closing in, I went too far.

Jonny Sexton is the Irish talisman at 10. He is as brave as he is brilliant, and he had taken a lot of bangs to the head. He had suffered another pounding against France, in a game which the Irish lost 10–9, and there was much speculation as to whether he would play against us. I spoke crassly early in the week of our clash with Ireland.

'I'd be worried about his welfare if he's had whiplash injuries,' I said of Sexton. 'I'm sure his mother and father would be worried about that. If you're saying a guy has got whiplash then he's had a severe trauma. Maybe they used the wrong term but if you've had severe trauma then you've got to worry about the welfare of the player. Hopefully, he's all right on Saturday to play.'

All hell broke loose. I copped an absolute hammering in the media for bringing a player's family into it. I had been careless and gone too far but I thought some of the coverage was unfair and unreasonable. I certainly had not intentionally meant to cause any offence.

Sexton played against us and came through the game unscathed. We led 6–3 at half-time and should have been further ahead. Early in the second half we conceded the first try against us since I took over. But, after Conor Murray dummied his way over the line, with Haskell in the sin bin, we responded. Billy Vunipola was magnificent and two tries from Anthony Watson and Mike Brown sealed a 21–10 win. Itoje did well in his first start and I upgraded him from 'a Viva to an Astra'. I also made the more serious point that, 'We probably left 10 to 15 points out there. We weren't quite sharp enough.'

After the match, I was still steaming about some of the harsher commentary and announced I was putting a media ban on myself. 'I don't want to do anything that offends the media or offends people's parents,' I said. 'If I don't say anything, you come away from the press conference and say it's boring. If I say something, I'm scaremongering. I can't win. So the easiest way is that I don't come to the media conference.'

It wasn't my finest moment. I'd lost my temper and control of the story. I was cranky with myself because I knew that effectively managing my daily communication would be a critical factor in our future success. At the midway point of the Six

Nations, the football was going well but I was struggling with my off-field game.

I also had sharp words with the squad when we gathered together to face Wales two weeks later. After the game against Ireland, most of the boys had been anxious to get home and seemed surprised that I expected them to get together with me and the coaches to enjoy a drink. So I made it non-negotiable. I wanted the whole squad to spend an hour together after all our home games so we could relax over a beer. I am pleased to say that this order soon turned into a pleasure for the players and they became closer.

Wales were also unbeaten when they came to Twickenham on the penultimate weekend of the Six Nations. It was rightly billed as a Grand Slam decider, but I played it very cool and made sure the players concentrated on the basics. I also wanted them to be more robust and adaptable and so we moved them out of Penny-hill Park two nights before the game. I was shocked that they had stayed at Pennyhill throughout the World Cup. It made life too comfortable for them. Before we played Ireland, I also shook them up by taking us to a hotel in Chiswick on the Thursday night. We did the same before Wales but, this time, booked into a hotel in Syon Park.

England play every home game at Twickenham. New Zealand, Australia and South Africa play their Tests at different venues in contrasting cities. The players get used to moving around. I was already thinking ahead to the World Cup in 2019 when we would have to criss-cross Japan, and so I wanted our players to sample a few changes to their pattern of home games.

We played well and were 19–0 ahead early in the second half. With seven minutes left on the clock we were cruising, 25–7, so I made a raft of changes. Suddenly, we conceded two tries in three minutes and our lead shrank to just four points. George North came close to snatching an underserved Welsh victory, but Manu Tuilagi forced him into touch. We won 25–21 to seal the Triple Crown.

16. Trying to pick Clive Woodward's brain during the 2002 Six Nations.

17. As part of our preparations for the 2003 World Cup, the Aussie team spent a night bonding in the Darwin bush.

18. George Smith on the rampage during the 2003 semi-final victory over New Zealand.

19. The aftermath of the devastating 2003 World Cup final loss to England.

20. The chastening press conference after being sacked as Australia's coach.

21. Taking a training session during my ill-fated time with the Queensland Reds.

22. Happier times with Jake White and South Africa during the 2007 World Cup.

23. No blazer, but a World Cup winner's medal will do.

24. Celebrating winning the All-Japan Rugby Football Championship final with Suntory.

25. My Japanese players savour our historic and brave victory over South Africa at the 2015 World Cup.

26. Being unveiled as England's head coach.

27. Celebrating the 2016 Six Nations Grand Slam with my assistant coaches Paul Gustard and Steve Borthwick a few months later.

28. With my old mate Glen Ella during the crucial first Test of the 2016 tour of Australia.

29. Although we lost against Ireland on the day, we'd done enough to be crowned Six Nations champions again in 2017.

30. Consoling George Ford and the rest of the players after the 25–13 loss to Scotland in the 2018 Six Nations. It was the first of seven losses during a difficult 2018.

31. England stare down the haka in a V formation, setting the tone for the comprehensive 19–7 victory over the All Blacks.

32. Utter dejection after the loss to South Africa in the 2019 World Cup final.

'We made a number of changes to test players and the strength of the team,' I explained. 'Maybe those changes didn't work. If you look at our first 60 minutes there was some fantastic rugby. The Grand Slam is a reality and we can't wait to get to Paris and to do the business.'

We soon had the championship wrapped up because, a day after we beat Wales, France lost to Scotland. England had won their first Six Nations in seven years. But the players knew that we had to win the Grand Slam to seal a successful tournament.

I did my homework and discovered that England had only won the Grand Slam on 12 previous occasions since the tournament started in 1882. They had been denied on four of the five previous occasions they had gone into the final round of the Six Nations in search of the Grand Slam. The last England team to win the Slam had been the 2003 vintage who went on to become world champions that year. We wanted to match them.

France performed creditably and we were poor in the first half. We still led 17–12 though and, after the French came close to a try early in the second half, when Robshaw saved us with a big hit on Bernard Le Roux, we clicked into gear. We were superb. Even when Hartley was carried off on a stretcher 12 minutes from time, I saw leadership from different players. We sailed home 31–21.

'I'm very proud of the boys,' I said as the words flowed passionately and sincerely. 'It's a great achievement by the team. Dylan Hartley has been fantastic and he has done a very good job. Billy Vunipola, Mike Brown and Owen Farrell have done very well assisting him along with James Haskell and Chris Robshaw. That nucleus has been very strong. The great thing is the best is ahead of us. We're looking forward to the summer tour to Australia.'

I paused and smiled just a little wider. 'We're only going to get better.'

14

A WINNING STREAK

My focus switched quickly to our tour of Australia. During the Six Nations we had played some tough rugby but we were still a long way short of the team we needed to become. Our back row lacked pace and so I called up Jack Clifford and Teimana Harrison. I wasn't sure if they would provide the long-term answer, but I needed to try something different – and I was desperate for us to play well.

I didn't just want England to go to Australia and compete with the Wallabies. I wanted a 3–0 whitewash of a team whose last match had been in the World Cup final at Twickenham. England's record in Australia was dire but I sensed a real opportunity. People who have not been in the position themselves have little idea of the emotional toll felt by a team who lose a World Cup final. You're so close to winning the greatest event in rugby and, suddenly, you've lost the game and all your hope. It's hard to recover, mentally and spiritually.

There is a bolter in every World Cup. It was France in 1999, Australia in 2003, England in 2007, France in 2011 and Australia four years later. Before the 2015 tournament few experts had given them much chance of even getting out of a group which included England and Wales. Michael Cheika had replaced Ewen McKenzie as Wallaby coach in October 2014 – with my two former Randwick teammates generating mixed emotions for me in Japan as I watched them swap places. Over the next year Cheika managed to rejuvenate Australia, as they had been in disarray, and he did a wonderful job steering them through the tournament. I listened to the final against New Zealand while I was in a taxi on the way to Heathrow.

Six months later I was convinced Australia would suffer a post-World Cup low. But I still knew it would be a mighty and unprecedented feat for England to win the series. I made my intentions plain when announcing my squad. 'We've got to take a side down there to play Bodyline. If we're going to beat Australia we've got to have a completely physical, aggressive team.'

I chose the Bodyline image deliberately to plant the first seed of doubt in Australian heads. It doesn't matter how old you are in Australia, because pretty much everyone has heard of Bodyline. It was a tactic devised by Douglas Jardine to help his England cricket team take down Australia's greatest icon, Don Bradman, in the 1932–3 Ashes series. Australia were expected to dominate again, with The Don almost impossible to get out, and so Jardine devised a campaign where his fast bowlers, spearheaded by Harold Larwood, attacked the body of Bradman and his fellow batsmen in a dangerous and intimidating fashion. The tactic worked and England won the Ashes 4–1.

I had always been fascinated by the series and, even as an Australian, admired Jardine's uncompromising approach against Bradman. He needed to find a way to overcome the king and his brutal strategy worked. I planned on something similar. Bodyline stressed the ferocious physicality of my game plan.

It was amusing when I made the first presentation to the team. There I was, all fired up by Bodyline, and the players looked at me like I had two heads. Most of them had no idea what I was talking about at first. But we showed some old film footage and they soon understood what I was looking for.

I also spoke openly to the press and said I was happy for us to be an arrogant team – just like Jardine's England had been during Bodyline. I thought I had set the right tone until I got an email from Pemby in Canberra.

'Beaver, how are you, mate? Congratulations on the Six Nations. Great start,' Pemby began in his familiar way. It was a detailed, two-page email with the title of 'Gratuitous Advice'. In reality it was deadly accurate analysis which made me rethink my approach.

'I liked "Bodyline" – that was nice and simple and clear,' Pemby continued before pointing out the flaws bluntly. 'But at the same time Bodyline was outside the rules, unsportsmanlike and dirty. If you use the line again you need to talk about it being shorthand for "tough, uncompromising, aggressive rugby." You don't coach teams to play outside the laws.

'I don't like the use of the word "arrogant" to describe your team. "Arrogance" suggests a lack of empathy and humility and that's not you. Nobody likes arrogant people or sporting teams. They like confident teams with a strong belief and a great work ethic. They like teams that respect their opponents and supporters. They like teams with integrity who are dreaming big dreams. "Arrogant" is an ugly word and you will struggle to sell it. There are other ways to say the same thing.'

Pemby suggested that most Australian sports fans wanted to see me 'having a laugh, brushing off the small things and having fun. Having good banter with Cheika during the tour, having your players excited by a three Test series in Australia, having the England players make a positive contribution off the field, play exciting games and bring real joy to the whole occasion.

'I know how things ended with the ARU was tough for you (I was there!) but that is well and truly in the past. Look what you've achieved since. And you did get the chance to coach Australia and the Brumbies (let's not mention the Reds!). You gave a lot and you got a lot. My view is that you need to be able to express your gratitude through deeds and the best way you can repay Australian Rugby is to come here with a fantastic, skilful and competitive team of outstanding young Englishmen determined to achieve great things and build a reputation. How you manage it and how you deal with the pressures will determine how high this kite will fly.'

He was right on every count. Our friendship and professional collaboration stretched over more than 20 years, to the very start of my coaching career with the Brumbies. Pemby knew me better than anyone else in rugby. I respected his advice and realized that I needed his expertise to help build a team to win the World Cup in 2019. No payment was involved – just an agreement that I would become an ambassador for contentgroup, his public sector content marketing company, while he would help me. Ian Ritchie approved the arrangement and the informal deal was done.

Away from rugby, we are working on a new business project. We are distilling all we have learnt about change, culture and building high-performing teams into a programme to support business transformation. Our aim is to help public and private sector organizations all over the world to build capability and resilience in their teams. It's an exciting project.

In terms of the Australian tour, we quickly got down to work and revised our plans. We don't talk publicly about our approach to communication but, to give you an insight, one of the first things he advised me in 2016 was to talk less. I needed to share the load with the assistant coaches and to build their capability in the lead-up to 2019. Pemby had been the communications director of the World Cup-winning Wallabies in 1999 – so he knew the British media well. His view was that I was never going to win any battle with them and so we needed to design a system to give the media regular access to the team. 'They're just doing their job,' he would say. 'Let's help them.' It was simple stuff but it made the world of difference.

When I next spoke in public about Bodyline I made a clear distinction. 'It's a figure of speech. We will play aggressive but fair rugby. We can't do what's been done by previous English teams. We've got to have a different mindset, a different way of playing the game against Australia to change history.'

I wanted the players to share my excitement and not to be frightened of failure. England had never won a series against the Wallabies in Australia and the chance to be the first needed to be embraced – while we enjoyed ourselves off the field. Whenever you can convince a squad of players that there is something special to be won, they will dig that much deeper to give you the best of themselves.

I felt it in my bones. We were ready to make history.

We touched down in Brisbane on 2 June 2016 and the fun began as soon as we were off the plane. I made sure to tell the Australian and English media exactly what had happened. 'I just went through immigration and got shunted into the area where you get checked,' I said after I had been picked out by officials to have my bags searched. 'That's what I'm expecting, mate. Everything that's done outside the game is coordinated to help Australia win. We've got to be good enough to control what we can control. Australia are second in the world. They've got the best coach in the world. They're playing in their own backyard. They're going to be strong favourites. Our record in Australia is three Tests won since Captain Cook arrived. So it's not a great record, is it?'

Many people thought that it would be deeply emotional for me to return home to Australia as the coach of a different country. But I felt no turbulent or wrenching emotions. I was having a good time and I already loved my England players. I was more intent on spanking the Aussies than feeling nostalgic about Matraville High, Randwick, the Brumbies and Wallabies.

I had persuaded Glen Ella, my oldest mate, to slip his considerable bulk into an England tracksuit for the duration of the tour. I trust Glen with my life; he was also a great skills coach who could help the England backline in the little time we had for training. Glen slotted into the role like a podgy hand slipping into a glove. He enjoyed meeting the England boys. They were a much more mixed bunch than he expected. There were plenty of ordinary working-class blokes who would have fitted into the life we knew back in La Perouse and Little Bay.

I had chosen two young props, Kyle Sinckler of Harlequins and Ellis Genge from Leicester, because I wanted to spice up the squad. Sinckler stood apart from most ordinary props. He had pace and a real feel for attack. I liked him and Genge because they came from the wrong side of the tracks and they were pretty wild boys. They needed to be watched carefully because, at that stage, they had little self-control. If they wanted to bash someone, they just went out and did it. If they wanted to run with the ball, they'd do it. They had so much raw aggression, which was unsurprising as they had survived difficult backgrounds. But I had faith they would both develop quickly. I felt this was particularly true of Sinckler and, since that tour, he has started to find an encouraging balance between that raw aggression and apparent hate of the world with a calmer discovery of his real self. He's also learning to love himself. I think he's only just over halfway through his rugby journey. In a few more years I am certain he will be a great player.

Of course you can't have a squad crammed with young tearaways like Sinckler and Genge. It's important that the bulk of the squad is mature and settled. But I love having a few rough diamonds to give you more grit and soul. Seeing young men like Sinckler and Genge succeed is the most satisfying thing of all for me as a coach. I appreciate how far they have come to reach a high, and remember my own unlikely journey through life and rugby.

The tour was a lot of fun. We settled on the Gold Coast ahead of the first Test and the players had a great time. At training the boys were amazed when, as dusk fell, a mob of kangaroos came onto the training field. There were also plenty of laughs as most people from England are fascinated and terrified, at the same time, by all the creepy-crawlies that can kill you in Australia. One night Dylan played a great joke on some of the boys. They were sitting around playing cards when, all of a sudden, he ran into the room screaming and holding a snake by the tail. The room emptied as they ran in fear of their lives.

It was a very realistic-looking plastic snake. After they had recovered, everyone enjoyed the joke. The atmosphere around the squad was positive and upbeat. We had travelled and trained well and were ready for the first Test.

Suncorp Stadium, Brisbane, Australia. Saturday, 11 June 2016

At Suncorp you sit in the coaches' enclosure, which is a glass box at the back of the main stand. The spectators close to the box can still make themselves heard. I settle down for kick-off, feeling the usual uncertainty and not knowing how the match will unfold, when a woman makes me look up. She's sitting right in front of the box and she has turned around to see me sit down. She's well dressed and wearing an Yves Saint Laurent scarf. But that doesn't stop her turning the air blue. She puts her middle finger up at me, shouts and swears at me very loudly. She calls me a traitor, among other insults, but it works mostly as a reminder that I have not divorced Australia to work for England. Australia has already divorced me. I cop the abuse and try to smile pleasantly.

I soon switch my attention back to the television monitor on my desk. Down in the bowels of the arena, the cameras have locked on the sight of the gold-and-green-shirted Wallabies hugging each other as they wait to step out onto the field. They look big and determined and a very tight unit. I know they are pumped for the Test – which I feel England have to win.

If Australia win the first Test, they will have dangerous momentum. It will be almost impossible for us to claw our way back and turn the series into a 2–1 victory. We need to win this opening game, even though England have lost all four previous Tests they have played in Brisbane.

The cameras cut away to Dylan Hartley walking calmly onto the pitch. He is followed by Mike Brown, Dan Cole, Owen Farrell and 19 others. The boys look ready and concentrated as they head down the echoing white tunnel.

England, since blowing up in the World Cup against Australia, have won seven games in a row. Greg Clark, the commentator, reminds us that the last time England won eight on the bounce had been back in 2003.

Stephen Moore leads the Wallabies out to a huge roar. Suncorp is one of the great stadiums of world rugby and when I was coach of Australia I considered it our home ground. In these last moments before kick-off, I think how hard Australia will be to beat. Michael Cheika seems to feel it even more, because he and his assistant coaches have chosen to go onto the paddock and line up with the Wallaby 23 for the anthems. Weird. It's not my style. I'm happy to keep a low profile even though I've just copped a foul-mouthed spray from one of the locals.

After 'God Save the Queen', a bellowing Cheika joins his Wallabies and the crowd in the buzzing Suncorp Stadium as they deliver a full-throated rendition of 'Advance Australia Fair'.

A fire has been lit inside Australia. This is England, the old enemy, and they are going to teach us a lesson. We're under immense pressure as they climb ferociously into us. After six minutes of dominating possession and territory they really crank it up. Eight phases into their next play the Wallabies are back in our 22. Nick Phipps, at 9, feeds Bernard Foley who misses out the centres to find Israel Folau joining the line at speed. Folau is electric and he burns a hole in our defence, before flipping a pass over the top to Michael Hooper. The great Aussie flanker powers down the right wing. We scrag him close to the line.

David Pocock, in his usual fetching role, picks up the loose ball and feeds Rory Arnold, the debutant lock and the tallest man ever to play rugby for Australia. The defence bring Arnold crashing down, but the ball belongs to Australia. Phipps passes it to Samu Kerevi and the centre finds Hooper who has ten metres to run before he touches down: 5–0 to Australia.

After 15 minutes we're reeling as wave after wave swamps us.

Eventually, Folau is set free by a peach of a delayed pass from Foley. Folau slices open a huge chunk of space and scores: 10–0. The cohesive play and slick skills of Australia's key players have been exceptional.

Farrell keeps us in the game with two penalties, but our problems are glaring after 28 minutes when Foley sets off on a slicing run. There was so much space between Farrell and Luther Burrell you could have driven a truck through it. We are in a mess as it looks like the Wallabies have scored a third try. We could be 17–6 down after the conversion, but the French referee, Romain Poite, immediately calls for the TMO to check for obstruction.

The infringement is obvious on the replay. Arnold had blocked Burrell who was scrambling to tackle Foley. I am not sure if Burrell would have caught Foley, but it is a clear obstruction. No try.

If it had been allowed, I thought the game was over. It would have been hard for us to come back from three tries down. I have always believed that the only way a coach can change the momentum once a game has started is to switch personnel. Usually those changes happen in modern rugby after 50 or 60 minutes. It is extremely rare for a coach to drag a player from the field before the break. But we're in trouble. Big time.

I pull the trigger after just 29 minutes and substitute Luther Burrell for George Ford. Luther is struggling with the pace of the Australian attack and they're making easy metres through his channel. I know Farrell will give us a much more physical presence at inside centre while Ford, such a skilful playmaker, will help us control our game. It's a bold but necessary move and, as he walks slowly from the field, the crowd give Luther the Bronx cheer. Inside the first 30 minutes, Australia have not only scored two tries but forced a tactical replacement.

I know it's a harsh call on Burrell but it has to happen if we are to have any chance of winning the game. After the match, and over the next few days, I will make sure that I speak to Burrell in detail about my reasons for replacing him so early. But, right now, after issuing the order for the substitution, I say nothing else. I am backing my rugby knowledge. The Australians have got us on the run and we need to stem the gold tide in which we are drowning.

Ford has been on the field for less than a minute when Farrell kicks the penalty that narrows the Aussie lead to one point. A 10–9 deficit is so much better than 17–6.

Our defence takes a lot of confidence when James Haskell smashes David Pocock in a perfectly legal tackle straight out of the Bodyline playbook. It sends a message to everyone that England will play tough, uncompromising and aggressive rugby. Immediately things start to improve. Our communication among the backs is so much better. The ball has been flying around on a warm Saturday evening and, until Ford comes on, the Wallabies are having a great time and the crowd has loved it. We begin to quieten a raucous Suncorp Stadium.

Maro Itoje wins the ball in our half and, from the ensuing maul, Ben Youngs sends a box-kick spiralling into Australian territory. Folau, at full back, gathers it near his ten-metre line and throws a sloppy pass to Foley. The ball bounces loose and, aware that our rush defence will soon be on top of him, Kerevi fails to control it. Jonathan Joseph sees his chance in a flash. He reaches the ball first and, with his outstretched boot, kicks ahead. Joseph looks as though he is playing football as he dribbles the ball towards the line. And then, rolling end over end, it suddenly bounces straight into his open arms and he crashes over. A Farrell conversion makes it 16–10.

'Sixteen unanswered points, by England, the Six Nations champions,' Clark the commentator shouts.

I am standing at the monitor, headphones on so I am in touch with my bench, with my arms folded. I am not aware of Horan's words on television. 'Eddie Jones, looking comfortable. He said earlier in the week that if England were ahead after 25 or 30 minutes they won't be caught.'

'Yeah, he backed himself on that,' agrees Phil Kearns. 'England have been very good in the last 15 minutes. They've lifted their intensity . . . and look at this lovely rolling maul, grinding away. This is what they love to do. It's not pretty but if they create anything it will be from this sort of stuff.'

A Foley penalty narrows our lead to three but Farrell doubles it before half-time. England lead 19–13 at the break.

I feel confident back in the shed. The substitution has changed the mood. Ford and Farrell look good together and, among the forwards, Hartley, Robshaw and Haskell have been magnificent in belting our opponents. We've taken the sting and bite out of the Australian attack and we can now cut loose.

After 44 minutes, a long Farrell penalty hits a post and bounces back onto the field. Robshaw, showing immense desire, runs hard and brings down Pocock who had picked up the bouncing ball. Australia are now under pressure and Phipps has to kick for touch to bring the home team some relief.

From the lineout, England set off on another rolling maul before Haskell, wearing a bright red scrum cap, charges though a hole in the Aussie defence. He makes significant progress before he is brought down by Hooper. Billy Vunipola is also held but we have the ball and Youngs passes it to Ford. We now see the difference that vision makes as Ford, such a pure player, floats a looping 30-metre beauty of a pass that cuts out our midfield and sails perfectly into the arms of Marland Yarde, our powerful wing. Yarde's dreadlocks fly behind him and he scores a vital try. Farrell converts and our lead stretches to 26–13.

A Farrell penalty adds another three points before, on 58 minutes, Hooper's try keeps the Aussies within touching distance. Another England penalty and another Wallaby try for Tevita Kuridrani, their strapping centre of Fijian descent, means the score is 32–25 with eight minutes left.

It feels a little nervy when Foley nails a penalty in the 77th minute: 32–28 to England.

We just need to maintain our composure as Australia come hard at us in search of the win. One phase follows another but our defence does not buckle. Then, amid the tenth phase, the ball is spilled and Farrell snaffles it for England. He sends Danny Care, on for Youngs, sniping through a gap. Care gains precious ground and then finds Haskell who pops it up for Ford. The Australians rush towards him but, occupying a calm little space of his own, Ford looks up and grubber-kicks the ball towards the left-hand corner. It is a subtle and perfectly weighted little kick which sits up and waits for the onrushing Jack Nowell. Ford has timed his kick with deadly precision. Nowell grabs the ball lovingly to his chest and races over for the decisive score, his blue cap gleaming under the hot lights as we jump up in our box.

'England have broken the drought of Brisbane, where they have never won,' Clark cries out on the commentary, 'and they go 1–0 up.'

Glen Ella and I, as well as Steve Borthwick, Paul Gustard and our other support staff, exchange high-fives and beaming handshakes. This is the best performance I have seen from England – at least until we produce a masterclass in Dublin against a heavily hyped Ireland in our opening match of the 2019 Six Nations. Against great odds, and amid fierce pressure, we have held our nerve and weathered a blistering start to seal a famous 39–28 victory over Australia. We stayed in the moment, stuck to our game plan, and did not get distracted by the scoreboard at any point. We showed a ton of courage.

'I don't know who is the most excited,' Horan exclaims, 'Eddie Jones or Glen Ella. Wow – what a finish and what a series this is going to be now.'

I understood the wider historical significance of the result. We had scored more points than any other England team against one of the southern hemisphere giants – Australia, New Zealand and South Africa. Most of the English press described it as the country's finest performance since winning the World Cup. I agreed, but there was no point in saying the words out loud. I tried to find a more cautious tone at the post-match press conference. 'All we have done tonight is give ourselves one more game in the series,' I said. 'We have made history today but it is not good enough for us. It is all about next week now . . . we can't get too excited.'

I pointed out where we would improve before the second Test in Melbourne. 'Australia put a lot of pace on the ball which we don't encounter in games in England. We're obviously happy with the result but we can improve significantly in terms of our ball-carrying, second-man work and defence spacing. We can also still put more set-piece pressure on Australia.'

It was very sensible and serious until, suddenly, the press conference turned briefly into a circus. I saw Stephen Hoiles approach with his camera crew. I knew Hoiles pretty well. He was a Randwick boy and, when I was Wallaby coach, I had picked him for his first Australia tour and even gave him his debut cap when he came on as a back-row replacement against Scotland in Edinburgh in November 2004. Hoiles was a decent bloke and, at the age of 34 and in retirement, he was building a new career for himself in the media. He had been asked to play a comic role on a new programme for Fox which was to be called *The Other Rugby Show*. It was meant to be an irreverent look at rugby, and poor old Hoiles was told to play the role of a clown. What followed was embarrassing.

'You seem to be in the press a bit more than Donald Trump this week,' he said to me, 'and the lads were pumped up. There was a bit of moisture out there, and I think you and Glen had a good moment, and looked really lubed-up. How did you enjoy that moment with your old mate up in the box?'

As soon as I heard that 'lubed-up' comment I took offence. I was not going to let him get away with it. 'Repeat the question, mate,' I said icily. 'I don't like the tone of the question, mate. Are we not allowed to enjoy a win, mate?'

The intended comedy routine had fallen flat and Hoiles squirmed. He didn't say anything else and the long silence was broken by a proper journalist who asked a decent question. But I was fuming. After the main conference ended and I was on my way out of the room, a couple of other journos came up to me. They wanted to know if I felt disrespected by Hoiles and by the Australian media in general. 'Without a doubt,' I said bluntly. 'Look at that ridiculous question from Hoiles. You've seen the Fox Sports television promos ridiculing our team and Chris Robshaw. I think they're pretty disgusting. The team has been treated in a disrespectful way. It's demeaning.'

But I didn't want such a sweet victory to be soured by Hoiles, and so I moved on to stress how much we were looking forward to the second Test the following Saturday in Melbourne. I grinned again. 'Australia have got the world's best coach so they have high expectations. All the pressure is on them next week.'

I always try and treat the media with respect because they've got an important job to do. On the whole, they treat me with respect in return. But when they don't, I will pull them up. After one England game, the BBC's Chris Jones demanded that the supporters hear from me. I told him to pull his head in. I'm just doing my best. The players are doing their best. Sometimes your best is just not good enough. I watch coaches being interviewed after football and rugby games they've lost and there is sometimes a lack of respect from the media. Every coach will have done his very best. The same goes for their players. I've coached over 150 Tests and I could count on one hand the number of players who I didn't think gave their best. So we deserve respect.

The Hoiles incident was an example of how rugby coverage has been influenced by other popular sporting codes and become more crass and personality-based. But I suppose it reflects demand and so I can't blame the media. I hold on to the fact that there is still some very good rugby journalism and that the Fox and Hoiles escapades are rare.

The Australians were under pressure. Losing at their favourite ground had been a real setback. We were accused of 'getting at' the officials and so, when we met the referees, the Aussies insisted they had representatives in the room. When we went to inspect the field in Melbourne, before the second Test, they also made sure they joined us. It was all fun and games but I felt we were getting on top of them. The big issue in Melbourne was the state of the turf. It had been a source of controversy ever since the stadium had been built. It was unstable and crumbled beneath the pressure of scrummaging. We forced Bill Pulver, the CEO of the ARU, into publicly defending a surface he knew was well below Test-match standard. I'm not sure Bill would have slept too well that week because if the surface collapsed, it was going to be his fault.

These are incidental battles to the real Tests which are played out on the field. But, after 20 years of professional rugby, I knew how you could affect the mood in the opposition camp and also steer the focus of the media in your chosen direction. Rugby takes up 95 per cent of my time in terms of preparation for a major Test – but the additional 5 per cent on the periphery of the game matters a lot. I felt that we were winning all these off-field skirmishes in Australia. But my focus always returned to my own players.

Before the Brisbane Test, Pemby had picked up on an interesting point from an earlier press conference: 'Beaver, perhaps the most revealing quote of the week was from Mako Vunipola who said that the biggest issue in the 2015 World Cup loss to Australia at Twickenham had been that "we couldn't react properly." That is a stunning admission. They were paralysed. That lack of confidence (or perhaps permission) to change things on the run compromised their performance. That obviously has to be an area of focus in terms of our building this team for 2019. We have to build a culture of learning, agility, adaptability, measured risk-taking and continual improvement; it will be critical for success on the way to, and in, Japan 2019. This weekend is a great opportunity to exercise that decision-making muscle.'

He was right. I knew I had shown the right 'decision-making muscle' in replacing Burrell with Ford, but it was more important that a hard core of five or six players had displayed real leadership in that first Test. Rather than being paralysed and unable to react to Australia's blistering start, they had adapted and found a way to seize back control of the game. They had shown so much initiative and, therefore, leadership, under intense pressure. We were starting to see the beginnings of our team for the World Cup.

But, first, we had two more giant stepping stones ahead of us – in Melbourne and Sydney. I would not be satisfied with anything less than a clean sweep of my home country.

Before the second Test, on 18 June 2016, Paul Gustard had reached into his box of tricks. Our defence coach had the boys reading some inspirational poetry. Dale Wimbrow's 'The Man in the Glass' had first been published in 1934 and, from its opening lines, the players were gripped. The poem told them that even when the world made them kings for a day, as they had felt in Brisbane, the only judgement that mattered belonged to the man in the mirror. He knew how much they had truly given. They might fool everyone else, but there were no secrets from the guy in the glass. All the cheers and the plaudits would count for nothing if they had cheated themselves.

The boys took it to heart and produced a monumental performance in Melbourne. Dylan Hartley was captain but his predecessor, Chris Robshaw, led the team out to mark him winning his 50th cap. He responded with a man-of-the-match performance. We produced savage defence and unwavering courage in a lopsided Test. We won 23–7, despite Australia having 70 per cent possession and running the ball 172 times for 962 metres. We only ran it 53 times and made 282 metres. We had to defend so much that England made 217 tackles compared to Australia's 81. But we scored two tries, through Hartley and Farrell, to Moore's lone Australian effort. Farrell kicked the rest of our points with three penalties and two conversions.

It reminded me of the way that, in the Rumble in the Jungle in 1974, Muhammad Ali had sunk back on the ropes and soaked up all that George Foreman could throw at him. Foreman, an intimidating ogre in those days, punched himself into exhaustion. Ali then shocked everyone by opening up and stopping Foreman. 'We had to play Rope-a-Dope today,' I said in a deliberate echo of the name Ali had given to his bold and resilient ring strategy.

We had to defend again and again and they got suckered and seduced into spinning it wide. The wider they played, the more it suited us. We kept them out, beyond that one try, and near the end they were mentally shot. We got a chance to throw a few punches and we knocked 'em cold. We had won the series 2–0.

'We have to be tactically flexible in Test rugby,' I said afterwards. 'That's why I'm so pleased. They had all the ball and then we had the opportunity to score a try and we took it. That's the sign of a good side.'

Our important victory summed up the way we wanted to play our rugby – and confirmed that we had the players and the genesis of a style to win the World Cup. We were on the right track. But we needed to add another layer to our game. We needed to learn how to score off the opposition's mistakes.

It was also the first time England had ever won a rugby series in the southern hemisphere. I felt extremely proud, but I was not ready to settle for anything less than 3–0. We had to win in Sydney to show the kind of ruthless streak that we would need in 2019.

'The boys started talking about it on the field,' I explained, 'and we're committed to doing that. We want to be the best team in the world. If the All Blacks were in this situation now, what would they be thinking? They'd be thinking 3–0. If we want to be the best team in the world, we have to think 3–0.'

In the build-up to the last Test I had a great week. I was back home in Coogee, training on my old home ground and catching up with a few mates, like Jeff Sayle. We had a few beers at the Coogee Bay Hotel. The great rugby league player Andrew Johns dropped by to work with Owen and George and we trained hard. The players were exhausted but we just had to push through it. On the way back to the hotel after one particularly hard session,

some of the players bought ice creams. One of the Fox journalists asked me: 'Do you think your players should be eating ice
cream?' He made it sound as if they had committed a crime. I
knew we had them then – the Australian media as well as the
Wallabies.

I'm an Australian and so I know you've got to stand up to the
Aussies. You've got to bully the bully. That's the only way you get
on top of them. It's the same when you play South Africa. You've
got to dominate them otherwise they're going to crush you.
Sometimes it's not pleasant. But you've got to keep doing it.

On a cool, clear night in Sydney, on 25 June, England won a rollicking game of Test rugby 44–40. We scored four tries, and Owen
Farrell kicked 24 points, but I was less impressed by the five tries
we conceded. I knew that the whitewash was an important moment in English rugby, and I had loved the whole tour of Australia.
But I avoided any sense of triumphalism after the game. I allowed
the writers to sum up the moment in their own words.

'And so ends the most extraordinary season in the history of
English rugby,' Robert Kitson suggested in the *Guardian*. 'When
the host nation stumbled out of last year's World Cup in the pool
stages no one imagined the same players would fly home from
Australia unbeaten in 10 games and trailing numerous historic
achievements in their wake. To their Six Nations grand slam can
now be added a 3–0 series whitewash of the Wallabies, an unprecedented feat for an England team in the southern hemisphere.

'To suggest Eddie Jones has slightly outflanked his compat-
riots is like saying Shane Warne took the occasional Ashes wicket
in his time. For England to round off a memorable series by
registering a record number of points in Australia, having trained
and played for 12 solid, aching months and endured such savage
World Cup disappointment, was remarkable. To do so in a
breathlessly quick game against opponents determined to deliver
a pressure-relieving victory was almost as noteworthy . . .

'Not that anyone would have guessed from Jones's immediate
post-match verdict – the wily wizard of Oz again stressing

England remain a long way behind the All Blacks and describing this performance as sub-par. As ever he was reluctant to sidestep brutal truths; England have never previously conceded 40 points and won a Test match and this was just the fourth time it has happened in international history. But rugby is about heart, soul and commitment as well as statistics and no England touring side since 2003 has come close to emulating what Hartley's mob have done this month.'

It had been a great series, played in the right spirit with massive interest and capacity crowds. The final Test match saw the biggest attendance at any match ever played at the Sydney Football Stadium. In difficult times we had also helped give Australian rugby a shot in the arm.

For England, beyond the results, the coaches and players were building strong and trusted relationships. But I knew we were far from the finished product. Changes would have to be made. We hadn't solved our lack of pace in the back row. Tom Curry and Sam Underhill had yet to arrive on the scene and we were getting by with the players we had.

But there was no question the revival of the team had brought great joy and relief to English rugby. It was satisfying and I was really pleased for Ian Ritchie. He had taken a punt on me and we had delivered.

I was, however, uncomfortable with some of the praise. It was over the top and there was a risk that the team would spend the next few months lolling around on the puffed-up pillows of prose. Instead of giving in to glory, I was circumspect. I knew there would be dips and setbacks ahead.

'Wait until the third season, mate,' I said in a few private meetings. 'We might hit a bit of a low then.'

I had reviewed the records of southern hemisphere coaches who had worked in Six Nations rugby. They all suffered a third-year dip. After a honeymoon first season, in which they radically improved the fitness of their northern hemisphere team, they continued to drive up skill levels in year two. By the time the third season began, the southern hemisphere lift sagged as familiarity set in and standards stagnated. I would try to do something different – ours was a four-year project. The way we dealt with a possible third-year slide would shape England's World Cup chances.

The Lions were touring New Zealand in the British summer of 2017 and I knew that there would be consequences. Players would be fatigued both physically and mentally for months afterwards. It was obvious that the following season, starting just six weeks after the Lions tour ended, would begin slowly for the players who had been in New Zealand.

In the space of seven short months, since I took over, we had moved from number eight to number two in the world. England were on a roll, but it was inevitable that the run of victories would end and we would be tested in new ways. I had already begun to plan ahead for the trials and tribulations which awaited.

I was also determined to keep pushing the players hard. As England coach you only get access to them for a short period of time and you have to make the most of it. You have to find ways to sort the wheat from the chaff, and the only way you can do that is by putting the players under pressure. I probably overdid it on occasions, but it was only because I was so eager to keep improving England.

At times there was criticism of my methods. But I wanted to find the players' limits. Remember perceptions of the four-minute mile prior to Roger Bannister? It was impossible. The body would disintegrate, they said. And now, with Eliud Kipchoge breaking two hours for the marathon, another impossibility has been achieved. I am never reckless, but my job is to find those limits. There were some issues adapting to the methods I had perfected in Japan. But it's not uncommon for there to be injuries under a new regime. When Jürgen Klopp took over at Liverpool there was a spate of hamstring injuries and he was widely panned. Look at Liverpool now.

Selection is a key lever in building teams. You are always looking to build depth and each year you want to bring in two or three new guys. If you look at the All Blacks, it's striking how they continue to evolve. Large parts of the New Zealand team are stable but there is always movement. The way they treat wingers is a good example. There is a constant rotation. I'm always looking for new English talent and to do that you have to go to the games. You can only judge a player by watching them live. You want to see how they interact with their teammates and how they work off the ball. In any selection period we have a draft squad of about 30 or 40 and, when the Premiership is on, we try and get to as many games as possible. I aim to go to games on Friday, Saturday and Sunday. The assistant coaches share the load of watching the key games.

As we headed into the autumn internationals, I was worried. Despite going to game after game, I wasn't seeing the talent we needed to keep refreshing the squad. My fear was that we would get comfortable because we had started winning and it's always difficult to make changes when the results are strong. Why break what's working, right? Wrong. A cold, hard analysis told me that our game was limited. We couldn't play with any real fluidity because we still didn't have everyone thinking the same way. Players come from a number of different clubs with different mindsets and, given that we have such limited time with them, I knew it would be hard to make dramatic changes.

We won all four internationals at Twickenham in the autumn of 2016 – beating South Africa, Fiji, Argentina and Australia again. Our winning run now extended to 14 Tests. The world record of 18 successive Test victories had been set by New Zealand. The English newspapers began to write up the prospect of our winning another Grand Slam in 2017 and our 19th Test match in a row in the final Six Nations game against Ireland. I let them get on with it and hunkered down with longer-term planning for Japan in 2019.

*

A game of rugby lasts for 80 minutes. The ball is in play for 32 minutes and out of play for 48 minutes. The game has now stretched to 100 minutes with stoppages for HIAs, sin bins, decision reviews and scrums. But the ball is still in play for just 32 minutes. The task for training is to understand and then devise drills that will make us most effective in those now massively intense 32 minutes. It's a brutal sport and the impact of the collisions and speed of ball movement are only increasing. Our analysis showed that 40 per cent of a tier-one international rugby match game time was structured and 60 per cent was unstructured. European rugby is almost entirely structured and that's what our players are good at and used to playing. Super Rugby, in contrast, is almost completely unstructured. We needed to find ways to be better at unstructured rugby.

I was also fascinated by how we could keep our players fresh and engaged during a season that places sapping demands on them. Being in Europe, the cradle of football, I became even more obsessed with what I could learn from the 'beautiful game'. The leading football teams play 60 games a year – so how do they prepare to perform?

Despite our winning run, the team was in danger of plateauing. There were signs in the autumn that our performances had flattened. My study of Guardiola, Klopp, Pochettino and the other top Premier League coaches showed that they trained specifically for games in super-intense, short sessions. I resolved to work the players even harder in training and test their leadership credentials even more forcefully. We would find out then which of the players had the resilience to go all the way to Japan.

Our opening two matches of the 2017 Six Nations were tight. We beat France 21–19 at Twickenham and then won 21–15 in Cardiff. Warren Gatland had taken a sabbatical from Wales to coach the Lions – but it was another important and welcome victory. Italy at home, on 26 February, was meant to be an easy stroll. Instead, it turned out to be an awkward and ultimately dispiriting afternoon which angered me.

Conor O'Shea, the former Ireland international and ex-Harlequins coach, had taken on the Italy job in 2016. He called in Brendan Venter, the South African coach who had succeeded me at Saracens in 2009, to help him in that year's Six Nations. In my view, Venter and O'Shea went against the spirit of rugby, in which we all believed, to take advantage of a loophole in the rulebook. They instructed their players not to commit to the breakdown. This meant that no ruck could form because the only Italian on the ground would be the player who carried out the original tackle. His teammates could not be ruled offside, under the old law, and so we had the farcical situation where the Italians were able to surround Danny Care, our scrum half, so that he could not release the ball to his backs. O'Shea and Venter also told other Italy players to position themselves so that they stood next to our centres – metres ahead of the advantage line without being penalized for offside.

My players were stunned by the tactic and they asked the referee, Romaine Poite, to explain what the hell was happening. 'What do we need to do for it to be a ruck?' James Haskell asked Poite. The Frenchman's response was cutting. 'I can't say. I am the referee, not a coach.'

The tactic worked and we were confused. At the break Italy led 10–5. We sorted out a few things at half-time, but it was still a scrappy, unsatisfying match, where gamesmanship got the better of rugby, and we were only 17–15 ahead with 11 minutes left. England then scored three tries to give an unsavoury match a respectable 36–15 scoreline.

I thought it was appalling. People said Italy were clever but that's ridiculous. They were not even the first to do it. The Chiefs had done it in certain sections of a game in Super Rugby and it had been successful for them. But, for me, it's against the spirit of the game. I'll admit that I had briefly considered using this tactic for Japan against the All Blacks in 2013. I was worried we were going to get beaten by far more than a hundred points. How could I stop them playing? I thought about the breakdown and the off-side law. If we didn't contest the breakdown, maybe it would mean we would only get beaten by 50 points. But what message would I have given to my players? We had to find another way.

When you consider all that Japan achieved in 2015, and again in 2019, maybe the Italians can now see the benefit in not taking the easy road.

If you don't want to have a contest for the ball, go and play rugby league. The spirit of rugby is to contest the ball and, for me, that's at the heart of our game. I'm old fashioned in this way, but we need to maintain our values. We all know that golf etiquette is so strict that players don't cheat. Without such values golf would not be the same game. It's the same with rugby. I loved the fact that it was a game of continuity and contests for the ball. I would have been happier losing by 150 points than breaking the spirit of the game. In the end, I fell victim to my stroke before we even played the All Blacks in 2013. But I am glad that I had resolved to play fairly.

People accused my players of not thinking on their feet. But if the opposition are blocking your half back, and standing in your backline without being penalized, how can your players be prepared? I had no anger towards my team – only towards the low tactics that had been used.

The farce of the match was resolved when World Rugby immediately changed the laws so it could not happen again. I had been proved right but it gave me no pleasure. The whole charade left a bitter taste.

Jim Telfer, the former Scotland and Lions coach, seemed intent on making the bitterness last. He launched a stinging attack on me and, in particular, the English before our next game. It didn't bother me. I concentrated on the rugby and we hammered the Scots 61–21. We played well and equalled the world record of 18 consecutive Test victories. The media were in a froth about this little milestone, but I knew that, when I eventually look back on my England record, I would remember the outcome of our World Cup in Japan rather than those 18 wins in a row. I was in this job for the long haul, and my eyes were on the prize that would be handed out to the World Cup winners in Yokohama City on 2 November 2019. We were already Six Nations champions for a second year on the spin. But far harder and more important battles were coming.

15

REBOOTING ENGLAND

Exactly one year, five months and 16 days had passed since England had last lost a game of rugby. But our long winning run ended on 18 March 2017 when, in a fevered but rain-sodden Dublin, Ireland stopped us dead in our tracks. Any hopes of a new world record were over. We remained stuck on 18 Test wins in a row with New Zealand. The All Blacks' own streak of victories had also been broken by Ireland, in Chicago, four months earlier.

Ireland deserved the win. It was strange because we'd had a really good week of preparation and everyone looked ready to go. But, psychologically, we slipped that day, and simply could not find the intensity and physicality to match the Irish. It was easy to tell the truth after we lost 13–9. 'You have these days,' I said straight after the game. 'Ireland played superbly. They were too good for us.'

Our run had been driven more by the courage of our players than the quality of our rugby. In most of the games, we played reasonably, but it was the players' refusal to give in that carried the run. They simply would not surrender and kept finding a way. They are tough bastards. When they get in the fight, they stay in the fight and never take a backward step. It's a tremendous quality for a rugby team. Effort is a key ingredient in high performance and our England team always give everything.

That loss was a reminder that rugby, particularly in Europe, is cyclical. Periods of success and failure keep following each other.

Rugby in the northern hemisphere is a harsh business. Ireland slumped in 2015 before Joe Schmidt found a style that suited them and they returned to the winners' circle. We were on the other side of our bell curve and headed for hard times. We had started to get comfortable and a little complacent. We were approaching the third year of our four-year plan and I knew this would be the most difficult time. If we were to be contenders in Japan we needed to change again.

I should have started well before the Six Nations, but I was like the players. The winning had seduced me into thinking we were going OK. Looking back, it became obvious that something wasn't right. We were not paying enough attention to the tiny details where even the smallest effort matters.

Fortunately our winning run meant we had plenty of credit in the bank. When our performances went off the boil, which I knew they would, we would be able to resist the inevitable calls for either my head or a return to old ways.

My planning cycle, which I adopted first with the Wallabies and then developed further with Japan, is built on selection and strategy. The first two years are about establishing a foundation. You want to settle on the 60–70 per cent of your core players while you are on the lookout for the other 30–40 per cent of players who will bring something different. Talent-spotting is the most important part of a head coach's role. The third season is the time to experiment, while in the fourth year you can hopefully settle on an effective game style that is tactically adaptable.

The World Cup is the tournament on which you are judged as a coach. It's the ultimate prize. In 2019, no one will remember who won the rugby championship or the Six Nations. But they will remember who won the World Cup.

While we lost the match in Dublin, we won the championship. As the fireworks exploded above Dylan Hartley, while he held up the Six Nations trophy, it was a real anti-climax. I was happy to have won another championship, but the loss had rubbed away most of the shine from our achievement. The boys were more sheepish than celebratory. As we packed up the dressing room that night and headed for the bus to take us back to the team hotel, I'd already started to consider the changes we needed to make.

A small part of me was glad the run was over.

Some players don't want to change. But the best players are curious and have the courage to improve. In talking to them one-on-one and as a group, I spelt out the obvious facts. International rugby was becoming increasingly athletic and so, while it wasn't a traditional English strength, we needed to find a new athleticism. We also needed to become more tactically adept. It was up to me and my fellow coaches, as well as the senior players, to find a way to develop our tactical thinking. The reputation of England and our hopes at the World Cup would be determined by how successful we were in building those dual strengths. This sort of challenge makes me want to get out of bed every morning. It's complex problem-solving in a high-pressure environment every day – and I love it.

If the mood around the team is too relaxed, I will generally try to create some sort of disturbance. High-performance sport is about being on edge. For example, I will go into the coaches' room and pick out a few aspects from the previous day's training and say: 'This isn't good enough. What were we thinking here?' It might not actually be too bad, but it will keep them and the players on edge. You can't do that every day of the week. There also needs to be an element of truth to your comments. But I am constantly looking to challenge people to improve and to think. I want people who work with me to be curious and ask questions.

There's a trend in both rugby and wider society to always be nice. We're told that everyone should feel involved and have their say. Everything is about good feedback and being positive. This works for a while and can achieve positive results. But ultimately you create a false environment if you don't speak the truth. And that's what happened to us. We had developed a polite and congenial environment where we had stopped asking the hard questions and being honest with each other.

As I was finding my way during my first 18 months as England coach, I'd often bite my tongue and let things ride. But that had to change. Many of the players and coaches were not going to like it, but I knew this more abrasive atmosphere would steel us for the World Cup.

I also started paying serious attention to some of the analytical work being produced at the RFU by a smart young bloke called Gordon Hamilton-Fairley. Gordon was a talented data analyst who was employed by Rob Andrew and Stuart Lancaster to investigate different problems in the game. Some of his projects included referee decision-making, lineouts and kicking. Rugby is dominated by video analysis, which has weaknesses. Often the video analysts who travel with the team listen to the views of the coach and then find the video evidence to back it up. Gordon was a devotee of the American sports-style independent data analysis that relies heavily on mathematics. Gordon had read politics and economics at the University of Virginia in the States and built a strong relationship with the Brooklyn Nets basketball team. He wanted to replicate – at the RFU – the Nets' research statistics department that built various models to examine team and player performance.

I had a meeting with him in my office at Twickenham and he presented a compelling case for his independent, maths-based approach. I was drowning in data and we didn't have the skills to make sense of it. I had a gut feeling about which statistics mattered most, but I didn't have the evidence. That bothered me. My hypothesis was that if we could use mathematics to work out what wins and loses games, we could design our training to make sure we improved.

Gordon undertook to do the research to unlock the secrets of success in international rugby and engaged his colleague, James Tozer, to help him. James is a data analyst, educated at Oxford, whose day job is writing for *The Economist*. After the 2015 World

Cup he had written a piece analysing the infamous Robshaw decision to kick for touch which cost England against Wales. Between them they set about building regression models and using machine learning to analyse five years of international rugby. Their discoveries were amazing.

Based on their analysis, James and Gordon, who have now set up a company called Prospect Sporting Insights, presented me with the six key metrics that matter in rugby. I won't reveal all six, but one metric is effective kicking.

They didn't stop there. They have continued to develop other models that help us to track and predict not only our own performance but those of our competitors. Their data, which was branded as Pressure Plus, gave us the information we needed to start developing our game. It has been worth every penny.

But, before I got around to making too many changes, my best players left on the British and Irish Lions tour of New Zealand in June 2017. I was delighted for all 17 of our players who were selected, although Ben Youngs and Billy Vunipola didn't tour. I was selfishly very pleased for England. Going on the toughest tour in rugby to play against the best team in the world with the finest players from England, Ireland, Scotland and Wales was guaranteed to improve every one of them. And it did. Jamie George came on in leaps and bounds as did Kyle Sinckler, Anthony Watson, Jack Nowell, Jonathan Joseph, Owen Farrell and Elliot Daly. Maro Itoje learnt to cope with being targeted while George Kruis, Joe Marler and Dan Cole realized that if they were to stay at the top of international rugby, they would have to work harder. I got out to see them all before the second Test. I was keen to find out what they had learnt from training and touring with the Lions but, most importantly, what they had discovered about New Zealand and All Black rugby. The tour was an another important stepping stone in the development of our team.

At the same time, as those players headed off to New Zealand, we had the chance to uncover a few gems on England's tour of Argentina. This is precisely what happened.

If I had to pick out three players who improved consistently throughout their Test careers, the first two names would be easy. George Smith and Will Genia. The third might surprise you. It's still a little early to say for sure, but I think Tom Curry might take that slot. He's going to be a special player.

I remember seeing him the first time, playing for Sale, and it reminded me of the feelings I'd had when I watched a young George Smith in Sydney grade rugby. After 30 minutes of watching Curry, who at the time was largely unknown outside of Sale, I thought, 'Why hasn't anyone mentioned this kid before?' He was head and shoulders above everyone else on the field. And I mean way ahead. He made hard, aggressive tackles, showed great commitment in attack and clearly had a natural feel for the rhythm and pace of the game. Like Smith, he was not a leader. He was a follower capable of playing great rugby. Sometimes the quiet ones, the hard workers, can be exceptional players.

Curry was still only 18 when I selected him, along with his twin brother Ben, who also played as a flanker for Sale, for the Argentina tour. I picked three other teenagers in Joe Cokanasiga, the London Irish wing, Harry Mallinder, the Northampton back, and Nick Isiekwe, the Saracens lock. They were all 19 when we flew to Buenos Aires. Jack Maunder, the Exeter scrum half, had just turned 20. Sam Underhill, the Ospreys flank, was also an uncapped 20-year-old. Ellis Genge, the Leicester prop who had made such a great double act with Kyle Sinckler in Australia the year before, was 22. Sinckler had been snapped up by the Lions, but I had great faith that Genge would really develop in Argentina.

'We have focused particularly on youth because we want to find players who are going to be better than the 17 England players on the Lions tour,' I said. 'To win the World Cup we need to have the best talent. That is our ultimate destiny.'

Piers Francis was older, being 26, but he was also little known. He had travelled an unlikely road. Born in Gravesend, Kent, he had moved to New Zealand at the age of 18 to improve his rugby. He had played at fly half or centre for Old Gravesendians, Maidstone, Auckland under-21s, Edinburgh, Doncaster, Counties Manukau, the Blues and Northampton. Only a few years before we picked him for the Argentina tour he had been working in Starbucks in Auckland while playing New Zealand club rugby.

I also selected Mark Wilson, an uncapped 27-year-old who was a hard-edged, grafting blind-side flanker from Newcastle. The talent of Henry Slade, who had won five caps at the age of 24, was obvious.

Cokanasiga, after Curry, excited me most. He was 6 foot 4 inches tall and weighed 280 pounds. I could tell he was a few years away from being ready, and he would not play against Argentina, but I wanted him to train with us. I thought he had the potential to become one of the most explosive and powerful wingers in world rugby. He's a Fijian boy, from an army background, and modest and quiet. You could tell that he's been brought up well by his family. He's a lovely kid.

Just over two years later, England's World Cup squad would include Cokanasiga, Curry, Francis, Genge, Slade, Underhill and Wilson. Luke Cowan-Dickie, George Ford, Joe Launchbury and Jonny May, who all went to Argentina, also made it to Japan. Marchant, who was part of the World Cup training squad, just missed out. Dylan Hartley, Chris Robshaw, Mike Brown, Danny Care and James Haskell – the older players in Argentina – did not make the cut.

The leadership of the senior players on tour was exceptional. They set the standards on and off the field and showed the youngsters what was required to play for England. They didn't let up and were generous in sharing their knowledge and experience. Their contribution accelerated the development of those young players. They also showed the younger players that rugby tours are great fun. I was grateful for their contribution and they were a credit to English rugby. But the biggest revelation in Argentina was Tom Curry. He was immense in the first Test, which we won 38–34. But it knocked him physically because, at that stage, his body wasn't ready for back-to-back Tests. Curry was the youngest England debutant since Jonny Wilkinson and I wanted to look after him because I knew he was going to be brilliant. Sam Underhill, another of our outstanding young prospects, replaced him for the second Test, which was another England victory, 35–25.

Curry and Underhill, just before the 2019 World Cup, would become my Kamikaze Kids as they played alongside each other as flankers.

It was a great tour – a low-budget, old-school rugby tour with the senior players leading the way. At one point we ended up staying in a rough and ready hotel in a town called Santa Fe. It was the home of a brewery that was a sponsor for the tour. It was also a ghost town. But the players made their own fun. Jonny May's quirkiness kept everyone entertained. It was a great experience and a brilliant way to spark change. I remember thinking on the flight home that the tour had delivered everything I had hoped for, and more.

There are 10,080 minutes in every week. A game of rugby lasts 80 minutes. How you use the other 10,000 minutes each week is vital when you want to win the World Cup. You have to deal with your players, fellow coaches, additional staff, executives and administrators, sponsors, the media and supporters – as well as giving precious time to your family and your own well-being. Preparing for three World Cup tournaments has taught me that there is never a minute to waste because every idea, word, action and their consequences have to be considered, calibrated and either adopted or discarded. Each day from 1 December 2015, when I started in the job, to 2 November 2019, the date of the

World Cup final, had been planned and mapped out in detail. I'm an obsessive planner.

I work to a clear and deliberate strategy. Even my sleeping patterns are ordered. Generally, I won't sleep for more than four or five hours at night. But I always try to slot in 30 minutes to an hour for a nap in the afternoon – otherwise I'll get quite tired. I need to keep an eye on my health and stress levels since the stroke.

This regime works well for me. It begins with a 5 a.m. alarm call. I am so used to getting up early that I produce some of my best thinking between five and six in the morning. I am in the gym soon after six. After a workout and a little breakfast, I turn this additional early morning time into a quiet period free from disturbances. By 8.30 or 9 a.m., when we join the players, my fellow coaches and I will already have done a decent chunk of the day's work. The days are long, but it is great fun. Before I get into bed, I reflect on the day and decide how I could improve. It keeps me honest and it's funny how the list is always pretty long. I'm hard on myself. It helps to guard against complacency.

As we approached the end of the second year, my desire to change the way the players trained and operated extended to myself and all the assistant coaches. We all needed a shake-up as we set about rebooting England. Only one game had been lost in the past 21 Tests, but I wanted to make us more flexible and resilient – physically and psychologically.

My positive experience in assisting Jake White at the 2007 World Cup encouraged me to appoint Neil Craig as the England team's head of high performance. Neil, who is a few years older than me, was 62 when he joined the team in October 2017. He brought vast experience with him. A former Australian Rules footballer, Neil had coached Adelaide and Melbourne and been the head of performance and coaching development at Essendon as well as the director of coaching at Carlton. The professionalism of Aussie Rules compares favourably with any other code anywhere in the world. They really know what they are doing. Neil did not have a background in rugby, but his understanding of coaching at the highest level in elite sport would be invaluable. And, most importantly, he is a good bloke.

His official title was pretty meaningless. Head of high performance did not resonate with either of us. He more accurately described his role as being a critical friend to me. Just as I had supported Jake, and eased the pressure on him whenever I could, so Neil became my observant right-hand man. His job was to watch closely and advise me where I might improve my interaction with my players and the other coaches. Neil understood the pressures and subtleties of a head coach's role and he brought a fresh perspective. I also wanted him to work with Steve Borthwick, Paul Gustard, Neal Hatley and all our coaches and key support staff. After all, who coaches the coaches?

Neil said that, rather than being a micro-manager, he saw himself as a micro-monitor. It was his task to watch our work closely and to offer a critical view. His initial feedback to me was positive. Neil had known me since before the 2003 World Cup and he felt that, while I was still demanding and sometimes intolerant, I had developed a greater empathy with my coaches. In the past, if a coach didn't know the answer to a question, I would erupt. Now I was more likely to give the coaches a bit more time. I would still make my dissatisfaction clear, but I was nowhere near as volatile. He also said that there was a clear gap between the media's cartoonish stereotype of me as this tyrant with funny eyes and the reality of my behaviour. I still have my moments but, over time, I've learnt to modify my more extreme reactions.

He agreed that one of my repeated frustrations with the England job was valid. Both the players and the coaches were, at least initially, reactive rather than proactive. This English reticence, in my opinion, reflects wider English society. I've never lived in a country with the cultural and class differences of England. It's an even more hierarchical society than Japan. This creates huge challenges when you are trying to build a united team where everyone's input is equally valued. One of our priorities was to level the playing field and bring unity to our mission.

I faced a similar problem in Japan, where a junior player would not dare speak to a senior player. I had to break that convention. I tried to do the same in England. My observation was that when a group of Englishmen get together they'll often behave like they're back in school. There will be characters who act like they're prefects and they will boss everyone around. The others will do as they are told. The Japanese and English are very similar in that there is always a facade of politeness to their interactions. People don't want to stand out and it appears as if cohesion is important to them. But there is no doubt that, beneath the surface, the English and the Japanese both love to bitch about everyone around them.

Now this is not to say that Australia is perfect. Far from it. We have our own problems but, as Australian outsiders, we were desperate to shake things up and change the team dynamic that was heavily influenced by these cultural traits. We needed to break the reticence. We needed to get everyone to feel confident enough to contribute and to speak up. I wanted a team from mixed cultures and backgrounds that reflected the strength of diversity in modern England.

You drive through Surrey and other privileged areas in the south of England, where the houses are palatial and the gardens are massive, and you see a society of accumulated wealth and status. People in the south seem much less open to change, as they look pretty comfortable. When I visit somewhere rougher in northern England, perhaps a town like Wigan, where Andy and Owen Farrell come from, it could not be more different. People are friendlier and more open. It is not for me to say one is better than the other, but I am happier and we are stronger when my squad contains a mix of these different English cultures.

Neil agreed with my observation that the English in general, not just in sport, want to be told what to do. They like clear instruction. In Australian culture there is more a tendency to question the instruction – and that is encouraged. But this more forceful approach is obviously foreign to the English players and coaches. Neil noticed that, occasionally, one of my fellow coaches would say: 'Just tell me what you want me to do, Eddie.' I would respond: 'Well, mate, I actually want your opinion. I want you to bring some different thoughts to the table. I want you to think and then act. I don't want you to do things only on my say-so.'

The English coaches found this hard but I didn't care. We are working in a brutal, unforgiving environment and it's my head on the block if it doesn't work out. If we are going to achieve our goal of being the best team in the world, we need to squeeze the very best effort and ideas from everyone on our team. I wasn't going to do that part of their job for them. Test rugby requires an aggressive mindset. This requires players to be clear about their role and accountable for their performance. They have to own it. No excuses.

Coaches can't be on the field with the players. But if coaches are not showing initiative in preparation, how can you expect the players to? Neil began to encourage the coaches to be more open, forceful and braver in voicing their opinions and insights. I loved it when we started to see their behaviour change.

We also needed the players to take more ownership of how the team operated if we were going to win the World Cup. After just a short time in our camp, Neil felt our boys had a great work ethic. But, again, they were more comfortable following orders rather than doing anything original. They all called Neil 'boss'. He would suggest they try something and they'd say, 'Right, boss' or, 'Yes, boss.' Neil was used to Australian players who would never call him boss and always ask him 'why?' We had to accept that we were working with English players; but we needed change. The positive was that the players were up for it and hungry to try new ways of learning.

Each player agreed their individual leadership plan and we made sure that we gave them plenty of opportunities to fail in camp. Failure is always painful but it's an important way of learning. We created scenarios that would test their attitude and resilience and encourage them to take risks and possibly fail. It was fascinating to see them grow in their own ways in their own time. But to a man, they were desperate to be a part of the team and desperate to improve.

Neil's work was supplemented by the great Frank Dick, the former head coach of UK Athletics who had led the GB team to four separate Olympic Games. Frank had also been Daley Thompson's coach when he won Olympic gold in the decathlon in 1980 and 1984. He might have had a few years on the clock, but Frank has one of the sharpest minds in elite sport. I had asked him to join our team in 2016 as a consultant and visit our training camps once a week. Neil is with us all the time, whereas Frank's occasional visits allow him to observe our progress with more detachment. His official title is 'strategic planning consultant', but in reality he is just a smart bloke with a lot to offer. He has made a huge impact on our progress.

I remember how, in one session, he spoke to us about the fact that, when you're in a team, there are four 'fatal fears'. The first is the fear of getting it wrong or making a mistake. But if you never make a mistake it means you've never challenged yourself to go beyond the limits. The moment you start something new, or step beyond the edge of risk, the chances of making a mistake are notably high. But every time you make a mistake you need to make a point of learning from it and not repeating it. When you become really brave, you don't wait for somebody else to see the mistake. You put your hand up straightaway.

Frank's second fatal fear is of losing. When you enter any contest in life you can only control yourself. But if you can deliver the performance that you're capable of, every time, the result should take care of itself. The third fatal fear is fear of rejection. This means you don't put yourself forward. But, by risking the fact you might be knocked back, you learn how to ask questions and to grow as a person. The final fatal fear is of criticism. But here, Frank said, the key point is to replace the word 'criticism' with the concept of 'feedback'. Once you start looking for feedback you will be much stronger and more resilient.

These four fatal fears are as relevant to non-sporting teams in business, government or the not-for-profit sector. Build a team of individuals who can conquer these fears and you will be well on the way to achieving your objectives.

Frank was interesting because, being Scottish, he was quite blunt in his assessment of the English national character. He felt that English people are pretty soft until their backs are up against the wall. It was a sweeping generalization, but the old spirit of Dunkirk and the Battle of Britain – desperate situations when you're one step away from a precipice – were still obvious in English sport. We wanted to reach a position where our team didn't have to wait until things were going off the rails before they produced their best effort.

We had achieved the stability and excellence implied by an 18-match winning run. But we had been fortunate to win some of those games while our motivation and intensity had dimmed. We needed to galvanize the players and coaches so that fresh impetus pushed us forward.

In late 2017, while speaking to the press, I had said: 'Players like to get comfortable. They like to have a nice house, drive a Range Rover, like to do the same thing every day in training. To get them to have the courage to try to be different is the biggest trick. Encouraging them to do that consistently, to be different, is vital. Don't be comfortable . . . be uncomfortable.'

Frank, like Neil, had seen a strong work ethic in the players and coaches – but he rarely saw them give each other any constructive feedback. The coaches, in particular, did not challenge one another. They were diligent but passive. It seemed to my two expert witnesses that I was driving the process too much on my own. People listened to me and carried out my orders – but what we really needed was debate and a questioning attitude if we were to grow as a team.

I'm always looking to improve every aspect of my coaching, and it was enormously helpful to have Frank and Neil point out to me that my relentless quest to get better could intimidate those around me. They would give me examples of when I had pushed too hard and compromised my impact. I always appreciated the radical candour of their feedback, no matter how uncomfortable it made me feel at the time.

The three of us wanted to break the mould. We saw ourselves as pioneers and we wanted to do things better than before. Continuous improvement was our goal. This explained why feedback and engagement were so important. It was not about belittling people. Encouraging constructive criticism and debate was an opportunity to improve.

As part of this drive to improve, we looked everywhere for advantage. In a conversation with the swimming coach Bill Sweetenham, he mentioned the work of the neurologist Professor Vincent Walsh from University College London. Knowing we had limited time with the players, we explored ways to maximize impact on their learning. Vincent introduced four key principles. The first was to ensure that the room in which you spoke to the players was open and well lit. The second principle was to introduce some sort of primer that would release dopamine from the brain. The third was built on the structure of only ever having three points. And so the fourth principle was to start and not to finish. We would leave meetings without resolution. This allowed the players to think more about the final solution. These changes worked a treat. Our players are with their clubs for 40 weeks a year and if you consider, on average, they have three meetings a week, that's 120 meetings before they get anywhere near us. We had to find ways to make it as easy as possible for them to learn.

In the autumn of 2017, the players were unaware that a radical reboot of our system was under way. Many of them were still physically and mentally tired after the Lions' drawn series with New Zealand. You could sense a real flatness about them in the

November internationals. But we kept on winning. The results looked impressive on the scoreboard. England beat Argentina 21–8, Australia 30–6 and Samoa 48–14. But just beneath the surface the cracks were clear. They were exhausted and only their toughness drove them on. But it couldn't last. We were heading into difficult terrain and it was going to take us almost a year to reach the other side.

The traditional southern hemisphere season is like a 400-metre race. You get out, you go hard and you finish strongly. Here, in the north, it's more like a 3,000-metre steeplechase. You need to pace yourself because it's a long and draining season – and there are plenty of obstacles in the way. Rather than give 100 per cent at every session or in each league game, you do just enough to stay under the radar. It explains why a southern hemisphere coach can come in and instil that toughness and pace and intensity from down under very quickly. But if you keep it up, it wears the players down and exacerbates the symptoms of third-season syndrome.

My third season coincided with the aftermath of the Lions, so I copped a double whammy. It was a disaster. Our best players were out on their feet but needed to return to their clubs to perform. A limited off-season meant they were in terrible shape physically and mentally when they got back to us. The clubs pay the players' wages so they owe them their best effort and loyalty. It makes it incredibly hard for the national team. Contrast that with the Kiwis, Irish, Scots and Welsh where the players are all under central contracts and are rested properly. The poor old English Lions were thrust back into club rugby far too early but, as expected, they were brave. They kept at it and their desire to work hard remained. But they were down a couple of percentage points – which was enough to take the edge off their normal standards.

When they came into camp before the Six Nations, I deliberately pushed them harder than ever in training because I needed to find out who really wanted to be there. It was the wrong thing to do in terms of achieving immediate results but the right decision in looking ahead to 2019. I knew we had a decent team but, at that stage, we weren't good enough to win the World Cup. I worked them relentlessly in training and took them totally out of their comfort zone. They hated it. But it sorted out the player group for me. It helped me work out which players I wanted to keep and who I was ready to drop. It was ruthless but it was massively important. I had to endure fierce criticism because, as a consequence, we had a terrible tournament. It obviously hurts but you try not to allow the barbs and jibes to get to you. Some of the same people who had hailed me as a brilliant coach nine months before now piled in and depicted me as a madman who had lost the plot.

We beat Italy and then scraped past Wales in our opening two games of the 2018 Six Nations. It meant we had won 24 out of my first 25 Tests as head coach. But then we lost 25–13 to Scotland on a freezing February evening at Murrayfield. We started badly and were 22–6 down at half-time. Scotland had not beaten England for ten years or even scored a try against them at Murrayfield since 2004. They bagged three tries against us and played with a ferocity which matched the passionate roar of their supporters. I tried to rationalize the defeat: 'We're human beings. Human beings aren't robots. We prepare to be intense, we prepare to be aggressive, but for some reason, we weren't. It's a great lesson.'

I guessed that we weren't as intense or aggressive as usual because I had pushed an already weary group of players to their limits. But the long-term strategy took precedence and so I kept working them hard throughout the rest of the tournament. In Paris, we needed to win big and score four tries to take the championship into the final weekend, as Ireland were streaking ahead. But we did neither as the zip and verve of 2016 was replaced by a heavy-legged fatigue. We looked physically and emotionally weary and France won 22–16.

I dropped George Ford and switched Owen Farrell to fly half against Ireland in a bid to find a physical spark. It was a repeat of the year before. A Grand Slam decider – with the only difference being that, this year, we were at home and Ireland had won their first four matches. We were under pressure and under threat of losing three matches in a row. Our prospects looked bleak.

I saw it differently. 'It's the best time in rugby, when you are under the pump and you have got to produce,' I said in my mid-week press conference.

On the eve of the match, someone released a video of me at a corporate event in Japan the previous July. I still don't know who did it. In my attempt to amuse the Japanese audience I referred to the 'scummy Irish' and Wales as a 'little shit place'. I was embarrassed. Not only because the slurs weren't funny but because they weren't my real views. I was going for a cheap laugh. While it was clear in the video that I was smiling and joking, it looked bad. It was bad. The leaker had timed the release to cause me maximum damage. Mission accomplished.

Immediately, both myself and the RFU apologized unreservedly. It had been a stupid mistake. No excuse. You might ask: what did I learn? Don't make jokes at others' expense. And, in my case, be careful when trying to be funny. I should leave the gags to the comedians.

Now, you would think I might have really learnt my lesson about making off-the-cuff remarks. But no. I'm not that bright. Just over a year later, in March 2019, I again dug a hole and tripped over into it. It was nearly as dumb as the embarrassment I caused myself in regard to Ireland and Wales.

I have for a long time wanted to coach the British and Irish Lions. I still hope that, one day, I might get the opportunity. Apart from telling Pemby, I'd kept it a secret that I had set my sights on the 2021 tour of South Africa. That will be one of the great tours in the history of world rugby. In preparation, we were keeping our powder dry and saying all the right things about how you have to be asked before you could consider it. But then I got a long-distance phone call from a journalist in Brisbane. I tried to have a laugh with him and said coaching the Lions was an ambassador job. 'The last thing I want to do is spend eight weeks in a blazer. That's an ambassador job. I'm a coach. I'd rather coach the Queensland Sheffield Shield [cricket] team.' Again, it was a terrible lapse of judgement.

Pemby was straight on the phone: 'Mate,' he said incredulously, 'I thought you wanted to do the Lions job?'

'I do,' I said sheepishly.

'Well you can safely say that ship has sailed, mate. Seriously, you really make it hard for yourself sometimes.'

It was another bad error on my part and, to this day, I don't know why I said it. But, as I've stressed before, I don't do regret. It's better to learn from these little disasters. Maybe one day I will get the chance to coach the Lions. Despite those very public and insulting comments, my genuine opinion is that it would be an honour and a privilege.

Back in 2018, we faced Ireland at Twickenham on St Patrick's Day. It was a grey afternoon made miserable by the perishing cold and my earlier stupidity. It was probably the coldest day I had experienced since arriving in England – and little about our performance provided comfort or warmth.

Ireland were more powerful than us. They were also sharper and smarter than us. We tried hard but they dominated the game and, if anything, the 24–15 score flattered us. I don't like losing but I was not as dejected as the crowd or the media. There was at least one bright moment. After we dominated the first five minutes, Owen Farrell chased a kick to Johnny Sexton and drilled him. We had been under pressure in the media and you could see Owen was trying to lift the team and lead by example. It's one of his great qualities and why I love having him captain my team. He knows no other way than straight and hard and never takes a backward step. At the end of the game I was not ready to reveal the full reasons for our lapse, but it felt important to address the differences between 2016 and 2018.

'We knew during that long winning run that we were not good enough to reach where we wanted to end up.' I said. 'A run like the one we are going through now is instrumental to the development of a team. It was easy to improve England initially, fixing this and that, but internal mechanisms, such as developing leaders, are slow burners. It is part of the process of becoming a better team. We are moving forward, even if results do not show that.

'A run like this tests your resolve, your purpose and the character of your team. That is what we are going through at the moment. I thought our effort today was outstanding. The players stuck at it but Ireland were too good. They are a tough, well-coached side with good leadership and they played exceptionally. We played with character but we just weren't good enough.'

Sections of the shivering Twickenham crowd booed as they saw me on the big screen. In the distance I could see the Grand Slam-winning Irish players frolicking in front of their ecstatic supporters. They had replaced us as champions, and as the second-best team in the world rankings – behind New Zealand. 'Good luck to them,' I thought. They had earned it.

I walked back to the dressing room beneath a darkening sky. Even in mid-March it felt as though we were back in the depths of winter. Ireland looked as if they were strolling down a sunlit path. I consoled myself with the private belief that Ireland had just peaked. They would be on a downward slope from this glorious high. We were again being mocked and ridiculed by the pundits. I was secure in the knowledge that the details of our World Cup plans were safe because the media, as a rule, are generally not curious and more interested in opinion than fact. No one was probing for the truth and, instead, they preferred to load up on the insults. But I knew that, in 18 months, at the World Cup, we would be stronger having endured days like these.

In preparation for 2019 we were still looking to develop the right training plans to generate an adaptable game style. We had to balance the demands of the game with the way we trained. Designing training is perhaps the most fascinating part of professional rugby because this is the only area, if controlled effectively, where you will improve. Raymond Verheijen is a Dutch football coach and an expert in conditioning. He had worked at three World Cups and three European Champion-ships with the Netherlands, South Korea and Russia. Raymond has also worked with Barcelona, Chelsea and Manchester City. He is an expert in tactical periodization and, as we wanted an external view of our approach, he held a three-day course for our coaches. It was brilliant.

Raymond also joined us on our tour to South Africa and the outcome was a new approach to our preparation. Instead of training Tuesday and Thursday we would switch to Wednesday, as it was the day where the players would be best able to train hard. We decided to dial up the intensity of that session. Our training would be really hard. We intended to push the players harder than ever on our tour of South Africa.

New Zealand and South Africa are the two greatest touring destin-ations in world rugby. The quality of rugby, and the significance the game carries for each country, mean that no other nation can match these traditional powerhouses. England have never won a series in South Africa, and so I considered our June 2018 tour to be another special opportunity. No one expected us to do well and I had the feeling that the media almost wanted us to lose because it would be a big story if we suffered a whitewash. I also knew it was going to be exceptionally challenging as we were missing 20 frontline players through injury or the need to rest them.

Dylan Hartley was the most significant loss. He was injured and I knew he was struggling. Owen Farrell was his obvious replacement as captain, and I was intrigued to see if we could discover some more leaders on a testing tour. Dylan had held us together for two and a half years but we could no longer rely on him. His body was creaking and, as much as I still hoped he could make it to the World Cup, it was imperative we had alternatives in place. I believed in Owen. He's one of the great players in world rugby and an inspirational figure in our squad.

Manu Tuilagi, Anthony Watson, Jack Nowell, Jonathan Joseph, George Kruis and Sam Underhill were all injured, while older players like Danny Care, Dan Cole and James Haskell needed a summer break away from rugby. Selection is always a difficult process, but I felt we had picked a promising squad with a good mix of established players, fresh faces and a few guys who were returning after a period away from England. Danny Cipriani had not played for England since 2015 and he had won only 14 caps after he made such an explosive start to his Test career. In March 2008 he was hailed as England rugby's saviour after he played brilliantly in a big win over Ireland in his first Test start. He had been meant to start the previous match against Scotland, but he'd been axed from the squad for 'inappropriate behaviour' in the week of the game. A tabloid photographer had snapped him leaving a nightclub.

I knew Cipriani was an outstanding talent in club rugby. I had coached Saracens against Wasps, when he was still a teenager, and Cipriani made the difference in that game. He had brilliant feet, a good eye for space and reasonable skills, so he always looked like he was going to be a very good player. He really caught the eye against Ireland, but then everything seemed to go awry. He was injured and his personal life was consistently chaotic. He was in and out of the newspapers for all the wrong reasons for years. I guessed that this was the main reason why his talent had not been matched by consistent performances.

Martin Johnson, the England coach in the 2011 World Cup, didn't trust or rate him and so Cipriani made a clean break. He left England and went to play Super Rugby for the Melbourne Rebels, who were a new team coached by Rod Macqueen. The Rebels struggled and, in 2011 and 2012, Cipriani was terrible. He looked to have lost his way completely. He was so bad that I thought there would be no way back for him. But since I became England coach I had been pleasantly surprised by how his game had improved. When I first came in, he wasn't playing well enough to be in the squad, but his quality over the next two seasons could not be ignored. He had a particularly good season with Wasps in 2017 and deserved an opportunity to play for England.

One of the reasons I had not picked him before was because I did not like the way he reacted to his teammates. But his language and attitude to the other players had improved enormously and he was having a much more positive effect on his team. The job of the number 10 is to drive the attack forward. Cipriani had been guilty of sometimes moving the game sideways rather than forward, but I saw a much more effective mix in his play. He had matured both as a rugby player and a person and I was happy to pick him to tour South Africa.

I regarded him primarily as a number 10, but I said I wouldn't dismiss the possibility that he might play at 15. I wanted to give him a good crack, even if, personally, I thought he lacked the gas to play full back. His relationship with the other players was the most important facet and I said that I only wanted him to appear on the back pages for good rugby reasons – rather than being splashed over the front page in yet another scandal.

It was not easy for Cipriani. There has always been an English fascination with someone who seems unusual and generates gossip. The media were obsessed with Cipriani and it was not entirely his fault. We played – and lost to – the Barbarians in a warm-up game before we flew to South Africa. A girl visited him at the hotel before the game and the press tried to turn it into a story. It was bullshit. The players were allowed visits from their wives or girlfriends and so Cipriani had done nothing wrong. But he was 'newsworthy'. This attitude filters down to the fans. Whenever I spoke to anyone in the street in England, one of the first questions they would always ask was: 'What do you think of Cipriani?' They wouldn't ask me about Owen Farrell – but I suppose that's because he's a tough, hard-working player whose story is dominated by rugby.

I was willing to see what Cipriani could do – despite often feeling frustrated because even the rugby reporters wanted to talk about him more than any other player. I agreed that this was a chance for him to convince me that he had a long-term future for England and that he was better than Farrell and George Ford. I've said before that I am very open to picking players who are regarded as X-factor talents, and who have come from the 'wrong side of the tracks'. Cipriani was different; I knew he'd had quite a tough upbringing and he owed a lot to his mum who drove a black cab in London to give him a good education and a real chance in life. I was encouraging, and Danny reacted with a good attitude.

My hardest task was not coaching Cipriani. Rather it was coaxing my players into being more creative. We needed to become bolder and more attacking. We could not thrive in Test rugby by playing conservatively. Rugby had become a high-scoring game. I knew we would need to score lots of points to win a Test, and we also had to uncover the mental toughness required to beat the Springboks in South Africa. I was set for a tour of real discovery.

Ellis Park is a brilliant place to play rugby. It's loud and it's raucous and, on a still and beautiful winter's afternoon in Johannesburg, on 9 June 2018, the atmosphere crackled with its own unique electricity. The significance of the occasion was amplified by the fact that the Springboks were being led for the very first time by a black captain. Siya Kolisi, a good rugby player and an inspirational man, had been appointed by Rassie Erasmus, who had replaced Allister Coetzee as Springbok coach. Allister and I had a good relationship, after we worked together for the Boks in 2007, but I knew Rassie was the better head coach. We were in for a mighty battle.

I could not have been happier with how we started. After two minutes we had a penalty ten metres inside our own half. Owen consulted with Elliot Daly, who has a monster boot, and we decided to have a crack at the sticks. Johannesburg is nearly 6,000 feet above sea level and, in the thin air of altitude, the ball flies. Daly nailed the penalty. Three minutes later, after a slashing cross-field move, Henry Slade fired a pass to Mike Brown, who I had switched from full back to wing. Brown went over for our first try and Farrell converted.

After 18 minutes we were 24–3 up as Daly and Farrell also scored excellent tries. It had been our best start as an England team in three seasons of my coaching. All the momentum was with us and then, suddenly, almost inexplicably, we allowed it to slip. I had been so impressed by our mentality because, usually, the away team crumbles at the outset at Ellis Park. We did the opposite. We fronted up and took total control of the game. But midway through the first half, when we should have just shut them out of the match entirely, we were sloppy. We allowed them back into the game. Faf de Klerk was a real menace at scrum half for the Boks and he got them flying. De Klerk's try was followed by three more in quick succession. From 24–3 up we went in at half-time trailing 29–27.

We had missed Hartley's calming influence, as well as a number of other experienced older heads. In the second row, owing to injuries, I had picked Nick Isiekwe. He had just turned 20 and he was one of the players who made it look as if, after our initial surge, we had a few too many boys playing against men. We simply lacked leadership. The Springboks were always going to come back strongly and get some advantage from the referee. That's the reality when you play the Springboks in South Africa. You just have to grit those periods out. Don't get too excited, don't get too frustrated. Hang in there and you will come out the other end. But the game swung away from us and we struggled to claw back our momentum.

We were chasing the game and trailing by ten points with eight minutes to play. Jonny May scored our fifth try, to match the five scored by the Boks, and it looked as if we might have one last shot at a famous victory. But the score stayed 42–39. We had lost an epic game of rugby.

The second Test in Bloemfontein followed a similar pattern. We raced into a 12–0 lead after just 13 minutes. Tries by Brown and May gave us another rollicking start after I had shuffled the pack by dropping Chris Robshaw. He had been a real warrior for me, and for England, but he was one of many players whose form had fallen away. But our positive start again melted away and shortly before half-time we were trailing 13–12. We didn't score another point in the second half and the Springboks, who kicked well, wrapped up the series with a 23–12 victory. It had been the same exasperating story. I was happy with Farrell as captain but there was a general lack of leadership, confidence and composure throughout the team.

We missed Hartley massively because he was our main 'glue guy' who holds the team together. He's a leader who comes into his own when the heat is on and the team are buckling a little. Hartley knows when to have a harsh or a calming word. As a coach you generally choose a captain in your own persona. The quiet coach prefers the quiet captain, the abrasive bloke goes for the abrasive skipper. But, with experience, you learn to coach and choose your captain in different ways. Hartley and Farrell fell into the abrasive camp. But Hartley had learnt to temper himself and be more in quiet control. Farrell was only 26 and I was sure he would grow as a captain. We still had 15 months left before the World Cup. I decided that, after the tour, I would experiment with Hartley and Farrell as co-captains and we'd see how the next few months unfolded.

Even the great leaders of world rugby take time to emerge. I saw it with George Gregan. He turned out to be one of the finest captains I've ever seen, but it took years for his real leadership powers to mature. John Eales, one of the great Test captains, struggled at the start of his career. He was a poor captain which, now, is hard to believe. Richie McCaw didn't have consistent success when he was first captain, though he went on to win two

World Cups. But McCaw went through the pain of 2003 and 2007. So he had an eight-year incubation period to learn those leadership skills. It takes time. Leadership often comes from failure because that's how the hardest lessons are learned.

Of course, the media love to write about failure. It gives them the chance to really put the boot in and to produce explosive and divisive coverage. I was reminded constantly that we had lost five Tests in a row. Most of the writers added the warm-up game against the Barbarians as a sixth defeat on the spin. I was told on the night we lost in Bloemfontein that 126 days had passed since England had last won a game of rugby.

Just as I had ignored the excessive praise during my first two years with England, so I refused to be bogged down in the spiral of negativity that followed us to Cape Town for the third Test. It's always difficult when you lose. But, in England, it gets amplified many times over. Your team goes from being the best in the world to the worst side England has ever seen. Your status as a coach plummets from brilliance to idiocy in a flash. There is an element of absurdity to the coverage because the English media feeds off hysteria.

The cold, hard reality is that you're never as good or as bad as they say.

When you're down, it is interesting to see how the players react. Once again, the England lads were outstanding. The greater the pressure, the stronger the unity and belief. On the rest day before the third Test, with the series gone and the losing streak stretching to five, the players took themselves to a park across the road from the team hotel for a game of cricket. They had a great time. Their laughter and camaraderie could be seen and heard from a distance. As they made their way back into the hotel, they were beaming. It was a powerful demonstration of the strong off-field bonds we were building.

The England job is particularly difficult because, beyond the media, there is a battle every day. You've got to box clever to stay on top of all the problems. I knew we were in a bit of a hole and

it was time to roll the dice for the last Test. I decided to call up
Cipriani at 10 and to give him a chance to run the show. Your
number 10 is the equivalent of a quarterback in American football. They set the tone and tempo at training and play a key role
in the organization of the week and the match. Ford was a little
unlucky to be dropped, but I felt we needed something different
and wanted to see what the team looked like under Danny's
guidance.

We were fortunate that, at Newlands, conditions suited us.
Instead of it being another fast track, we faced South Africa on a
slow deck on a wet day. It was a real arm-wrestle and, once
again, we were courageous. The score was tight all the way. We
led 6–3 at half-time and the game was still in the balance with
eight minutes to go. England were ahead 15–10 but the Boks
were firmly in the match. Cipriani then produced a little magic.
His delicate and precise cross-field kick found May, who had the
simple task of scoring the try which made the game safe.

Cipriani did his job and I was delighted that we had won the
match. At the last press conference before the game, I said that
we were looking for that special moment from him – and he
produced it. But the reaction from the press was outrageous.
They thought Cipriani had proved he was a rugby genius. It was
one good moment, but he had been very quiet throughout the
rest of the game. I remember Farrell producing something similar with a kick which also set up a May try at Twickenham. But
no one said much about it then because it was Owen. When
Danny did it he was exalted for his 'unbelievable' and 'incredible'
skill. I judge the players on how they prepare, how they train and
how they play. Every day is a selection day. At the end of the
week in Cape Town, Danny was still a distant third behind Owen
and George Ford.

I was more interested in the fact that, for the most part, we
outplayed South Africa. I was also really proud of the way we
played tactically under enormous pressure. It was good to break
the cycle of defeats. When you've coached for a long time, you

accept that you get these fallow periods. I've had them every seven or eight years and you've got to battle through them. It helps to know that, if you've got the right players and the right staff, you and the team will be stronger for coming through adversity.

I have been on many rugby tours in my career as both a player and a coach. I rate this one as my most enjoyable. The team was tough and dedicated and they kept wanting to improve. You could see the belief growing. It was exciting to see the progress on and off the field.

In tough times I always remember the first year I coached the Brumbies. We finished third from bottom in the Super 12 and it looked like we were miles off the pace. But when we assessed everything carefully, I felt we were only a few percentage points away from making the top four and the play-offs. At Test level the margins are even smaller. We might have won the series in South Africa 3–0, or suffered the same score in reverse, with one or two slight differences here and there. You need to be realistic and accept that you tread such a fine line between success and failure. But impartiality is not part of most sports reporting. People want to read about triumph or catastrophe. There is nothing in between. But the truth is that, for most sports teams, you're generally somewhere in the middle, occasionally touching the opposite extremes.

I was heartened by the way the squad had moved forward. Their attitude and application, as well as their willingness to absorb pain and get on with it, had been fantastic. We had lost the series, but we had come a long way in a short time. We had turned a tight corner.

On the way home from South Africa, I assessed our games in detail. I focused on the first two Tests. We had come out firing in both games. Our attack was brilliant and the structured parts of our game were solid. But we couldn't sustain the momentum. Our game style wasn't working and I couldn't quite put my finger on it. Our opponents had kicked well and won both matches. I

wondered if there might be something in it. When I landed at
Heathrow I called Gordon Hamilton-Fairley. I wanted the maths
men to take a look at tier-one rugby matches and see if they
could build a hypothesis for a new game style as we approached
the last long run to the World Cup.

Danny Cipriani was back in trouble just two months later. He
had joined a new club, Gloucester, and on their pre-season tour
to Jersey, he was involved in another incident. Cipriani pleaded
guilty to hitting a bouncer at a club and resisting arrest. He
was fined £2,000 and agreed to do ten weeks' community service. I was not too surprised or let down. When a player
consistently does stupid things, you don't expect him to change
much. Players make choices and they have to live with the
consequences.

But the incident in Jersey did not have any bearing on my future
selection. I just thought Farrell and Ford were both better players
at Test level than Cipriani. I made it clear to him that he remained
in my thinking and if either of the two blokes ahead of him were
injured or lost form drastically then I would have no qualms
about picking him. From Danny's perspective his cause was done
more damage when he played for Gloucester against Saracens. It
was billed as a showdown between Farrell and Cipriani, but it was
no contest. Saracens and Farrell were dominant.

Away from the Cipriani soap opera, I was much more
absorbed and excited by the coaching changes that had occurred.
For the South Africa tour, I had persuaded Scott Wisemantel to
come in as our attack coach. He worked with me at the Wallabies as our skills coach between 2004 and 2007, and he had done
brilliant work with Japan before and during the 2015 World Cup.
Wisey's a really good, energetic coach with a real knowledge of
the game, after also working in Super Rugby with the Waratahs
and in France with Lyon and Montpellier. The players like him
and he is full of new ideas. He offered us an injection of vitality.

Wisey's role in South Africa was on a consultancy basis, but he was so good that I worked hard to convince him to join us full time until the end of 2019. I was thrilled when he agreed because he offered the contrast we needed with the two excellent English coaches in Steve Borthwick and Neal Hatley. There is no one better than Steve when it comes to the detail of the job, and he gels well with Neal who is also very popular with the players. But Scott is much more of an extrovert and he gave the coaching staff a real spark and zip.

There had also been a change in our defence coach after the South Africa tour. I worked well with Paul Gustard and I was happy with all he had done for England. But I could not stand in his way when he was offered the chance to become director of rugby at Harlequins. Gussy also has a young family, and so I could understand why he wanted to take the job and get off the international treadmill. Our parting was very amicable and it helped that I felt I had quickly found an exceptional replacement in John Mitchell.

John and I had been in opposition in the 2003 World Cup semi-final when he coached the All Blacks against my Wallabies. He had been in charge of a very good team, but anything less than winning the World Cup is a disaster for New Zealanders. John lost his job. But I knew he was a talented coach with gravitas and experience. John had worked around the world and he also knew English rugby inside out. He had been England's forwards coach under Clive Woodward from 1997 to 2000. John had also been head coach of the USA and looked after five Super Rugby teams in New Zealand, Australia and South Africa. He had worked at Wasps and at Sale in the English Premiership, and so he had one of the most wide-ranging CVs in world rugby. John, like all veteran coaches, had been through some tough times, but he was a survivor. And, like me, he loved coaching.

We had evolved the role of the assistant coaches. We now call them positional coaches. While they still coach an area of the game, they are now responsible for a specific group of players. Neil is the scrum coach, but he is primarily responsible for all the front-row players. He's got to make sure they are fit and on task. If there are any issues, he deals with them before they come to me. Steve is the forwards coach but he's mainly responsible for the locks. So if the locks aren't performing, it's his responsibility to fix it. John focuses on the back row. I look after the inside backs and Scott takes the outside backs. Most of our meetings are now in these positional groups.

Getting Mitch on board completed my coaching jigsaw. I was convinced that we had just the right back-room team to take England to the World Cup.

The 2018 autumn internationals were played less than a year before the tournament which would define my England legacy. Every Test match counts, and you want to win each one you play, but the closer you come to the World Cup, the more it feels as if the other games are sparring sessions compared to the real deal. Our two hardest Tests that November were the first matches we played – against South Africa and New Zealand.

My plan to field co-captains in Hartley and Farrell had its first trial run against the Springboks. Farrell led the team out, but Hartley was back at the heart of the scrum and in joint charge of the team. I sprang a little surprise by picking Mark Wilson at number 8 as Billy Vunipola was still injured. I like the grit and graft of Wilson. Tom Curry was at open side and Brad Shields completed the back row. There was a real freshness to the team, but we had to show so much old-school determination to stay in the game.

The Springboks enjoyed 78 per cent possession and 80 per cent territory for a long period in the first half; we were on the ropes and absorbing one attack after another. South Africa had beaten New Zealand in Wellington, and narrowly lost the return match at home, and they were on a roll under Rassie Erasmus. But they weren't clinical enough against us and we hung on to reach the break only trailing 8–6. It could have been so much worse.

A fourth Farrell penalty in the 73rd minute meant that we inched ahead 12–11. But the Boks came back at us and, in the very last minute, their big replacement centre André Esterhuizen set off on a bullocking run from just over the halfway line. He looked intent on saving the game, but Farrell stood in his way. Farrell hit him really hard and Esterhuizen went down in a heap. The ball spilled to the ground and we booted it out as we had passed 80 minutes on the clock. Our players celebrated, only to suddenly see that the referee, Australia's Angus Gardner, had asked the TMO to check the legality of the tackle. He specifically wanted to establish whether Farrell had used his arms to bring Esterhuizen down, rather than hitting him with his shoulders. I thought it was a fair hit, but I knew it was very close – and the legitimacy of Farrell's tackling technique would come under fierce scrutiny after the match.

This time the decision went our way. We had won a brutal Test match by a single point.

I was delighted. 'There was a lot of toughness from us out there,' I said after the match. 'We stayed in the arm wrestle and turned the game around. We were not quite good enough to take advantage of a couple of opportunities we had but we scored the winning points. We played some of the big moments really well and I could not be prouder of the players.

'The young players did exceptionally well and we can look forward to New Zealand now. I cannot wait to play them. New Zealand are different to South Africa. They'll want an athletic contest. But we will not be wearing singlets and running shorts. It will be a proper game of rugby. You want to face the best in the world and the Kiwis are that. Bring it on.'

Our plan was to choke the life out of them. The All Blacks are the kings of unstructured play. Sit back and watch them play and they will cut you to pieces. You have to take their space and hit them hard. When you attack you need to run powerfully to tire them out. You have to get in their heads and make them very uncomfortable. Australia, under both myself and Rod Macqueen, had great success against the All Blacks because we had the play-ers to keep it tight and deny them opportunity.

It was a thriller with the All Blacks at Twickenham on 10 November 2018. A see-sawing beauty came down to another very late decision from the TMO. We had started like a train. In the second minute, after a rock-solid scrum, Ben Youngs fed Ben Te'o, who set up a forward rumble as Sinckler and Itoje blasted a hole in the black wall. Youngs then found Chris Ashton with a fizzing pass and the wing went over. A Farrell drop goal made it 8–0 after ten minutes. We were soon 15–0 up when, from a crisp England lineout, Hartley crashed over on the back of a rolling maul.

New Zealand always come back and they edged into the lead, 16–15, as we entered the last quarter of the game. It wasn't the usual bursts of All Black brilliance. Rather, on a miserable day at Twickenham, the world's best side proved that they had learnt how to arm-wrestle under Steve Hansen. When the game is tight, like our clash, they just stick at it. Their scrum and, in particular, their lineout had improved immeasurably. Brodie Retallick was supreme and they hurt us in the lineout. But we hung in, with just as much toughness, and then went in search of the win.

There were just five minutes left when Courtney Lawes charged down TJ Perenara's kick. The ball bounced loose and Sam Underhill, who had been immense all afternoon, scooped it up. He sidestepped Beauden Barrett and scorched across the Twickenham turf, eating up 40 metres to score. The crowd and the players celebrated a match-winning try – until the referee Jérôme Garcès turned to the TMO to ask whether Lawes had been onside at the ruck when Perenara put boot to ball. It was another agonizing wait, just like the week before. This time the decision went against us. Marius Jonker, the TMO, ruled that Lawes had been fractionally offside. We had lost the match by a few centimetres.

I was justifiably upbeat after the game. 'We had a team of 400 caps and they had a team of 800 caps. That is a hell of a difference, and your ability to handle those difficult situations comes down to experience. We've got Mako and Billy Vunipola to come back into contention so it's a good situation for us to be in. It's been a tough year but we needed a slump to reignite ourselves and we've done that. The next time we play New Zealand it might be a different story. We feel like we have the game to take to them.'

It felt written in the stars. I was pretty sure that we would next play the All Blacks in Yokohama City on 26 October 2019 – in the first World Cup semi-final. I expected we would both win our pools to set up a titanic battle which would matter so much more than an autumn international in 2018.

I knew that we had got some luck against the Boks, but not against the Blacks a week later. 'Sometimes the game loves you and sometimes it doesn't,' I said with a little smile as another tumultuous rugby year wound to a close on a rainy night at Twickenham. 'It always balances out. We'll get some love from the game further down the track.'

16

BLUEPRINTS AND LESSONS

We were on the final lap of our four-year journey. The World Cup was less than a year away and we were back on track. A turning point had been reached and we had shown the courage to take it. In pushing so hard to change the culture of the team we had suffered some setbacks – but we had grown stronger. I approached 2019 with renewed purpose and resolve.

The history of English rugby in the World Cup does not make for pretty reading. Winning the tournament in 2003 is the outlier in an otherwise disappointing pattern. Reaching the final in 1991 and 2007 does not make up for the failures in 1999 and 2011, nor for the demoralizing exit in the pool stages in 2015. Winning the World Cup is all that counts. The misery of 2015 had left deep mental scars for many of my current players. I had experienced the disappointment of losing a final at home – but that bears no comparison with the turmoil of being dumped out of a home tournament in the pool stages.

The players were reminded constantly in the media that they had been at the heart of, apparently, a national embarrassment. Different players deal with the fallout in their own way but, collectively, it was a millstone that could have dragged us down. In the three years since my appointment we had made good progress. The players had moved on from 2015, and now only used it as motivation whenever they were asked about it. We were building a resilient and adaptable team to win the World Cup but, as always, there was more to be done.

It was important that my fellow England coaches and I kept developing in the ten months we had left before flying to Tokyo. My quest to improve as a coach and a leader sharpened every day. It helped to remember a story John Eales once told me. John had been a fantastic captain of both Queensland and Australia and he appreciated playing for driven and inquisitive coaches. He described how, in 2001, a coaching development day had been held in Brisbane, as Queensland were then at the peak of Australian rugby. They had a new coach called Mark McBain who had taken over from John Connolly. Bob Dwyer also attended the course and Eales told a story about their contrasting attitudes to knowledge. Mark was a new Super 12 coach while Bob had won the World Cup ten years before. Yet, while Mark sat quietly at the back, Bob was right up front, lapping it up and asking more questions than anyone after they had listened to the invited speakers. It did not matter to Bob that he had already lifted the World Cup. He was still curious and eager to learn.

Courage and humility are required to ask questions in front of your peers. The fear is that you might end up looking stupid. It's easier to sit back and say nothing. But the best coaches are risk-takers. They are not, however, aimless gamblers. The risks they take are calculated. They are quite happy to ask difficult or seemingly obvious questions to discover something new. It's the only way to avoid life in the dreaded comfort zone.

People are fascinating. You can travel through a new town with two different people. One of your passengers might spend the time on his or her phone while the other person will be looking out of the window, asking, 'What's this?' or, 'What's the significance of that?' Some of us are born curious while others are more self-absorbed. Professional curiosity is vital in elite sport and so I set about planning a trip to Australia for Steve Borthwick, Neil Craig, Tom Tombleson (our strength and conditioning coach) and myself in the brief gap we had between the 2018 autumn internationals and the 2019 Six Nations.

We could have taken a holiday, but we had little time to waste as we searched for more knowledge and composure to improve our squad. People have spoken about marginal gains in sport for years but, in our game, there are so many ways to win a rugby match. You can win it through the set piece, by dominating the scrum or the lineout, or by kicking more effectively than the opposition. You can win the game by running or tackling better, or by getting on top at the breakdown. But, in all cases, success begins and ends with a mastery of the basics. Eighty per cent of your preparation is improving the basics. The other 20 per cent of your time is devoted to strategy, tactics, communication and psychology. All the top teams apply a similar mix of effort, so even the slightest gains are important. It's often the smallest of factors that decide a crucial game of World Cup knockout rugby.

We had a packed six-day programme in Australia and met coaches in Aussie Rules (Essendon), rugby league (Melbourne Storm) and rugby union (Melbourne Rebels). The highlight of our trip was a day with Ric Charlesworth. He had been a state cricketer for Western Australia, an Olympic medal-winning hockey player, a doctor, a federal member of Parliament for ten years and a bestselling author. Ric Charlesworth is the most interesting coach in world sport.

Apart from coaching Australia's women's hockey team to Olympic gold in 1996 and 2000, and the men to silver at London 2012, Ric has held consulting roles with the New Zealand Test cricket team, the Australian Institute of Sport and an Australian Rules football team in Freemantle. He has also written three books which offer mind-opening insights into elite sport.

During our visit, one of the most interesting conversations centred on the topic of 'downtime' – or how a team manages itself when the ball is out of play. We discussed the fact that it might take four hours to play 18 holes in a round of golf, and yet you're only standing over the ball, and hitting it, for five out of the 240 minutes. Rugby is also a game where the ball is out of play for long periods. We're not alone, as so many other sports, from American football to tennis, have downtime. Ric's theory is that you have to be more productive in your downtime to gain an advantage over the opposition.

So we had an intriguing session with Ric about how England's players could best use that 'dead time' in the middle of a match. It related directly to the performance mindset that can help them win a tight game. We considered how to measure the quality and impact of those strategies and how to improve them.

Ric showed us a video of his Australian team being beaten in the semi-finals of the 2012 Olympics. He believed that they lost because their players did not engage in any meaningful conversations when the ball was out of play. The set-up was wrong and one of their players had strayed into the wrong position. But the environment was not robust enough for the players to take charge and talk to each other in the midst of a sporting battle. It was one of Ric's few failures in a major tournament and he was honest in pointing out how he and his team had not created the right atmosphere to communicate constructively when they were under the pump. We call it the performance conversation, and I knew it was imperative that my England players could produce it when they needed it most.

Ric introduced us to Corinne Reid. Although she is an academic, and was then Director of Research and Chair in Psychological Therapies at the University of Edinburgh, Corinne had worked with Ric's most successful hockey teams. She had contributed two outstanding chapters to his latest book. The first chapter was called 'The Excellence Delusion' and the second was 'Come to the Edge'. In essence we learnt that an exceptional sporting performance is rooted in an exceptional environment.

It sounds obvious, but Corinne was penetrating in explaining how these critical and candid performance conversations require a specialist skill set. It takes a subtle skill to call out a teammate and explain, in a clear manner, that they need to change the way they are playing. The last thing you want to do is crush an individual's confidence. You need to relay your message without judgement.

I knew immediately that Corinne could teach our players to deepen their relationships with each other. They did not have to be best mates, but they had to work together effectively. During a World Cup camp, as a player, you have to spend a lot of time with 30 other blokes. It's impossible to be friends with everyone. But, to maximize the performance of the squad, we needed the players to be curious. We had to get them to open up and say to each other: 'I need to know you better. I need to know how you think. How do you handle pressure? What do you want from me? What can I tell you about myself that will help us both perform better in the World Cup?'

Togetherness is forged through conversation. Players needed to get to know each other much better in person, either on a one-to-one basis over a relaxed coffee, or in a group session run by Corinne. They would be encouraged to talk about life away from rugby.

We decided to mix seating arrangements at dinner and in team meetings. We forced the players out of their familiar groups so that they could mingle with the teammates they didn't know as well. You can only begin to understand someone when you're face to face, sharing a meal or spending constructive time in each other's company. There would be no room for cliques.

This also applied to the coaches. I decided to sit with the younger or newer boys who did not really know me well. The other coaches did the same and, soon, the players quite deliberately went out of their way not to sit with their club teammates but to actively engage with the blokes they knew least.

Corinne held six sessions with the staff and the players, and the impact was immediate and remarkable. It would have been great if she could have stayed with us, but she was offered a prestigious academic post back in Australia. However, she had laid the groundwork in helping the players bond even more tightly together. Dr Andrea Furst, a psychologist who had helped the GB women's hockey team win gold at the 2016 Olympic Games in Rio, assumed responsibility for this important work.

Andrea was excellent during our hot-weather training camps in Treviso, when she worked with the squad before the World Cup, and she remained in regular contact with Neil and specific players who benefitted from her wisdom throughout the tournament. It's hard to overstate the impact that these two incredibly impressive and intelligent women had on the development of our group. The impact will extend well beyond the World Cup in Japan.

We saw the benefit of that bonding in one of our World Cup training sessions against Georgia, which we staged during the Six Nations. A torrid scrum session against the Georgians exploded, and both the young and experienced players got stuck in to defend each other. It was very sparky. I am glad that it settled quickly, and we all left on good terms, but it was encouraging to see how our players responded. It was a sign that they cared about each other and confirmation that the atmosphere around the squad was building ahead of the World Cup.

When the time came to leave Ric Charlesworth in Melbourne, I had another 'Pep Guardiola' moment. I knew we had spent time in the presence of greatness. A combination of Ric's curiosity and insight produced some of the most testing questioning I had ever faced. Short, sharp and varied queries forced me to consider yet again my approach to high performance. I was left with the overwhelming feeling that the older I get, the less I know. Ric offered a masterclass in curiosity which was delivered with credibility and humility. It encouraged me to continue to ask questions and to seek new insights. They are always there if you care to look.

As we prepared for the 2019 Six Nations, and during the World Cup, it was clear that we had achieved our goal of establishing a happy team full of noise, niggle and laughter. It was to be the soundtrack of our 2019 Six Nations and World Cup.

Both tournaments are stressful, but the World Cup is far more intense. It's the competition that determines the best team in the world. The World Cup demands everything. If you want to win it there is no choice – everyone has to give their best every day. As we prepared for the Six Nations, we knew we were getting just that little bit tighter and stronger.

It's a strange life being the head coach of an international rugby team during competition. Your natural habitat is the team hotel. In the week of big games, it's hard to get out because of the attention. Half the people you run into want to pat you on the back and take a photo, while the other half, often in good humour, offer you a frank character assessment. It's easier to stay out of sight. It's why I always enjoy catching up with my fellow international coaches whenever we get the chance. We are members of a small tribe, so it helps to make the effort to get on.

I don't see Steve Hansen as much as I'd like because we're on the other side of the world – but we've known each other since the early days of the Brumbies when he was at the Crusaders. Steve's a great bloke who has done fantastic work with the All Blacks. With Steve, what you see is what you get. He knows the game, he understands people, and he is super sharp. Steve loves his family, rugby, beer and the horses, in that order. He's a straight shooter and he always puts the interests of the game first. So it's always good to see his name pop up on a call on my phone or in a text. It's easy to understand why he has enjoyed such remarkable success throughout his career. His relentless focus has always been on improving his players and he has delivered for them every day.

With the Six Nations looming early in 2019, I had a chance to talk to the guys working closer to home. I first ran into Warren Gatland back in 2004 when I was at Suntory and we wanted to develop one of our young tight-head props. Wasps were the gold standard for scrummaging at the time, so we made contact with Gats and he was happy to help out. We now schedule catch-ups and grab a curry and a few beers prior to games between Wales and England. The conversations are good-humoured, open and honest because we all have the same access to information. And, of course, we gossip. It's all good fun. Gats is another of the Kiwi coaches who has done so much to improve the standard of rugby around the world over the past 20 years. In Gats' case, away from his home in New Zealand, it's been with Connacht, Ireland, Wasps, Wales and the Lions. Not a bad record for a boy from Hamilton. He will coach the Chiefs in Super Rugby and I have no doubt that, one day, he will be a great coach of the All Blacks.

I didn't know Ireland's Joe Schmidt too well prior to arriving in Europe because his stint in Super Rugby with the Auckland Blues came after my time with the Brumbies. He was a little frosty in my early days as England coach, after I made those comments about Johnny Sexton, but we had a good chat at the draw for the World Cup in Kyoto. I came down to breakfast one morning and found Hiroko and Joe in a conversation which helped to warm up the room. Since then, it's been all good. As we prepared for the opening match of the 2019 Six Nations in Dublin, Joe and the Irish management invited our staff over for a pre-match drink, which was really good of them. This sort of socializing, which is the bedrock of rugby, seems to be returning more to the elite game.

Gregor Townsend, meanwhile, scares me. He is a seriously bright bloke. I've presented papers alongside him at a few conferences and I'm always impressed with his thinking. As coach of Scotland, he has to stay on the edge of innovation to try and gain parity with the world's larger rugby nations. Scotland need to back him, and I know that, if they do, he will deliver.

Conor O'Shea is another great bloke. A charming Irishman who has come to the end of his time with Italy, Conor did not achieve the results he wanted at elite level, but he grew the game elsewhere. The performances of Treviso are a credit to his programmes.

These bonds between the coaches made it feel as if the tournament had rekindled much of the old camaraderie that made the Five Nations such a fascinating and inviting tournament when I was a kid following it from Australia. It also remained one of the hardest competitions to win in world rugby – as we would learn again in 2019.

Most of all, this particular Six Nations rollercoaster would emerge as the perfect tournament for England before the World Cup. We would find a blueprint for future success, make some bad mistakes, learn more about each other and come out of the competition feeling thankful for every last twist and turn we went through in Dublin, Cardiff and London.

The leaders in our squad, whom Billy Vunipola calls the 'generals', picked up on the powerful spirit of socializing together. Before they joined the coaches in Portugal for a pre-tournament training camp, the senior players organized a night out for the squad. They made sure that there was no trouble and, echoing the work done by Corinne Reid, set about having a night which would leave them with some stories to tell and a real sense of togetherness. I was delighted, because there had been little of this spontaneity, leadership and unity when I began working with them three years earlier.

We had a really strong and productive camp on the Algarve, and we did a few off-the-wall exercises to get them ready. There was much amusement initially when Steve Borthwick brought out a stepladder and buckets of soapy water to help our lineout forwards get used to dealing with the kind of slippery ball we expected to encounter on rainy afternoons in Dublin and Cardiff. It soon worked and our lineout looked increasingly assured.

Away from everyone else, Steve also hunched over his laptop for hour after hour as he studied Ireland and helped plot some moves that we thought might catch the Six Nations champions cold. Ireland, who had beaten New Zealand in Dublin the previous autumn, were being proclaimed as the best team in the world, while we were being written off by everyone. I was happy to begin our World Cup year by flying under the radar.

There were still some difficult selections to make. I initially shook up the press by suggesting that Jack Nowell, our talented and combative wing from Exeter, could conceivably play as a ninth forward. I explained how Ric Charlesworth, who is not a follower of rugby, had helped me rejig a few old ideas. 'Why not try Jack as a seven?' I asked at a press conference ten days before we played Ireland. 'I know Sam Burgess was used in the centre and in the back row during his time in the game, but Jack is a rugby player, one of the most highly skilled players at the breakdown. He could play as a ninth forward because he understands the game.'

The media weren't convinced and the Colonel Blimps amongst the old school frothed, gnashed their teeth and wailed: 'He's gone completely mad . . . it would never work.' I've always found the reluctance to analyse new ideas amusing. While they lunch and we work, they misplace opinion for fact. The vanity is astounding.

But I made my case: 'Rugby has become very methodical. You watch teams now and you can tell what they are going to do. I went to a Pro14 match the other week and you could almost call the game. You have to look at opportunities to do things differently. The game goes through phases. When I was at the Brumbies, we would hang on to the ball. Some saw it as boring, others as fantastic. There were up to 95 kicks a game in the 2007 World Cup. Some hated it but 65 million people in South Africa thought it was the best thing that ever happened.

'You have to be radical in your thinking, but the most important thing is to prepare for it. Jack is such a good player he could play in a number of positions for us and it is something I have been thinking about for a while. The only time the eight forwards are together is at a scrum when the ninth could stand on the blind-side wing. It is like when Barcelona won the Champions League playing with a false nine. You always have to look at how you can add more to your team. Our strength is our forward pack. How can we make it even stronger?'

This was not just a pre-game smokescreen. I had actually used nine forwards when coaching Japan against Georgia in our final game before the 2015 World Cup. We had played Georgia twice before then and, while we had won the first game, they destroyed us upfront in the second match. So we deliberately picked Georgia to be our last game before facing South Africa in that now famous match. We had to test how far we had come in the forwards and we thought, 'Why don't we beef up our pack?' I knew the backs wouldn't get much work against Georgia, so I thought we might as well try and use a ninth forward as a blind-side winger. We won the game and not one person asked me about it afterwards. The idea was to keep our forwards fresher by spreading the load and, in the last ten minutes, Japan had the legs to win the match.

Rugby in 2019 is much faster, and Nowell plays like a forward a lot of the time. I feel he's good enough to come off the bench as an open-side flanker. There was an element of fun to the debate, but it was also a serious example of looking at the game in new ways. The work rate of forwards is exponentially higher than that of the backs, so it makes sense to find a way around that problem. There's no reason why, in the future, many more teams won't consider using a ninth forward.

In the end I kept Nowell on the right wing and chose a back row of Mark Wilson, Tom Curry and Billy Vunipola. Asked about my choice of Nowell, I said: 'He's a street-fighter, mate. When you go to Dublin it's not going to be a nice game. It's going to be a tough old match. It is well documented no one thinks we can win, but I can tell you everyone inside our camp believes we can. I'd hate to go into a game thinking we weren't better than the opposition, that we need surprises or tricks to win the game. We don't need that. Praise can make you weak but the good teams always expect to win and play well and that's what we are.'

As I had done in the major matches in the autumn, I chose Owen Farrell at 10. George Ford is one of my favourite players, whose application and intelligence has made him such a brilliant contributor to the team. But when we face big ball-running inside backs who are fast-moving and really physical, like the

Wallabies' Samu Kerevi, I tend to pick Farrell as my fly half, with Manu Tuilagi at 12 and Henry Slade at 13.

It was an important moment for Manu, as his selection marked his first Six Nations start in six injury-ravaged years. He had suffered for so long, and made his fair share of mistakes as well, but he had returned to the squad with a Zen-like calm. Apart from turning his hotel room into an impromptu coffee shop for the boys, Manu gives us another dimension physically. Henry's vision and subtlety is the perfect complement. He is a sublime talent. But I knew George would remain a key member of the World Cup squad and I valued his talent and leadership. The quality of Owen and George made it easy to resist the persistent calls from the lunch club for Danny Cipriani's inclusion.

As the Six Nations began, our key communication themes were starting to stick. 'Our ambition is to be the best team in the world', 'continuous improvement' and 'staying in the day' echoed throughout the squad. Relevance and repetition were key to underlining the message. Both the players and the coaches were now pushing themselves to meet higher standards and focusing on the next task. They refused to get ahead of themselves. Steve Hansen has a great saying: 'Your head needs to stay where your feet are.' It's so true. The best way to reduce performance anxiety is to narrow your focus to the next task.

On the field my selection also marked a milestone. It was the first time in three years that I had been able to pick Tuilagi, the Vunipola brothers and Maro Itoje together. Those four players, with Farrell, were vital to our World Cup campaign. So I approached the trip to Dublin with a real sense of anticipation. I was encouraged because I could sense the resolve in the squad. Listening to the entertaining chatter over breakfast, lunch and dinner, I was struck by the positivity, determination and unity of the players. I could tell that there was a real hunger among the boys. Ireland were officially number two in the world, the defending champions and a very good side. But so were we, and the players wanted to make a statement.

Ireland had won 18 out of their last 19 Tests, including a series win in Australia, but ever since they had beaten us at Twickenham we had studied them closely. With each game they won, they were kicking less. They were being seduced into playing more attractive rugby. The easiest teams to defend against are the sides that kick less because then you don't have to worry about the back field. The only way they could trouble us was by getting momentum through their forwards to create space. But the new system that John Mitchell had embedded, to stop their momentum around the ruck, was working and our forwards were growing in confidence.

We decided to play in short phases and, once our forwards gained momentum, kick earlier than usual. A strong performance in Dublin would be a great way to start our World Cup year. The game plan to beat Ireland would also become the blueprint for how I wanted us to play in Japan.

My good mood disappeared during the captain's run on the Friday before the match. We were terrible. After a fantastic week the players were dropping balls and running into each other. An outsider would have thought the players didn't know each other.

But I wasn't too concerned because I remembered the awful captain's run that Japan had had under Michael Leitch the day before we beat South Africa. Sometimes it happens because the players are nervous. Or maybe they are too relaxed.

As a way of clearing my head on the Friday afternoon in Dublin, I went for a haircut. There's not much hair to cut these days so I just wanted a simple head-shave before the game. Soon after I stepped out of the hotel, people were bagging me. Some of it was good natured, but one bloke in particular was really aggressive. He tried to egg me on into a confrontation. He bumped into me and I could see he had his phone in his hand. It was obvious that he was hoping to goad me into reacting so he could post it online and be briefly famous.

I gave him nothing, smiled and walked on. It actually felt good because that kind of edge matched the mood I expected we would encounter at the packed stadium, where the Irish fans would really be up for their boys giving us another thrashing.

The players executed our strategy brilliantly. After 38 seconds, at the first lineout of the game, Jamie George threw a long ball right over all the forwards and straight into the arms of Manu running at full tilt. It was a move we had planned and practised and it worked a treat. Manu came crashing through and, even when he was brought down, a series of rucks gave us a chance to really stretch the Irish defence. The breakthrough came after just 90 seconds when, following seven phases, Owen threw a brilliant pass that cut out two men to find Elliot Daly, who immediately fed Jonny May flying down the left wing. Jonny went over in the corner and Owen's conversion matched the excellence of his pass to make it 7–0 after two minutes.

We endured a little blip when Tom Curry was sent to the sin bin for a late tackle on Keith Earls. We kept Ireland out for the next ten minutes but, soon after Tom's return, Cian Healy completed an Irish drive for a try. Sexton's conversion, following an earlier penalty, meant that Ireland were in front, 10–7, after 26 minutes.

I was impressed by our response. Three minutes later some slick interplay between Ben Youngs, Tuilagi, Farrell and Daly opened up Ireland. A deft little grubber kick by Daly was chased hard by Nowell, who pressured Jacob Stockdale into a fumble across his own try line. The ball bounced loose and Daly was on it in a flash to score.

Mako Vunipola came agonizingly close to a third try, only for the TMO to decide that he had not crossed the line. But a Farrell penalty just before the break gave us a 17–10 lead at half-time.

We were just as dominant in the second half. Even a Sexton penalty, which cut our lead to just four points, didn't bother me. England were in control and we really took hold of the game after 65 minutes. We won clean ball from a scrum on our 10-metre line and Youngs released Slade who threw a long pass to May. Slade pointed straight ahead and May took the hint with an electrifying run. Before he could be caught, May kicked deep into Irish territory and, following up, Slade collected the bouncing ball and dived over. He was engulfed in a bear hug by a roaring Tuilagi before a simple kick was converted by Farrell. A much longer penalty, just inside the Irish half, extended our lead to 25–13 with ten minutes remaining.

Ireland were desperate. Trying to start a move from his own 22, Sexton threw a sloppy pass which Slade intercepted for his second try in the 76th minute. Farrell converted. Ireland 13, England 32.

Even some rare slackness in our defence, and a late Irish try, could not take the shine off our thumping victory. Our 32–20 win was a first home defeat for Joe Schmidt in the Six Nations and a significant turnaround from our limp defeat a year earlier. I didn't say this in public, but it was one of the two best performances by England since I took over as coach. Only the first Test against Australia in Brisbane, in 2016, could rival our display in Dublin. As always, my message to the players and the public was that we had to improve.

'We're still growing,' I said. 'We are nowhere near our best. This match has nothing to do with the World Cup: it was a stand-alone between a very good Ireland side and an improving England team. It's always physical when you play here and we knew we had to win that battle to win the game. We shaded a top side in that area and the players deserve all the credit. We executed our game plan well. The front row was outstanding, as was Jonny May with his selfless work, Manu Tuilagi darted well at 12 and Henry Slade is getting better with every game. Maybe, at first, he did not think he was good enough to play for England, but now it is a question of how good he can be. We kicked today to create space and the chase was very good.'

We were thrilled, as coaches, to see the growing confidence and communication of the players. At one point, with the score still relatively close and England defending hard against an Irish attack, Mark Wilson turned to his fellow forwards during a break and said, with a big smile, 'How good is this?' It was exactly the appetite for battle, with the ball out of play, I wanted. The fact it was voiced by one of our newest players made it even more satisfying. Wilson is one tough rooster and his hunger for work on and off the field rubbed off on his mates.

Before a World Cup you have to build belief in the side without showing the opposition everything you've got. Against Ireland we proved that we can beat very good teams under real pressure. But I was not heartbroken that our performances in the Six Nations were patchy after Dublin.

On Sunday 10 February we played really well again, especially in the first 50 minutes, as we blitzed France 44–8 at Twickenham. Jonny May scored a hat-trick of tries even before the first half-hour of the match had passed. The pace, power and speed of thought of the whole team was hugely encouraging. Curry and Wilson had big games in the back row and their energy and effort never flagged. They had helped force 14 turnovers in Dublin. We pushed the French even harder and they turned over the ball 21 times as we showed how our transition game, turning strong defence into unstructured attack, had improved.

Owen was masterly. He scored 17 points, including a try, and Jamie George said of his friend and Saracens teammate: 'The bloke's a genius. I never see him have a bad game and that's why he's one of the best players in the world, if not *the* best player in the world.'

I felt Owen, like all of us, could still improve, and I also knew he was not immune to having an off day. But England's overall performance was as encouraging as our record Six Nations margin of victory over France.

Rugby, however, has a way of knocking down a team that starts getting ahead of itself. We lost Mako Vunipola to an ankle injury during the game – and the post-match assessment was dire. Mako had damaged his ankle ligaments and he would be out for at least ten weeks. I knew how much we would miss him throughout the rest of the Six Nations, and hoped like crazy that he would be ready again for the World Cup. Mako doesn't say much, but he has an enormous influence as a superb player and an even better human being. It's a privilege to coach him.

We really felt his absence two weeks later, when we played Wales in Cardiff. We missed his cohesive and calming presence in our team. Owen is still learning the art of captaincy, and Mako does so much to lead the team in an understated way. The gaps in our leadership were still evident because we let the match against Wales slip away. We were ahead 10–3 at half-time, with a converted Curry try being the difference between the sides, and held the lead with just 13 minutes left.

It was a brutal encounter and the fact that we made over 50 tackles in the first 15 minutes gives an indication of the huge physical effort we put into the game. But we lacked composure, and the game swung away from us when Dan Biggar came on. He set up Cory Hill with a long pass and then kicked a difficult conversion to inch the Welsh ahead 16–13. Three minutes from the end, Biggar's clever cross-field kick was caught by Josh Adams, who outjumped Henry Slade and scored another try to seal a 21–13 win for Wales.

We had been outstanding in the first half. Combining aggressive defence with good kicking and running lines, we had set out to pressure Wales as much as we had Ireland and France. But there was a difference. Rather than Robbie Henshaw or Yoann Huget at full back, Wales had the peerless Liam Williams. In the second half, he took us to school. Our kicking game became one-dimensional and he killed us in the air. We didn't react quickly enough to change a strategy that wasn't working. It was a big lesson for the players, and they were bitterly disappointed to concede 18 points after the break while only scoring three.

Neil Craig was excellent in reminding the players that the Principality Stadium is as tough a venue as any in world rugby and that the defeat mattered less than the preparation the game had given us for the World Cup. Although it's never pleasant, you learn the best lessons in defeat.

Owen said he was 'filthy' with himself for not changing our kicking strategy as Williams took full advantage of our inability to think clearly. I knew he would be a better captain for the loss. But Kyle Sinckler was the most obvious example of someone who would emerge from defeat as a more mature player. Our rough, tough, young, tight-head prop had been targeted by Wales. Even before the game, Gatland had been stirring the pot. He had coached Sincks in the Lions when they toured New Zealand in 2017, and was now trying to get inside his head.

'There is sometimes a challenge with Sinckler's temperament,' Gats said in the build-up. 'He is aware of it, as are other players. He has been involved in a couple of incidents this Six Nations. Emotionally he can be a bit of a time bomb. We will not be going out to antagonize him, but the big challenge for him is to keep his emotions under control.'

Gats was just doing his job by attempting to pressure a talented young opposition player. Sincks was superb for 50 minutes and, in the first half, he made an incredible 16 tackles. He also won the scrum penalty that opened up our lead. But as we approached the hour mark and, with tiredness kicking in, Sincks lost his cool under sustained pressure from Alun Wyn Jones. He conceded two penalties before I replaced him. Gats claimed it as a scalp because, from that moment, the game swung Wales's way. Fair play to Gats. I've made similar claims myself, but in fact we had always planned to replace Sincks. Press-conference talk is part of trying to gain an advantage for your team. Players have to be strong enough to ignore it.

The following week, John Mitchell made a spirited defence of Sincks which reflected our united view of a special young forward. 'In this generation of players, you don't have many who play on the edge,' Mitch suggested. 'So Kyle is unique in the way that he does play on the edge and the last thing that we want to do is ever take that away from him because it is something that he can bring to us in a very positive way. Gats won the Test, didn't he, so he can say what he likes. At the end of the day, most teams are targeting the best players; the great thing is that they see him as one of our best players. In itself, that is a great accolade. So now that he understands he is in that bracket, he can actually use it to his and our advantage.

'Kyle is 24 years of age and he is an exceptionally gifted athlete as a tight head. He's already a very good player for England. As he matures, he is going to be outstanding. He is just going through a process, like any young man, learning and growing in self-awareness. I think we are blessed with an outstanding player. Kyle is a guy with an abundance of talent and all we're asking is for him to contribute to the team, when it really matters, without losing his ability to play on the edge.'

Eight months later, in a World Cup quarter-final in Japan, Sinckler was again put under real pressure by Australia. The Wallabies hooker went out of his way to provoke him by rubbing his head. This time Kyle didn't react. He just moved on to the next task. It was proof of his restraint and growing maturity. He also got the last laugh against Australia when he ran onto a beautiful flat pass from Owen, sprinted through a gap and steamrolled Kurtley Beale on his way to the try line. It was a thing of beauty.

After Wales beat us, Gats was clearly feeling pleased with himself. He couldn't resist a dig at us for choking. 'I've always had my doubts that England can win the big matches,' he gloated as he twisted the knife. Soon after he said it, my phone pinged with a message from Pemby. 'Don't worry, Beaver,' he wrote. 'I've banked it. We will make good use of it when the time is right.' A long memory and keeping a close eye on everything your opponents say is a critical part of international rugby.

The best lessons are invariably the most painful. After a routine 57–14 win over Italy, we played Scotland at Twickenham on 16 March. We were brilliant in the first half and raced into a 31–0 lead. The rugby was superb but, suddenly, the match turned in the most outrageous way. One of Owen's kicks was charged down shortly before the break and a try put Scotland on the board. Five more followed in a madcap second half. With just four minutes left, the score read England 31, Scotland 38. It was shocking and, yes, it was embarrassing.

We had allowed the Scots to turn it into a free-for-all. We lost control because at 31 points up and with five minutes left in the first half, we just needed to shut them out until the break. But we kept on trying to play with extravagance. It was naive and costly. When you play extravagantly, you give the other team the opportunity to attack. Our minds went blank and we kept on inviting them back into the game. The Scots took the invitation in brilliant style.

Our players had, once again, been seduced by the scoreboard. Just as they had done twice against South Africa in 2018, and even against Wales in this tournament, they had frittered away a lead by playing so thoughtlessly. The Welsh game had been tight throughout, but we had been 24–3 and 12–0 up in successive Tests against South Africa and lost both games. It looked as if we had added an even worse calamity to the list.

But then, in a moment which gave me immense pride, George Ford saved us. Having come on for Owen, he held his nerve and proved his quality yet again. George is such a natural and resourceful player, but he's one of those rare talents whose effectiveness can be diminished if you put too much structure around him. At Leicester he is often told to play a certain way, in a pattern, and it takes away some of his creativity. We did a good job initially in bringing that back out of him when I took over as England coach but, after losing his place at 10 to Owen, George had retreated into his shell a little. However, he came on against the Scots with England reeling and he gave us a point of difference through his clear thinking and decision-making.

Under enormous pressure, and staring down the barrel of a shocking defeat, George took charge 20 metres from our try line in the last few minutes of the game. If we made one mistake we were dead, but he proceeded to drive our team up the field like he was Tom Brady orchestrating a Super Bowl-winning play. George scored and then converted the try which earned us a 38–38 draw in one of the most unlikely matches in Six Nations history. He had shown the mental resilience and clarity of thought that we had lacked as a team. We had taken our collective foot off the gas when far ahead and allowed the game to drift out of control.

I spoke bluntly in the aftermath. 'It is 100 per cent mental. There's no physical difference out there at all. It's 100 per cent the way you think. And we'll get that right. We've got good time before the World Cup. These are possibly things the team have had for a long time, even before I've coached them. So we need to make sure we get the right people in to help us and we'll sort it out. It's a lesson. The hardest lessons are the best lessons. You want them before you go to a World Cup. If you do that in a pool game against Tonga, for instance, you can find yourself in a difficult situation. We'd rather have those lessons now and we'll do everything we can to learn from them and make sure it doesn't happen again.'

For me there were three massive lessons to take from this helter-skelter game against Scotland. First, it reminded the players that when you get in front you have to find a way to sustain momentum. Second, our composure and control were essential to any World Cup hopes we harboured. We lost our discipline towards the end of the game and we played some of our third-stringers. The third lesson was for me alone. I had listened too much to the other coaches when it came to making substitutions.

Mitch is an optimistic person; Steve is more cautious. I have always been a reasonably aggressive coach in terms of replacements but, against both Wales and Scotland, I got caught up trying to keep everyone happy. Rather than trusting my instincts, and my understanding of what I could see with my own eyes, I'd allowed a consensus of opinion to cloud my thinking. It probably cost us two victories.

Coaching, after all, is not a democracy. I promised myself that, with the World Cup closing in on us, I would never again allow my control to slip in the midst of a match. The key decisions would be made by me – and by me alone.

After all the hurly-burly – the exultation of Dublin, the pain of Cardiff and the madness of Twickenham – we finished second in the Six Nations behind the Grand Slam-winning Welsh. I did not enjoy losing to Wales, or drawing with the Scots after conceding 38 unanswered points, but I felt strangely satisfied at the end of the tournament. People on the outside were already writing us off as World Cup contenders. These same people would have said we were nailed on to win the tournament if we had held on to our lead against both Wales and Scotland. But they would have been wrong then; and they were wrong now.

I am not sure how much we would have learned about ourselves if we had sailed through another Grand Slam, as we had done in 2016. Neil Craig agreed with me. We both felt that the Six Nations, for all the upheaval and disappointment, had been just the tournament we needed to steel and sharpen ourselves for Japan. The road to a World Cup is never smooth and flat. All the twists and turns, the bumps and falls, help build a team that, eventually, can truly believe in itself as future world champions.

17

RIDING THE ROLLERCOASTER

Typhoon Faxai hit Tokyo before we did. On Monday 9 September our team flew into Narita International Airport and discovered that the storm had swept through the city and surrounding areas the previous evening. Winds of 105 mph, heavy rain and large waves had caused chaos. The main roads linking Narita to our hotel were closed and all trains into Tokyo had been suspended. After a three-and-a-half-hour wait on the tarmac, we remained stuck at the airport for five hours. England's fast start to our World Cup campaign was gridlocked.

Throughout our build-up we had prepared for the unexpected. I was familiar with the weather at this time of the year and knew that such delays and disruptions were always possible. Typhoons in Tokyo were reasonably commonplace. I had lived through enough of them during my years in Japan, even luckily avoiding one on the day of my stroke. So I was not worried and the players also responded well to the delay. They started a game of cricket to fill the time. They were ready for anything.

I was thrilled to be back in Japan. I had been looking forward to this tournament for years. Japan was familiar. The country flowed through my family like a river. It came from the very source, from my Japanese grandparents and mother. Of course it had been in Japan, too, that my parents had met and fallen in love. They had overcome prejudice in both Japan and Australia to provide me and my sisters with the foundations to build happy and fulfilled lives and careers. In my own immediate family with Hiroko and Chelsea, Japan was a cornerstone.

I was bound to the country through my stints coaching Suntory and the national team. Japan was the country that gave me the chance to return to international rugby at my lowest point. I allowed myself a brief thought. If I were to win my first World Cup as a head coach, there would be no better place to do it.

It was hot and steamy at the airport as the transport chaos piled up around us. 'We are excited to be in Japan,' I said in our first meeting with the press. 'It's a great honour and privilege to represent England and we are looking forward to the tournament. This is a unique World Cup. It's the first time in Asia and in a tier-two nation. Our ability to adapt quickly to situations like today will be imperative. We have prepared well and have put ourselves in a good position.'

England had played four warm-up games and produced strong performances. We beat Ireland by a record score, with Tom Curry and Sam Underhill playing in the back row together for the first time. They were a revelation. After 58 minutes and leading 43–10, I'd seen enough and was convinced we had a partnership that would make a name for itself in Japan. Post-match I referred to them for the first time as the 'Kamikaze Kids'. It was a nod to Japan but, really, it was a tribute to their fearlessness. They nailed anything that moved.

In the 2015 World Cup, England had struggled without the skills of a genuine open-side. In my first two seasons in charge of England it was much the same. We made do with great players like James Haskell, who was not a natural number 7. But by 2018, after so many barren years, England had produced not one but two potentially great open-side flankers to fill this key position. Injuries and the emergence of an excellent blind-side flank in Mark Wilson meant I only had the chance to play them both in the same back row in the late English summer of 2019.

I picked Tom at 6 and Sam at 7 to play against Wales at Twickenham on 11 August. But Sam picked up a knock in training and was replaced by Lewis Ludlam. It was another two weeks before I could see how Underhill and Curry might work together. They were simply outstanding against the Irish. John Mitchell and I believed that Tom had the versatility to switch to blind-side. He's a slightly bigger ball-carrier, which suited the more patient role of a number 6.

Lewis Ludlam was a bolter. A year before he was on the fringes at Northampton with his future in question. But he was given a final chance at his club when Haskell was injured. Lewis played in the Premiership play-offs and impressed everyone. I was encouraged enough to invite him to train with us before the Barbarians when Teimana Harrison was called away to the birth of his child. I could see that he had something just a little bit different about him. I decided to watch him more closely.

He then did well against the Welsh, and he was one of the surprise inclusions when I announced my final 31-man squad the following afternoon. Lewis was stunned, so much so that when he saw that he had been added to the squad's WhatsApp group he asked one of the boys: 'Are you sure? Is this for real? Is this the World Cup squad?' He had shown precisely the attitude and effort that I wanted and got his reward. He is a fine player with a big future.

Before announcing the final squad, I'd already called the players who had missed out. Selection is the hardest part of the job. There are always too many players for too few spots. It was gutting giving the news to Chris Robshaw, Mike Brown and Danny Care. They had played vital roles in our success in 2016 and 2017 and had done so much to mentor the younger players on our tour of Argentina. They're all great guys. The call to Dylan Hartley was made easier by the fact that both he and I knew that his knee was still not right and it would be impossible for it to stand up to the rigours of a World Cup campaign. Robbo, Browny and Danny wanted redemption for 2015. But I had to do what I thought was best for the team.

We won three of our World Cup warm-up games, including

a win over Italy in Newcastle, and lost to Wales in Cardiff. I said to the media: 'We used our warm-up games effectively. We were able to experiment with selection and tactics and have developed a solid platform. Our ability to adapt to different conditions, teams and referees has improved. We are ready to play an English-style rugby that can win a World Cup.'

We eventually made it to the hotel for one night in Tokyo before travelling to our training camp in Miyazaki, in the south of Japan. Miyazaki means a great deal to me. It was here that I plotted Japan's campaign to Beat the Boks in 2015. It was a place soaked in the sweat and memories of all the hard work done by my Japanese players. England's mission to win the 2019 tournament was equally as ambitious in its own way and our training regime matched the intensity of our goal. The boys worked bloody hard. They gave it everything.

I was encouraged by the growth in the team and the communication and leadership that flowed through the squad. Owen Farrell, as captain, began a series of player-only meetings. Supported by the core leadership group – George Ford, Mako Vunipola, Ben Youngs, Maro Itoje and Elliot Daly – Owen created a trusting environment where players could be open and honest with each other. They could share concerns and doubts without any fear of judgement. So much of successful high performance comes from teams being comfortable with each other. You must have trust. I loved that the players were taking more control. I often talk about making myself redundant. The players are the ones who play the game so it's important that they own as much of the preparation as possible.

It hadn't always been the case with this group. During the earlier training camps in Treviso there had been tension. There was the highly publicized blow-up between Ben Te'o and Browny, but that had not been the only conflict. English rugby is fiercely tribal and, often unknowingly, the players bring those prejudices and biases into camp. They are fiercely competitive and in many cases have been at each other for years. There are feuds, old and new, like in all teams. It got to the point earlier in our campaign that I needed to point out to the players that some of the competition was not productive. To their credit, they took it on board and worked hard to resolve the tension. By the end of the campaign, we had set a new standard for collaboration and unity. The boys loved being in each other's company. For any England team I coach in the future, this team has set a new benchmark. We will never go back to the old days.

As we worked through the long days in Miyazaki, I loved every minute of it. In the four-year World Cup cycle, the build-up to the tournament is the only time you get the players for over ten weeks. It means that you can make a difference. You can try new things and make them stick. You can prepare in a way that is impossible during a short tour or a Six Nations.

Owen was growing into his role as captain. It was gratifying to see him mature in Japan. He does not waste time or words. He is pretty much all business. But he was learning to think carefully about what he wanted to say and, with the entire squad hushed and attentive, he often spoke with electrifying power. He was also getting better at noticing things away from training and games.

He was fortunate that he led an outstanding group. When I'd announced the squad a month earlier, one of the journalists had asked me how consensus on selection had been reached. I told him that, 'There's no such thing as a democracy, mate. The other coaches put forward their ideas but I make the final decision. I've been handed the responsibility and it's a judgement that I make. At World Cups I pick 1 to 15 first, then I pick numbers 28 to 31. They are your absolute keys. They are possibly not going to have much game time, so the character and behaviour of those guys is super important. Then you try to pick a blend from 16 to 27. So I follow a clear process.'

Jack Singleton, our third-choice hooker, Piers Francis at centre, and Ruaridh McConnochie and Joe Cokanasiga on the wing, had just 19 caps between them. I knew that, unless there were injuries, they wouldn't play much rugby in Japan. But importantly they were good men who would put the team's interests ahead of their own. We had picked them for their talent and character.

After the pool stages there is always danger for your World Cup squad. The siren call of the nightclubs is hard to resist for players who are not required to play on the weekend. But if we were to achieve our goal of winning the title, we needed their complete attention. Each of them delivered.

Pemby and I had both experienced World Cups where the 'double dirties', as they are known, were not committed, and it had a corrosive influence on team morale. Given the boys had been training so hard throughout the tournament, we decided after the pool stages that we would award them a Test jersey for their efforts. At the players-only meeting on the Friday night before the remaining World Cup matches, every bloke who had the privilege of being in the match-day squad presented jerseys 24 to 31 to their teammates. In that ceremony our commitment to the 'Team of 31' was brought to life.

In Miyazaki, the mood was calm and upbeat. You could see and feel the happiness and the deeper unity of the team during both the meal-time chatter and the serious intensity of training.

It was not as hot as we had expected but the humidity was suffocating. We started some sessions as early as 7.00 a.m. and worked brutally hard. With each session, the belief and confidence grew. But it was important for the boys to get away, relax and enjoy life in Japan, which is so different to what they are used to back home. They loved the paddle-boarding and watching the surfers from the Beach Burger House – a local restaurant on the seafront. For me, Miyazaki was a time to reflect, refine our plans and consider what was ahead. As far as I could see, we were in increasingly good shape as we waited for the tournament to begin.

We left Miyazaki on the Wednesday and travelled to Sapporo for our tournament opener against Tonga on Sunday 22 September.

At our final press conference, the significance of what lay ahead hit me. My voice thickened and my eyes became misty as I discussed the challenge and opportunity of a World Cup in Japan. It meant a great deal to me to be coaching England. It meant just as much to be coaching such a talented and competitive group of young men. I spoke from the heart.

'It's humbling, mate. It's a great honour to coach England . . . and I just want to make sure I do my best. World Cups are always emotional. You get to do something that is pretty special. To coach a nation and to be responsible for that nation at a World Cup, where you know it's not just rugby fans watching, is different. Families watch World Cups together and it becomes an event for the country rather than just for rugby followers. It's definitely going to be a big event in Japan. To be involved in that is a real honour.

'I'm massively nervous and I'm massively excited. If I didn't have that feeling, I'd be a little worried. But the one thing we don't control is the results of games. We control the preparation and every coach – all 20 coaches out here – is having this conversation now. They all think they've done a great job preparing their team, but we don't know, do we?'

The raw emotion tumbled out of me and I had to draw breath. I looked out at all the television cameras, the massed ranks of journalists and photographers who were ready to send words and images from Japan around the world. And then I smiled as I told the truth of how we all felt. 'The World Cup is like a rollercoaster. We are at the top of the ride now. We are looking down – everyone's nervous, everyone's excited. You get down the first slope, you are not sure if you are going to throw up or hang on.'

Of course, deep down, I believed we would do more than hang on. I was confident that if we maintained our focus and effort every day, we could challenge for the title.

Tonga, coached by Toutai Kefu, were first up. Kef is one of the great blokes of world rugby and a member of my first Wallaby team. He was a brilliant and skilful number 8 who scored the try which helped us beat New Zealand at the death in Sydney to win the 2001 Tri Nations just six weeks after I became Australia's head coach. In his press conference, Toutai spoke my language. 'When Tonga are ferocious and direct that's when we play our best football,' Toutai said. 'It's a massive challenge for us, but we have got nothing to lose and we are going to throw everything at it.'

I met the Tongan challenge that Toutai had laid down in such impressively stark language. 'We want to take them on,' I said at my final media conference. 'We are England and we want to take them on up front so no one will come out of there guessing. We're ready to go.'

Some of the lessons of the summer helped in the Sapporo Dome. I had invited Sir Alex Ferguson to talk to the boys in Bristol, at one of our early World Cup training camps, and the advice he offered that day worked on a very different afternoon against Tonga. World Cup openers are always tricky and we didn't play well. But we were always in control and, with three minutes left, were 28–3 up after Manu Tuilagi scored a couple of tries and Jamie George another. But we all knew the importance of getting a bonus point for scoring four tries. After 77 minutes that decisive try looked elusive.

Sir Alex had talked about the need for patience when the clock was ticking and the result you needed was seemingly out of reach. 'Fergie time' was a Manchester United mantra. It often sparked images of him tapping his watch and shouting at the officials to make sure that they added on enough extra time. But it was really about controlling your emotions and skills in the dying stages of a match. 'Fergie time' was about maintaining composure and not panicking. We all thought of his words when Luke Cowan-Dickie crossed the line to seal our 35–3 victory and our bonus point. We had kept our heads in 'Fergie time'.

'Sir Alex's message was be patient and that's what I enjoyed about our team today,' I said after the game. 'There was no sign of panic and they kept on playing good rugby. It might have been easier if the try had come a little earlier, but it came and that's a good sign. Whenever you get great people in, they make an impact and you pick up one or two things. And that particularly resonated. Naturally there's some urgency but you don't need to do anything different. You've got to be patient and just do the simple things over and over again. That showed today.'

Maro Itoje made a similar point. 'A lot of the time when the pressure's on – with Fergie time – he [Fergie] said: "Don't shoot. You'll find a way to get into a better scoring position." We can take a lot from that. When the pressure is on, it's not about the elaborate play. It's about doing the right thing.'

We did the right thing again, and were patient once more, as we beat the United States 45–7 in our second pool match. We spent 81 per cent of the game camped in the US half and scored seven tries. It was still a very physical game. Piers Francis, under instruction to make an impact, got it marginally wrong and hit one of their players high straight after the kick-off. Much later in the match, John Quill, the US flanker, became the first player to receive a red card in the tournament after his shoulder charge smacked into Owen Farrell's head. It was a mistimed tackle that looked pretty ordinary and, in a tournament where any contact with the head was being heavily punished, it was no surprise to see him sent off. Owen went down but of course he played on. Owen was hit hard again and I joked after the game that he was 'missing part of his nose'. Despite the temptation to say something more, I kept quiet. The goal was to get out of the pool stages without any controversy, so I kept my thoughts to myself.

Two matches down and we had ten points in the bank. Our first big test, in what had been billed pre-tournament as the 'Pool of Death', was against Argentina in Tokyo on 5 October. Four days before that game I received terrible news. Jeff Sayle, my former Randwick coach and mentor, had died in Sydney at the age of 77. It rocked me. Sayley had taught me to love the game and its people. My first instinct was to see if I could fly overnight to Sydney for the funeral, but I quickly realized that, in the thick of the World Cup, it was never going to happen. Sayley would have insisted I stayed in Japan and put the team first. I asked Glen Ella to pass on my best wishes to his family at the service.

I spoke to Neil Craig about the loss of Sayley. I explained all that he had done for me over the years. Neil, as he always does, just let me talk. He listened and let me get it all out. In high-performance coaching, the way you make people feel defines how well you do your job. Neil was patient and sincere and I appreciated his empathy. Sayley was a great old amateur rugby man and, in a way, it was fitting that he passed away during the biggest event in our sport. Every rugby club in the world has a Sayley, and they need to be treasured.

The next obstacle was talking about it publicly. I knew I would be asked about Sayley at the press conference before the Argentina match. The best tactic would be to just walk straight into the press conference, pick the microphone up and start talking. I did exactly that.

'I'd just like to start today by paying a tribute to Jeff Sayle. He was a great mate of mine.'

I paused and choked up a little; but I soon composed myself. 'It's a very sad day for rugby because he was a good person. He gave a lot to the game, to a number of players he coached and a number of teams he looked after. Even with England in 2016 he was the most welcome host. I remember going for a few beers with him at the Coogee Bay Hotel. Just a great fella and a real loss. We've got to make sure we keep those characters in rugby because they're so important to our game.'

Against Argentina we made a fast start before the match was ruined at the 20-minute mark. The huge Argentine lock Tomás Lavanini dropped his shoulder and hit Owen square in the face. Owen had set himself to take the tackle and Lavanini got his timing wrong. He was red carded. Argentina, having lost narrowly to France on the opening weekend, knew that they were on their way home as we cruised home 39–10, scoring six tries. We would have won by a lot more had Owen not missed all four of his first-half kicks for goal.

The result sealed our qualification for the knockout stages. Our final pool match against France would decide who topped the group. Getting out of the pool was a major milestone for England after the disappointment of 2015. When we qualified, a lot of tension was released. We had buried the previous tournament and we would go at least one better. The players who had endured the misery of that result were happy to move on.

As Japan braced itself for the onslaught of a super-typhoon, our game with France, alongside a few others, was in jeopardy. Typhoon Hagibis was heading straight for Tokyo. Of most concern, in strictly rugby terms, was that Scotland might not play Japan and would be knocked out of the tournament having lost to Ireland in their opening fixture.

The World Cup had been set alight by Japan's wonderful victory over Ireland – then the world's number-one ranked team. It was a wonderful display by Japan and sent the country into delirium and the tournament to the next level. I was delighted for Michael Leitch, who was still Japan's captain, all his teammates, and their coach Jamie Joseph, who had done remarkable work in building on our achievements from 2015.

Rugby was soon irrelevant as the scale of the typhoon and its path became apparent. It was described as a 'once-in-a-generation' storm. The organizers made the brave decision to cancel games – including our match with France. As soon as we got this news, we made plans to head for Miyazaki. Our logistics team were superb. In a few hours we were out of the hotel and on a plane flying south, where we knew we would be able to prepare in the sunshine and away from the chaos of the storm.

Eighty-seven people died, some are still missing, and 346 more were injured. It was a reminder of how vulnerable we all are when a storm of this force tears through a city.

While we had been ready and looking forward to facing France, I was just as happy to not play the match and bank the rest. It would also give us more time to prepare for our quarter-final against Australia.

The impact of the typhoon cast a pall over Japan. But the Japanese people are remarkably resilient, as they showed when blue skies and sunshine spread across a devastated Tokyo the next day. Local people worked incredibly hard to make sure that Japan's game against Scotland could still proceed, despite the flooding and damage.

There was a great moment for rugby when the Canadian players, following news that their match with Namibia had been cancelled, headed out to give the locals in Kamaishi a hand with the clean-up. Rugby is different to most other sports. We are bound by a universal set of values, including integrity, passion, solidarity, discipline and respect. The generosity and care of the Canadians made me proud to be a part of our great sport.

Japan's players drew on an even deeper spirit as they beat Scotland convincingly to top their pool and set up a quarter-final against South Africa. The winners would play either Wales or France in the semi-finals while, on the other side of the draw, New Zealand faced Ireland. I expected the All Blacks to win that game and they would then meet either Australia or England. We had entered the serious business of knockout rugby.

'It's do-or-die time,' I said bluntly in the build-up to the match. 'Every time the samurais fought, one lived and one died. It will be the same on Saturday: someone is going to live and someone is going to die. The best eight teams are all playing for their lives.'

I was not about to sugar-coat the situation. The hard truth of losing a World Cup quarter-final loomed over both teams. If we had a bad day, and the Aussies hit their peak, we would be flying back to London to face a barrage of abuse that we were utter losers and chokers and I was an idiot whom everyone had always known would fail with England. But I was also being truthful when I stressed my anticipation. I far prefer the white-hot pressure of a World Cup knockout than some humdrum game where neither team feels they have much at stake.

Australia's coach Michael Cheika did his best to put some pressure on me, picking up on my remarks about the benefits of our trip to Miyazaki. 'Their coach says they've had the best preparation, so they better win.' I resisted the temptation to say anything publicly, but I thought it was a statement of the obvious.

I was pleased with how the players were managing themselves and their workloads. They were composed and there was a sense of equilibrium in our camp. We were just as calm before the Australia match as we had been in preparing for any of the pool matches. People find it boring, but it's true that the best way to deal with any challenge is to focus on doing the next task to the best of your ability. It was important we continued to concentrate on the process which had got us this far. It doesn't sell newspapers or generate web traffic but it does help you prepare for important matches. Often there is a lot of resting and quiet time as you get closer to the game. It's quiet and sedate. Most journalists and fans, looking in from the outside, can't see the real picture. So they want to hear or even drum-up stories of conflict and drama. But we liked keeping our emotions in check and focusing on all we needed to do to play well.

We got a little taste of the familiar old hunger for controversy among those on the outside when there was a furore over my decision to start Owen at 10, with Manu and Henry Slade at centre, while George would come off the bench later in the game. I had no complaints about people saying that George had been our best player in the World Cup. I thought he was having an exceptional tournament. But it seemed as if my critics believed I should not take the opposition into account and just stick to the same line-up in every game.

Samu Kerevi, playing at 12, was an immensely powerful attacking force. I had no doubt that George would play a key role later in the game but, at the start against Australia, it was right to opt for a more physical axis of Farrell, Tuilagi and Slade.

Externally there is still a stigma if you don't start in the opening XV. You are said to have been dropped. That has to change. Neil Craig and I are emphatic that, in Test rugby today, where all 23 players usually play and games are often decided in the last quarter, such thinking is outdated. I was mercilessly bagged a few years ago when I promoted the idea of starters and finishers. Most coaches share my view and you could argue that, in Japan, Rassie Erasmus selected his bench first. Some of his best players were held back so that they could come on at the end to finish teams off.

It was easy for me to ignore the outside noise because of George's reaction to the decision. He was clearly disappointed but could see the logic. The players want to play as many minutes as possible and the way you do that is to start the game. But George knew that I was making the decision in the best interests of the team and he got on with his work. Again, I had been laughed at when I said our inconsistent Six Nations had been the perfect preparation for the World Cup. As a squad we had addressed the bizarre second half against Scotland and, once we had dealt with the lessons of squandering such a large lead, we had analysed what George had given us from the bench. He showed such mental strength and lifted the whole team after we'd conceded 38 points in a row. The way in which he drove us across Twickenham to secure a draw in the very last minute had inspired us all.

His preparation for Australia was again exemplary. He was an absolute credit to England and our World Cup squad, which had become so tight ever since the 31 players had been picked. All the relationships we had built with each other were strong and I approached our quarter-final with the certainty that, physically and mentally, we were in the best shape we had been during my nearly four years with the squad. Billy Vunipola had overcome the ankle injury which would have kept him out of the French game and Mako was looking close to his best in the front row. The Kamikaze Kids were ready to fly out of the blocks against two of their back-row heroes in David Pocock and Michael Hooper. Everywhere I looked I saw young England players who were confident and eager for battle. It calmed the pre-game nerves and allowed me to settle into an expectation that we were about to see something very special.

Oita Stadium, Oita, Japan. Saturday, 19 October 2019

Jonny May, winning his 50th cap, leads out England just as the black sticks are hit and the big drums are hammered by four young Japanese men on the edge of the pitch in this coastal city on the island of Kyushu. Australia and England line up alongside each other as they wait for the anthems after a short silence to commemorate the victims of Typhoon Hagibis. When the first notes of 'God Save the Queen' resound around the arena, Owen Farrell is concentrating so hard that he forgets the mascot standing next to him. But the little Japanese girl bravely stretches out her hand and, with a smile, Owen reaches down to take it. Like all the mascots, she has dutifully learnt the anthem of the country she is representing. She sings more sweetly than the giant players whose bellowing voices are loud, proud and often off-key. Afterwards, Owen bends down to thank her. It will be a last sign of tenderness for the next 80 minutes and more.

The Wallabies attack from the outset in gold and green waves, with one booming phase after another, as England are forced to defend with fierce resolve. There are too many hits to count but Daly, Itoje, Curry, Watson, Curry again, Lawes, Farrell, Sinckler and Lawes again all bring down the rampaging Australians before, after 18 phases, a big tackle from Tuilagi forces the 19-year-old centre Jordan Petaia to knock on. Our finishers are up in a flash, jumping from the bench to roar their approval at the intensity of our defence. George Ford leads the way, standing and clapping and shouting his encouragement.

The first scrum is set repeatedly and, eventually, Kyle Sinckler gives away a free kick. Tolu Latu, the Wallabies' Tongan-born hooker, laughs at Sincks and does his head-rubbing gesture as if he, the bearded Australian master, is consoling a wayward London kid. I am proud of Sincks as he refuses to be provoked. Instead of taking the kick, Hooper opts for another scrum. It looks to me as if they are out to rile Sincks. But my gifted young tight-head has absorbed the lessons of leadership we've been trying to share for the last three years or so and, taking his example from Jamie George and Mako Vunipola, he retains his composure. They go down again, and again, and soon it is Australia's turn to be penalized. The pressure on us eases a little.

We are 3–0 down, following a Lealiifano penalty, when we begin to turn the screw. Australia are now rocked and the play between our backs and forwards is slick and purposeful. Watson is brought down in the Wallaby 22 and Farrell feeds Tuilagi, who makes another small dent in their defence. Australia are being battered and stretched.

Suddenly, we cleave them open. The ball spins out from Youngs to Farrell to Curry. Our brilliant 21-year-old shows real guile as he delays his pass and draws Hodge towards him. Then, at just the perfect moment, he slips it to May, who completes an easy score. Farrell, who has worked hard on his kicking since the Argentina match, shows that he is back in the groove as he nails a difficult conversion from close to the touchline.

We score another try two minutes later when Slade intercepts a pass from Naisarani just as the Wallaby number 6 is clattered by Itoje. Slade bursts away and, as he approaches the halfway line, with two defenders trying to close him down, he sees May shoot out his right arm and point to a spot deep in Aussie territory. The angled little grubber kick from Slade is a thing of beauty. It rolls end over end before sitting up and begging for May to wrap his hands around the ball. May is away, the ball tucked safely under his arm as he arrows towards the corner flag. He has too much gas for anyone to catch him. Once he is over the try line, he is soon swallowed up in a huddle as Ford and Ludlam embrace him. The finishers had been keeping loose and warm and I am again so impressed by Ford's immersion in the game from the sidelines. Farrell makes another hard conversion look easy: 14–3.

We swap penalties and England lead 17–6 as a thunderous half winds to a close. Australia need a score badly but even when Hodge looks threatening, Curry knocks him back with a monstrously good tackle. Underhill, his Kamikaze sidekick, is immediately there to get over the top of the ball and turn over an Australian attack into an England scrum. Tuilagi, Farrell and Itoje gather round our two young flankers to show their appreciation.

The last scrum of the half collapses and England are penalized. Lealiifano kicks his third penalty and the players head for the dressing room. England 17, Australia 9.

We are calm as I remind them of what we need to do after the break. They listen and get ready to go again. We are halfway there but much more work is needed.

Australia come back hard. Hodge throws a big looping pass which finds Lealiifano who releases Koroibete. The winger is too fast to be caught by Slade, Watson and Daly as he scores close to the sticks. An easy Lealiifano conversion means that our lead of ten has been cut to a single point just three minutes into the second half.

There are echoes of leads lost to South Africa, Wales and Scotland but, this time, it is different. The lessons have been absorbed and, within a minute, after some slick and relentless play, a beautiful pass from Owen cuts out Itoje and Billy V and sets Sinckler free. Sincks has pace and power and he is almost impossible to stop. Beale tries hard but Sincks sees him coming and, at full tilt, turns his body so that he can absorb the impact without spilling the ball. Sinckler crashes over for a blistering try. The force of his dive spins him round and, after the score has been confirmed, he lies chest down on top of the ball and spreads his arms wide in celebration. Farrell converts: 24–16.

The hits keep on coming, with Curry and Underhill at their most imposing, and three more Farrell penalties extend the lead to 33–16.

Our finishers are on and the momentum keeps building. Watson pulls off a stylish interception and blasts through a hole to score an easy try; 40–16 is England's widest margin ever, and Australia's heaviest defeat, in a World Cup knockout game. I am more interested in the fact that Sam Underhill (20), Mako Vunipola (18), Jamie George (17) and Owen Farrell (17) have all surpassed the previous highest number of tackles made by an England player in a World Cup match. Tom Curry, meanwhile, is deservedly named the man of the match.

Every single one of my players has been a warrior and, afterwards, I can't resist celebrating their samurai spirt. 'The best samurais were always the guys who had a plan they could adapt. They had calm heads but were full of aggression. I thought we were like that today.'

I pause and then grin as my mind has already turned to the next challenge. 'But there's always a better samurai around the corner. We will be even better next week.'

Around that sharp corner, in the unknown shadows of a different game, the next samurai was dressed all in black. This samurai was, to some, an almost mythic giant. The mystique of the All Blacks could be felt in Japan. There were so many Japanese people wearing replica New Zealand jerseys that, if we allowed it, we could have felt as if we were stepping into the samurai's own menacing backyard. When he had been England coach, Clive Woodward had been so determined to sidestep the hyped-up aura that he banned his players from using the words 'All Blacks'. They were just New Zealand. It made some sense because there is an almost comic-book awe to the way in which the All Blacks are so revered and feared in world rugby. Many in the media, particularly in the UK, are fully signed-up members of the All Black fan club. BBC radio broadcast a documentary in the week of the game as a mark of their respect.

But I wasn't so convinced. I had beaten them enough times to know the truth. They were neither gods nor monsters. I could say the words 'All Blacks' without quaking. But I had also lost enough times to New Zealand to appreciate that they are not just another team. They are the most successful team in the history of sport. I don't just mean in rugby but across any team sport around the world. They have an unbelievable win–loss ratio and their conveyor belt of talent runs with smooth and formidable power. Like a great heavyweight champion, whether it's Sonny Liston or Mike Tyson, the All Blacks can intimidate many of their opponents into accepting defeat even before the first big hit is made. They carry that force with them whenever they step onto the field and, in the quarter-finals, against Ireland, they won 46–14.

We were up next. There was no point fretting about the fact that New Zealand had not lost a World Cup match for 12 years and were gunning for an unprecedented third straight title. It was more important to remember that we had only played them once since I became head coach. Just under a year earlier, we had gone after them from the opening whistle. We scored a try in the first minute and built a 15–0 lead. Even when they came back, and we were trailing 16–15, we kept hammering away. We all thought we had won the match until Sam Underhill's late try was disallowed by the tiniest of margins. It was then that I had made my point that 'sometimes the game loves you and sometimes it doesn't' and suggested that 'we'll get some love from the game further down the track.'

A World Cup semi-final, against New Zealand, was a mighty challenge. But I meant it when I said we had not played our best yet. I was convinced we would be so much better against New Zealand than against Australia. We would need to be superior because we were facing a stronger team in a ferocious contest. World Cup semi-finals are brutal. Both teams are desperate to reach the final and every single player empties the tank. The threat of elimination burns even more brightly and it explains why our training environment is so unforgiving.

Yet it remains crucial that decency and honesty frame the

work of both players and coaches. Your team is not made up of machines. The humanity of your players, even in peak physical condition, is paramount. Steve Hansen, New Zealand's coach and one of the best men in world rugby, understands this simple truth as well as anyone in the game.

It felt important to stress my huge respect for Steve. 'He's a good bloke, to start with,' I said in one of my media conferences. 'That's number one. Secondly, he's got a great record in Super Rugby with the Crusaders, when we started coaching against each other, followed by Wales and then New Zealand. You don't get a better record than that. Having a respectful relationship is important in the game. You just have to see what this World Cup has done. The things that happen in this tournament don't happen in other sports. You've got the Canadian and Namibian blokes cleaning up the ground. Could you imagine Ronaldo or Messi doing that if Barcelona or Real Madrid were washed out? And that's why relationships with players, coaches and fans are so important in our game.'

But, as much as I admired Steve, this wasn't a week for friendship. It was a week for competition, and on the Sunday night following the win over the Australians, I received an email from Pemby that would set the tone for the week. It was titled 'Flick the Switch'.

I had been deliberately low-key and unprovocative throughout the tournament and left most of the media work to my assistant coaches and the players. When I did speak, I was complimentary and uncontroversial. But this week would be different. Very different.

Pemby and I discussed getting on the front foot and staying on the front foot until full time. We had to be aggressive and provocative on and off the field. The All Blacks were feeling the pressure so we had to remind them of it. We needed an attention-grabbing approach that would be two parts mischief, one part menace.

The goals were clear.

1. Get Steve answering questions about things he didn't want to talk about, namely pressure.
2. Make sure that every time the All Blacks checked their phones during the week they were reminded of the pressure they were under.
3. Ensure our boys prepared without expectation.
4. Ensure the squad noted that I was relaxed, confident and ready for the fight.

But in creating a stir we needed to be respectful of Steve, Kieran Read and the All Blacks. They are rugby icons and whatever we did or said could not reflect on them in any adverse way.

The media are obsessed with 'mind games'. Most dismiss it as some sort of frivolous sideshow, but they would do well to reflect on history. The Ancient Greeks and Romans certainly believed that there was something in the value of rhetoric and the art of persuasion. Words matter just as much to a head coach as they do to a lawyer, politician, business leader or diplomat. It's how you inform, persuade and influence. I read somewhere that Stuart Lancaster spent 40 per cent of his time planning what to say to the media. I don't apply anywhere near that sort of effort, but I do think carefully about what I say and when I say it. It can be a very effective tool in influencing the context of a match.

We crafted a narrative that was funny and sharp. There were verbal bullets in the chamber and, with Owen at my side, we walked into the media conference room and I fired them. It worked a treat. Inside the hour, our 'pressure' narrative was up and running and dominating both social and mainstream media.

I also had some fun and diverted attention from my players. I pointed out that someone had been spotted with a camera on a balcony in an apartment block overlooking our training ground. 'There was definitely someone filming, but it might have been a Japanese fan. I don't care, mate.'

I was asked if I was trying to give the All Black management something to read over their coffee. 'Well, someone has to ask them a question because the New Zealand media doesn't.'

I looked at the Kiwi scribes and flashed another grin. 'You guys are just fans with keyboards.'

But I also had a reminder for the UK media. 'One week ago I was going to get sacked, Owen Farrell couldn't kick, and someone wrote that there would be blood on the walls of Twickenham. Now we are in a World Cup semi-final with a chance of going through.'

I was keen to drive home the point and so I asked the assembled media to raise their hands if they thought England would make it to the final. 'I didn't see too many hands go up there,' I said five seconds later. 'Your first reaction is always your most honest reaction and, if you don't put your hand up straight away, you don't believe it. And you don't.'

The clear implication was that, in contrast, we believed. I was asked to explain. 'We don't have any pressure, mate. No one thinks we can win. There are 120 million Japanese people out there whose second team are the All Blacks. So there's no pressure on us – whereas they've got to be thinking about how they're trying for a third World Cup in a row. That brings pressure. New Zealand talk about walking towards pressure. Well, this week the pressure is going to be chasing them down the street.

'The busiest bloke in Tokyo will be Gilbert Enoka, their mental skills coach. It is potentially the last game for their greatest coach and their greatest captain, and they will be thinking about those things. It's always harder to defend a World Cup and that will be on their minds as well.'

I reiterated that most of my players had already beaten the All Blacks in New Zealand with the 2017 Lions. 'They went down there and played in the All Blacks' backyard. They know they're human. They bleed, they drop balls, they miss tackles like every other player. It's our job to take their time and space away and put them under pressure. Pressure is a very real factor.'

It was easy to end the build-up with another memory and a

surge of anticipation. 'I can remember being in Kyoto for the draw two and a half years ago. Even an Australian could do the mathematics – we were going to play New Zealand in a semifinal. We've progressively built a game that we think can beat New Zealand. We've done this for the last two and a half years. And now we're just excited by the possibility.'

The next day was Wednesday, the All Blacks' rest day, and they clearly decided to leave our ruse alone so as not to give it any credibility. But we had stoked a raging bushfire. By the time Steve addressed the issue at his team announcement on the Thursday, it was too late. We had shaped the discussion for the week and it was all running our way.

In fact it was running so well that we changed plans on Thursday morning. We had stockpiled a heap more 'ammunition' to drop, but agreed to stand down. We risked losing our advantage if we pushed it too far. I went back to being Nice Eddie Jones.

But we had one more trick up our sleeve. In 2017, a year before we played the All Blacks in London, Pemby had been in London. He'd been at the game against Australia and we'd agreed to catch up at Twickenham on the Sunday evening for a drink.

'Mate,' he said as we greeted each other, 'I've had a great idea.' He went on to make his case that the only time we had ever had any success against Kiwi teams in either Super Rugby or in Tests was when we took them on – when we stirred them up before the game and stood up to them on the field. The haka, he said, was not off-limits and, within the bounds of respect and courtesy, it was a challenge that needed an active response. His idea was to have the captain line up directly opposite the AB's captain, with two flanks of players heading off to the right and left. When the haka began, the players would start walking towards the All Blacks. They would never take their eyes off their opponents and they would listen respectfully. Once the captain was ten metres from the haka, the flanks would fold and surround it in a circle.

'The crowd will go nuts and the players will get the benefit,' he said.

I thought: 'He's gone mad.' I shook my head. 'Mate, that will cause an international incident. You can't do that.'

'Yes we can, mate,' Pemby insisted. 'That's the point. We can and we must. If we are going to get in their heads, we have to take them on.'

We argued the toss for about ten minutes but it wasn't going to happen on my watch. All I could see was trouble. When the barman came over and asked if we wanted another drink, Pemby said: 'Thanks, mate. I'll have a beer and you can get my friend here a saucer of milk.'

'You've gone soft,' Pemby said. 'Polite Eddie Jones . . . now I've seen everything.'

Two years later he was at me again. In the early stages of the World Cup he was softening me up further by sending articles about the haka. An Irish journalist wrote that, 'It's a magnificent celebration of New Zealand culture and an iconic part of our sport. Long may it be celebrated.'

Pemby argued that 'the All Blacks are up for a challenge and, as long as we are respectful and don't get in their grill, they will be fine. And what sort of message does it send to our boys if we spend all week stirring the pot and then we encourage them to take a passive line during the haka? Our theme for the week is stepping forward and we have to take them on.'

For the last four years I had been working hard to remove reticence and politeness from the players. The semi-final was an opportunity for them to make a statement. I was still nervous, but I agreed to take the idea to the players.

They loved it. Straightaway they could see the benefit. It was respectful, but it was an act that told the All Blacks 'we are ready for you.'

Agreement was quickly reached. We would accept the challenge of the haka, and respond. We would take on the All Blacks.

18

THE FINAL

Yokohama International Stadium, Yokohama, Japan. Saturday, 26 October 2019

The players make the long walk from the dressing room to the tunnel. The usual echoing sound of studs clattering down a corridor is silenced by the blue carpet underfoot. They walk quietly and steadily, one player following another as they head for the cauldron of heat and noise outside. England are led by Billy Vunipola, who wins his 50th cap today, and soon they stand at the entrance of the tunnel.

The All Blacks, led by Kieran Read, wait alongside them. They say nothing and, like the England players, look stoically ahead, trying to ignore each other in these anxious moments.

Just before six in the evening they get the signal. They walk out into the glare of the flashing cameras and the roaring acclaim of 70,000 spectators inside the stadium, with over a hundred million people watching them on televisions around the world. Dark clouds roll across the sky and add to the sense of a gathering storm about to begin as the Japanese drummers add to the tumult and the drama.

There is a call for a poignant pause before the anthems. We remember again, in silence, the 87 victims of Typhoon Hagibis and the seven people who are still missing. Another 4,000 Japanese people are still living in evacuation shelters. This is real life. We, meanwhile, are just waiting for a game to start.

The seriousness of that game, however, pulses through me

after the anthems, as the two teams peel away into their separate halves. We know what is coming and we have prepared.

Our respect for the haka is profound. We understand that the All Blacks, drawing on Maori culture, are laying down a challenge to us. We also know that they respect any opponent who accepts that challenge.

We gather in a V formation because we are not willing to just stand in a humble line. The V starts on our ten-metre line and stretches into New Zealand territory. Four of our players, with two at the tip of each line of the V, are warned by match officials, who try to push us back into our own half.

Joe Marler, at the end of the left-hand fork of the V, is defiant. He has come closest of any England player to the New Zealand ten-metre line and there is no shifting Joe. His hands are on his hips and his magnificent beard and Mohican gleam under the lights. Nigel Owens, the referee, again gestures for him to move back. Joe lifts a questioning eyebrow and does nothing. Billy Vunipola, who heads the other V, also refuses to budge.

The crowd makes a ragged roar as people recognize the nature of our challenge.

TJ Perenara begins the ancient call of the haka. He is in the midst of the black huddle which fans out into an imposing phalanx with Read at the front. Perenara's voice booms around the stadium, for it has been amplified by television to crank up the theatre both inside the stadium and in sitting rooms and bars around the world.

Tongues stick out as the All Blacks lower themselves into a squatting position and hold their arms parallel to each other in front of their chests. Perenara cries out even more urgently as his fellow warriors flare their nostrils and get ready to launch into their unified chanting and beating of limbs.

At the apex of the V, Owen Farrell catches the unblinking eye of the television cameras. He stares straight at Read, his face creased by a knowing smile. It's a great moment which is seen up on the big screen. People would describe it later as a smirk but that reduces his reaction to one of disdain or disrespect. This is the opposite of what he and England mean. Rather, his smile is an acknowledgement of the power of the haka as well as our readiness to match the Kiwis with fire and intensity. It is a smile of anticipation rather than apprehension.

The All Blacks slap their forearms and bellow out the first words of the haka before, slowly, they sink down onto their haunches with a hiss. Sonny Bill Williams can be seen on the big screen, his cheeks puffed out as if he is snorting fiercely before he gets set for the next stage.

The lone voice of Perenara rings out again and then, slowly and deliberately, the All Blacks pick up the rolling chant in time to the smacking of hands and arms. They lower themselves again to the ground and then, once more, Perenara calls them to action. The pattern is repeated and then they rise up as one, their hands and heads lifting skywards as they look up and cry out still louder. The rhythm of the haka grows and grows; but we stand resolute in their territory, facing them down.

It ends in a blur and, as the last voices fade away, Read, as the All Black leader, takes a big step in our direction. It is his way of telling us that this is it. The moment is upon us.

England's players, calmly and methodically, remove their white tracksuit tops. I am pleased to see how unfazed they look – even as one of the commentators on New Zealand television yelps: 'You want box office? You've got it! How about *that* challenge from England?'

We know New Zealand would not have been expecting our V response and we want to keep them thinking. So we stick to the plan we have for kick-off. To the All Blacks it looks as if George Ford, who starts again at 10 in a sign of our attacking intent, will kick to the right. But he quietly informs the referee that we are doing the opposite.

Ford flips it to Farrell who sends the ball spiralling up into the dark sky to the left. We are ready to shake up the All Blacks. At the first lineout, Lawes climbs high to win the ball. It is soon in the hands of a charging Tuilagi. Curry makes more headway and then down the line it zips, from Youngs to Ford to Daly, who breaks through half a gap and releases Watson flying down the wing. Three defenders eventually bring him down, but Watson is immediately back on his feet as he makes a few more precious metres.

One England phase after another unfolds in a white rush, and New Zealand are forced to defend desperately. A long pass from Daly finds George on the wing. The hooker cuts back inside and brushes off two tackles before he is brought down. In the next two phases Lawes and Sinckler come close and then Lawes goes again. He is stopped just two metres from the line and Curry and Itoje follow up hard to protect the ball. Tuilagi is on their heels and he is unstoppable as he scoops up the ball and crashes over the line for our opening score. New Zealand gather in a dark huddle behind the posts as Farrell kicks the easy conversion: 7–0 after two minutes.

We keep dominating and look to have doubled that lead when Ford feeds Sinckler after 25 minutes. Sincks looks to jink right but he then shimmies to the left and delays his pass until Underhill can take it and smash into clear open space. Underhill bursts away and touches down under the posts. The try is awarded but Owens goes upstairs to the TMO. He wants to check that Curry is not offside. Replay follows replay and the decision is reached. Curry has cut in front of Moody and Whitelock, who both failed to stop Underhill. Crucially, he is also fractionally in front of Underhill. He is just offside and, like last November, an Underhill try is erased from the record books.

Farrell suffers a dead leg when he tackles Goodhue. He limps for a while but makes it clear he is going nowhere. After 30 minutes we have had 61 per cent of possession and our defence has been enormous. New Zealand have not been able to create much and they are making mistakes. But we are still only seven points clear.

Towards the end of the half, the television cameras lock on

me. Ben Kay, the 2003 World Cup winner who offers analysis on ITV, suggests that, 'Eddie Jones will be desperate. With three minutes to go, having had all the possession, he would have wanted more than seven points going into half-time.'

Nick Mullins, the chief commentator, replies. 'No other coach has got the better of New Zealand more often than Eddie Jones. Those wins include the 2003 World Cup semi-final when he was in charge of Australia.'

Lawrence Dallaglio, another World Cup winner, chips in to say that, 'This break comes at a good time for England to breathe life back into Owen Farrell because he's been really struggling with whatever injury he is carrying at the moment.'

I am oblivious to the chatter and concentrate on the match. It is heartening to see how Itoje, Lawes, Curry, Jamie George and Mako Vunipola are using their downtime. They are involved in an animated conversation, with Itoje leading the way, which is just what we wanted; Ric Charlesworth taught us so much about how best to use time when the ball is dead.

New Zealand come again and, with two minutes left on the clock, we have to defend attack after attack. Farrell brings down Savea and, in the fight for the ball, Lawes and Underhill form a white net which chokes the black shirts. Underhill has his hands on the ball and Scott Barrett makes a basic mistake. He is penalized and, at the award of the penalty for England, Itoje lifts his right arm in triumph. Curry smiles broadly and Youngs claps his hands in delight.

England's pressure is forcing cracks in the black wall. We are 8–3 up in turnover ball and soon 10–0 clear on the scoreboard after Ford curls the penalty between the sticks as the half-time gong sounds.

There is just time for New Zealand to kick off and for us to keep our heads. Lawes leaps high to tap the ball down to Watson who hoofs it into touch.

'Eddie Jones has spent all week assuring his players and everyone else who might be listening that New Zealand do bleed,'

Mullins tells his television audience as we head for the dressing room. 'They do drop balls, they do miss tackles, they are still only human. Half-time in the semi-final. England 10, New Zealand 0.'

Three minutes into the second half we look to have scored another try when, after a smart interception, Youngs slashes through space and crosses the whitewash; 15–0 flashes up but, soon, we are back in the world of the TMO as Marius Jonker agonizes over a possible knock-on in the rolling maul that preceded the try. He eventually decides Jamie George had knocked on, even though Mako Vunipola helped keep the ball up. George protests that his hands were always on the ball but Jonker's decision is final. The try is cancelled and it's a black scrum.

We remain undaunted and even the New Zealand substitutes feel the pressure. Sam Cane is penalized for tackling Billy Vunipola without the ball. Ford slots it home: 13–0.

Another big moment comes after 55 minutes when Underhill knocks Read off his feet with a devastating tackle. Our intensity remains as high as it has been from the opening whistle.

But a minute later our lineout implodes. The call is muddled and George's throw sails over Itoje, Kruis and Curry and straight into the arms of Savea, who will never score an easier try.

'The All Blacks are back in the house!' Mullins yells.

'Boy,' Kay agrees, 'do we have a finish on our hands now.'

Having worked so hard to keep New Zealand out, we have just offered up the softest of tries. We are about to be tested again.

In the previous 18 months we have let many big leads slip away but not today, not after everything we have learnt and tried so hard to implement. Two minutes after that error, Underhill smashes into Jordie Barrett with another legitimate big hit. That turnover is just one of 19 we will produce in the match.

We also keep the scoreboard ticking over and two more Ford penalties lift our lead to 19–7.

England's supporters can switch back and forth between singing 'Swing Low, Sweet Chariot' and 'Oh ... Maro Ito ... je!' as our supremacy today is obvious. It has been the most commanding England performance against the All Blacks in history and we march into the World Cup final.

At the whistle, it is noticeable that the England players do not really celebrate. It looks as if they knew, all along, that they would win today. Another huge obstacle still looms, against either South Africa or Wales, but we can at least savour a momentous victory.

'New Zealand are the god of rugby, so we had to take it to them,' I say after the game. 'We wanted to try to put them on the back foot as much as we could. They are a great team. They have won two World Cups in a row. They have got a great coach, a great captain, so we had to battle hard. You have got to give so much credit to New Zealand, the way they kept fighting right until the end. We had to dig deep.'

Steve Hansen has to suffer the indignity of some crass questions at his own press conference. Someone is dumb enough to ask him if he thought England had more hunger to win. 'My players were desperate to win,' Steve says angrily. 'Just because I've asked them at half-time to get hungrier doesn't mean they didn't turn up hungry. There's a big difference and if you want to spend some time outside, I'll give you a rugby education on that one. To say that an All Blacks team comes to a semi-final of the Rugby World Cup with our ability and history but lacks hunger? That's a pretty average question.'

There is generous praise from Steve in saying that we had been the better team and deserved to win. He also mentions the fact that he had spoken to Graham Henry, whom we all call Ted. Henry and Hansen had coached the last All Black team to lose a World Cup match. 'I had a chat with Ted about 2007,' Hansen says. 'We agreed that it's no different. It's a gutting feeling. Then Ted and I spoke about how well George Ford had played. Ford put us into positions where we had to really work to try to get out of our own territory. He made us force things.'

I am even more gratified when hearing George's measured

reaction to beating New Zealand: 'We came into the game with huge belief, thinking we could win. We had to be somewhere near our best to do so. We want to enjoy the win but the feeling now is that we've given ourselves an opportunity – that's literally all it is.'

A World Cup final week is different to anything else in rugby. I was about to begin my third, following 2003 and 2007, and I remembered how the pressure turned Jake White inside out when he was in charge of South Africa in Paris. Sitting in the number two seat is easy. My job as Jake's adviser was to try and take some of the heat away from him. Now it is my turn to deal with the pressure. I know it's critically important to our preparation that I stay calm.

From the day of our arrival in Japan I had set out to share my enjoyment and enthusiasm for the World Cup. It was easy because I was having such a good time. What's not to enjoy about competing in the biggest tournament in our sport, in a country I love, with a group of people who were giving their best effort every day? Rather than being weighed down by pressure I wanted people to see that I was the happiest bloke in Japan. As head coach you are the lightning rod for the team. I knew that my upbeat mood would rub off on the players and staff and would help keep everyone relaxed as we prepared for the massive challenge of facing South Africa – who had beaten Wales in an abrasive and dour semi-final.

Finals can make you do strange things. You can sometimes find yourself jumping at shadows or second-guessing decisions. I've been guilty in the past of working the players too hard in the build-up to big matches. But less is usually more when you're about to play a fourth major southern hemisphere team in five weeks. We had beaten Argentina, Australia and New Zealand in successive games. South Africa are the most brutal opposition, and so it felt right that we gave the players more time to recover from what had been an exhausting few weeks.

There is also a psychological challenge after the kind of big win we achieved against the All Blacks. While we did play well, I thought the analysis was a bit over the top. Everyone was slapping us on the back, saying how fantastic we were, how it was the best ever performance by an England team and the best ever win at a World Cup. The praise was everywhere. The challenge is to bring the players back to reality. Bring them down to then lift them up again. It changes the structure and narrative of the week. In this case we did nothing on the Sunday and Monday before heading back to work on the Tuesday.

Our preparation for the big match was solid. Clearly, it still wasn't good enough because, ultimately, you judge the preparation by the game's result. But in terms of the way we trained, behaved and looked forward to the game, it felt good. We also did well to diminish the feverish noise outside. There were reports that tickets for the game had soared to £12,000 and there had been a huge surge in flights booked from the UK to Japan.

'I think it's great,' I said. 'You want to give the country something to cheer about and, with Brexit at the moment, they probably need something to cheer. The crowds at the World Cup have been fantastic and I thought our supporters on Saturday night were massively instrumental in getting us home. Their singing and general support of the team were fantastic and we urge them to keep doing that. It's the job of the team to make the country happy – but people are not as happy as they can be because there is still a game to go.'

I was asked about the mood of the team. 'The great thing for us is we know we've done the preparation,' I said. 'We've spent four years getting ready for this occasion. That's why the players can be relaxed, that's why I can be relaxed. But we know South Africa will come hard at us. They've got a history of being the most physically intimidating team in the world and they have a massively aggressive forward pack. There are not many Springbok teams that don't come through the front door. So we've got to be ready at the front door and have enough cover at the back door, too. Rassie [Erasmus] is a cunning coach and has done a great job with the Springboks. We've prepared for the unexpected as they are going to be difficult to beat.'

I wanted to convey a sense of self-belief and anticipation. 'We will play with no fear. How fantastic is it for our young guys? Saturday is the biggest sporting event in the world. And our players get to play in a World Cup final. What an exciting opportunity to be themselves, to play with spirit, to play with pride and an English style of play.'

We'd last played South Africa one day short of a year ago. On 3 November 2018, we had beaten them 12–11 at Twickenham. It was, like it always is against the Boks, a very hard day. They pride themselves on handing out beltings. They physically test you in every part of the game. Seven of the Springbok squad also had experience of Premiership Rugby; and Faf de Klerk and Francois Louw spoke of their respective friendships with Tom Curry at Sale and Sam Underhill at Bath. We knew what we were facing and there wasn't a suggestion of complacency. Our boys have too much respect for them.

Louw set it up nicely. After he had praised Sam, he said: 'It will be an immense battle on Saturday. We are at the final stage of the ultimate competition in our game. Both groups of players will have to dig really deep and front up, but afterwards I will have a good time with my five Bath colleagues who are in the England squad.'

Early in the week I reacted sharply to a question from the media when asked about Warren Gatland's comments following Wales's loss to South Africa when he said, 'We have seen in previous World Cups that teams sometimes play their best in semi-finals and don't always turn up for a final. So it will be interesting to see how England perform.'

Gats loves sticking the boot in, as do I. After we had lost to them in the Six Nations earlier in the year, he'd said he always felt that 'England struggle to win the big games.' Sensing he was having a dig in Japan, I shot back: 'Well, guys, can you just send my best wishes to Warren and make sure he enjoys the third/ fourth place play-off.' It was a good line at the time and it got a laugh; but with hindsight maybe there was some truth in Gatland's comment.

There was an option, as always, to change the team and select with the opposition in mind. I considered bringing in Henry Slade to start – with George Ford moving to the bench. But our game plan against South Africa relied on strong kicking and George is clearly one of our best field kickers. So the only change was Ben Spencer for Willi Heinz. Poor old Willi had injured his hamstring in the final minutes of the semi-final and was ruled out immediately. In the dressing room after the game he was inconsolable. He was a key member of the team and had made a massive contribution on and off the field. His dream was over. You could see the other players thinking it could have been any one of them. It was a sobering time for all of us.

We had just two scrum halves in our squad and so our head of logistics, Charlotte Gibbons, jumped on the phone to Ben Spencer who flew into Tokyo on the Monday. Our team of 31 was now 32 as, happily, Willi wanted to stay on with us. He was brilliant in helping Ben slot easily into the squad. Ben was in great shape, having completed a preseason and played in the Premiership with Saracens. I had repeatedly said that I wanted the players back in England to be ready if they were needed. Ben was ready.

On the Friday, I felt relaxed enough to take a coaching session with one of the local schools. The Japanese people had been such gracious hosts, and I thought it might show England's gratitude in a small way. With their parents beaming on the sidelines, the kids had the time of their lives. I hope the legacy of this tournament is greater participation in junior rugby in Japan. For me, standing on a field with a whistle in my mouth while ordering people around is my happy place. I love coaching, and to spend even a small amount of time with these kids connected me once again to my love of the game. It was the perfect way to spend the afternoon before a World Cup final.

Yokohama International Stadium, Yokohama, Japan. Saturday, 2 November 2019

We had started like a train against New Zealand but, seven days on, the final is very different. After 38 seconds we concede a penalty when Courtney Lawes tackles Frans Malherbe, South Africa's beefy loose-head prop, and fails to roll away in time.

Handré Pollard, unusually, misses his kick at goal. But trouble is heading our way.

Just over a minute later a Tom Curry drive is blocked. Ben Youngs, at the base of the ruck, waits and then kicks a high ball into South African territory. It's gathered by Makazole Mapimpi and the Springbok right wing sets off on a jinking run as Jamie George, Maro Itoje and Kyle Sinckler all rush towards him. There is a sickening collision as Sincks' head catches Maro's elbow. He is knocked out. For five long minutes the medical staff assess Sincks' condition and it's obvious that his night is over.

A stretcher and then a golf cart arrive on the pitch. Happily, Sincks is eventually able to walk off the field. But in the opening two minutes we have lost our starting tight-head prop and one of our best players. He will spend the rest of the game in a track-suit. You prepare for these circumstances, hoping they never occur, but this is a genuine setback. It makes our task of winning the final just so much more difficult.

Dan Cole, our replacement tight-head, is 32, and he will have to play 78 minutes of a World Cup final. It's a huge task for anyone – especially when you consider he will have to battle Tendai 'The Beast' Mtawarira, who will then give way to a fresh young loose-head prop in Steven Kitshoff early in the second half.

At the first scrum, the Beast puts the squeeze on Dan. We concede a penalty. De Klerk taps and runs with the ball, moving from Mapimpi to Le Roux, Kolbe and Pollard. Inside the first five minutes, South Africa have run further than they did in the semi-final against Wales.

After six minutes we have another scrum. It collapses and is reset. We win the ball but we're going backwards. Billy Vunipola gathers the ball from the base and sets off on a run before throwing a pretty average bounce pass to Farrell inside our 22. Farrell scrambles to regather control but he is monstered by Vermeulen and Kolisi. He is penalized for not releasing and Pollard kicks an easy penalty bang in front of the sticks: 3–0, South Africa.

We try something a little different after ten minutes when Farrell stands at the front of the lineout. Lawes soars above him to win the ball. He offloads it to Farrell who finds Youngs. Tuilagi comes storming through to take the pass. He makes good ground before Lood de Jager and Malherbe gather him in. Youngs looks to start the next phase but his pass, intended for Watson, sails into touch. It's a nervy start.

We have neither the precision nor the power which had been so obvious against the All Blacks. For some unknown reason we're just not clicking. Some days are just like this and we don't know the reason. We soon lose a lineout on our own throw – and are penalized again at the next scrum when Mako Vunipola struggles to deal with the force of the Bok pack.

But, slowly, we begin to build a little momentum. After nine phases of controlled play, Kolbe sticks his hands into the ruck and gives up a penalty. Owen makes it 3–3. The match is a hugely physical contest with both sides ripping in. South Africa also have to make a double substitution as Marx replaces the concussed Mbonambi at hooker and the lock Mostert is on for De Jager, whose shoulder has been destroyed. The Boks have a 6–2 split in favour of their forwards on the bench and their pack is now even more formidable than the starting eight.

Two minutes later our scrum struggles again. The Bok pack really hammers us in the set piece and we're on the back foot. In these big games, when it's close, South Africa have a decisive advantage. We begin to concede more penalties and leak three points every ten minutes.

Marc dal Maso, the great French prop and my scrummaging coach with Japan, always used to say: 'No scrum, no life.'

Marc understood rugby. A losing scrum has a trickle-down

effect. Everyone gets a bit edgy. The forwards lose confidence and the backs overcompensate and force the play.

We're 12–6 down at half-time. Despite having played poorly, we're still in the game. I believe we can turn it around. This team has proved time and again that they can hang in and win tough games. They can do it again. The scrum is at the core of our problems. Neal Hatley, our scrum coach, brings the props and hookers together to find a solution.

I accept that I made two selection mistakes for the final. I should have chosen Joe Marler ahead of Mako and I should have reverted to the Farrell–Tuilagi–Slade midfield we used against Australia. George Ford could have come off the bench when we had got into the game. But you never know until the game starts. You use the best available evidence and rely on your gut. I had been right against Australia and New Zealand but, as it turned out, in the biggest game of our four-year cycle, I got it badly wrong. Hindsight is a wonderful teacher.

Kruis replaces Lawes at half-time and, after five minutes, I bring on Marler for Mako. A minute earlier Kitshoff and Koch, the replacement Bok props, had just forced another scrum penalty. Pollard is in the groove: 15–6, South Africa.

Slade is on for Ford and the introduction of Marler and Kruis has stabilized the scrum. We have our best spell of the match. A Farrell penalty cuts the lead to 15–9 and, after 54 minutes, he has another chance to reduce the deficit to just three. We would have been right back in the game then but his kick drifts agonizingly wide.

The Springboks, meanwhile, are outstanding. They keep pouring into us, playing on the edge of the offside line, making big defensive hits and running with menace. But, still, we hold on. Pollard and Farrell swap penalties and, with just 15 minutes left, South Africa lead 18–12. A converted try would put us in the lead. There's still hope.

But all the momentum is with the Boks and a sharp backline movement down the left ends in a Mapimpi try. I know now that the dream is over. Kolbe scores another try and the World Cup is out of sight. It's lost in a green and gold blur.

South Africa 32, England 12.

In the final minutes my mind starts to wander. My first thoughts are for the players. They will be distraught. They have been brilliant, coming together as a powerful, united England team which has done everything asked of it and more. They have played with flair and tenacity and, during a difficult and uncertain time at home, they have given people something to smile about. The subsequent news that the final was watched by the biggest television audience in the UK this year (over 12.5 million), and that supplies of replica jerseys had sold out, proved the boys had made a lasting impact.

I look around at my coaching staff and management. They are gutted. They've all put in so much work to get things right for the players. There is nothing more I could have asked of them.

I gaze across the stadium at the masses of white jerseys. That noisy, boisterous white wall has been with us throughout the tournament. I think of the people who have flown in to be at the game and are leaving first thing the next morning. The lazy cliché of our fans is that they are arrogant. It's bullshit. They love the game and the team, and the team loves them. I understood that they would be disappointed but I knew that, with a little time, they would reflect on everything the boys achieved and be proud. We're miles away from 2015 and they know it.

A feeling of dread then fills me as I contemplate the time I will have to spend with my friends in the media. Sure as night follows day, those who threw bouquets and went completely over the top in their praise of our win over the All Blacks one short week ago will grab the pitchforks, light the torches and demand immediate answers. They will talk of 'failure' and rail against my selections and the game plan that didn't work. It's a necessary and important part of the job but, trust me, it's exhausting. True to form one of them suggested later we choked, and I snapped. I was having none of it. Our players didn't choke. We were beaten by a better team on the night. I often wonder who marks their homework.

Having shuffled up to get my silver medal, I stand with the boys as we watch the Boks and consider what might have been. There is nothing you can say. We just have to live with the fact that, despite our best efforts, we have come up short. Most of the boys gaze into the crowd with faraway stares. They aren't thinking much; but they feel a lot of hurt.

In our misery we watch the World Cup being presented to the Springbok captain, Siya Kolisi. I'd caught some of what he said after the match over the public address system. I heard him speak of the example this victory could set his country. Here is a symbol of what can be achieved when people work together. South Africa's first black captain, a young man from the townships, who had little food to eat as a boy and who had sat in a shebeen to watch our World Cup victory in 2007, now holds up the greatest prize in rugby. It's a powerful symbol of progress for South Africa. A part of me is pleased for Siya and for South Africa. I sincerely hope it makes a difference.

I offer my congratulations to Rassie and we share a minute together. It's a quick chat. The winning coach doesn't want to talk much to the losing coach, because he feels like he's being patronizing and you, in turn, haven't got much to say to him beyond 'well done' and 'well played'. As Bobby Robson used to say after a game, 'There's one happy dressing room and one unhappy dressing room.'

We're in the sad place without any champagne or noise. I know the happy place far better because, over the years, I've won more than I've lost. But, right now, there is no escape. We lost a dream tonight.

The hours pass on World Cup night and the gloom lifts. Of course I know that when I wake in the morning there will be a dull ache as soon as I remember the game. The hurt will be there on Monday morning, and Tuesday, and every day for weeks to come. In some ways, it never goes away. This is familiar territory. I've won a World Cup final, with South Africa, but I've now lost two. The pain of 2003, and Australia losing to England at home in extra time, ran so deep that it really did take me a couple of years to get over it. This feels different. It feels nowhere near as bad. I feel all right because I know we have done everything possible in our power to win the game. The players have been magnificent. They gave their all.

My eyes are clear and my heart lifts just a little on a clear night in Tokyo. Age teaches you a better and calmer understanding. I am not going to call it wisdom because I don't feel very wise tonight. I made a few mistakes, but the honest truth is that I really don't know why we failed to produce the kind of perform-ance we found within ourselves a week ago in this very stadium. I haven't got all the answers; but at least I know enough now not to hang on to this disappointment like I did after 2003. I will go through a grieving period, because the loss of a World Cup final cuts that hard. But experience has taught me to let it go.

If we had won I would not have allowed myself to linger over victory for months and years on end. I would have enjoyed it for a week and then I would have started planning for the next chal-lenge and the next adventure. If I can keep a win in perspective, it's not such a leap to do the same when confronted by defeat.

We played six games in Japan and we won five. South Africa did the same, as they lost their opening pool game to New Zealand. No other team had won the World Cup after losing in the pool stages, but South Africa have proved that history is always there to be made. Out of the five games we won I will always remember two with affection. Australia were desperate to beat us but we were too good. And our semi-final against New Zealand was spe-cial. Martin Johnson, England's only World Cup-winning captain, was generous. He said it was the best World Cup performance he had seen from England.

For me it goes down in a quartet of particularly memorable games I've coached. It belongs with the Brumbies defeat of the

Sharks in the 2001 Super 12 final, the Wallabies beating the All Blacks in the 2003 World Cup semi-final, and Japan's victory over South Africa in 2015. Each one means so much to me. I would never pick one over the other because, seen in unison, they show my capacity to successfully coach different teams, who play diverse styles of rugby, in all kinds of conditions and countries. I have had so much joy, through rugby, in Australia, Japan and England. South Africa and New Zealand have rarely been far from the heart of these stories. Memories of all these encounters wash away some of the sorrow.

The art of good coaching is turning an idea in your head into reality on the field. I would love to play running rugby all the time, because that was my background at Matraville High and with Randwick in Sydney, but the reality is that sometimes the players you're coaching need to play the game in different ways to match their culture and identity.

It was special to see Bob Dwyer after we beat New Zealand in Yokohama. Bob, who loves the Randwick Way, was thrilled with our English-style rugby. Australians always enjoy seeing the All Blacks lose but, beyond that basic national instinct, he appreciated the way we played. During my time with England I've taken most pleasure from the fact that we've been able to generate our own power style of rugby which matches our players and delights our fans.

We've taken a side that couldn't get out of the group stages in a home World Cup to being the second-best team in the world. We aimed to be first, but we ended up second. There was one team ahead of us, and 18 behind us.

I am definitely staying as England's coach for another two years. My contract runs until 2021. I'm excited by what our young team can achieve. It won't be the exact same team for lots of reasons. Some players will lose their hunger or form, or succumb to injury. Younger and better players, motivated by what they have seen in Japan, will emerge. But the core of this 2019 team will grow and improve. They are the youngest team ever to play a World Cup final, with an average age of 27. The potential is massive. Not only are they great rugby players but they are better people with outstanding character. I believe I can keep making a difference with them over the next two years. We can and we will improve. We want to become the powerhouse of world rugby. After that? We'll see. It's too early to know and, right now, I am happy to just hit the pause button.

At the end of such a long and arduous World Cup campaign in Japan, a country which has helped shape my family alongside my native Australia, it is time to reflect. Hiroko has been with me for all our games and Chelsea, who works for the Wallabies, only left after England beat Australia. She had to keep working while watching us on television. My dear old mum, the mighty Nell, also watched every game on TV while my sister Diane travelled to the final.

The tournament has been a wonderful showcase for the game I love – and to see the whole of Japan consumed by rugby has touched me deeply. When I returned to Japan in 2009, this country really was a rugby backwater. People told me that I would ruin my career by coaching in Japan. My gut told me something different. My gut told me that I needed to come to Japan to try and make a difference.

Someone had to believe in Japanese rugby. Someone had to try and shake up the culture of a rugby country that used to accept defeat meekly. Christopher Columbus said you can never discover anything new unless you leave the shore. I left the shore and sailed to Japan. I helped start the change and then other people have taken it on. Japan were magnificent, beating Ireland and Scotland, reaching the quarter-finals before losing to South Africa.

I know the clock is ticking on my time at the top of international coaching. But I know I will become a better coach with England. In another two years we will see where I am and which way I move forward. I feel privileged to coach England and, for however long that lasts, I will continue to give my best effort every day.

In the days and years ahead, wherever I am, either on a muddy or a sunlit field, I will always want to make a difference. I remember how Cyril Towers used to wander down to Matraville High every afternoon to share his sheer joy and passion for our game. Maybe, like Cyril, I will find a high-school team that will have me. Wouldn't that be great?

ACKNOWLEDGEMENTS

This book is full of great memories and has made me realize, once again, just how fortunate I have been to spend my life in rugby with so many great people. Thank you to all my former teammates, my former and fellow coaches and, especially, to all the wonderful players I've been fortunate enough to work with over the years. You have enriched my life.

I would like to say a special thanks to those who were kind enough to relive some of their own memories while we worked on the book – Steve Borthwick, Neil Craig, Frank Dick, Fourie du Preez, Bob Dwyer, Glen Ella, George Gregan, Junichi Inagaki, Rod Kafer, Michael Leitch, Ewen McKenzie, David Pembroke, Ian Ritchie, Mark Sinderberry, John Smit and Chris Webb.

Craig Livingstone, my agent, was instrumental in making the book happen. Thanks, mate.

Thanks to everyone at Pan Macmillan for all their support and belief in the book. In particular, Robin Harvie, my editor, has backed this project from the outset and helped us throughout the three years we've worked on it. Matthew Cole and Laura Carr have also done great work and thanks to Penny Isaac for her copy-editing.

I do owe David Pembroke (Pemby) a special thanks. Our partnership stretches back over 20 years and, as the commitments of the World Cup closed in, I handed over to him to work with Don McRae to fine tune and check everything. He was, as always, invaluable in helping us find the right stories and the right words. Thanks, mate. As always, I appreciate your help.

And Don. Thank you so much for your professionalism, perseverance and curiosity. You have done a superb job in helping me tell my story.

Finally, I would like to thank my family. Without them, I would have accomplished nothing.

INDEX

PICTURE ACKNOWLEDGEMENTS

1. *The Advocate*
2. Author's own photographs
3. Author's own photograph
4. Ibid.
5. Ibid.
6. Peter Naklicki
7. Author's own photograph
8. Peter Rae/Fairfax Media via Getty Images
9. Steven Holland/Fairfax Media via Getty Images
10. Gary McLean/Fairfax Media via Getty Images
11. Kenneth Stevens/Fairfax Media via Getty Images
12. (i) & (ii) Brendan Read/*Sydney Morning Herald*
13. Colorsport/Shutterstock
14. Matthew Impey/Shutterstock
15. Matt Turner/ALLSPORT via Getty
16. David Ashdown/*Independent*/Shutterstock
17. Author's own photographs
18. Manuel Blondeau/Photo & Co./Corbis/VCG via Getty Images
19. (i) DAMIEN MEYER/AFP/Getty Images (ii) PETER PARKS/AFP/Getty Images
20. Chris McGrath/Getty Images
21. Jonathan Wood/Getty Images
22. Matthew Impey/Shutterstock
23. Tom Jenkins/*Guardian*/eyevine
24. Sankei via Getty Images
25. Charlie Crowhurst/Getty Images
26. David Rogers/Getty Images
27. David Rogers – RFU/The RFU Collection via Getty Images
28. David Rogers/Getty Images
29. David Rogers – RFU/The RFU Collection via Getty Images
30. Michael Steele/Getty Images
31. Richard Heathcote – World Rugby/World Rugby via Getty Images
32. David Rogers/Getty Images